NO CONDEMNATION

A NEW THEOLOGY of ASSURANCE

Michael Eaton

InterVarsity Press
Downers Grove, Illinois

Published in the United States of America by InterVarsity Press, Downers Grove, Illinois, with permission from Paternoster Press, Carlisle, U.K. Published in the U.K. as A Theology of Encouragement.

InterVarsity Press® is the book-publishing division of InterVarsity® Christian Fellowship, a student movement active on campus at hundreds of universities, colleges and schools of nursing in the United States of America, and a member movement of the International Fellowship of Evangelical Students. For information about local and regional activities, write Public Relations Dept., InterVarsity Christian Fellowship, 6400 Schroeder Rd., P.O. Box 7895, Madison, WI 53707-7895.

Cover photograph: Cowgirl Stock Photography

ISBN 0-8308-1888-X

Printed in the United States of America

Library of Congress Cataloging-in-Publication Data

Eaton, Michael A., 1942-
   [Theology of encouragement]
   No condemnation / Michael A. Eaton.
     p. cm.
   Previously published: Theology of encouragement. Carlisle, England:
Paternoster Press, 1995.
   Includes bibliographical references and index.
   ISBN 0-8308-1888-X
   1. Assurance (Theology) 2. Grace (Theology) 3. Law and gospel.
4. Freedom (Theology) 5. Eaton, Michael A., 1942- . I. Title.
BT785.E28   1997
234—dc21
                                      96-48381
                                          CIP

23	22	21	20	19	18	17	16	15	14	13	12	11	10	9	8	7	6	5	4	3	2	1
16	15	14	13	12	11	10	09	08	07	06	05	04	03	02	01	00	99	98	97			

Foreword by Dr. R.T. Kendall

Those of us who are committed to reformed theology but have been uneasy with its failure to give consistent encouragement and robust assurance will welcome this book. Although this particular volume will appeal largely to the more serious reader, the theology that emerges from it will, when grasped, give incredible relief to the simplest Christian, whatever one's background. Every minister and church leader should read and digest its content, then simplify it by teaching those who want to believe the good news of salvation but are afraid it's not true. The author is capable of writing very simply indeed, as his other books demonstrate; but this kind of work is needed to anticipate questions and objections that come from the highest critical level.

And yet the book *is* written simply! It is merely that the author has delved deeply into the original biblical languages and interacted with scholars the average Christian has never heard of. This kind of treatise is therefore most necessary before ministers and serious Christians can feel they can truly treat its arguments. This will take time, but I suspect that this crucial study will influence Christianity in the twenty-first century more than any book like it that has been written in the present century.

Dr Michael Eaton ministers in Nairobi, Kenya. He and his wife Jenny are members of Westminster Chapel. He turned up here on Friday evenings, early in my ministry, when we were inching our way through Galatians. He is rather shy and self-effacing and, to be honest, I hardly took notice of his presence. But over the years he was to turn out to be one of my greatest encouragers and supporters. When I would go out on a theological limb, taking positions I had not heard of, it was Michael who would come alongside to say, 'You've got that right.'

He kindly states that my own *Calvin and English Calvinism to 1647* (to be republished by Paternoster) helped him on his way. I used to dream of filling out that book myself and answering my own critics. Perhaps not too unlike Jude who wanted to write a soteriological treatise but was compelled to take a different direction (Jude 3), my present ministry has been almost entirely preaching and pastoral so that someone else would have to carry the torch of 'developed Calvinism' to the world. Dr Eaton has done that.

And yet I was not prepared for this book. He has moved beyond me and has come to conclusions I had not envisaged, possibly because he has more courage and most certainly because he has had greater insight and a better mind. He has few peers in the world in terms of learning and quality of intellect. Better still, he is a godly man and loves the Lord Jesus with a passion that, when all is said and done, should be the chief reason why readers will take Michael seriously.

There are two categories of people who, I predict, will eventually modify their views after reading this book. First, the traditional Calvinist. There are thousands of reformed people with integrity who have assumed that there is only one way to think when it comes to the doctrines of grace. Some of them who have had access to the manuscript of this book already, or Michael's doctoral thesis (from which this monograph is derived), have testified to the new freedom it gave them. To those who are truly open and have no axe to grind, even if they have published views they have felt obliged to defend, this work will be like a breath of fresh air from the Throne of Grace. Secondly, to the person holding Arminian views there will be one awesome awakening after another. It would not surprise me if many come to espouse views they had thought they must oppose.

I appeal to the reader to read this book carefully, as though on one's knees before God, to see if, just maybe, there is in it a life-changing word from the Lord.

R.T. Kendall
Westminster Chapel
London

Preface

This work is a revision of my doctoral thesis presented to the University of South Africa in 1989 under the title *A Theology of Encouragement – A Step Towards a Non-Legalistic Soteriology*. The present work has involved abridgement of the main text, addition of some material on eternal security, omission of chapters on James and 1 John, and a severe reduction of footnotes.

I am conscious of many gaps in this study. It covers a vast field. Old Testament studies, New Testament studies, theology, theological history, are all relevant and find some place in this work. However a pastor is a general practitioner, not a specialist. I am a preacher first and cannot specialize too narrowly as I would if I were a 'pure' scholar. For the purpose of this particular book (and its underlying dissertation) I chose to confine my expositions to selected areas of Scripture. I have not forgotten that Deuteronomy exists, and I have plans to see through the press further works that might answer questions arising from this one. *How To Live A Godly Life* (Sovereign World, 1993) might answer some questions, and *Living Under Grace: Romans 6:1–7:25* (Nelson Word, 1994) is popular in style but includes a 25,000 word exposition of Romans chapter 7. An exposition of 1–3 John, due to be published by Christian Focus, will incorporate the material on 1 John.

Without implicating him in any of my opinions I must thank Professor Adrio Konig of the University of South Africa for his help and guidance during the original research on which this work is based. I count it a privilege to have been able to learn from Professor Konig's questions, his friendly criticisms, and his encouragement.

R.T. Kendall resolved some difficulties I had in the early stages of my explorations into the matter of law and grace. For his continued encouragement I am most grateful. However, I have ploughed my own furrow and not all my opinions can be blamed on him!

My thanks to my wife and family for their consistent encouragement.

Michael Eaton, Nairobi, 1995.

Part 1

A Theological Problem

1

The Quest for an Encouraging Theology

'The most that I have ventured to say respecting myself is, that I think it possible I may get to heaven.'[1] So said Asahel Nettleton, a powerful evangelical preacher in 19th century America. His understanding of the Bible was influenced by the Protestant Reformers, the greatest of whom was John Calvin. As a 'Calvinist' Nettleton believed that he was saved totally by the grace of God, 'justified' through faith in Jesus. He believed that the salvation of every Christian cannot possibly be lost because the grace of God is sure to keep him safe. Nettleton however had a problem. He was sure that salvation could not be lost but not so sure that he personally was 'saved'. If he was genuinely saved he could be sure he was permanently saved, but he was not sure he *was* genuinely saved.

Consider another famous preacher. In the eighteenth century, John Fletcher, a friend of John Wesley, held a rather different view. He thought it was quite wrong to think that 'faith alone turns the scale of justifying evidence at the bar of God' and spoke of 'evangelical legality'.[2] Despite his background of the Protestant doctrine of grace, Fletcher often presented his teaching in a way that by making 'good works' so integral a part of salvation, he was virtually urging that the Christian has to work for his salvation. In 1770 Fletcher argued that the Christian was 'working for life'; 'every believer, till he comes to glory, works for, as well as from life'. 'We have received it as a maxim that 'A man is to do nothing, in order to justification. Nothing can be more false.' Every person, taught Fletcher, must perform good works 'in order to find favour with God'.

In consequence, Fletcher spoke of 'conditional perseverance' in salvation. He contrasted this with the Calvinist doctrine of 'unconditional perseverance'. If the Christian did not pursue holiness, then, Fletcher believed, loss of salvation would follow.[3]

These great men exemplify a theological problem that has troubled evangelical churches and preachers since the 17th century, if not before. On the one hand, Nettleton's doubts related to the *genuineness* of salvation. On the other, Fletcher said no Christian could be absolutely sure about the *permanence* of their salvation. Nettleton's teaching has been popularly summarized in the phrase 'Once saved, always saved' – but he was not quite sure that he was even once saved! John Fletcher taught 'Once saved, maybe lost'! I find neither doctrine very encouraging. In fact, both seem rather terrifying. My certainty of salvation is Jesus. My trust is in him. But am I to believe, with Nettleton, that my salvation may not be genuine, and that what I think is my salvation may turn out delusive? If so, I shall spend all my life wondering whether I am really saved or not. Or am I to believe with Fletcher that my salvation may not be permanent and I have to work hard at keeping it? If so, I shall live my life in the fear that perhaps I shall not keep going.

A PERSONAL EXPERIENCE

It may help clarify the issue if I describe how it came home to me in a personal way some years ago. The first time I ever seriously read the New Testament was in my teens. As a schoolboy interested in languages I tried to teach myself Classical Greek and found in a book called *Teach Yourself Greek*[4] a section of the Greek New Testament for translation. I had never before read the Bible voluntarily and my interest was linguistic rather than spiritual, but I enjoyed reading from John 10 about 'the Good Shepherd' in Greek. I had never listened to any Christian preaching or attended any Christian worship but, despite my neo-pagan background, I was persuaded by a friend to go along to a Christian youth group at an Anglican church in north London. Within a few weeks I had trusted Jesus as my Saviour. I knew that Jesus had died for me, that I was on my way to heaven, that I would never be the same again.

About eighteen months later I spent a Saturday morning walking from my parents' home in east-central London to Wigmore Street in west-central London where I had been told there was a large Christian bookshop. There I bought my first Christian book, one of J.C.Ryle's volumes on John's Gospel. Over the next few weeks I spent my treasured pocket-money on Christian books. My interests were Puritan and Reformed. Early acquisitions were an exposition of Jude by the Puritan Thomas Manton and William Hendriksen's commentary on 1 Timothy, 2 Timothy and Titus. On Christmas Eve that year I bought Robert Haldane's *Romans*, which I eagerly devoured through the Christmas break. My ideas of the Bible would have horrified many Christians and when I casually mentioned what I knew of biblical criticism to the curate of the church I had begun to attend, he looked aghast and urged me to read a book that had not long been published, J.I.Packer's *'Fundamentalism' and the Word of God*. I found the book quite devastating; it changed a number of my ideas about 'fundamentalism' and brought me to a firm belief in the reliability of the Bible.

One Thursday afternoon I found a second-hand copy of volume 3 of Hodge's *Systematic Theology* on sale for a pittance. At the same time I wanted to tell everyone of the things that I was discovering and started a Christian Union at school. I conducted virtually every meeting, the first one, I recall, being a 75–minute regurgitation of Luther on Galatians! Just before my eighteenth birthday I preached my first more formal sermon (in a village called Yelling!) on Romans 10:8,9. In this way, throughout the two years from the time I bought my first Christian book to the time I went up to study theology at Tyndale Hall, Bristol, my interest in Christian teaching grew steadily. My mother's sympathy and generosity enabled me to acquire about 300 volumes of theology. My constant companions were Louis Berkhof's *Systematic Theology*, John Owen's *The Death of Death* with its introduction by J.I.Packer, and Charles Hodge's three-volume *Systematic Theology*. I also discovered Charles Higham's secondhand bookshop, at that time housed in a basement within walking distance of my home. There I bought works by Goodwin, Owen, Sibbes and others, and sets of the complete works of Stephen Charnock, Goodwin and Owen became my favourites.

While I studied at school for 'A' level examinations, I attended evening classes in New Testament Greek at the London Bible College, at that time in central London. By the time I was eighteen I was able to read the New Testament in Greek, was beginning Hebrew, and was becoming familiar with 17th century theology. A friend recommended the preaching of Dr Martyn Lloyd-Jones, whom I first went to hear during his series of sermons on 'Revival'. From that time on I went whenever I could to hear Dr Lloyd-Jones's famous sermons on Romans preached on Friday evenings at Westminster Chapel. Within a few years I owned a thousand books, most of them Reformed. This set the direction of my thinking and had an effect upon my Christian experience for many years. I gained a degree in theology, spent a year in Old Testament research at Tyndale House, Cambridge, was an Anglican curate for a year, and married. Jenny and I moved to Africa where I started the Christian Union in the University of Zambia, later affiliated to the International Fellowship of Evangelical Students. At the same time I worked for the Zambian Ministry of Education. We were members at Lusaka Baptist Church where some years later – much to my surprise – I became the pastor. A constant theme of my preaching was – and still is – what are sometimes called 'the doctrines of grace'.

It was my experience as an elder and pastor at Lusaka Baptist Church that drew my attention to something that forced a change in my thinking. I began to feel very dissatisfied with some aspects of the 'Reformed' teaching which I knew so well and with which I had lived for so many years. As I looked at myself and at some of my friends, our 'Calvinism' did not seem to be the genuine article. Many things made me wonder. My preaching seemed to be producing converts who were narrow-minded, introspective and pharisaical. How could it be that the preaching of God's grace could produce such resemblance not to New Testament Christians but to the New Testament description of the Pharisees!

I was beginning to think along these lines when suddenly my father had a heart attack. So it was that the day after one of my children was born, I had to leave wife and child in the care of friends in Zambia. Within a matter of hours I was by my father's bedside in London. When I arrived I found that my mother was dying of cancer but neither of my parents realised how rapidly she was declining. It was a very traumatic time and it reinforced my conviction that many Christians I knew were somehow removed from the New Testament.

I was alone in London for some time, my wife and children far away in Africa. On Sundays I went to various 'Reformed' churches, some of them famous for their preaching. I found them cold, formal and legalistic. Even when their purpose was evangelistic they seemed so uninterested in people that I could not imagine anyone being saved by their testimony.

I went to a famous Reformed church to hear a man who was well known for his preaching. Although his exposition of Hosea 14 was accurate, well prepared and delivered in a way that held my attention, no one in the fellowship seemed to have the slightest interest in an 'outsider' like me. Homesick for Africa, I was amazed that no one said a word to me. I decided I would simply stand at the back of the church and wait. Surely someone would say something to me. Slowly the worshippers drifted off. It was a cold rainy night and I had nowhere to go to except a 20–mile journey to dying parents. Finally there were just two of us left on the steps of the church – me and the preacher, who had apparently been left to lock up the building. He put on his raincoat, stepped out into the rain, and, as he walked away from me, shouted over his shoulder: 'Goodnight!' I stood in front of the church building for some minutes with the wind blowing the rain in my face. Was this, I asked myself, really Christianity? Or had I lost my way?

I was distressed at what seemed to be a kind of legalistic harshness in the 'Reformed' people I knew. But worst of all I knew that some of that hard legalism was present in my own life and I possessed neither the assurance nor the spiritual power I had had as a teenager. I didn't even like my own converts, people I had led to the Lord or who I knew admired my preaching. Why was it that the Reformed tradition seemed to consist of an ossified legalism, a crippling introspection, and a harshness of spirit that seemed nothing like the Jesus of the Bible?

Feeling that something was wrong somewhere, I asked the Lord to show me what it was. I determined to go back to the Bible and start all over again. I knew that Galatians had delivered people from bondage before and remembered how I had loved Luther on Galatians in my teenage years. I sensed that if only the Holy Spirit would show me what Galatians was all about I would be all right. I felt sure the answer was theological. My Christian friends in Zambia were very legalistic yet I felt that it was I who had made them that way and what was wrong with them was wrong with me. If I could find out what they needed I would help myself in the process! I began reading everything I could on Galatians and, after doing everything possible for my parents, went back to my family in Zambia with boxes of books following me as unaccompanied baggage.

There followed years of theological pilgrimage. I worked through Galatians clause by clause, writing dozens of pages of notes. Three years later I was still dissatisfied with everything I had read on Galatians but was slowly coming to see that the epistle was saying more than I had ever realized. I discovered that many commentaries on Galatians seemed somehow to draw back from following Paul. 'Liberal' commentators who did not feel obliged to accept what Paul taught seemed in some respects to be more accurate and honest than those who, holding a 'high' doctrine of Scripture, were anxious to subscribe to Paul's teaching. These evangelical commentators seemed to offer freedom with one hand, only to take it back with the other. Having liberated the believer with wonderful expositions of grace, they then took everything back again with dark mutterings about temporary faith and works confirming salvation and talk about self-examination. The bottom line always seemed to be that after the law had been dismissed through one door it came back through another, and in the end stayed with dark threats and heavy frown. I could see I was going to end up taking Galatians more seriously than ever.

My years in Zambia came to a sudden end and I found myself in London enjoying what turned out to be a ten months' sabbatical leave. I had time on my hands and in between sessions of Old Testament writing continued to read everything I could on law and grace.

During the next few months the theological pilgrimage which had started in Zambia gathered momentum. I saw that the message of Galatians really was more radical than the teaching I had been used to and more liberating than anything I had dreamed of. I borrowed R.T.Kendall's doctoral thesis on *Calvin and English Calvinism to 1649*, which explained much that had perplexed me in Reformed theological history.

During the hours I spent reading in the British Museum and the Evangelical Library it increasingly came home to me that the story of Reformed history was one of decline rather than development. I recall reading alongside each other the commentaries on Galatians by Luther and William Perkins and being struck by the contrast. Perkins was struggling with the problem of introspection but was unable to resolve it. The best he could do to help the introspective Christian was to reduce faith to an act of the will. In Galatians 2:20 Paul speaks of having been crucified with Christ and of living 'by faith in the Son of God, who loved me and gave himself for me.' For Perkins: 'if there bee also a will and endeavour to believe' one could then make the words of Galatians 2:20 one's own. 'God accepts the true and earnest will to believe, for faith.' Luther's bold confident invitations to assurance of faith were far different. Surely the 'Reformed faith' had

gone backwards not forwards! Luther was liberating, Perkins intimidating. I loved Luther but was not so sure about Perkins.

On one occasion the mistake of a British Museum librarian meant
that instead of the works of Tobias Crisp I found myself reading about
the death-bed experiences of 17th century Puritans. I was shattered to
discover that their assurance of salvation at such a time was not what I
would have expected. Then I came across the remark of Asahel
Nettleton, quoted above, which expressed the very essence of everything I felt was wrong with the approach to grace that I had grown up
with: 'The most that I have ventured to say respecting myself is, that I
think it possible I may get to heaven.'

Surely, I thought to myself, there is more joy and assurance in the
New Testament than that! Yet I knew only too well that such
introspection and doubt was widespread in the Reformed circles I
knew. The life-changing assurance of salvation that I experienced
when I first believed in Jesus had been eroded rather than enlarged by
my theological reading. Soon I had gone through a theological and
spiritual revolution and had entered into a deeper liberty in the Holy
Spirit than I had known for some years. But not only was I a new man;
those who listened to my preaching seemed to change too, and I saw
assurance and joy on the faces of others as I preached my new
discoveries. What made me absolutely sure that I had found a
goldmine was the joy and peace my new preaching brought to others.
Sometimes I would stay awake into the early hours of the morning
preaching Galatians to my wife. Never did I preach with more liberty
than in those days when I had a congregation of one! I was now ready
for my next pastorate (at Nairobi Baptist Church) and knew what my
first series of sermons would be based on: Galatians!

As I continued to think about these matters I slowly discovered that
freedom from Mosaism had repercussions in many areas of theology.
It correlated with what I had long believed concerning the Holy Spirit.
Since my earliest days as a Christian I had believed in distinct and
conscious workings of the Holy Spirit, and I had experienced what I
believed in. I can only regret it took me so long to accept Galatians
5:18 in its totality. I had believed in the first half – that Christians 'are
led by the Spirit' but had not seen the full implications of the second
half: that 'you are not under law'.

DEVELOPED CALVINISM AND EVANGELICAL ARMINIANISM

Over the years of Christian history evangelical theology has experienced controversies about 'law and grace' without reaching any
satisfactory conclusion. Two main branches of evangelical theology
have arisen. What I am calling 'developed Calvinism' is a theology that
derived from the 16th century Reformation in Europe, and received
some distinctive emphases and changes from Theodore Beza, John

Calvin's successor in Geneva, and the Puritan preachers of 17th century Britain. 'Arminianism' – deriving from the name of Jacobus Arminius – appeared in the last decade of the 16th century. It was a reaction to what seemed to be a strand of fatalism in the teaching of Beza. In the English-speaking world Arminianism was supported and also underwent some changes in the teaching of the 18th century evangelist John Wesley, and his supporter John Fletcher of Madeley.

The controversy between developed Calvinism and evangelical Arminianism revolved largely around predestination and the place of works in salvation. The role of the law of God was not very much at dispute between them. Yet it seems that this was a major omission from the debate. For the Evangelical Arminianism and the kind of Calvinism that developed in English-speaking evangelicalism after the end of the 16th century have, I believe, both been legalistic. Developed Calvinism has also exhibited, I suggest, strongly introspective tendencies. Yet both of these two major forms of evangelical theology have been concerned with Christian godliness.

'THE LAW'

The doctrine concerning 'the law' has been a major ingredient in the legalism and introspection of much Christian tradition. The term itself is used in a quite confusing manner. In evangelical theology, 'the law' does not refer, as it ought, to the totality of the Mosaic legislation given by God through Moses to Israel. It refers instead to a code of morality and spirituality heavily influenced by the teaching of Thomas Aquinas in the 13th century AD and further developed by the Reformers of the 16th century and the Puritans of the 17th It is quite amusing to read in an evangelical writer[5] that one might keep the fourth commandment by gathering round a cosy fire on the Sabbath (i.e. Sunday) to read John Bunyan – when one knows that what the fourth commandment really stipulated for gathering around a fire on the Sabbath (i.e. Saturday) was the death penalty (Ex.31:15; 35:2f.)!

In evangelical thinking 'the law' (understood in this Thomist-Reformed-Puritan way) has been regarded as a guide to Christian sanctification, as a means of 'convicting of sin', and as a means of testing true salvation. All obedience has been considered law-obedience. Whenever the word 'command' is used in Scripture it has been taken for granted that the Thomist-Reformed-Puritan idea of 'the law' is in view. The thought that there could be 'obedience' that has no relationship to the Mosaic law code has scarcely been considered, in spite of examples such as that of Philip in Acts 8:26f. I shall argue in this work that the time has come to reconsider the traditional evangelical view of 'the law' in its relation to salvation and assurance.

I doubt whether the concept of 'preaching the law before the gospel' is correct. Nor is it right, I believe, to define repentance as 'turning from all known sin' and then insist that repentance precedes faith or that repentance and faith together are the way of salvation. Nor do I think it biblical to encourage introspection with regard to 'the law' with a view to determining or confirming one's salvation. The most aweful introspection follows if this is seriously attempted. Examining the relation between the Abraham stories and the presentation of the giving of the law in the book of Exodus reveals a strong platform for a radical doctrine of freedom from Mosaic law, and the epistle to the Galatians is radical in its doctrine of freedom from legalism. Although other parts of Scripture have often been thought to pull in a different direction, it seems to me that the New Testament is less introspective a book than fellow evangelical expositors often make it to be.

I must emphasize that my dislike of this misuse of the Mosaic law concerns the doctrine of salvation more than theological ethics. The distinction I draw between morality and godliness implies an analogous distinction between 'ethics' (which I see as primarily relating to the political task of bringing Christian thinking to bear in a fallen world so as to bring about a measure of morality) and 'spirituality', which outstrips public morality. If Mosaism is an epoch in salvation-history which has now terminated, the Christian's interest in public morality may derive wisdom from it, but will not directly apply the Mosaic covenant to modern society. My study has implications for a Christian view of ethics and the relationship between church and state. Yet my work does not tackle these issues directly and deals rather with what I conceive of as a starting point further back: soteriology – including the Christian's assurance of salvation and obedience to the Spirit. Modern legislators may learn from the Mosaic covenant. Yet the statement in 1 Timothy 1:9 that 'the law is not for the righteous man but for the sinner' must also be weighed. It is the relationship – or the lack of it – between the law and the righteous person that I pursue in the following pages. I would not be surprised if the Christian politician or social reformer were to be hostile to what I write here. Such hostility would arise from their particular concern for society. Agreed, 'the law is . . . for the sinner'. I have no dispute with that. However the relevance of the law to culturally mixed society is one matter; the irrelevance of the law to justification, assurance of salvation and Christian spirituality is another. 'The law is not for the righteous man.' The law, by which I mean the legislation given by God to Israel in the 13th century BC, is, I suggest, irrelevant to the doctrine of salvation, not because Christian spirituality accepts anything lower than the law, but because it aims at something higher. 'The law' is not brushed aside by Christ; it is fulfilled by Jesus.

The point is made clear if we think of the animal sacrifices. Christians do not offer animal sacrifices, because the greater Sacrifice has come; the sacrifice of Jesus fulfils and utterly transcends for ever the system of animal sacrifice. In a precisely parallel way, the Christian does not live under the law because the greater gift, the Spirit, has been given. The Spirit fulfils and utterly transcends for ever the system of living under the law of the Mosaic epoch. Those who believe in Jesus fulfil the animal sacrifices accidentally. Those who walk in the Spirit fulfil the law accidentally. Those who believe in Jesus are not under a system of animal sacrifices because they do not have to be. Those who walk in the Spirit are not under the Mosaic law because they do not have to be. Animal sacrifices typify the great Sacrifice but must not be identified with the great Sacrifice of Jesus on the cross. Similarly the law-obedience of the Mosaic covenant typifies Christian obedience but actually Christian obedience outstrips it vastly. Even for society the Mosaic law is too low a standard for a nation influenced by the Christian gospel. Would William Wilberforce have worked to abolish slavery if he had been implementing the Mosaic law?

It is a commonplace of evangelical theology to understand much of the law typologically. 'Typology' is the phenomenon in which one event is analogous but not identical to another event. Animal sacrifice is typological of the sacrifice of Jesus. The passover festival of the Old Testament is typological of his death upon the cross. The entry into Canaan is typological of the Christian's entering into a spiritual inheritance in Christ. The work of the high-priest in the tabernacle of early Old Testament days is typological of Jesus' presentation of his sacrifice to the Father. Yet an essential element in typology is that analogy is not identity. Animal sacrifices are not identical to the death of Jesus upon the cross. The law is only a shadow of the good things to come; it is not the good things themselves (Heb.10:1).

All of this is widely accepted, yet the possibility does not seem to have been adequately considered that even the moral principles of the law given by God through Moses are also typological of Christian spirituality, and that Christian spirituality itself is something greater and more exuberant and joyful.

The following chapters make a start in proposing a more encouraging theology of salvation. At its heart will be a reconsideration of the place of the Mosaic law in Christian theology. I propose to consider what I think to be the weakness of the two major alternatives current in the evangelical Christian world. Over against those weaknesses I will put forward a somewhat revised evangelical theology. I also have in view, to be published later, expositions of particular books of the Bible that are the source in my own thinking and preaching of the theology proposed here.

The present book will argue that the Christian is released from the law and that Christian godliness is a matter of walking in the Spirit upon the basis of complete assurance of present and final salvation. On this view, the righteousness of the law is not lost in the Christian but is embraced in something altogether greater. Christians 'fulfil' the law without being 'under' the law. They walk in the Spirit deliberately and so fulfil the law accidentally. Only by a radical freedom from legalism may there be a theology which avoids the snares of both legalism and introspection.

ANTINOMIANISM

In the history of the Christian church the term 'antinomianism' has generally been used with overtones of disparagement. It arose in Luther's conflict with Agricola and was used by Lutheranism to denigrate what was felt to be Agricola's heresy. Similarly in 17th century England and America 'antinomianism' designated what mainstream Puritanism viewed as the 'heretical' party in the debate concerning the law of God. 'Antinomian' was always an insult, never a compliment.

It is arguable however that from the earliest days in the history of the Christian church Christians have too easily disparaged 'antinomians' and have often themselves lapsed into moralism, legalism or introspection. T.F.Torrance points out that the earliest Christian writers had an insufficiently radical view of grace. For the Didache, Clement of Rome, Ignatius, Polycarp, Barnabas, the Shepherd and the author of 2 Clement,

> What took precedence was God's call to a new life in obedience to revealed truth. Grace, so far as it was grasped, was subsidiary to that. And so religion was thought of primarily in terms of man's acts toward God, in the striving towards justification, much less in terms of God's acts for man which put him right with God once and for all.'[6]

Torrance attributes this moralism partly to the influence of Judaism and partly to the influence of Greek naturalistic thought:

> 'The converts of the first few generations had difficulty in apprehending the distinctive aspects of the Gospel, as for example the doctrine of grace'.[7] 'Their theology represents a corrosion of the faith both from the side of Judaism and from the side of Hellenism, because the basic significance of grace was not grasped . . . The most astonishing feature was the failure to grasp the significance of the death of Christ.'[8]

From an altogether different (Roman Catholic) standpoint Guy Bourgeault surveys the early use of the Decalogue from about AD 60 to AD 220. Unlike Torrance, he writes with greater approval of early Christian moral teaching. But the general conclusion is much the same. His survey of the Didache, Barnabas, the Shepherd, Ignatius, Polycarp, Justin, Tertullian, Irenaeus and other less significant writers reveals that all of them made use of the Decalogue. Their usage is radicalized and spiritualized in ways that resemble the Sermon on the Mount, and so they do not speak of being under the law with regard to the details of the 'ceremonial' law. Yet the Christianized version of the law 'does not abrogate the decalogue and does not annul the requirements of the natural law'.[9] Similarly Hugo Röthlisberger speaks of 'the journey of the Church to Sinai', saying that 'Christ was viewed in the second century not as a Mediator but only as a Lawgiver'.[10] It is not only in the first generation that we find this tendency.

A similar slide into moralism is noticeable after the Reformation. C.F. Allison's survey of the proclamation of the gospel in Britain between Hooker (1554–1600) and Baxter (1615–1691) follows an analogous pattern. After the solafidian doctrine of the early Caroline divines (such as Hooker, George Downame, Joseph Hall, James Ussher, John Donne, Lancelot Andrewes) a steady decline into a moralist soteriology is observable.[11] It has affected British evangelical Christianity ever since. Both the Anglican and the nonconformist theologies have their roots in this period of British evangelical theology. Puritanism also had its legalistic aspects and in the end British evangelical theology was riddled with legalism and moralism.[12]

Over against this tendency in the church I shall argue that there is a valid emancipation from the Mosaic law, and a grasp of such emancipation is essential to a vibrant doctrine of assurance. The apostle Paul was certainly vulnerable to accusations of licentiousness as the arguments of Romans and Galatians make plain (Rom.3:8; 6:1; Gal.2:17). My thesis is that the Christian is totally free from the Mosaic covenant, that it is a mistake in theology to take the law as recorded in the Decalogue as a 'rule of life'[13] or as a needful tool in bringing about conviction of sin[14], that the Sinai covenant is in radical antithesis to the movement in history that began with Abraham, that it was an intrusion into the history of redemption, was innovative, unnecessary, exclusively an interim measure and therefore is now of no direct relevance to the Christian. Because of this release from condemnation Christian godliness may proceed upon the basis of a high level of assurance of salvation. The positive side of this negative contention is that Christ and the gift of the Spirit are sufficient to justify, to sanctify, to glorify. Christ alone 'without the law' is the ground of justification. Christ alone 'without the law' is amply adequate to guide and to sanctify. Christian faith is directed towards the sufficiency of Jesus in revelation, justification, sanctification and glorification, without the law. Christian obedience is 'obedience of faith' unmediated by the law of God, sustained by fellowship with Jesus Christ, illuminated by the Spirit, checked by one's total understanding of Scripture, fulfilling the law of God 'accidentally' yet surpassing the law of God as recorded in the Pentateuch and leading to a level of godliness that puts the Mosaic law into eclipse.

In all of this I am not referring to any kind of licentiousness but to a style of living that in complete independence of the Mosaic covenant seeks to glorify God. A Christian who walks by the Spirit deliberately fulfils the Mosaic law accidentally. The Christian is moral and more-than-moral; he or she does 'fulfil' the law but is not 'under' it.

In the history of the Christian church it has often happened that those against whom there is no suspicion of a sinful lifestyle have been called 'antinomian'. One thinks of Johannes Agricola[15], John Cotton[16], certain English Puritans,[17] the early 'Plymouth brethren'[18], and individuals such as the 19th century preacher César Malan[19]. Yet no one could easily accuse these people of moral laxity. Agricola's behaviour in the sixteenth century was not inferior to Luther's.[20] 'Antinomian' was a theological term of disparagement often used against godly believers who held a particular theological position regarding law and grace.[21] Such 'theological swear-words' are well-known. The earliest was 'Christian'.[22] The 'antinomianism' which was propounded by Agricola, Cotton and others, ought to be given an entirely different label from that of immoral cults who have taught that morality is in no way needful. Drawing such a distinction would contribute to clear thinking and Christian charity. The point of the 'antinomianism' of Agricola and Cotton was not to question whether the Christian should be moral but how such morality could be attained and how assurance of salvation could be enjoyed in liaison with striving after godliness.

There is room for a 'non-legalistic' theology that will also hold to a doctrine of justification by 'faith only' more radical than is customary. Such a teaching is found supremely in the writings attributed to the apostle Paul, but is consistent with the whole Bible, if due allowance is made for the interim character of the Mosaic covenant. It is charismatic in that it lays stress on the direct work of the Spirit, evangelical in that it bases such a position upon the Bible, incidentally moral in that it holds that the Mosaic law is incidentally fulfilled, and godly in that it looks for a level of godliness that outstrips mere morality and has likeness to Jesus as its major goal.

2

Developed Calvinism

In the history of evangelical theology since the Reformation contro-versies concerning grace have revolved largely around such issues as election and justification. In the English-speaking world a major divide came in the 18th century when the 'methodist' movement, which emphasized experience of God, divided into Calvinist and Arminian sections. It may be suggested that neither side satisfactorily handled the issue of the place of the law in the Christian life. Both theologies resulted in legalism, but the Calvinist often bore the added burden of introspection. At this point we shall survey a few of the concerns of these two classic forms of evangelicalism, focusing especially on the English-speaking scene. Later I shall present a similar outline of a theology of grace which does not exactly follow the contours of either theology outlined here.

In evangelical theology freedom from Mosaism has been treated with suspicion, generally evoking the fear of licentiousness. Recent writings suggesting a less legalistic approach to the doctrine of perseverance have received hostile reviews from fellow Calvinists.[1] But are such fears justified? Classical high Calvinism has taught a doctrine of 'final perseverance' which, despite its apparently encourag-ing tendency, actually includes strongly introspective and discouraging elements. Much modern theology follows what has historically been known as 'Arminianism', accepting the possibility that salvation may be lost. The viewpoint I shall present differs from both.

DEVELOPED CALVINISM

I am assuming that there is such a thing as 'developed' or 'scholastic' Calvinism, a theology which differs in numerous ways from the teaching of Calvin himself. This is now widely accepted, and I have touched upon the matter in a previous book.[2] There are a number of distinctive emphases in scholastic Calvinism.

LIMITED ATONEMENT

Scholastic Calvinism has held to what has been called 'limited atonement' or 'particular redemption'. The atonement of Christ is correlated with the doctrine of election so as to produce the logically extended doctrine that Jesus did not die or atone for all humankind.

The doctrine has early roots. A 'limited atonement' has sometimes been distinguished in the teaching of Augustine[3] and certainly was taught by Gottschalk in the ninth century[4]. Peter Lombard's formula for denoting the extent of the atonement was: 'sufficient for all men and efficient for the elect'[5]. This was accepted by Calvin although he did not think it entirely adequate.[6] Luther and Calvin did not discuss the matter very explicitly. The matter was raised by Gottschalk. Calvin's allusion to Lombard shows that he was conscious of the question, and he cannot have been unaware of the predestinarian conflicts that surrounded Gottschalk. Luther's view of 'the many' in Romans 5:15 was reminiscent of the Augustinian view[7] but Calvin explicitly took a different view of Romans 5:15 from that of Luther[8]. He does not seem to have tightly woven together election and atonement after the manner of later Calvinists. Although the matter has been debated, my view is that Calvin should be classed with those who hold to universal atonement. In later Calvinism, Beza, Perkins and late English Puritanism held to a limited atonement, but there were always Calvinists who held to a universal atonement.

There is more than one way in which a doctrine of unconditional election can be correlated with the doctrine of atonement so as to deduce a doctrine of limited atonement. In a brief article Hywel Roberts has distinguished three ways in which the teaching was presented among Welsh-speaking preachers.[9] According to Roberts the Baptist preacher Christmas Evans argued that the death of Christ was not of infinite worth but was exactly equivalent to the sins of the elect. The Congregationalist John Roberts held that the atonement had a general purpose which gave rise to temporal blessings as well as a particular purpose in which Christ designed to save only the elect. The Calvinistic Methodist, Thomas Jones of Denbigh, argued that Christ's death was of infinite worth, yet was intended only for those whom God had given to his Son.

Roberts went on to urge that the third of the views summarized is the correct one and was held by the Reformers, the Puritans, the leaders of Calvinistic methodism, as well as by Andrew Fuller, Daniel Rowlands, Howell Harris and William Williams. Our concern at present is to draw attention to the significance of the doctrine in relation to an evangelical view of assurance of salvation and freedom from legal condemnation. It has, I suggest, at least the following implications.

(i) It depersonalizes the 'free offer' of the gospel. The 'limited atonement' theorist cannot and generally does not say to anyone: 'Christ died for you.' A 19th century advocate of universal redemption thought that even the 'sufficient for all' formula is inadequate.[10]

'If the inhabitants of a city were perishing by famine what would it avail to be informed that a store of provisions had arrived amply sufficient, and more than sufficient, to satisfy the wants of all, if at the same time they were told that the provision was actually designed only for a few? Would not the attention of the starving multitude be immediately withdrawn from the amplitude of the supply, to the more nearly interesting inquiry whether or not they individually were included in the favoured number'

The limited atonement theorist is in difficulty, because a salvation offered to a particular man or woman seems to imply a salvation already provided for that very person. At this point the particular redemptionist must draw back. The most he can say is, in generalized terms, that Christ died for sinners. He cannot personalize the gospel offer. In practice the particular redemptionist gives the impression that Christ died for the individual non-Christian but avoids saying so.

(ii) Limited atonement presents a threat to a genuine free offer of salvation. Outsiders initially get the impression that Christ died for them, when that outsider or newcomer does not notice that the preacher or evangelist holds back from personalizing his message. The uninitiated non-Christian may not know of 'limited atonement' and may get the impression that Christ died for him whether he is elect or not! The Baptist preacher Charles Spurgeon could be mentioned in this connection. He believed in limited atonement and had a sermon preached on the subject at the opening of the Metropolitan Tabernacle in the 1850s.[11] Yet anyone who reads his 62 volumes of sermons constantly receives a strong impression that Christ died for everyone, elect or non-elect.

However the doctrine of limited atonement also becomes a threat to assurance of salvation. It correlates atonement with election in such a way that it is not possible to look directly at the cross of Jesus to get assurance of salvation. If a would-be believer is familiar with such teaching, threatening thoughts will cross his mind when he looks at the cross. It will occur to him that the work of Jesus might not be for him. To talk of trusting Christ without knowing definitely whether what Christ did on the cross relates to oneself is in practice rather difficult. In conjunction with other aspects of developed Calvinism it becomes impossible.

(iii) It is characteristic of scholastic Calvinism that it has difficulty with statements in Scripture concerning the objectivity and universality of the work of Jesus. Statements that Jesus died 'for all' or for 'the world' or that he 'tasted death for every person' do not fit easily with an approach that tightly links election and atonement. Probably only a scholastic Calvinist could say 'The term world as used in John 3:16 presents a serious difficulty of exegesis.'[12]

(iv) It is somewhat difficult for the limited atonement theorist to give real significance to faith. Admittedly scholastic Calvinists want to give significance to faith. Yet they say: 'The Cross makes certain the salvation of all those for whom Christ died'.[13] 'It is not the possibility of salvation, not simply the opportunity of salvation. What is offered is salvation'.[14] On such a view the cross purchases faith. As John Owen put it 'Faith . . . is itself procured by the death of Christ.'[15] But this makes it difficult to see how faith has any independent significance. If the cross applies its own benefits and is God's only saving instrument- ality, what place does faith have? In scholastic Calvinist thinking it 'is the duty of all men everywhere to believe'[16]. But to believe what? Not to believe that Christ died for me. Such a statement is thought to be without warrant and no part of the gospel. Is it then that the individual must believe in the person of Jesus without having any assurance that what Christ did is for him? Apparently this is what the scholastic Calvinist desires. Yet Calvin puts the problem when commenting on John 3:16: 'Men are not easily convinced that God loves them; and so, to remove all doubt, He has expressly stated that we are so very dear to God that for our sakes He did not spare even His only begotten Son.' Calvin is clear that any introspective doubts are needless. In John 3:16 'whosoever' is 'a general term, both to invite indiscrimin- ately all to share in life and to cut off every excuse from unbelievers. Such is also the significance of the term 'world' which He had used before. For although there is nothing in the world deserving of God's favour, He nevertheless shows He is favourable to the whole world when He calls all without exception to the faith of Christ, which is indeed an entry into life'.[17]

(v) Limited atonement thus relegates assurance of salvation to the future and makes it the long-term goal of faith rather than an immediate possibility. For the authors of *The Grace of God in the Gospel* the kind of assurance Paul expressed in Galatians 2:20 is not an immediate possibility for the Christian. 'It is the zenith, not the beginning, of faith to appropriate to oneself this verse.' William Perkins said the same thing in the seventeenth century[18]. It is part of the logic of limited atonement that such personal assurance has to become the 'zenith' of Christian experience.

(vi) Limited atonement thus introduces 'preparationism' into the doctrine of salvation. Consider, for example, the following sentence. 'No-one who has not first repented and trusted in Christ to save him, may legitimately believe that Christ has died for him personally.'[19] This may be contrasted with a statement of Calvin: 'How shall we be convinced that He loves us until those sins for which He is justly angry with us have been expiated? Thus before we can have any feeling of His fatherly kindness, the blood of Christ must intercede to reconcile God to us.'[20]

A consideration of the two sentences reveals that they make diametrically opposite points. In the one case, it seems one must know one has repented and know one has trusted in Christ before one can know that Christ's death is 'for me'. Calvin makes the opposite point. One must know Christ's death is 'for me' before one can have any feeling of God's fatherly kindness. In other words, on a universal atonement view there is nothing preparatory to certainty that Christ's death is 'for me'. For the authors of *The Grace of God* there has to be (if one takes them seriously) a consideration of oneself before there can be a knowledge of Christ's death being 'for me'. This is the key point: there is an introspective tendency built into the very foundations of scholastic Calvinism.

ASSURANCE OF SALVATION

The reformation tradition has always made much of assurance of salvation. For Luther and Calvin faith is assurance. Subsequent theological reflection drove a wedge between initial-faith which may or may not include full assurance of salvation, and developed-faith which reflects upon itself and reaches assurance of salvation. From the days of the Westminster Confession (1649) the latter has been dominant in English-speaking Reformed theology, especially among the Puritans and their successors. John Murray called initial faith the 'direct or primary act of faith'. He called developed faith the 'secondary or reflex act of faith'. The latter he thought to be 'logically subsequent' to the former.[21]

On this view, assurance of salvation may be much delayed in the life of the believer. Infallible assurance, says the Westminster Confession, 'doth not so belong to the essence of faith, but that a true believer may wait long, and conflict with many difficulties, before he be a partaker of it'.

The point I wish to emphasize here is that Reformed thought claims that a believer may have present assurance of final salvation. Yet it is vital to note that, as often presented, the high Calvinist view of final perseverance has legalistic elements. In another work Murray acknowledges that he dislikes the expression 'the security of the believer' and prefers the Puritan expression 'perseverance of the saints'. The latter term 'guards against every notion or suggestion to the effect that a believer is . . . secure as to his eternal salvation quite irrespective of the extent to which he may fall into sin'[22]. For Murray, assurance of salvation is not 'without works'. Rather it is based upon the doctrine that believers do inevitably persevere; 'it cannot be too strongly stressed that it is the perseverance of the saints'; 'the security that is theirs is inseparable from their perseverance'; it requires 'the most intense and concentrated devotion to those means which God has ordained for the achievement of his saving purpose'. Murray reveals his concern when he says his doctrine wishes to avoid both 'the Arminian tenet' concerning possible loss of salvation, and also 'antinomian presumption'[23].

I suggest that Murray is perhaps closer to evangelical Arminianism than he ever realized. What is the value of a doctrine of assurance with such a strongly conditional element? The evangelical Arminian says the Christian shall attain salvation as long as he perseveres. Murray also says the Christian shall attain salvation as long as he perseveres. Is there any difference between them? The Arminian says that despite all the appearances of salvation, salvation may be lost. Similarly, John Murray holds to a doctrine of 'temporary faith' and speaks of 'the lengths and the heights to which a temporary faith may carry those who have it'. There are (he says) 'forces that are operative in the kingdom of God' and 'very uplifting, ennobling, reforming, and exhilarating experience of the power and truth of the gospel' which fall short of salvation.[24]

It seems that Arminians must not assume the *continuance* of their faith, and scholastic Calvinists must not assume the *reality* of theirs. In the one case awareness of sin threatens the Arminian's confidence about continuance in the faith; in the other case awareness of sin threatens confidence about the reality of salvation. Again one notes how the developed form of Reformed thinking has a tendency to introspection.

A high Calvinist who does indeed come to a present assurance of salvation can have an assurance of final salvation. This is the implication of relating election to perseverance. It is extremely comforting if the person concerned does indeed reach assurance of present salvation. Yet the legalistic tendencies of this view and the doctrine of 'temporary faith' form a great barrier. Such a person's doctrine is likely to be of no practical help.

On the scholastic Reformed view, assurance becomes 'the duty and privilege of assurance'. How then is the duty to be performed? It is a matter of obedience to the commandment of God; 'obedience . . . constitutes the evidence that we love God'. We must not take salvation for granted.[25] The Christian's task includes the responsibility for self-examination. 'There is much reason to fear' (says Murray) 'that the Christian church has to a large extent neglected the duty of self-examination.' We are to ask such questions as: 'Am I an heir of God? Do I bear the marks of the children of God? Do I have the title deeds to the resurrection of life and to the house not made with hands eternal in the heaven?' Murray thinks this is not 'morbid introspection' but a necessary part of the pathway to assurance of salvation.[26]

However I also have some questions. Is assurance of salvation represented in the New Testament as a duty? Are Christians ever invited in the New Testament to ask such questions of themselves? How many people who take such a doctrine serious actually arrive at the kind of assurance Murray envisages? Is not such a doctrine so conditional upon passing certain tests as one looks at oneself, that doubt and insecurity are bound to be the result? May not the verses of Scripture that Murray quotes from 1 John and elsewhere be interpreted in an entirely different way? Is it not a fact of history that the Calvinist has tended to have less assurance of salvation than the Arminian? The Arminian is at least sure of his present salvation. As the result of the high Calvinist doctrine the Calvinist often doubts his present salvation and thus has a less contented frame of mind than his evangelical Arminian friend.

GODLY LIVING

Thirdly, the Reformation tradition has always had a concern for godliness. A sincere motive underlies the theological constructions we have been surveying. It is the fear that an extreme doctrine of grace might lead to a real licentiousness. Despite all accusations to the contrary, concern for godliness has undoubtedly been a dominant concern in Reformed as well as in Arminian theology. We need not question the sincerity of either side. The history is well known. Luther emphasized two aspects of the Christian use of the law. It both restrained sin in society and was also of value in inducing conviction of sin and thus preparing the way for the gospel. Agricola's main concern was apparently with the first of these uses of the law. He believed Mosaic law was primarily for the magistrates; to preach it to induce conviction of sin was needless. Calvin agreed with Luther but added a third use of the Mosaic law; it was of importance too in guiding the Christian life.

From these early Protestant origins the Reformed doctrine developed and has remained much the same until this day. Christ's words about the law in Mt.5:17–20 have made this a key text in Reformed thinking. Romans 6 and 7 have been interpreted as referring to freedom from law with regard to justification but not with regard to sanctification.[27]

WARNINGS OF FAILURE

Fourthly, the Reformed tradition has handled the warnings of Scripture in a distinctive way. The New Testament contains many warnings concerning failure of faith. There are warnings concerning forfeiture of the kingdom (1 Cor.6:9; Gal.5:21; Eph.5:5), conditional statements where some aspect of future blessing is introduced with the word 'if' (Rom.8:13;17; Col.1:23), statements addressed to disciples which warn of loss of grace in some manner. For example, the recipients of the Sermon on the Mount included disciples (Mt.5:2), and there is no reason to think that the warnings about gehenna (5:22,29,30), loss of reward (6:1), judgement (7:1–2) and the broad road that leads to destruction (7:13,19) do not concern them. We find warnings about 'enduring to the end' (Mk.13:13) and about being 'destroyed' by neglect of attention to one's conscience (1 Cor.8:11; Rom.14:15). There are remarks about 'falling from grace' and being 'cut off from Christ' (Gal.5:4), and making shipwreck of the faith (1 Tim.1:19; 6:21; 2 Tim.2:18). In a category of their own come the warnings of the letter to the Hebrews. In Reformed thinking, such warnings are generally taken to refer to an unreal salvation or an appearance only of salvation. Murray quotes the 'tests of life' in 1 John without any indication that they could do anything other than threaten the reality of salvation[28] and interprets 2 Peter 1:10 as an invitation to diligence in cultivating assurance of salvation.[29] He thus follows a tradition going back to the days of William Perkins[30]. For Calvin, 2 Peter 1:10 'should not . . . be referred to conscience'[31]. He did not understand 2 Peter 1:10 introspectively. The verse is positive ('Prove you are called and elected') not introspective ('Conduct tests to see whether or not you

are called and elected'). 2 Peter 1:10 assumes that the readers know
their calling and invites them to prove it. It could be discussed whether
or not this is an accurate reading of the verse. It at least demonstrates
that the introspective interpretation may not be assumed without
discussion.

Similarly Heb.6:4–6, in Murray's opinion, must make us fear that
exhilarating experiences of God may turn out to be delusive[32]. At
every point the warnings are taken in an introspective manner.

If one explores Calvinist biblical commentaries from the early 17th
century onwards one discovers that the introspective approach to the
warnings of Scripture dominates this tradition. There is a lengthy
history that includes the large expositions of the English Puritans and
their Scottish colleagues. It takes in the work of the Calvinistic Baptist,
John Gill, the 19th century expositions of John Brown, and the
expository writings of Charles Hodge and J.A. Alexander. More
recently it is seen in the volumes of the New International Commentary with – in the early days of the series – its Reformed contributors.
Stridently Calvinistic exposition has also been apparent in the expository writings of W. Hendriksen, S. Kistemaker, G.B. Wilson, A.W.
Pink and D. Martyn Lloyd-Jones.

Throughout these works the warnings of Scripture are taken, by and
large, to refer to an unreal salvation; Christians are frequently invited
to search their hearts to see whether or not they are true heirs of
salvation. The documentation of this point could run to tens of pages –
but space forbids and it would not be useful. We shall later glance at
how Reformed writers have generally taken Hebrews chapter 6 in this
introspective manner. Two examples must suffice, one ancient and one
modern. In the teaching of the 17th century preacher and commentator, George Petter, repentance is defined as 'turning from all sin'.
Petter analyses the matter is great detail. Repentance has two parts.
We have to be aware of sorrow for our sin. This must be with 'constant
purpose in heart'[33]. Our turning must be from 'all sin'. Petter has five
tests for us to use to discern whether we have in fact turned from all sin
in this way. One of them is that our repentance is 'universal' and
'constant'; it must be from 'all' sin; it includes the practising of 'every
good duty'; 'late repentance is not acceptable'; the repentance must
not arise out of fear of hell. We must 'try ourselves whether we be
angry at our selves for our sins'. 'Let every one ask his own heart' says
Petter. Repentance leads to faith and good works and we must 'by
these marks try ourselves' and 'rest not in temporary faith.'[34] Only
with such repentance may there be any forgiveness of sin. Throughout
Petter's pages on repentance there is a strong atmosphere of introspection. I doubt whether anyone ever came to assurance by acting on such
teaching.

A modern Reformed commentator is G.B. Wilson, who has written
eleven volumes of popular 'Digests' of Reformed comment. The fact
that he is specifically offering a 'digest of Reformed comment' makes
his works all the more significant as we consider the Reformed

approach to exposition. Wilson is not as heavily introspective as his Puritan predecessors, yet he interprets the key 'warning' verses in much the same way. Thus the Corinthians were told to test the genuineness of their faith lest they should be 'counterfeit Christians'[35]. No other view of 2 Cor.13:5 is considered. Even the apostle could turn out not to be truly Christian at all, and it would help the Corinthians to know it! Col.1:23, according to Wilson, contains an 'if' that is cautionary. The salvation of the Colossians is to be evidenced by the continuance; Paul 'puts a question mark against their fidelity'[36]. When approaching a verse like Rev.22:18f. ('. . . God shall take away his part from the tree of life . . . ') Wilson takes it to refer to one who is only apparently a Christian. Such a Christian would forfeit his share of eternal life, 'i.e. he would lose what he seemed to have by profession, though as such an act would prove, not by possession'[37]. All of this is typical of the Reformed tradition we are considering. Revelation 22:18f is not interpreted as referring to apostasy; rather it means that what seemed to be salvation turns out not to be salvation after all. Wilson apparently sees no way of understanding the warnings of Scripture except along introspective lines. He does not wish to go the Arminian route and teach the possibility of apostasy, so he is shut up – so it seems – to the introspective interpretations beloved of English Calvinism.

INTROSPECTION

Fifthly, arising out of these motifs, traditional late Reformed theology has a problem with introspection. I have already urged that introspection is implicit in many aspects of the Reformed doctrine of grace in late Calvinism. Now I wish to underline the fact that the most intense introspection follows if many or all of these emphases are combined. If Christ did not die for all, and if it is possible to have a sorrow for sin which is not true repentance, a faith which is not true faith, a possessing of the Spirit which falls short of true regeneration, if despite any and every 'experience' of the gospel there is 'a way to Hell even from the Gates of Heaven'[38], if Paul himself feared loss of salvation, then what remains of the Calvinist's assurance? It has died the death of a thousand qualifications. No wonder a great Calvinist evangelist could say, 'The most that I have ventured to say respecting myself is, that I think it possible I may get to heaven'.[39] Puritanism was notoriously introspective; many Puritan preachers themselves had difficulty in the matter of assurance of their own salvation. O.R.Johnston, who was an admirer of the Puritan Thomas Shepard, nevertheless called him 'notoriously a melancholic' and spoke of his difficulties with depression.[40] O.C.Watkins makes similar points concerning John Bunyan, who showed great introspection in *Grace Abounding*, the account of his early Christian experience.[41] Elizabeth Braund records how Puritans might set aside a whole day for self-examination.[42] I.Murray notes that the preaching of the doctrine of election might be used to deliberately induce despair in the hearers; this was thought often to be a salutary experience.[43]

A characteristic of Reformed practice in this stage of English life was the time that Puritan pastors spent in counselling 'troubled souls'. However the question may be asked: was it their distinctive teaching that gave rise to so many 'troubled souls'.[44] For example Richard Greenham, pastor of Dry Drayton from 1570, gave considerable thought to 'distressing states of mind and heart', including especially lack of assurance of salvation.[45] P.Cook, in summarizing the teaching of Richard Greenham and Richard Rogers says that by their standards 'many professing Christians would fail the test of being truly Christians',[46] which is another way of saying that their teaching undermined assurance of salvation. R.Horn refers to the 'weight of emphasis which [Thomas] Hooker places on the law', and criticizes him for disregarding biblical material on evangelism, for example the evangelistic sermons of Acts, because it would not fit into his scheme of ideas.[47]

In addition, Puritans often wrote books seeking to help their people into assurance of salvation, William Guthrie[48] and Thomas Brooks[49] among them. One of the few Puritan diaries that have survived is that of the Puritan Oliver Heywood (1629–1702). Again one notices its introspection. W.H.Davies notes what he calls Heywood's 'intense self-examination' and comments: 'One thing is consistently to be noticed in Heywood's life and that is his habit of continuous heart searchings.'[50]

The studies of Puritanism quoted here show that even those who admire it concede that it is introspective. The danger is especially severe when all of the various aspects of developed Reformed doctrine are held in combination. The picture is as follows. Jesus died for sinners – but fuller knowledge reveals that he died for only some sinners. He makes an offer of salvation to anyone who believes in him. When he saves, he saves utterly and for ever. He is able to keep. Once one has believed in Jesus one's salvation is secure for ever. One lives a godly life not in order to obtain salvation but as grateful response to salvation.

So far so good. Many people – including the present writer – have come to life, joy and liberty under the influence of such a theology. Yet as knowledge of the full teaching of scholastic Calvinism is received it becomes increasingly threatening. The way for faith has to be prepared by repentance. Repentance is turning from all known sin. Was my faith preceded by repentance? Have I turned from all known sin? I fear I may not have done so! Jesus did not die for everyone. Am I perhaps one of those for whom he did not die? Is there any way of knowing? If I believe, then I may know I am indeed one of the ones for whom Jesus died. Yes, but at the moment I am questioning whether I really did believe or not. Worst of all, there is such a thing as imitation-salvation. It is possible to be enlightened, to have tasted of the heavenly gift, even to have one's life changed, and yet not be a true Christian.

The last threatening paragraph is long enough. But it could go on for ever! This is the snag of scholastic Calvinism. It leads into an abyss of ever-increasing introspection.

That my description above is correct will be admitted by anyone who has much experience of developed-Calvinist circles. The more sincere the Christian the more they are haunted by these doubts. In my own ministry I think of the words of a well-known Christian leader who shared with me his anxieties: 'all my life I have wondered whether I really am saved'. I think of the words of a theological student I once sought to help: 'I have always been troubled by the feeling that I am only harrowed ground and the Word has not gone into my heart.' Reformed theology has been a great power for good in the history of Protestantism. The theology presented in the following chapters is decidedly Calvinist. Yet one needs to remember that there are subtle variations among different versions of Calvinism. The introspective variety is decidedly not totally derived from the New Testament, and its all-pervasive view of the law needs reconsidering.

3

Evangelical Arminianism

Evangelical Arminian theology has much in common with other forms of evangelicalism: its regard for Scripture, its trinitarianism, its forensic doctrine of justification, its doctrine of new birth. In this chapter however we shall consider those aspects of evangelical Arminianism that relate to our theme of law, grace, security and introspection.

UNIVERSAL ATONEMENT

Firstly, *evangelical Arminianism was notable for its doctrine of universal atonement*. The scholastic doctrine of 'limited atonement' was sharply repudiated by English-speaking Arminianism. John Wesley, who may be taken as one of the founding fathers of contemporary English-speaking Arminianism, inherited from his parents an intense and abiding dislike of any form of predestinarianism. Wesley entered into sharp conflict with his friend George Whitefield over this point, and gloried in universal atonement, even to the point of bringing it into his hymns in a polemical manner:

> O for a trumpet voice,
>   On all the world to call!
> To bid their hearts rejoice
>   In Him who died for all;
> For all my Lord was crucified,
> For all, for all my Saviour died.[1]

In at least two ways the Arminian doctrine of universal atonement has implications for a doctrine of assurance. It connects with an assurance of availability of grace. While limited atonement theologians may teach a 'free offer' of grace, any doctrine of limited atonement is likely to prompt the suspicion that such an atonement is 'not for me'. Wesley was conscious of this tendency. Having written

> The world He suffered to redeem;
> For all He hath atonement made;

> For those who will not come to him
> The ransom of his life was paid -

he went on to ask

> Why then, thou universal love,
> Should any of thy grace despair?[2]

In addition, a doctrine of universal atonement *gives significance to faith*. On this view, the cross is *not* efficacious in itself. Here Calvin may be classified as holding an Arminian doctrine of the extent of the atonement, if the anachronism may be allowed, for he does not portray the cross as inherently efficacious and he attaches great significance to faith.

ASSURANCE OF (PRESENT) SALVATION

Secondly, *evangelical Arminianism holds to assurance of present salvation only*. On Arminian presuppositions a present assurance of final salvation is not possible. Among his *Articles To Be Diligently Examined*, Arminius included a section on 'Assurance of Salvation' in which he denied that a believer could be sure than he would not fall away from the faith. Such a conviction, he thought, engendered security, 'a thing directly opposed to that most salutary fear with which we are commanded to work out our salvation and which is exceedingly necessary in this scene of temptation'.[3]

This approach has become common in one strand of modern English-speaking evangelicalism. E.M.B.Green, writing on 'Salvation and Perseverance', concedes that there is teaching in Scripture to the effect that a Christian cannot be utterly lost, and which teach 'the absolute security of the Christan'. He thinks however that there is 'a contrary body of evidence' also. In his discussion of the matter Heb.6:4–6 (understood as teaching the possibility of apostasy) is allowed to have the last word. This means that the promises of Scripture are not absolute (despite his use of that word); they are conditioned by the Christian's 'free will' (a term which Green also uses). As Green explains what this means it turns out that the Christian's assurance is only assurance of present standing. When one looks into the future such assurance is conditional. One cannot 'fossilize God's future' says Green – a phrase which apparently means one has no assurance about it except one conditioned upon one's own faithfulness. Salvation must not be regarded as a 'possession'[4], another term, which seems to mean that I may enjoy salvation here and now but have no guarantee that I will keep it, except a guarantee that I myself must sustain. Here then is the view that, for want of a better term, I am labelling 'Arminian'. It holds to a present assurance, but has only a conditional hope for the future, not an absolute one.

GODLINESS

Thirdly, *evangelical Arminianism has had a concern for godliness*. This indeed has been one of its notable characteristics and deepest concerns. Historically it has led into the 'holiness movement' of which the largest representative is the Church of the Nazarene. It is significant that when John Fletcher, the friend of John Wesley, felt it necessary to write against Calvinism, the title of his work was 'Check to Antinomianism'.[5] Fletcher was acknowledged as a godly man by all who knew him. D.R.Smith rightly says that 'whenever the Calvinist / Arminian controversy is discussed, the name of John Fletcher must arise . . . The subject of holiness . . . was the cornerstone of his arguments relating to the Calvinian position'[6]. He is therefore of particular interest in the present study, and we may focus on him briefly as one of the most admirable of Arminian evangelical Christians.

WESLEY AND FLETCHER

There was considerable controversy between John Wesley and the Calvinist George Whitefield, during the years 1738–1745. But from 1745 to the day of Whitefield's death (1770) the two men agreed to differ and there was a relatively peaceful relationship between the sympathizers of the two men. However in the minutes of the 1770 Wesleyan conference, Wesley produced an extreme statement concerning justification and works. As a result the Calvinists, no longer restrained by the pacific George Whitefield, took up the controversy once again. Fletcher wrote to defend Wesley, and vigorous controversy followed for about four years (1770–1774).

We may take Wesley and Fletcher as representatives of the theology we are considering. Three points are of importance.

They regarded holiness as indispensable to salvation, so much so that there was even a tendency to teach what seemed to be salvation by works. Fletcher maintained that holiness is the outer proof of our inner salvation' (citing Mt.7:16–17; Gal.5:24; Jm.2:18; 1 Jn.3:3) and is a preparation for heaven (citing Mt.5:8; Gal.5:19–20; Eph.5:5; Heb.12:14; Rev.11:27).[7] The works of believers contributed to their final security[8]; the Calvinist doctrine of 'final perseverance' Fletcher rejected.

In addition, Fletcher taught a doctrine of 'second justification by works'. He argued from 1 Timothy 6:19 and Romans 2:6f. that final salvation depended on ethical achievement as well as upon the atoning work of Christ. He denied that 'faith alone turns the scale of justifying evidence at the bar of God'.[9] Fletcher thought that this doctrine of second justification by works would 'rouse Antinomians out of their carnal security'.[10]

Fletcher felt that Calvinism was promoting looseness of life within the methodism he loved, and was alarmed at the 'almost general

Antinomianism of our congregations'[11]. He feared that Calvinism encouraged sin: 'I have seen them carelessly follow the stream of corrupt nature, against which they should have manfully wrestled'[12]. He also detested the Calvinist doctrine of imputation of Christ's righteousness ('a trick of antinomian hearts').[13]

LEGALISM

Fourthly, one has to note that *evangelical Arminianism has been characterized by legalism*. Through their overriding concern for godliness Wesley and Fletcher were responsible for leading evangelicalism into legalism. Fletcher spoke explicitly of 'evangelical legality', saying that 'legality is excellent, if it is evangelical'.[14]

Fletcher taught that although dead to the *ceremonial* law and to the *curse* of the moral law, yet the Christian is obliged to keep the moral law – which he saw summarized in the ten commandments in the traditional fashion.[15] In this, Wesleyan Armininianism was thus in agreement with Arminius himself. For in his 'Seventy Nine Private Disputations' Arminius urged the need of 'special acts of obedience . . . prescribed in the Decalogue' and went on to expound parts of the Decalogue with such conscious obedience in mind.[16] In its Wesleyan form Arminianism was led into a very heavy emphasis on works, often in such a way that it was easily possible for the Christian to be virtually working for salvation. In 1770 Fletcher recalled the 1744 minutes of the Wesleyan Conference ('we have leaned too much towards Calvinism') and argued that the Christian was 'working *for* life'. 'Every believer, till he comes to glory, works *for*, as well as *from* life.' 'We have received it as a maxim that 'A man is to do nothing, *in order to* justification. Nothing can be more false.' A person, taught Fletcher, must perform good works 'in order to find favour with God'. Salvation is 'not by the *merit* of works, but by works as a *condition*'. As a result Fletcher spoke of 'conditional perseverance' in salvation, contrasting this with the Calvinist doctrine of 'unconditional perseverance'. In his view salvation was lost by the Christian who did not pursue holiness.[17]

Related to this emphasis on godliness was an insistence that the Mosaic law was directly relevant to the life of the Christian. Fletcher assumed that 'fulfilling the law' in Gal.3 is identical to being under the law as a moral code[18] and took for granted without discussion that the 'law of liberty' of the Epistle of James is the Mosaic law. On this he and his Calvinist opponents were agreed.

ARMINIAN EXPOSITION

We have seen that there is a Reformed tradition of interpretation. What of the Arminian counterpart? A precisely comparable tradition is not found in evangelical Arminianism. Yet in the exegetical work of

John Wesley, Adam Clarke, J.Agar Beet, and late-Lutheran expositors such as R.C.H.Lenski, one comes near to a tradition of Arminian
biblical exposition. One would have to turn to Roman Catholic works
to find comparable series of biblical commentaries but they tend not to
have the depth – or at least not the length – of the Reformed
commentaries mentioned above. A review of these commentaries,
particularly the way they handle the key 'Arminian' sections of
Scripture, reveals that they invariably maintain the possibility of
apostasy for the sinful Christian. Thus Lenski's exegesis of key texts
takes for granted the possibility of apostasy. Of Paul it is said, 'The
fact that he is an apostle is not yet proof to him that he will be saved.'[19]
For Lenski, Judas was a believer who apostasized. Yet Lenski seems
to have difficulty with Jn.17:12 because he wishes to say both that
Judas was a believer yet also that, as a result of God's foreknowledge,
he was never given by the Father to Jesus. He does not face the
question whether this does not remove all comfort from the notion of
Jesus's protection since anyone's lapse might be similarly foreknown
and thus the threat of forfeiture of Jesus' protection is open for
anyone.[20] Along similar lines, R.Shank lists 80 passages which he
thinks teach conditional security.[21] G.Duty argues similarly[22], as does
I.H.Marshall.[23]

The Arminian viewpoint may also be said to characterize works that
hold to a view of Scripture other than an evangelical one. In this
connection the popular expository works of W.Barclay are notable for
urging the possibility of apostasy. For him Phil.2:13 may be translated,
'Carry to its perfect conclusion the work of your own salvation.'[24] I
need not produce extensive quotations to demonstrate the Arminian
approach. It is the commonplace manner in which the warnings of
Scripture are handled. It does not contain the introspective subtlety of
the Reformed expositions. Whether its approach is correct is a matter
to which we shall return.

The preceding chapteers have supplied a brief outline of some of the
distinctive points of two evangelical theological traditions, examining
only their emphases concerning security, godliness and law. The
question to be considered is whether either of these two approaches is
right in these emphases. In a later chapter I shall suggest a variant
version of the Calvinist approach, which takes seriously the Pauline
teaching concerning freedom from Mosaism.

4

A Challenge to Tradition

.

Why have so many Christians been so threatened, as we have seen, by legalism and introspection? The answer to this question should take account of at least the following elements:

(i) the tendency within the church to make excessive and simplistic use of the Mosaic covenant in expounding Christian theology,

(ii) the difficulty the Christian church has always had in interpreting Hebrews 6,

(iii) the way the concept of repentance has tended to clash with the concept of faith and has tended to become a form of working for salvation both in medieval times (with its concept of 'penance') and in the Puritan theology (with its concept of 'turning from all known sin').

All these aspects of the matter need to be explored in the totality of Scripture, in the history of theology and in the story of the church. Not all of this can be tackled within one book. The present work aims simply to survey the two main options and give an overview of some major aspects of a different approach.

I am conscious that the proposals I am making are in some respects a breach with tradition. For any who are familiar with Scripture or are theologically informed, to raise the possibility of a Christian's being radically free from the Mosaic law stimulates an explosion of questions and protests. What about the demands for good works? What about the warnings concerning apostasy? Does not Matt.5:17–20 say the law is not abolished? Is not obedience to 'commandments' the test of salvation according to 1 John? There are questions concerning spiritual guidance ('Is love to be unguided by anything propositional?') and motivation ('Is Christian obedience without sanctions or warnings?') Any teaching concerning a reign or lordship of grace will invariably lead to the question, sometimes with a splutter of protest or hostility, 'What shall we say then? Shall we sin that grace may abound?'

In other words, to seek to expound a non-legalistic soteriology along Pauline lines immediately raises, in evangelical circles, questions concerning Scripture. Evangelical theology has generally held to the principle that 'Scripture is its own interpreter'. Thus a radically non-legalistic theology raises questions concerning one's harmonistic her-

meneutic. Did Paul adequately understand the Torah? Or did he
develop an 'antinomian' theology that lost touch with the realities of
straightforward reading of the Torah? How does Jesus' message fit
with Paul's? Does Matthean 'legalism' cohere with Pauline antinomianism? Is James at odds with Paul? A non-legalistic emphasis on the
Spirit alone will lead into questions concerning relationships within the
Old Testament (Abraham, Moses), across the Testaments (Torah,
new covenant), and within the New Testament (Jesus versus Paul,
Paul versus James).

HERMENEUTICAL PRE-UNDERSTANDING

It has rightly been said that 'every theology stands or falls as a
hermeneutic and every hermeneutic stands or falls as a theology'.[1]
Every theologian has a 'hermeneutical circle'. This expression has
come to be associated with Rudolf Bultmann, yet it is worthy of wider
use. Everyone comes to Scripture with some kind of 'pre-
understanding' whether it be a Heideggerian anthropology (as with
Bultmann), a Christomonist ontology (as with Barth) or radical
scepticism (as with many critics of traditional Christianity). Sheer
neutrality is a myth. All students of the Bible have their 'hermeneutical circle', just as everyone, consciously or unconsciously, has a
systematic theology. The evangelical comes to Scripture with certain
basic commitments. One basic ingredient of an evangelical hermeneutic is that it will be progressive in that traditional formulations will
be challenged as the exegetical and expository task proceeds.

I have used the model of a 'circle', yet there is much to be said for
speaking instead of a spiral. For the 'pre-understanding' which takes
evangelicals to scripture to look for God's mind in the minds of God's
men will constantly lead to discoveries that challenge or even refute
what they have hitherto taken for granted. They will find themselves
moving round the circle (so to speak) at a higher level. The circle will
become a spiral and as they come back to what they thought they knew
they will find themselves in a higher position. They will meet with
disruptions in the circle of their ideas about God. To be explicit: an
evangelical view of Scripture ought to lead to the challenging of
traditional formulations. The danger is that one will view Scripture
through the eyes of one's denominational, confessional, theological or
academic confreres. I can imagine no better way of expressing this
point than to make parabolic use of Luther's famous story concerning
his 'Reformation break-through'. Let Luther himself tell the story.[2]

> I had indeed been captivated with an extraordinary ardour for understand-
> ing Paul in the Epistle to the Romans. But up till then it was not the cold
> blood about the heart, but a single word in Chapter 1, 'In it the
> righteousness of God is revealed,' that stood in my way. For I hated that
> word 'righteousness of God', which, according to the use and custom of all

the teachers, I had been taught to understand philosophically regarding the formal or active righteousness, as they called it, with which God is righteous and punished the unrighteous sinner.

Though I lived as a monk without reproach, I felt that I was a sinner before God with an extremely disturbed conscience. I could not believe that he was placated by my satisfaction. I did not love, yes, I hated the righteous God who punished sinners, and secretly, if not blasphemously, certainly murmuring greatly, I was angry with God.

At last, by the mercy of God, meditating day and night, I gave heed to the context of the words, namely, 'In it the righteousness of God is revealed, as it is written, "He who through faith is righteous shall live." There I began to understand that the righteousness of God is that by which the righteous lives by a gift of God, namely by faith. And this is the meaning: the righteousness of God is revealed by the gospel, namely, the passive righteousness with which a merciful God justifies us by faith . . . Here I felt I was altogether born again and had entered paradise itself through open gates. There a totally new face of the entire Scripture showed itself to me.'

Here is a man who has a traditional theology. He is used to reading his Bible through the eyes of late Augustinian theology. He has a 'circle' of traditional ideas. But now, because of his new responsibilities as exegete in the newly founded university of Wittenburg he is wrestling with Scripture for himself. He stumbles upon something that will not fit into the circle of his ideas. He can find no way in which the righteousness of God can possibly be good news. Eventually he looks at it in a new way and is lifted to a higher plane. He still has a 'circle' of ideas. He still believes there is a coherent teaching in the scriptures, yet he has been through the experience of changing his mind, allowing new insights to break through. His faith in the harmony of scripture has kept him seeking to discern the relevance of scripture for one seeking a gracious God. The process has to continue. A decade or so after Luther a new tradition had been set up and there were theologians looking at scripture no longer through the eyes of Augustinian traditionalism but through the eyes of Lutheran traditionalism!

Is it possible that evangelical theology has to take a step forward in its view of law and grace? Could it be that there is scope for a new evangelical synthesis which takes more seriously than ever before the possibility of a radical freedom from the Mosaic system, even from a direct subservience to the decalogue? Such an approach will leave one highly vulnerable, but were not Jesus and Paul vulnerable to (unjust) accusations of licentiousness?

We must find a more satisfying approach to law, grace, security, admonition, obedience and the nature of Christian spirituality. Such a theology will need to be a harmony. Until the nineteenth century it was traditional in the Christian church to regard the canonical scriptures as a harmonious unity. Expositors and theologians within the church generally regarded themselves as duty-bound to show the harmony and consistency of Scriptural teaching. Scripture in their view (i) possessed normative content, (ii) showed internal coherence, (iii) was open to multiple application, and (iv) was viewed in terms of the divine legislator who has issued his law.[3]

The contemporary emphasis, by contrast, majors on the diversity of Scripture. It stresses (i) conceptual variety, both diachronic and synchronic, (ii) comprehensiveness in the historical canon (i.e. the idea that conflicting teaching can be happily accommodated), (iii) one-sidedness and selectiveness in all biblical expositors, who inevitably work with a 'canon within a canon', for doctrinal insights. J.I.Packer has challenged evangelical theologians about this. He urges that the Reformers' viewpoint 'will only appear viable or credible if it can be shown that a unitive biblical exegesis . . . is actually plausible'.[4] Clearly if Paul is interpreted as having a radical doctrine of grace and other parts of Scripture are thought to be in disagreement with or even in radical antithesis to Pauline teaching, as even Luther thought,[5] a harmonistic hermeneutic is severely threatened. It might be thought that to show a consistent theological position regarding law and grace is a difficult enough task when considering Paul alone. More than one expositor has thought his teaching incoherent.[6] Yet the task of seeking the harmony of Scripture should not be lightly abandoned.

Part 2

Towards a Fresh Theology of Grace

5

A Fresh Approach to Grace

The relationship between grace and obedience, especially obedience to the Mosaic law, has never been clearly settled. Neither of the two evangelical approaches is satisfactory. Emphasis on a moral system extrapolated from the 'Ten Commandments' has produced theologies which are legalistic. Yet an altogether different approach is possible, one which is more gracious and more encouraging, and yet which still does justice to the serious admonitions of the New Testament. Over against scholastic Calvinism and evangelical Arminianism I wish to present some features of such a non-legalistic theology.

As I see it, the Christian position is one of invincible assurance of salvation combined with awesome warnings concerning forfeiture of blessing (but not of salvation itself). There are both reassuring and admonitory aspects. Freedom from Mosaic law is one of the reassuring features but this needs to be put in a wider context and related to the warnings of Scripture. Among other reassuring aspects are at least the following: objective and universal atonement, the faith of Christ, transfer to a realm of grace, eternal security. Among the admonitory aspects of New Testament teaching are: the possibility of loss of experience of the kingdom, 'falling' (*parapipto, paraptoma*, a possibility that I do not identify with loss of salvation), salvation 'by fire', eternal loss of reward. Some of these matters are likely to be contentious. As should be the case with any expositor or theologian, my statements may need to be modified, as more is discovered in days to come. No doubt I shall have made some exegetical mistakes, but he who never made a mistake never made anything. The following pages seek to unfold this New Testament paradox of great assurance plus earnest warning.

'SHALL WE CONTINUE IN SIN?'

A major factor in these matters is the fear of licentiousness, and (such is the fear we have of others' opinions) vulnerability to accusation concerning licentiousness. Sometimes it seems we are more troubled about accusation concerning licentiousness than we are about actual licentiousness. We fall easily into the mistake of wanting our gospel to be respectable, and are afraid to be 'fools for Christ's sake'.

There is an understandable anxiety lest talk of 'freedom from the law' might actually lead to sheer immorality or licentiousness. Yet according to the New Testament, Jesus and Paul themselves faced this reaction. Paul evidently expected his readers to ask: 'What shall we say then? Shall we continue in sin that grace may abound'. Arguably, therefore, unless one's theology leads to a similar response it cannot be said to approach that of Paul.

Paul's theology was vulnerable to the charge of licentiousness, just as his doctrine of sanctification was vulnerable to the charge of perfectionism, and his doctrine of election vulnerable to the charge of injustice (see Rom.9:14). If our theology claims to be Pauline but is not vulnerable to these accusations, is it Pauline after all? Dr Lloyd-Jones of Westminster Chapel used to say that 'if our preaching does not expose us to that charge [the charge of licentiousness] and to that misunderstanding, it is because we are not really preaching the gospel'. 'There is this kind of dangerous element about the true presentation of the doctrine of salvation'.[1] Whatever Paul's teaching was in fact, it was clearly rumoured that he was teaching, 'Let us do evil that good may come.' If Paul's emphasis on grace was so great that he was vulnerable to this kind of rumour, it is fair to ask whether a theology so moralistic that no one could conceivably misunderstand it to be licentious, does resemble Pauline teaching? Not all theologians are concerned to conform to Paul, but I have in mind largely those whose doctrine of Scripture is such that they do wish to subscribe to Pauline teaching, just as they do to the whole of Scripture.

A THEOLOGY OF MOTIVATION

In order to ensure a sense of direction in the following sections, it may be helpful if I outline the theology of motivation that I wish to unfold.

Arminian theology takes the warnings of Scripture as *relating to* salvation and as warning *against* apostasy or forfeiture of salvation. Final salvation hinges upon the Christian's good works. Calvinism likewise has also taken the warnings of Scripture as relating to salvation. If a high Augustinian doctrine of perseverance is maintained, then the Calvinist sees the warnings of Scripture as addressed to *the danger of pseudo-salvation*. Thus an introspective note is introduced. Real salvation is so inseparably tied to *good works* that they constitute a *test* of *genuine* salvation, a test which is meant to be used by the Christian in self-examination.

In some respects these two theologies are similar. Both assume that salvation and good works are tied together. In the one case salvation requires good works; in the other salvation inexorably and irresistibly produces good works. In both theologies salvation and good works stand and fall together.

The essence of the theology which I wish to explore is that salvation and good works are not inexorably tied together. They are associated, since salvation should be thought of as preparing the way for good works, making good works possible. Yet they are not so rigidly tied together that they are two sides of a coin. I draw a clear distinction between salvation and reward. The biblical doctrine of the Christian's security relates to salvation, to justification, to a secure position in grace, to freedom from condemnation, to eternal membership of God's people. I do not believe the admonitions of Scripture addressed to Christians relate in any way to gaining or losing salvation. Salvation is so wholly of grace that to one who has already believed admonition concerning losing or gaining salvation – in the sense of regeneration or justification – is entirely unnecessary and is not found in Scripture at all. The admonitions of the New Testament rather relate to present experience of the blessings of God's kingdom, to reward in this life and beyond, to usefulness in God's kingdom.

Whereas Arminianism and Calvinism – especially in their later forms – have thought of these two matters (salvation, reward) as so closely tied together as to make them virtually one category of thought, I conceive of them as decidedly two categories of thought. 1 Cor.3:15 puts this in a nutshell: 'he shall suffer loss . . . he shall be saved'.[2] Reward may be lost, although salvation is retained. Thus they should be thought of as two categories. The reassuring aspects of New Testament teaching concern *justification*. The admonitory aspects of New Testament teaching concern not justification or its loss, but *reward* and the possibility of loss of reward. The two matters may be kept distinct in our thinking. The following pages consider first the reassuring aspects of the Christian salvation and then the admonitory aspects of New Testament teaching, especially the most severe warning of the New Testament, Hebrews 6:3–6.

6

Objective and Universal Atonement

For Calvin, faith is assurance. When one looks at the death of Jesus Christ one does not need to ask such introspective questions as: 'Is this for me?' or: 'Am I elect?' The death of Jesus Christ is for everyone unconditionally.

UNIVERSAL ATONEMENT

Within traditional Reformed theology the doctrine of limited atonement has been deduced from a doctrine of election.[1] The doctrine is often presented more as a matter of logic than of direct scriptural testimony. Serious appeal is made to two central passages only, Jn.10:15 and Eph.5:25.[2]. Scriptural testimony, on the other hand, points in the direction of objective universal atonement. In evangelical theology the matter is of considerable importance. The following paragraphs summarize the biblical data concerning universal atonement.

SYNOPTIC GOSPELS

In the synoptic gospels a doctrine of atonement is not highly articulated. Only Matt.20:28; 26:28; Mk 10:45; 14:24 relate to the extent of the atonement. Protagonists of limited atonement generally see special significance in the term 'many' (*polloi*) rather than 'all'[3]. Others urge that the atonement is universal but that 'many' implies a limitation of salvation because faith is needful and not all believe.[4] Others feel that to make deductions from these verses concerning the efficacy of the atonement is unwarranted[5]. However, as Calvin noted, 'many' denotes all![6] *Polloi* may denote 'the multitude' or 'people in general' and so come to mean virtually 'everyone'. Where Mk 3:10 has 'he healed many', Matt.12:15 has 'he healed them all'. 'Many spread their cloaks' (Mk 11:8) appears as 'The very large crowd spread their cloaks', in Matt.21:8. In Matt.4:16, Mk 1:34, Lk.4:40 'all', 'many' and 'each one' are equivalents. The usage is a Hebraism and while Hebrew has a unitary word for the totality of a group (*kol*, 'all') it does not possess an individualizing word 'everyone'.[7] 'The many' (*rabbim*) is an individualizing way of saying 'everyone'. Certainly these verses of Scripture cannot be used in the interests of limited atonement.

JOHN

There is a strongly universalist strand of thought in the Johannine literature. Here the term *kosmos* refers to the objects of God's grace (Jn.1:29; 3:16f., 4:42; 1 Jn.2:2); the 'bread of life' is given ('my father gives you . . .', Jn.6:32) whether faith is present or not ('yet you do not believe', Jn.6:36). Scholastic Calvinism seeks to urge that *kosmos* means the total number of the elect or the elect of every nation or man in his ethically 'worldly' character,[8] yet by far the most natural way of taking *kosmos* in the Johannine writings is to refer it (with Calvin) to 'the human race' or to 'all without exception'.[9]

A passage where a weakened sense of 'all men' is plausible is Jn.12:31–36. Yet a closer scrutiny is illuminating. Jesus' death will draw 'all men' to himself. Though it no doubt alludes to the widening scope of Jesus' mission to all nations yet it cannot be weakened to mean 'all types of men'. Earlier in the account certain individuals had come seeking Jesus (Jn.12:20–21); the later section of the chapter is surely related to this and is intended to provide encouragement not only to Greeks at large but to any individuals (*Hellenes*, *tines*, Jn.12:20) from among the Greeks who might seek Jesus. No questions concerning election need be raised; at this point Jesus is said to be lifted up for 'all' (v.32). It is noteworthy that in the following verses (Jn.12:35f.), the 'light' is said to be the possession (*echete*) of the contemporary Jews whether they believe or not. It is for them; they have it (*echete*); they are urged to believe. In this chapter we are far from any doctrine of limited atonement.

PAUL

It is perhaps the Pauline writings that most clearly teach a universal atonement. In Romans 5, when Paul says 'sin entered the world' (Ro.5:12) and immediately goes on to deduce that 'death spread to all men because all men sinned', it is clear that 'world', 'all men', and 'all' (*kosmon*, *pantas anthropois*, *pantes*) are referring to the same group. When a few lines later Paul says 'the many died' there has been no change in the group of people being referred to; 'the many' are clearly those denoted by 'world', 'all men' and 'all'. This reference to the grace of God as abounding 'to the many', concerns the same group that has been referred to all along – the entire human race. Similarly there is no natural way of changing the meaning of 'all people' when it is used twice in Ro.5:18. 'All people' are condemned; 'all people' have 'justification of life' in Christ provided for them.

The outstanding proof that 'many' in Romans 5:12–21 refers to the entire human race is Romans 5:19. In Paul's teaching the entire human race are constituted sinners; likewise by Christ's obedience the same group – *hoi polloi*, the human race – are constituted righteous in Christ. Whatever questions this may raise in our minds there can be little doubt that *hoi polloi* has not changed its meaning and that, according to Paul, there is an objective provision of grace for the human race.

The same point appears in 2 Cor.5. When Paul says that 'one died for all' (v.14) it is difficult to see how this could refer to a limited or elect number. The whole point of the passage is that on God's side nothing more need be done: 'Be reconciled to God.' The basis of the appeal is the fact that on God's side reconciliation has already taken place. If this is a correct understanding of the argument, then 'all' (v.14) and 'world' (v.19) refer to the entire human race. Verse 14 will men that objectively the entire human race was put into a different position because of the death of Christ. The human race has 'died' to what it was; God is reconciled. One thing remains: response to the appeal: 'Be reconciled to God.'

Much the same teaching is evident in 1 Tim.2:4f. If speaking of 'God, who wishes all people to be saved' does not express universal grace what other phrase in Hellenistic Greek could express the point? How could one say in Hellenistic Greek, 'God wishes all people to be saved', meaning the entire human race, in any way other than in the words used by Paul (or his editor)? The passage goes on to assert that Christ is the mediator between God and people (*anthropous*). Paul could easily have made it clear if Christ's mediatorial work was for a limited or designed group. He could have spoken of 'one mediator between God and his people' or 'between God and those who believe' (*heis mesites theou kai laou autou* or *heis mesites theou kai ton pisteouon*). But Christ's mediatorial work was suspended, according to 1 Tim.2:5, neither upon faith nor upon election, but upon man's existence as man. The objective work of Christ is never presented as preconditioned by election.

Titus 2:13 has been translated, 'The grace of God that brings salvation has appeared to all men' (NIV). A more likely translation is: 'The grace of God has appeared for the salvation of all men' (RSV). Six Greek words intervene between 'has appeared' and 'to all people' but 'saving' and 'all people' are alongside one another. The natural interpretation is to take 'saving all people' as a coherent phrase.[10]

HEBREWS

The same teaching is found in the letter to the Hebrews, where the Son of God is said to have made a 'cleansing of sins' (*katharismon ton hamartion*, Heb.1:3). The absence of any genitival expression (such as 'of our sins') plus the aorist tense of the participle point to an accomplished objective event that makes a provision for the sins of the race.[11] Later in his work the writer explicitly takes up the question of who were the ones for whom Christ died. It was not angels because

Psalm 8 asks, 'What is *man* that you are mindful of him' (Heb.2:6)? The author goes on to say that Jesus did not taste death for angels; he tasted death for 'everyone' (*pantas*). Limited atonement theorists have tried to understand this in the light of verse 10 where 'many sons' are mentioned. The 'many' then refers to the 'many sons'. The difficulty with this interpretation is that at Heb.2:9 the writer had not yet mentioned the 'many sons'. If the writer expected us to read his letter in order, 'many' could refer only to the entire human race just mentioned in Heb.2:6–8.

In Heb.9:28 we find another reference to the 'many' for whom Christ died. Again inclusive and exclusive interpretations of the phrase have been debated. It would take us far afield to explore the theology of Hebrews but it seems to the present writer that there is a difference in Hebrews between (on the one hand) the death of Jesus, which, in the imagery of the tabernacle, takes place in the open courtyard of this world, and (on the other hand) the presentation of blood, which takes place in the heavenly sanctuary, and secures atonement. There is a difference in Hebrews between a promise being available and a promise being received (see Heb.6:12). When Hebrews speaks of the heavenly ministry of Jesus it uses limiting phrases (we have a high-priest in the sanctuary; we have a hope behind the curtain; he lives to make intercession for them[12]). When Hebrews speaks of the death of Jesus on earth there are no limiting phrases (he made a cleansing of sins; he tasted death for every man; he dies to deliver all from lifelong bondage; he dies for the sins of the people[13]). There is a difference between public death and open availability on the one hand, and hidden application of the blood of Christ and intercession behind the veil on the other hand. If this is a correct observation it corresponds to the usage of 'the world' in John's gospel where Christ dies for the world (Jn.3:16) but does not pray for the world (Jn.17).

2 PETER

2 Peter 2:1 is another verse that has been much discussed in connection with limited atonement. Of all that we have considered thus far this is the text that causes the greatest concern to those who believe in 'limited atonement'. The 'false teachers' of this verse are described as 'denying the Master who bought them'. Clearly, the writer is envisaging persons who do not believe yet who have been bought by Christ. Owen argued that 'Master' refers to God the Father, not to Jesus; that the 'purchasing' refers to deliverance from trouble, not spiritual redemption; and that the writer speaks according to the heretics' claims rather than according to the real situation[14]. In the course of a full discussion, A.D.Chang points out that 2 Pe.2:1 is similar to Jude 4 and refers to Jesus, arguing that 'Master' refers to a change of ownership on the basis of redemption, and noting that the non-mention of the price of redemption is irrelevant (it is not mentioned in Rev.13:3f. either but the context is soteriological). His conclusion

must, I think, be allowed to stand: 'The main thrust of this verse is the change of ownership as a result of redemption.'[15] The idea that 'Master' is never used of Jesus is falsified by Jude 4 (so long as one does not follow the inferior texts behind the KJV).

THE GROUND OF ASSURANCE

The universal atonement of Christ is one aspect of the ground of Christian assurance of salvation. I have also suggested that the doctrine of limited atonement is a partial cause of introspection. A person seeking salvation, who is also deeply persuaded of a correlation between a doctrine of election and a particular and inherently effective atonement, will be hindered from looking directly at Christ. If there is no guarantee that the work of Christ is 'for me', apart from the personal conviction that I am 'elect', then there is no possibility of my receiving any encouragement as a result of looking at the cross. Election is a highly threatening concept if viewed directly. Calvin understood the problem and constantly warned against viewing election in such a way. 'What revelation do you have of your election?' he asks. Calvin says that the thought of election, if approached directly, 'overwhelms and unsettles the conscience from its peace and tranquillity towards God' ; 'we must carefully avoid this rock, against which no one is ever dashed without destruction'.[16] There is only one remedy, thinks Calvin, and that is to look directly to Christ and come at election afterwards and via the 'mirror' of Christ.[17] Thus it is possible to grasp hold of election without its being a labyrinth in which one loses assurance of salvation.

But – and here is the vital point – if one correlates a limited atonement with a limited election then nothing to bring assurance can be found by looking directly at the cross just as nothing to bring assurance can be found by looking directly at election.

Calvin had an answer to his own question: 'What revelation do you have of your election?'. If one could see, with assurance, that Christ was the pledge of God's love, that in itself was the proof of the sealing (i.e. regenerating, illuminating) work of the Spirit in one's life, proof of one's election. This is what lies behind Calvin's remark, 'If Pighius asks how I know I am elect, I answer that Christ is more than a thousand testimonies to me.'[18]

One notes here the difference between Calvin and Beza. According to Beza, when one has doubts concerning election, one cannot look directly at the cross (because the cross and limited atonement are correlated). Where then should one look for assurance? Beza's answer was that one should look at oneself! 'When Satan putteth us in doubte of our election, we maye not searche first the resolution in the eternall counsell of God whose majesty we cannot comprehende . . .' So far, so good. Beza follows Calvin at this point. Then he adds ' . . . but on the contrary we must beginne at the sanctification which we feele in our selves . . .'[19] This is a disastrous move. It is almost the opposite of the reply Calvin said he would make to Pighius: 'I shall not oppose to him the feelings which the faithful experience'.[20] Christ – said Calvin – spoke the way he did 'to divert men's eyes from themselves to the mercy of God alone.'[21]

Limited atonement is a cul-de-sac. Assurance comes by not correlating atonement and election. Scripture puts things in such a way 'that no doubt may be left.' 'The heavenly Father does not wish the human race that He loves to perish'. 'Before we can have any feeling of His fatherly kindness, the blood of Christ must intercede to reconcile God to us.'[22]

7

Freedom from the Law
(The Abraham Stories)

According to Galatians 3:19, 'the law was added because of transgressions, till the offspring should come to whom the promise had been made; and it was ordained by angels through an intermediary.' According to one understanding of this verse, the law of God is a punitive, subsidiary and temporary institution in the history of redemption. Via a harmonistic hermeneutic this leads to many questions concerning our understanding of other parts of the Bible. For our present purpose we need to ask whether the provisional understanding of Galatians 3:19 set forth above is confirmed by the exegesis of the Torah itself?

In this book I examine the stories of Abraham, the Book of Exodus, Matthew's Gospel and Galatians. Deuteronomy and 2 Corinthians 3 need to be considered, but I leave those aside for later work. Publication of work on Romans has already commenced, beginning with the vital sixth and seventh chapters.[1] I have also written on James and 1 John and hope to make work on these books available.

This study of the Abraham stories assumes that the first five books of the Bible are a unity, whatever may be the story of editorial work that may be behind them.

STRUCTURE OF THE PENTATEUCH

The Pentateuch in its present form may be regarded as a unity; first an introduction dealing with origins and primeval history (Genesis), next a large central core revolving around the theme of the exodus (Exodus-Numbers) and finally a sermonic recapitulation (Deuteronomy). The whole work bears indications of deliberate structure, which may be schematically analysed as follows.

Origins and Prehistory of Israel's Redemption (Genesis)
Primeval History (1:1–2:3)
The Succession of Heaven and Earth (2:4–4:26)
The 'Book' of the Succession of Adam (5:1–6:8)
The Succession of the Sons of Noah (6:9–9:29)

The Succession of Shem (11:10–26)
The Succession of Terah (11:27–25:11)
The Succession of Ishmael (25:12–18)
The Succession of Isaac (25:19–35:29)
The Succession of Edom (36:1–43)
The Succession of Jacob (37:1–50:26)

The Redemption of Israel (Exodus-Numbers)
Redemption by the Blood of a Lamb (Ex.1:1–15:21)
  The Flight of the People (Ex.1:1–22)
  Preparation of a Mediator (Ex.2:1–4:31)
  Conflict with Pharaoh (Ex.5:1–7:7)
  Miracles Without Redemption (Ex.7:8–10:29)
  The Redemption (Ex.11:1–14:31)
  The Song of Redemption (Ex.15:1–21)
Establishment of Israel as the People of God (Ex.15:22–40:38)
  Events of the Journey (Ex.15:22–17:7)
  Two Gentile Reactions (Ex.17:8–18:27)
  The Covenant (Ex.19:1–24:11)
  The Tabernacle (Ex.24:12–31:8)
  The Rebellion (Ex.32:1–34:35)
  Again: The Tabernacle (Ex.35:1–40:38)
Law and Ordinances of the Sinai-Covenant (Leviticus)
  The Offerings (Lv.1:1–7:38)
  Inauguration of the Priesthood (Lv.8:1–10:20)
  Rules and Rites for Clean and Unclean (Lv.11–15:33)
  The Day of Atonement (Lev.16:1–34)
  Injunctions Upon People and Priests (Lv.17:1–25:55) o62
  Blessings and Curses; Vows (Lv.26:1–27:34)
Journeying From Sinai to Moab (Numbers)
  Preparation for Leaving Sinai (Nu.1:1–10:10)
  Journey to the Plains of Moab (Nu.10:11–21:35)
  Events in the Plains of Moab (Nu.22:1–36:13)

Sermonic Recapitulation (Deuteronomy)
Preamble (1:1–5)
Historical Prologue (1:6–4:49)
  From Horeb to Hormah (1:6–2:1)
  Advance to Arnon (2:2–23)
  Conquest of Transjordania (2:24–3:29)
  Summary of the Covenant (4:1–49)
Stipulations: Covenant Life (5:1–26:19)
  The Great Commandments (5:1–11:32)
  Ancillary Commandments (12:1–26:19)
Sanctions and Covenant Ratification (27:1–30:20)
Arrangements for the Future (31:1–34:20)

LAW IN THE PENTATEUCH

It is in this setting that we must consider the legislation of the
Pentateuch. This material is primarily narrative in format. Its legal
material is presented within the setting of a story telling the origins

first of the earth, then of the family of Abraham, then of the nation of
Israel. Its dominant notes before Ex.15:22 are those of creation,
election and redemption. Ex.15:22–27 makes mention of 'a decree and
a law' (*choq hoq umishpat*) and thereafter (Ex.15:22–Dt.34:12) there
is frequent mention of the Sinai legislation. Within the narrative
setting of Ex.15:22 – Dt.34:12 the outlines of Israel's laws are given.
The Pentateuch as a whole is neither 'law-code' nor 'constitution' of
Israel[2]; those of later ages who wished to use it as a constitution found
it necessary to supplement it with oral law. Omissions may be noticed
when Pentateuchal laws are compared with other collections of the
ancient near east.[3]

Where does one find the first biblical reference to God's law?
Genesis contains allusions to the laws of surrounding peoples (e.g.
Gen.23:3–20).[4] There are also mandates for dominion, procreation,
geographical extension (Gen.1:26,28) and labour (Gen.2:15). But
there is no record of any law given by God to his people before Sinai.
Within the story of life in Eden we find the single command of Genesis
2:16f. The ordinance of marriage in (Gen.2:24) has a law-like ring. Yet
none of these really amounts to 'law' unless we define law in such a
way as to make the term include any and every command. (For a full
discussion of this, see pp 51f., 68f. below.) The nearest to a collection
of law is the Noahic mandate in Gen.9:2–7.

The introduction of 'the law' occurs at and after Sinai. It is difficult
to decide which portions should be accorded the status of legal text;
even the narrative should be viewed as illuminating the law. Under the
influence of form criticism certain sections have been isolated and
considered in isolation: the decalogue (Ex.20:1–17), the Book of the
Covenant (Ex.20:23–23:19), the commands of Ex.34:11–26, the 'Holiness Code' of Lev.17–26, and Deuteronomy considered as having its
own character and identity.

THE FIRST PRESENTATION OF THE LAW

In the Pentateuch as its final editors have presented it to us, there are
two presentations of Sinai law. Ex.15:22–Num.10:10 tell the story of
the approach to and the events at Sinai; Num.10:11–36:13 completes
the story. Interspersed throughout the narrative itself, after Ex.15:22 –
chosen because it is a dividing line according to the analysis above – we
see the introduction of Sinai law.

Much of Exodus consists of sheer narrative. Instructions concerning
the Passover, the festival of unleavened bread and the consecration of
the firstborn, are presented as given while the people of Israel are still
in Egypt (Ex.12:1–11,14–20,24–27,43–49; 13:1–13). These verses have
a law-like ring about them and are intended to function as law
concerning these institutions. Ex.15 and 16 contain further allusions to
laws and decrees before Sinai. Ex.15:25b–26 presents itself as a single
principle concerning obedience and health. Ex.16 introduces us to a
single text concerning the obedience of the nation. At this point the

Sabbath is presented as testing whether the people will obey Yahweh. It is not yet integrated into the Sinai covenant. Yet as it is later made part of the Sinai laws, and as Ex.16:33 especially looks forward to the arrangements for the tabernacle, it is best to consider the key legal verses (Ex.16:4–5,23,25–26,28,33) as part of the direct legislation of the Pentateuch.[5] Other directly legal sections are found in 20:1–17,22–26; 21:1–23:33; 25:1–31:17; 34:11–26; 35:1–3.

Almost the whole of Leviticus consists of further legislation, continuous with Exodus. The narrative is entirely stationary; the people remain at the foot of Sinai throughout the book. There are only a few snippets of narrative (Lev.8:1–10:20; 24:10–23).

Numbers continues the account. At this point it is more difficult than before to disentangle sheer legislation from narrative designed to exhibit legislation. Although the people move from Sinai at Num.10:11, legislation continues to be given to them until the end of the book. It is best to regard the whole of Ex.15:22–Num.36:13 as one presentation of Sinai-law, combining sheer legislation with narrated or exhibited legislation. Although differences of opinion are natural in deciding which texts to label direct legislation, the sections may be identified thus: Ex.12:1–11, 14–20, 24–27, 43–49; 13:1–13; 16:4–5, 23, 25–26, 28, 33; 20:1–17, 22–26; 21:1–23:33; 25:1–31:17; 34:11–26; 35:1–3; Lev.1:1–7:34; 11:1–24:9; 25:1–27:34; Num.3:5–10, 25–26, 28b, 31, 36; 4:4–33; 5:1–6:21; 15:1–41; 18:1–19:22; 28:1–30:16; 35:1–34.

THE LAW IN DEUTERONOMY

A second presentation of Israel's law is found in Deuteronomy, which presents itself as a farewell address – or series of addresses – given by Moses on the plains of Moab. Apparently Deuteronomy is analogous to a treaty document attesting in written form the covenant between Yahweh and Israel. Because of its treaty structure it contains a major section (5:1–26:19) of stipulations concerning covenant life. Within this section there is a division. Deut.5:1–11:32 deal with the main stipulations governing the people; 12:1–26:19 (beginning 'These are the statutes . . .', 12:1) present the detailed ancillary commandments. What strikes one's attention as one surveys this large body of material is how little of it would be thought of as 'the law' by Christians today. The central demands for morality that the modern Christian tends to think of as coming from 'the law' in actuality centre only on the decalogue. Of the verses listed above, only the 33 verses that comprise the decalogue are dominant in modern ethical discussion. Apart from the 'theonomy' school in American evangelicalism, evangelical discussion of 'the sanctity of God's law' almost invariably confines its attention to the decalogue. We shall do well to remember that this does not reflect the proportional balance of the Pentateuch itself.

Paul himself observed that God gave to his people no law before Sinai (Ro.5:20; Gal.3:19), he makes so much of Abraham that his theology of salvation could be called his theology of the life of Abraham. Hebrews and James also make use of the life of Abraham and relate it to their distinctive doctrines of salvation and Christian spirituality.

ABRAHAM

What was it in the Genesis account of the life of Abraham that attracted New Testament writers to use it as a source of their theologies? The stories about Abraham reveal a number of distinct stages. We must consider Abraham's salvation (Gen.12; 15), the covenant with Abraham (Gen.15; 17) and the event of Gen.22.

Consider first the nature of Abraham's salvation. Paul regarded Abraham as a model of the way in which a person experiences the salvation[6] of God and saw Gen.15:6 as a definitive statement of his gospel. Several features of the narrative that leads up to Gen.15:6 merit attention.

Firstly, we note the absence of any statement concerning Abraham's worthiness. Admittedly, arguments from silence are notoriously insecure. Yet if one is looking for the origins and the causes of Abraham's salvation one cannot but notice what is *absent* from the text. Abraham – or Abram as he is called during the early parts of the story – appears abruptly in the narrative. He is passingly mentioned in Gen.11:27,29,31. Here his family are said to originate from Ur, a town whose principal deity is known to have been Nannar, a god also worshipped at Haran.[7] There are no indications of Yahweh-worship in that locality, and Jos.24 records a tradition that Terah and Nahor 'worshipped other gods' (24:2). The same passage confirms our sense of the abruptness of the introduction of Abraham when God says 'I took your father Abraham from the land' (Jos.24:3).[8]

The first introduction to any relationship between God and Abraham shows God speaking to Abraham, apparently without any precedent, and giving to him a series of promises ('I will show . . . I will make . . . I will bless . . . and make . . . I will bless . . .', Gen.12:1–3). At this stage no ethical demands are made on Abraham that would clear the way for God's activity in his life. On Abraham's side only one thing is said. Promise was met by response. Abraham left. The text makes it clear that this was a response to God's word to Abraham; Abraham left as the Lord had told him.

The response is followed by further divine promise. Yahweh appears and repeats the promise now defining where the land is located ('To your seed I will give this land', Gen.12:7). Again Abraham responds, this time with worship ('and he built there an altar', 12:7).

We note the absence of any statement of worthiness on Abraham's side. No hint is given as to any reason why God should have spoken to Abraham. Here surely is the root of Paul's doctrine of election. So far as the text indicates God simply steps into Abraham's life. Neither worthiness nor unworthiness is considered. The obedience with which Abraham responds is what Paul would later call the obedience of faith (Rom.1:5; 16:26). Abraham responds to God's word, believes God's promises. His leaving Haran is his response to the promises put before him.

In the following chapter, in accordance with the command to leave family (12:1) Abraham and Lot separate (13:8–12), and the promise is renewed (13:14–17). There is still no mention of any kind of worthiness. (I leave aside Genesis 14; it is a unit on its own and detailed consideration would demand too much space.)

Equally notable is the total absence from these chapters of any reference to law. Abraham is not in any way responding to a decalogue or to anything comparable to it. God is viewed as speaking directly to Abraham, whose response of faith and obedience is presented as his response to the direct voice of God. Neither law nor anything approaching explicit law appears at any point.

DEFINING 'LAW'

To clarify this point we must consider what is meant by 'law'. In the history of the Christian church any kind of obedience is often thought of as responsiveness to law. Yet not all 'obedience' is law-obedience, and not every command must be conceived of as law. It is helpful to distinguish different kinds of directive.

'Law', as I am using the term, is characterized by:

(1) codification in written or memorized form,

(2) inflexibility (because any directive written or memorized in set form is thereby inflexible),

(3) distinctness or precision (law that is vague, open to a wide variety of interpretations, or is so general as to create doubt in specific situations, is to that extent unable to function as law),

(4) accompaniment by penalty for default (a command which may be totally ignored with no consequences has become 'advice' not 'law').

'Principle' is similar to law but (in the way I am using the term) is more general and allows of varied actions in different situations. The principle of love is not exactly a law.

A 'discipline' I think of as something that is not mandatory in every situation but is self-imposed or imposed upon another simply to give structure to one's life. An item of 'discipline' is not thought of as morally obligatory but as a practical piece of wisdom imposed, perhaps only temporarily, for practical purposes.

A 'specific directive' ought to be viewed as a distinct category. There may be a situation where a single command or a small number of commands are given, yet where one should not think of such directives as being 'law'. The English Puritans often regarded the command given to Adam (Gen.2:16) as 'law'.[9] Yet it is doubtful whether a single directive such as that in Gen.2:16f. ought to be thought of as a 'law'. Admittedly it has a number of characteristics in common with law (obligation, precision), yet it should be viewed distinctly. The instruction in Acts 8:29 ('Go to that chariot') is a similar case. It is a specific directive, invested with angelic authority, yet it can hardly be called 'law'.

In the case of Abraham, there are guidelines to his life (the responsiveness of faith, heeding God's voice, obedience to specific commands), yet none of them is called 'law'. There is no legal system resembling that in the Sinai narrative. The demand for Abraham to leave his country is directive but not law. The instruction is not written; it did not have to be memorized for future occasions; it was not a standing command concerning ethical matters. The divine words of Gen.12:1–3 consist of promises and revelations of God's will for Abraham's life. Abraham responds to these in faith; his faith leads him to leave land, tribe and family.

Thirdly, Gen.15:6 draws attention to Abraham's faith. Nothing else is mentioned. No obedience to law contributed to Abraham's being righteous in God's reckoning.

FAITH IN GENESIS 15:6

Gen.15:6 is so prominent in the New Testament as to call for closer study. It says: 'And he believed on Yahweh; and it was reckoned to him for righteousness'. The precise force of the Hebrew *hiphil* 'and he believed on Yahweh' has been debated. Jepsen is surely right in urging that usage must be the primary way of determining its significance.[10] Apart from Gen.15:6, there are 22 occurrences of the verb (*h'mn*) with 'on' (Hebrew *b*). The other occurrences reveal that the expression normally denotes trust in a person especially when there is reason to regard the object of trust as trustworthy. In the usage of the verb this latter point is prominent. Normally the surrounding context stresses the credibility of the one who is to be the object of trust.

Thus Ex.14:31 speaks of the people who believed God and Moses; Ex.14:1–30 has set forth the ground of trust. Ex.19:9 emphasizes the 'thick cloud' and then explains that this is 'so that the people may . . . believe in you for ever'. In negative statements the evil of unbelief is underlined when there is ground for trust yet trust is not shown. Num.14:11 speaks of unbelief despite signs. Deut.1:32 speaks of unbelief despite God's word. Jer.12:6 speaks of lack of faith despite fair words (see also Prov.26:25). Ps.78:34 speaks of unbelief despite God's wonders. In these passages it is noticeable that the ground for credibility is mentioned. Job 4:18 and 15:15 speak of God's not trusting his angels. The point is that God does not trust even his angels, who might be thought to be objects worthy of trust.

'GOD RECKONED IT'

Thus, despite some uncertainties regarding the precise force of the *hiphil*, the general meaning of *h'mn* is clear; it speaks of a trust in a person or in his words because the person is thought to be trustworthy. In 'and he reckoned it' (*wayyachshebeha*) we have an imperfect *qal* of *ch-sh-b*, with a 3rd person singular suffix. The subject is clearly God.[11] The suffix refers back to the whole previous statement ('Abraham believed God') as in the Hebrew of Ex.10:1 and Job 38:18. The *qal* of *ch-sh-b* ('reckon') occurs 75 times in the Massoretic text. Many of these instances do not resemble our verse and therefore do not illuminate it. The participial form may refer to what is 'skilful'. The verb may speak of one's intentions (Gen.50:20), one's opinions (Job.35:2) one's regard or approval of someone (Is.33:8), one's inventiveness (Am.6:5). More important for comparison with Gen.15:6 are those instances where the verb has a double object and refers to what one person considers or counts another to be: Gen.38:16 ('he thought her to be a harlot'); 1 Samuel 1:13 (Eli 'considered her a drunken woman'); Job 13:24 ('Why . . . count me your enemy?') and others (Jb.19:11,15; 33:10). The nearest linguistic parallel to our verse is Ps.106:31, 'It was reckoned to him for righteousness'. In that instance however it was a righteous deed that was credited for righteousness; in Gen.15:6 it is faith that is credited for righteousness. Despite the absence of a precise parallel, the meaning of the phrase is clear. The suffix is a case where the feminine singular stands for what in many languages would be a neuter, and refers to Abraham's believing. '(God) reckoned it' means that God reckoned Abraham's believing for righteousness.

Here then is a definitive statement of the nature of Abraham's salvation. In the unfolding of the narrative any mention of law is significantly absent. Faith results in obedience but the obedience concerned is not mediated by law. Rather it is 'obedience of faith'. One could also call it 'charismatic' obedience since God's word apparently comes to Abraham in direct form, not via the instrumentality of any 'Scripture' or written document.

THE PURPOSE OF ABRAHAM'S CALL

Gen.15 introduces us to the first stage of the covenant with Abraham (Gen.15). Immediately after the statement that Abraham's faith has been reckoned as righteousness, we are told that Abraham is again informed of the main purpose of his call ('I . . . brought you out . . . to give you this land', Gen.15:17).

Abraham's salvation is thus said to contain a further purpose. Lying behind faith (15:6) and election ('I brought you out', 15:7) is God's purpose concerning the land of Israel, as it later came to be called. What follows is an expression of anxiety on Abraham's part: 'How can I know that I will gain possession of it?' (15:8). It is thus in the context of a present uncertainty concerning a future inheritance, that we have the story of God's making a covenant with Abraham. A ceremony is described, promises are given, and this is said (15:18) to be God's making a covenant with Abraham.

COVENANT, GRACE, PROMISE, LAW

At this point we must face certain questions that arise concerning covenant, grace, promise and law. I will argue later that there are three kinds of covenant, or that numerous differentiations among covenants fall into three groups. There are (1) parity covenants between two equal partners, (2) covenants of grant in which the emphasis falls upon the beneficence of the senior partner and in which the oath is taken and the promises made by the senior partner, and (3) treaties or covenants of law in which the emphasis falls upon the obligation of the junior partner and in which the junior partner takes the oath. It is (as I shall argue) the different position of the oath that signally differentiates the three types of covenant.

At this point we shall examine only the covenant described in Gen.15, a covenant which falls into the second of the categories just mentioned. The following points are worthy of note.

(i) The covenant is related to assurance. The promise of the land has been given before (12:1,7). What comes in distinctively at this point (15:18) is Abraham's request for deeper assurance concerning God's promise. The covenant is introduced in reply to the question 'How can I know . . . ?'

(ii) The covenant is preceded by election and faith. On God's side there has been election ('I . . . brought you out', 15:7). On Abraham's side there has been faith (15:6).

(iii) The covenant is related to neither a request for obedience nor any statement of obedience. There has indeed been the 'obedience of faith'. Abraham's conviction of the truth of God's promise led him to venture into what was initially unknown. Thus obedience has been implicit in Abraham's faith. But nothing is made of this and it is not brought into relationship with the covenant. Later in the narrative one finds a request for obedience (17:1) and later still an emphatic statement of Abraham's obedience (22:12). At this point obedience has not been mentioned as the ground of the covenant.

Equally Abraham's lapses are not mentioned, and apparently do not hinder the covenant. For despite the call to go to Canaan, Abraham has at one point left Canaan (12:10) and returned to it only in circumstances of disgrace (12:10–13:4). Despite the call to leave family (12:1), Abraham has only slowly disentangled himself from proximity to Lot (13:1–13). The renewed promise of Gen.13:14–17 is explicitly said to have been given after Lot had parted from him. Abraham has had doubts concerning his lack of reward ('I am your salary, *sakar*, Gen.15:1, after the generosity of 14:20 and the deprivation of 14:21–24). He has had doubts concerning his safety ('I am your shield', Gen.15:1, after the battle of 14:13–16). He has had doubts concerning his childlessness (15:2) and his landlessness (15:8). The covenant comes in at the point where Abraham has shown faith, but is not entirely free from doubt. It also comes in at a point before obedience has been invited (17:1), before it has been tested (22:1), and before it has been confirmed (22:12, 'Now I know . . . '). It is for this reason that one must say that while Abraham has exhibited the 'obedience of faith', yet the covenant is not built on Abraham's obedience.

(iv) Central in the covenant is sacrifice. The sacrifice is required for God. Although its arrangements are managed by Abraham, the sacrifice has a God-ward orientation. God both requires it and provides it. 'Take for me an heifer . . . ' is the divine command (15:9). As J.A.Motyer puts it: 'Sacrifice is not a technique whereby man twists the arm of God; sacrifice is God's own provision'.[12]

(v) Central in the covenant is the taking of an oath. Here the oath-taking is entirely on God's side. It seems that the ceremony in Gen.15:17 is a form of oath-taking. Passing between the animals seems to be a way of saying 'So be it done to me if I do not keep my word'.[13] In this ceremony God is the sole agent. Not only does Abraham not pass between the pieces, he is put into a deep sleep and the oath-taking takes place in circumstances where Abraham had been explicitly prevented from taking part. 'He is immobilised', writes Motyer, 'in order that God might be the only one active in this situation . . . God takes upon himself the total obligation of the covenant'.[14]

(vi) Accompanying the covenant is predictive prophecy. Abraham is to know for a certainty the outline of history for the following four centuries. The delay before inheritance (15:13), the enslavement of Israel (15:13), the punishment of the enslaving nation (whose name is not mentioned, 15:14), the prosperous beginnings of the nation ('with great possessions', 15:14), the fact that the inheritance of the land is beyond Abraham's lifetime, the persistence in sin that will character-ize the Canaanites (15:16) – all is given to Abraham in predictive outline. Revelation consists in a word which is subsequently confirmed by a deed.

(vii) Abraham functions as a covenant mediator. Just as God speaks to Noah of 'my covenant which I make with you (singular) and all flesh' (Gen.9:17), so he says to Abraham 'In you (singular) shall all the families of the earth be blessed' (Gen.12:3). The narrative of Gen.15 stresses the centrality of Abraham. God's people will be 'Abraham's seed' (15:5). The predictions relate to Abraham's descendants (15:13f.). Although it concerns a people as numerous as the stars (15:5) yet the covenant is made with Abraham himself: 'Yahweh made a covenant with Abraham' (15:18). Abraham may therefore legitimately be called the mediator of this particular covenant. His descendants will inherit the land because of promises made to Abraham himself.[15]

(viii) In its origins, as with its continuance, the covenant with Abraham is characterized by the absence of law. It was this that would mean so much to Paul in the argument of Galatians. Abraham was elected without law, came to faith without law, was told of a 'seed' and of a land and of reward, received prophecy – all without the involvement or even the presence of law.

So far then the Abraham-narrative has almost exclusively pointed to God's grace. The obedience of Abraham has been responsiveness to

God's promises, in the context of directly experienced fellowship with God. It has been a fellowship in which God speaks to Abraham and Abraham speaks to God, with no involvement of any law-code. Failures in obedience (the matter of separation from family, and disgrace in Egypt) have not abrogated God's purpose.

GENESIS 17

A major step forward in the story of Abraham comes in Gen.17. The events of that chapter are clearly intended by the final redactor of the book to be thought of as taking place many years after the events of the previous chapters. The events of Gen.16 in which Abraham takes Hagar as a slave-wife and begets Ishmael are to be viewed as Abraham's attempt to get the promise of a 'seed' fulfilled in view of the long delay since the promise was given. The time-reference in 17:1 indicates that yet further years have gone by, so much so that by any human reckoning the birth of a child to Abraham and his elderly wife would seem impossible. Fourteen years have elapsed since the birth of Ishmael (see 16:16; 17:1).

In this context God speaks again of his covenant with Abraham, but now several additional elements are added.

EL SHADDAI

(i) God draws attention to his sufficiency in enabling fulfilment of the promises. The statement in Gen.17:1–2 relates three matters together: the name of God as El Shaddai, the request for loyalty, and the confirmation of the covenant that has already been made.

Although the etymology and meaning of El Shaddai as a word are uncertain[16], there is good reason for thinking that the name was especially used in contexts of human helplessness. In the patriarchal narratives the usage is fairly consistent. It occurs in contexts of human desperation. In Gen.17 it comes immediately after the failure of Abraham to get the 'seed' born (Gen.17). In Gen.28:3 it again occurs in a sitation of human helplessness, immediately after a signal failure in Jacob's life (27:41–44). In Gen.35:11 it again occurs in a situation of need (as 35:7 indicates) and explicitly recalls the 'day of distress' (35:3) when 'El Shaddai' had appeared. In Gen.43:14 it occurs at the distressing stage in patriarchal family history when Jacob is (seemingly) for the second time about to lose a favourite son. In Gen.48:3 the dying Jacob recalls the desperate plight he had been in when 'El Shaddai' had revealed himself. In Gen.49:25 El Shaddai is the one who rescued Joseph when 'with bitterness archers attacked him' (49:23).

Thus El Shaddai is consistently used in Genesis to speak of God's ability to transform human incapacity. J.A.Motyer notes that in passages that use the term El Shaddai there is also a consistency as to the manner of working.[17] (We return to this below.)

OBEDIENCE

(ii) For the first time in the Abraham stories God requires that Abraham should walk before God and be perfect. This is the first explicit demand for Abraham's obedience. This has been implicit from the beginning, but nothing in the text before chap.17 implies that God's grace was in any way based upon Abraham's obedience.[18]

Like the Akkadian *alaku*, Hebrew *halak* is used metaphorically of one's behaviour or lifestyle.[19] The precise phraseology (an imperative of *hithalek*, walk, in combination with *lipenei*, before) occurs nowhere else in the Old Testament, yet there are a number of occasions when (*hit*)*halek* and *lipenei* are found. The combination may speak of divine leadership (Ex.13:21; 14:19; Nu.14:14; Dt.1:30; 31:8; Is.52:12) or royal leadership (1 Sa.12:2). On other occasions it seems to denote service, as when Goliath's shield-bearer 'went before' him (1 Sa.17:7) or Ahio 'goes before' the ark (2 Sa.6:4) or as when the priest 'goes before' the Lord's anointed.

More important for understanding Gen.17:1 are a series of allusions to the Davidic king who is to 'walk before' God. Thus Solomon speaks of God's servants who 'walk before you with all their heart' (2 Chr.6:14). The expression is combined with phrases like 'in faithfulness, with all their heart and all their soul' (1 Ki.2:4), 'with all their heart' (1 Ki.8:23), 'in faithfulness, in righteousness, and in uprightness of heart toward you' (1 Ki.3:6), 'with integrity of heart and uprightness' (1 Ki.9:4), 'doing according to all that I have commanded you' (2 Chr.7:17), 'in faithfulness and with a whole heart' (2 Ki.20:3; Is.38:3).[20]

Three times such phraseology occurs in Genesis. Apart from 17:1, we discover that Abraham's servant claims to 'walk before' Yahweh (24:40) and Jacob speaks of Abraham and Isaac who 'walked before God' (48:15). In the light of such usage it seems that 17:1 concerns Abraham's loyalty, service and openness to God.

Abraham is also asked to be perfect (*tamim*). The term has cultic associations. In 51 of its 91 occurrences in the Massoretic text, it is used of the required health and soundness in animals to be offered in sacrifice, and means 'without discernible defect'. On six occasions it is best translated by such terms as 'whole' (Lv.3:9; Jos.10:13; Prov.1:12) or 'complete' (Lv.23:13; Ezk.15:5) or 'full' (Lv.25:30). It is found in 1 Sam.14:41, where the text is apparently corrupt.[48] Four times it is used of God's activities (Dt.32:4; Ps.18:30; 2 Sa.22:31; Ps.19:7) and twice of completeness of knowledge (Jb.36:4; 37:16). A survey of the twenty-eight occurrences which are closer in usage to Gen.17:1 reveals that *tamim* combines the idea of sincerity and absence of pretence with that of absence of visible defect. Sometimes the emphasis is on blamelessness, the difficulty which others will have in pointing to obvious defects. Thus Noah is said to be *tamim* among his contemporaries (Gen.6:9). When Israel is required to be *tamim* in Deut.18:12 the allusion is to the absence of obvious ugly sins mentioned in 18:10–12.

When in Jos.24:14 the people are to be *tamim* the reference is to the absence of the worship of other gods.

At other points the emphasis is on basic genuineness. We read of the integrity of the people who made Abimelech king (Jdg.9:16,19), who acted 'in truth and in *tamim*'; elsewhere we have mention of 'straight' talk (Am.5:10). Sometimes David is portrayed as claiming such blamelessness (2 Sam.22:24; Ps.18:23,32), as also is Job (Jb.12:14).

Such 'blamelessness' is thought of as being possible. On numerous occasions it is taken for granted that it is possible to live without obvious defects, having the various areas of one's life as they ought to be be (2 Sam.22:26,33; Ps.15:2; 18:25; 37:18; 84:11; 101:2,6; 119:1; Pr.2:21; 11:5,20; 28:10,18; Ezk.28:15). That both inward and outer aspects of sincerity are involved is clear from the fact that we have references to both the blameless 'way' and the blameless 'heart'. (Ps.119:1,80 have both within the same psalm.)

Such claims are not sheer self-righteousness. God himself uses similar language of Job (Jb.1:8; 42:8) without implying total sinlessness. The claim is not to sinlessness but to basic straightforwardness, absence of duplicity. The righteous man may search his heart and be sure that he is not deceiving himself or others (2 Cor.1:12). As Kidner comments on Ps.5:4–6, the psalmist acknowledged 'that if God were to try his character instead of his case, he would be undone'. When people use such language, 'they know they are in the right vis-a-vis their opponents, as disputants in, so to speak, a civil court; and in general relation to God and his law their heart is 'perfect'; they are totally committed'.[22]

It is this kind of commitment that is asked of Abraham. God is not demanding utter sinlessness, a moral faultlessness like that of God himself. Rather what is required is all-round integrity, absence of duplicity, a sincerity that is obvious to men and pleasing to God.

It is likely that the second imperative in Gen.17:1 is dependent on the first, and means 'Walk before me and so be perfect.'[23]

In the context of this assurance of God's aid ('I am El Shaddai') and the demand for Abraham's obedience ('Walk before me . . . '), the covenant is again announced and further features are added. First (17:3–8) we have the promises given to Abraham; Abraham himself is prostrate and therefore again passive before Yahweh. Then in 17:9–14 demands are made of Abraham ('You shall keep my covenant . . . This is my covenant which you shall keep . . . every male shall be circumcised'). Uncircumcision in any member of the family of Abraham is to be punished by the offender's being 'cut off' from his people, i.e. from the people of Abraham. In a further section (17:15–21) God addresses Sarah, promising her a new name/nature, as he had Abraham. The seed will come through her, and the covenant will continue through Isaac. The prayer concerning Ishmael is heard, but the covenant line will go through Isaac not Ishmael.

(iii) As mentioned above, the ability of God to transform human incapacity follows a consistent method in the patriarchal narratives.

Human frailty is met with God's bestowing a new name, speaking of a new ability to meet God's demands. In the 'El Shaddai' passages three patriarchal figures are renamed. El Shaddai renames Abram, who cannot produce the seed, and designates him 'father of a multitude'. He renames Sarah, the wife through whom the true seed will come (17:5, 15, 19). Again it is immediately after the renaming of Jacob that God is called 'El Shaddai' , in the Jacob-narrative (Gen.35:10f.). It is also in connection with the name El Shaddai that the promises of the land are given to the patriarchs despite their obvious weakness. As Motyer says: 'It was the claim of El Shaddai to be powerful where man was weakest.'[24]

Thus the renaming of the key figures emphasizes that the God of the patriarchs is one who works in the lives of those to whom he speaks, transforming their natural incapacity so as to enable them to receive by continuing faith-and-obedience the promises that have been put before them. Evidently the promises are not simply inherited. On-going faith is required; transformation of character is needed. Only in this way will the promises be inherited. However the demand for obedience is followed by enablement for obedience. A child had been promised many years previously. Ishmael had been born but Abraham had gone on waiting for at least thirteen more years. At the time when God draws attention to his character as El Shaddai a new name is given to Abraham, emphasizing, at this juncture, that Abraham will be enabled to be what the promise had always said he would be – the father of a multitude. God's power comes 'to make the man into a new man, to make Abram what he was not before – Abraham – to give him capacities which he did not possess before, to make the childless man a father on a colossal scale'.[25]

CIRCUMCISION

(iv) Circumcision is incorporated into the Abrahamic covenant. In 17:4–8 God says he will establish his covenant. Since what is found at that point is a series of promises it appears that the covenant is here viewed as consisting in promises. In 17:9–14 we have a fresh unit ('And God said to Abraham . . . ', v.9), in which the covenant is defined in terms of the sign of circumcision. Abraham must 'keep' the covenant. Keeping the covenant, at this point, consists in circumcising every male within the family. The promises are personal ('between me and you (sing.)'), and family-based ('I will make you (sing.) fruitful'), but will eventually become international ('father of many nations') and territorial ('all the land').

It is important to note the setting and context in which circumcision is introduced. It comes in connection with the new name, speaking of the new nature and power that Abraham has received, to enable him to father many nations. Circumcision could be said to be the sign of regeneration, if one may be allowed to use a New Testament term in elucidating the Abraham story.[26] Circumcision comes many years after

Abraham's salvation and so may be said to 'seal' Abraham's salvation, ratifying what has gone before and signifiying the capability of God in empowerment and enablement with a view to the receiving of the promises. Put in modern Christian language, circumcision 'seals' Abraham's salvation and signifies the regeneration which will enable the promises to be received.

(There is however no reason to think that circumcision sealed the salvation of anyone other than Abraham. Paul later protested against regarding circumcision as a general seal and as a certification of the salvation of whoever possessed it in Abraham's line. It was Abraham's faith which circumcision sealed, pointing to faith as the only way to continue in Abraham's line. Those in Abraham's line who possessed the sign but did not follow in Abraham's faith had nothing).[27]

Circumcision thus pointed to Abraham as the model of salvation. It was later incorporated into Mosaic legislation and became part of obedience to Mosaic law. Yet circumcision did not originate with Moses, according to the Genesis story. It pointed to faith and regeneration rather than to legal obedience, although at a later stage legal obedience involved the keeping of the sign of faith. Jesus was making a theological point when, according to the Johannine testimony, he said 'Moses gave you circumcision' but added 'Not that it is from Moses but from the patriarchs' (Jn.7:22).

The possibility of breaking the covenant is mentioned in Gen.17:14. Anyone who will not identify with Abraham's way of relating to God, and with the purpose of God through Abraham's seed, is thereby no part of Abraham's seed, and is to be cut off from it.

If the interpretation above is correct it means that circumcision seals justification by faith, symbolizes regeneration and summons Abraham to obedience. When given to the physical descendants of Abraham it recalls the story of Abraham and summons the seed of Abraham to follow in his steps. If I am right in seeing significance in the stages in which the life-story of Abraham unfolds, it is also significant that circumcision comes in not at the point of faith, nor at one of the earlier announcements of promise, but at the point where demands are laid on Abraham in order for the covenant promises to be fulfilled. The covenant sign spoke of covenant promises. Yet it also spoke of those promises being given to Abraham at a time when demands were made on him. When Abraham saw the marks of circumcision on his own body he could say to himself, 'I am a man to whom promises have been given'; he would also have to say (for the two aspects came at the same time), 'I am a man upon whom demands have been laid.'

(v) Nowhere in the narrative is there any demand for obedience to law. At this point it is important to keep in mind the analyis of the term 'law' which appears above (pp 51ff.). If any kind of obedience implies 'law', then law must be thought to be present in the Abraham story, for certainly obedience is demanded of Abraham. But it is confusing to use the term 'law' in this way. J.A.Motyer, whose work I admire and have quoted above, is confusing at this point. He says that 'the covenant man is a man under the law of God' and continues, with Abraham in view, 'At the very moment when the promises light upon a man, he is turned into an obedient man. At the very moment when God gives him the promises, the obligations will be arising, and these two things cannot be sundered. As soon as Abraham marks his body with [the] knife of circumcision, he glories in the promises and is summoned to obedience'.[28] I agree with this entirely, except that it seems confusing to use the term 'law' in this connection. The obedience to which Abraham is summoned is a direct obedience, unmediated by any 'law'. It may seem only a matter of words whether or not this should be called obedience to law. Yet if the New Testament interpretation of Genesis is to be understood and one is to align oneself with the total biblical interpretation of Abraham, it would seem helpful to use Paul's terminology and view 'law' as something that comes in only at Sinai. Paul would have said that it was the Spirit that was leading Abraham, and would call the gift of the Spirit 'the blessing of Abraham' (Gal.3:14).

In Gen.17:9 Abraham is asked to 'keep' (*sh-m-r*) the covenant. The verb has a wide range of meanings but in this context the usage is similar to references to 'keeping' a festival (Ex.23:15), the sabbath (Dt.5:12), a vow (Dt.23:15), commands (Jer.35:18) and 'keeping' a covenant (Ezk.17:14). Again the lateness of this demand within the Abraham stories should be noticed. There was nothing to 'keep' in Gen.12, and no mention of 'keeping' the covenant when it was first introduced in Gen.15. In 17:9 'keeping' the covenant refers to maintaining the relationship already in existence, and to obeying the particular requirement that circumcision should be maintained as the sign of the way of salvation to which Abraham had been introduced.

Gen.17 is the point where the demand for obedience is introduced in intense form in Abraham's life-story. Implicit in the promises of Gen.12, it becomes explicit only at this later stage of the story. It is a demand for obedience yet does not involve law. No vows or promises are asked of Abraham. He does not have to say he will be obedient. It is characteristic of the Mosaic law that prior pledges are involved (as in Ex.19:8). Vows are part of the Mosaic system but not part of the relationship between Abraham and God. Rather than say he 'will be' obedient, Abraham 'has to be' obedient. His relationship with God operates by direct contact, involves response to God's promises and direct obedience to the voice of God.

GENESIS 22

The event of Genesis 22 is clearly of crucial significance. It is no accident that a New Testament writer will pinpoint this as the occasion when Abraham was justified by works.

The record of Gen.12–21 shows a steady progress in Abraham's obedience. Chapter 12 offers a glimpse of Abraham's first faith in responding to God's voice by departing from home, family and country. Chapter 13 reveals a greater disentanglement from kindred in the separation from Lot. The departure to Egypt seems to have been a lapse of faith. God does not speak to Abraham there. The incident is a lapse in the movement of the narrative towards Canaan. Only when Abraham returns there does God speak to him again. Chapter 14 shows Abraham trusting God with regard to material possessions. Chapter 15 is the occasion of the covenant. Chapter 16 discloses another lapse of faith, as Abraham turns to what Paul would call 'the flesh'. Chapter 17 presents for the first time God's demand for obedience. The following chapters portray Abraham as a godly man, leading his family into ways of righteousness (18:19), able to share the secrets of God (18:17), an intercessor (18:23–33). A further lapse of faith in Gen.20 does not abrogate God's purposes, and Isaac is born.

Thus chapters 12–21 show Abraham living in the obedience of faith, subject to lapses, but nevertheless on close terms with God.

ABRAHAM'S OBEDIENCE

The phrase, 'After these things' which opens the story (22:1) pinpoints a specific event that takes the narrative of Abraham's life a step further. No challenge such as this had yet occurred. The text is well-known and we need not look at it in detail. The important points are that it calls for great faith, great obedience, involves much self-abasement and is an apparent threat to all of Abraham's hopes. Abraham is obedient; he passes the test. As a result of his obedience a number of fresh elements are introduced into his relationship with God. Key verses which require fuller consideration are Gen.22:12 and the oath of Gen.22:16. Again the details may be itemized in several points.

i. Abraham's obedience reaches an unprecedented height. The introductory sentences of this section disclose a climactic test. Gen.22:12 lets us know that the test was passed and Abraham was commended. The commendation is explicitly stated and linked to a specific occasion. God says 'At this time I know'.[29] Abraham's obedience has reached an unprecedented height; he has passed a supreme test.

ii. Abraham's relationship to God is taken a stage further. The particle ʿattah – 'now' (22:12) may be a note of time ('At this time') or, less likely, a note of inference ('In the light of what you have done'). Either way it explicitly relates the obedience of Gen.22 to a development in the relationship between God and Abraham. James 2:21 describes it as 'justification by works'. ('Was not Abraham . . . justified by works when he offered up Isaac?') The relationship between God and Abraham is not static and predetermined. The phrase ʿattah yadaʿti points to a real change and improvement.

GOD'S OATH

iii. As the result of the new level of obedience God swears by himself when renewing the promises to Abraham. What is an 'oath' of God?[30]

It is closely related to the question of whether or not God changes his mind. In classical Christian orthodoxy, influenced by Greek thinking, the doctrine of God's immutability was so influential that statements concerning a change in God were played down. God 'could not' change his mind. Yet the Bible portrays God as changing his mind on a number of occasions[31]. God is represented as able on the one hand to withdraw his promises and on the other to abandon his threats. According to Jonah 3:4 Nineveh was told that judgement would fall upon it in forty days' time. No conditions were set; no possibility of change was mentioned. Yet after the king of Nineveh had said to his people 'Who knows whether God will not . . . repent?' and had summoned them to amend their ways, 'God repented' (3:10). Saul, by contrast, although he was chosen to be the head of a lineage of kings had the kingdom removed from him because he sinned (1 Sa.15:28). God would have established his kingdom for ever but the point came where Samuel could say, 'But now your kingdom shall not continue' (1 Sa.13:13–14). Clearly the biblical representation is that God may amend his purpose. The oath of God relates to this; the oath is the point after which God will not change his mind. Thus after God decides to reject Saul it is said that God 'is not a man that he should repent' (1 Sa.16:29). The rejection occurs after Saul has persistently failed in obedience and God has 'made up his mind' about the king. There is a correlation between God's 'making up his mind' and his oath. Thus Psalm 110:4 says of the priest after the order of Melchizedek: 'Yahweh has sworn, and will not repent . . . '. The oath is the point at which a decision is made as to whether the promises will in fact be inherited, or whether the threats will in fact be executed.

One can see this usage of the oath-language in Gen.22. Promises have been given to Abraham for many years; they have to be inherited by faith and patience. Obedience is required if they are to come to full fruition. They conceivably could have been aborted, as in the case of Saul. Then comes a decisive test (Gen.22:1); Abraham passes the test by responding in supreme faith and obedience. At that point God takes the oath concerning the promises. God has 'made up his mind' about Abraham. From now on the purposes of God are immutably fixed with regard to the 'seed of Abraham'. The promised 'seed' will bring international blessing through Abraham's line. The land of Canaan will indeed be given to Abraham's people.

It is notable that in books of the Old Testament that refer to later times (regardless of whether or not their editing really was later) the incident referred to as the crucial occasion of Abraham's life – the occasion when the land was pledged – is not Gen.12 or 15 or 17, but Gen.22 (see Jer.11:5 with its explicit mention of 'the oath which I swore to your fathers'). Similarly the Song of Zechariah mentions, not 'the promise which he gave to Abraham', which could refer to Gen.12, but 'the oath which he swore to Abraham', which refers to Gen.22. The occasion of the oath is the decisive one after which God would not change his mind. It is to this that Hebrews 6 refers when it mentions

Abraham's inheriting the promises by faith and patience (Heb.6:12), and when it speaks of heroes of faith who 'obtained promises' (Heb.11:33). In Hebrews there is a difference between 'having' and 'obtaining' a promise. Obtaining the promise correlates not with initial faith, but with faith and patience; it occurs when one's faith has been tested and has been proved to be an abiding faith. Only at such a point does God take an oath and say, 'Now I know . . . '. At this point and not before, the promise is immutably secure. It is to this that James 2:21 refers. James calls it 'justification by works'.[32]

There are four major occasions in the Old Testament when God takes an oath: the oath to Abraham (Gen.22:16), the oath taken in anger concerning the forfeiting of the land of Israel for the first generation of Israel (Nu.14:20–23), God's oath to the Davidic dynasty (Ps.89:19–37), and his oath concerning the Messianic priest-king (Ps.110:1–4).

While the oath may receive only brief treatment here it clearly is a matter of major significance. It connects with questions concerning God's immutability and 'repenting'; it relates to a doctrine of 'justification by works'. It is of key significance in the interpretation of Hebrews 6:4–6 (which surely refers to the point at which God 'makes up his mind' and 'entering into rest' is no longer a possibility for the Christian).

The introduction of the covenant in Gen.15 and 17 and the oath in Gen.22 imply that there are various levels of promise. One may distinguish casual promise (in which a promise is made but there is no legal commitment) from legal promise (in which the promise is bound by covenant). Within covenant-making one may distinguish the introduction of the covenant (Gen.15:17) and the consummation of the covenant-making in the giving of the oath. Concerning the oath in the life of Abraham one notes: (i) it takes place after Abraham's initial experience of salvation, (ii) it is a certifying word from God that Abraham has acted in great obedience, (iii) it introduces reward into Abraham's life, for it is based upon his acting in obedience, and (iv) it introduces the actual acquirement of that which has been promised to him, his 'obtaining' the promise.

COVENANT AND OATH

A difficult but important question, touched upon in the previous paragraph, is: what is the relationship between covenant and oath? What makes the matter important is that oath is embodied in covenant. There is no covenant without oath-taking[33]. How then is it possible that the covenant should have been made with Abraham in Gen.15 and 17, yet the oath is given after the crucial event of Gen.22?

The link between covenant and oath is plain from many parts of the Bible and in all types of covenant. Thus in the parity-covenant between Abimelech and Isaac, Abimelech's men say 'Let there be an oath now between us . . . and let us cut a covenant with you'

(Gen.26:28). In the parity-covenant between Abram and Abimelech the two themes are side-by-side ('the two men made a covenant . . . the two men swore an oath', Gen.21:27,31). In the covenant between Laban and Jacob the two terms, covenant and oath, are identified ('Come now, let us make a covenant . . . so Jacob took an oath', Gen.31:44,53). Likewise in the case of the covenant between David and Jonathan we read: 'So Jonathan cut a covenant . . . Jonathan made David reaffirm his oath' (1 Sa.20:16f.). Similar links between oaths and covenant in parity covenants are found in Hos.10:4, Ez.16:8 and other instances.

Every covenant involved an oath, and the oath was 'the formality which made the covenant valid'[34]. At times it is difficult to draw any distinction between the two. To 'make a covenant' and 'to swear' are virtually synonymous. One term replaces the other in the synonymous parallelism of Ps.89:34f.:

> My covenant will I not break,
> Not alter the thing that has gone out of my lips.
> Once for ever have I sworn by my holiness
> I will not lie . . .

How then is it possible that there should be such a disjunction between covenant and oath in Gen.15, 17 and 22? Gen.15:8–11 is an oath-taking ceremony. Why was the oath not thought of as given then? I suggest that the covenant of Gen.15 and 17 was viewed as not entirely completed. Promises were indeed given (15:18–21; 17:4–8) yet at that point God did not swear by his holiness. One swears by someone greater as guarantor (as Heb.6:13 points out); this did not take place in Gen.15 or 17. In Gen.22 however, after the faith-obedience of Abraham has been tested and confirmed, God completes the oath and swears not by someone who is greater but by his own life (Gen.22:16). As sure as he is God, the promise will indeed be fulfilled.

If this is correct it means that the covenant and oath of Gen.15,17 and 22 belong together and all make one covenant taken over the course of many years. In the early stages the covenant had something missing; it was open-ended and could have been aborted by unbelief and disobedience. Oath-taking procedure had commenced yet the swearing by someone greater had been omitted. The covenant is 'on offer' yet not completed. The completion would not come until Abraham's obedience had been confirmed. Thus the covenant-making procedure was not entirely finished until Gen.22. Just as Gen.15 and 17 were part of one covenant yet separated by a time-gap, so Gen.22 was still a continuation of covenant-making with a further time-gap between the elements of the one covenant.

(v) Abraham was allowed to know that he pleased God and that the inheriting of the promise had been secured. It is conceivable that God could have taken a decision entirely within himself and not revealed to Abraham that it had been taken. He could have said to himself 'Now I know that Abraham fears me.' However what we are in fact told is that Abraham was informed that he had passed the test, that God himself accepted and vindicated his piety. On a previous occasion God debated within himself whether or not he would reveal his purpose to Abraham (Gen.18:17); a hidden purpose is conceivable. There too God revealed his secret to Abraham (Gen.18:19–21). In Gen.22 God's secret purpose is revealed, and Abraham is informed that the seed of Abraham will continue, and that the purpose through the seed of Abraham will go forward and is henceforth entirely secure. This too must be understood in direct or mystical terms. Abraham is evidently portrayed as knowing God's mind as the result of direct fellowship between himself and God.

We come then to an interim conclusion. Our exposition of the highlights of the story of Abraham has been given with a view to looking for the place of the law (if any), and of obedience and 'good works' in the life of Abraham. This, in summary, is what we have seen:

(i) The narratives reveal the dominance and priority of grace. Abraham's life of obedience began in election and faith. No explicit call for obedience is found before Gen.17:1. Grace is first; the call for obedience second. There is a time gap between the giving of the promise and the call for obedience.

(ii) The knowledge of God's will is not mediated through anything written or legal. It is directly communicated knowledge.

(iii) Thus Abraham's obedience is obedience to God's will in the context of direct fellowship with him.

(iv) The narratives are conspicuous for the total absence of law-code – a point which will be developed in the next chapter.

8

The Law of the Mosaic Covenant

In Galatians 3 Paul draws a sharp distinction between Moses and Abraham. It is appropriate then to move from the Abraham stories to the narratives concerning Sinai and the Sinai covenant, to see whether a review of the Sinai narratives does indeed reveal such a great contrast. It will also help in considering whether the contrast Paul draws between Abraham and Moses resides in the Old Testament narratives themselves or whether (as is often asserted) Paul is referring not so much to the law as to a particular interpretation of the law given by his theological enemies.

We begin by noting the absence of the law before Sinai. Legislation for God's people comes in as a somewhat dramatic innovation in the stories of the Pentateuch. Paul asserts (Gal.3:19) that the law was 'added' (*prosetethe*) to the gospel, and thus was an intrusion into what had originally been given to Abraham. Paul's language gives the impression that he regarded the Mosaic covenant, with the decalogue at its heart, as no part of God's original plan; God had at a certain point departed from a previous approach and 'added' the Mosaic covenant. A study of the Exodus account gives much the same impression and there is therefore every reason to think that it was Paul's reflection upon the Exodus story which brought him to the conviction expressed in Gal.3:19.

LAW AND THE COVENANT

J.A.Motyer lists eight main words in the vocabulary surrounding law: ʻedah, torah, dabar, choq, mishpat, mitsweh, piqqud and derek.[1] We may agree with him that these eight terms pinpoint eight different aspects of the law. 'Testimony' (ʻedah) speaks of the revealed-ness of the law; it is God speaking from his own mind. 'Teaching' (torah) speaks of its impact upon man, its purpose to inform his mind and shape his life. 'Word' (dabar) speaks of that which is intelligible, a deposit of information to be pondered. 'Statute' (choq) speaks of permanency. 'Judgement' (mishpat) speaks of royal authority, author-itative decision. 'Commandment' (mitsweh) reminds us of authority and the right of a command to be considered as mandatory. 'Precept' (*piqqud*) reminds us that the law is to be broken up into specifics. 'Way' (*derek*) tells us of the path of characteristic behaviour that results from obedience to the law.

Where does this legal language commence within the Pentateuch? When did legislation begin to occupy a role in the relationship between God and his people? The answer is that this terminology appears in the pages of the Pentateuch almost exclusively in connection with the Sinai covenant.

LEGAL VOCABULARY IN GENESIS

Before *'edah* is used of the Mosaic law in Deuteronomy, Joshua and Psalms the word occurs only in Gen.21:30 and 31:52. In neither of these does it refer to anything written or codified; *'edah* is thus not used of any law prior to Sinai.

The word *torah* occurs seven times before Ex.24:12. Its first occurrence (Gen.26:5) comes a considerable way through the Abraham stories. God's charge (*mishmeret*), God's commands (*mitswoth*), statutes (*chuqqot*) and instruction (*torah*) refer to the various directives that have been given to Abraham, without the utilization of any written document or law code. Leupold believes that the reference is to the command to leave family, the instructions concerning the sacrifice of Isaac and to similar instructions given by God directly to Abraham.[2] The reference to *chuqqot* is more difficult since the background of the word gives the impression not of anything occasional but of something permanent. It probably refers to the instructions of Gen.17:2 and the command concerning circumcision. Only at this point do we have an instance of *torah* that refers to any kind of pre-Mosaic instruction. (I have in mind the date of the time referred to, not the date of any source). The instances of the term at Ex.12:49; 13:9; 16:4,28; 18:16,20 are found shortly before the story of Sinai, and receive comment below.

Dabar occurs about 60 times in Genesis. On three occasions it refers to God's word (15:1,4; 30:34) but on none of these occasions is the reference to any kind of law comparable to Sinai.

Before the Sinai stories, *choq* occurs only in Gen.26:5, mentioned already in connection with the use of *torah* in the same verse. The term also occurs in connection with the Egyptians' laws in Gen.47:22,26; Ex.5:14.

Mishpat is used on three occasions in Genesis (18:19,25; 40:13) but never in connection with law. It is used in Ex.15:25; 21:1 (and often thereafter) of aspects of the Sinai legislation.

We find *mitswah* only in Gen.26:5, mentioned already. Then it appears in Ex.15:26; 16:28 in incidents that take place as Sinai is approached.

The word *piqqud* has no pre-Mosaic usage. It is used only in Psalms, where it refers to the Sinai legislation.

Derek is found 31 times in Genesis. On several occasions it refers to the godly life. Thus in Gen.18:19 we have reference to the 'way of Yahweh'. In that case it clearly refers to the godly living that flows from an intimate relationship with God. As we have seen, no law code is involved.

To conclude: legal language can scarcely be said to exist in the patriarchal stories. Such language occurs only spasmodically and then has no connection with legislation such as we discover in the Sinai law codes.

LEGAL LANGUAGE AFTER SINAI

On the other hand, legal language commences in abundance in the narratives telling of the approach of the people to Sinai, and in the remainder of the Torah. After its isolated use in Gen.26:5, *torah* first occurs in connection with the passover (Ex.12:49). Since at Ex.12:49 no reference to any laws has yet been made it is likely that at this point the ongoing ceremony of Passover is envisaged as a permanent requirement. However the incorporation of this into a larger legal code is not initially mentioned. Exodus envisages the people as settled in the land with an alien population among them. Ex.13:9 envisages the Passover as a permanent requirement. Then *torah* is also used in connection with the Sabbath in Exodus 16:4,28, thus anticipating the decalogue.

The word *choq* is used in much the same way of the Passover (Ex.12:14,17,43; 13:10). We find *'edah* used of Mosaic legislation in Deut.4:45 onwards, and *dabar* is found frequently of items of legislation. The ten commandments are introduced as *hdbrym h'lh*. In Ex.15:25f. where *choq*, *mitswah* and *mishpat* are found, the 'law' envisaged refers to the people's obedience to specific directives and the consequent promise of freedom from Egyptian diseases. It probably envisages the approaching Sinai covenant.

Of course law may exist without precise legal language. Yet the fact that legal language first appears only in Exodus 12 is a confirmation of what has already been noted in the Abraham stories. The people of God before the days of Moses were not in any way under codified legislation. There are references to local law, but these have no special divine mandate. The first hints of divinely mandated legislation come in events preparatory to Sinai. Ordinances are introduced at the time of the redemption of the nation. First mentioned is the directive concerning Passover (Ex.12:14,17,23,43,49) and the feast of unleavened bread (13:10). Later we find a hint of the many demands of obedience that are to come (15:25f.) and a rule concerning the Sabbath (Ex.16:4,28). The Pentateuch presents a picture of a large amount of legislation upon arrival at the mountain. Whatever one may conclude about how far every legal clause of the Pentateuch actually originated at this time, the representation is clearly that much detailed legislation originated at this point which had not characterized the relationship of God with his people before the Exodus events. The law was 'added'.

THE NATURE OF THE COVENANT

This leads us to a second matter: the nature of the Sinai covenant. In Ex.19:5 the relationship between Yahweh and Israel established at Sinai is designated by the term *berith*.[3] In the order of events presented in the finally edited Pentateuch, this is the third 'covenant' between God and man explicitly mentioned, the previous two being those connected with Noah and Abraham. This prompts several questions: what is the nature of the Sinai covenant? what is the connection between what happens in Exodus 19 and the covenant mentioned in Genesis 15 and 17?[4]

A major break-through in biblical studies occurred in 1954, when G.E.Mendenhall published in the *Biblical Archaeologist* his studies of covenant forms. He urged that a study of the covenant forms known in ancient documents would throw light on Israelite religion. He pointed out that records of international treaties, known especially from the Hittite empire *c.*1450–1200 BC but deriving ultimately from Mesopotamian sources and being the common property of many cultures in the second millennium, showed resemblances to biblical covenants and could be used to illuminate their background and interpretation.[5] He distinguished between suzerainty treaties and parity treaties. In a suzerainty treaty the junior partner took an oath of obedience as stipulated by the senior partner. By contrast, in a parity treaty both partners were equally bound by oath to identical obligations.

Mendenhall urged that at least three collections of material, in Exodus, Deuteronomy and Joshua, are linked with this legal tradition, and that 'innumerable incidents and ideas in the entire history of Israel can be adequately understood only from this complex of covenant patterns of thought'.[6]

Since 1954 an immense body of literature has come into being. The six-fold structure of second millennium treaties (preamble, prologue, stipulations, provision for reading, witnesses, curses and blessings) has been frequently rehearsed[7]. Many have accepted Mendenhall's view that the decalogue is to be viewed as having treaty-like structure and background. Many aspects of Old Testament thought and religion have been reviewed in the light of new discoveries concerning treaty and covenant. Yet not all of Mendenhall's views have won approval, and his 'covenant-formulation' interpretation of Ex.19–24 has especially been criticized. Furthermore, not all have agreed with Mendenhall's drawing a distinction between first and second millennium covenants, and his Mosaic dating of the decalogue.

Although I believe that Mendenhall's work remains basically valid, there is no need at this point for detailed involvement in the debates concerning Hittite and Assyrian covenants. Three matters, however are important for our purpose. Firstly, it must be remembered that what we have in the Old Testament are not themselves covenant documents but are one or more steps away from the events they narrate. They describe the giving of the covenant and its various renewals, but are not themselves covenant documents. Ex.19–24 might still bear the marks of a treaty, without being itself a treaty document. The nearest document to a treaty would be Deuteronomy, but even there it is arguable that Deuteronomy reflects rather than consists of treaty.[8]

Secondly, there can be no doubt that the treaty form (known to us from Hittite sources but of wider Mesopamian origins) is still visible in Exodus, Deuteronomy and Joshua. Consider the following table (based upon the work of K.A.Kitchen).[9] Kitchen wishes to add traces of oath-taking and solemn ceremony (Ex.24:1–11; Dt.24; fulfilled Js.8:30–35) and the threat of sanctions (the *rib* motif starting from Dt.32 and continuing throughout the Old Testament).

Treaty *Title/*	Exodus	Deuteronomy	Joshua
Preamble	Ex.20:1	Dt.:1−5	Jos.24:1f.
Historical Prologue	Ex.20:2	Dt.1:6 − 3:29	Jos.24:2−13
Stipulations, *basic and detailed*	Ex 20:3−17,22−26 +21−12,25−31 (law) & Lv 1−25 (ritual)	Dt.4:5−11 + 12−26	Jos.24:14f. + 16−25
Deposit of text	Ex 25:16, cf 34:1,28,29 (cf retrospect in Dt.10:1−5)	Dt.31:9, 24−26	Jos.24:26
Public reading	−−	Dt.31:10−13	− (but see 8:34)
Witnesses	Ex.24:4 (cf Jos.24:27)	Dt.31:16−30, esp v.26; 32:1−47	Jos.24:22
Blessing	Lev.26:3−13	Dt.28:1−14	Implicit in 24:19f.
Cursing	Lev.24:14−33	Dt.28:15−68	

However disputed certain sections might be, it seems incontrovertible that enough of the treaty form shines through all three sections of the Old Testament (Exodus-Leviticus, Deuteronomy, Joshua 24) for it to be possible to make use of the fact in theological exposition.

Thirdly, it is important to let the biblical material speak for itself. Although our knowledge of the ancient world might make us notice aspects of scripture that otherwise would have been overlooked, in the final analysis it is the biblical documents themselves that must be allowed to speak. One must always be sensitive to the possibility that amidst general similarities to the culture of the ancient world there may be modifications and contradictions. For example, while the gods of paganism might be invoked as witnesses in Hittite treaties, something else has to function as witness in the faith of Israel. Instead of pagan gods we read of memorial stones (Ex.24:4; Js.24:27) or a song to be memorized (Dt.32:1–47) or the deposition of a document (Dt.31:26) or the people themselves as witnesses (Js.24:22). Thus we shall not be surprised to find many resemblances to the ancient cultures, but we shall keep our minds open to the possibility of modification or disagreement.

In 1970 M.Weinfeld drew attention to another type of covenant in addition to the parity-covenants and treaties that had already been widely investigated. Weinfeld pointed to the royal grant, classically found in the Babylonian *kudurru* documents (boundary stones).[11] Although the royal grant is very similar to the treaty the obligations are in direct contrast. In the treaty the vassal owed allegiance to his master; in the royal grant the overlord pledges himself to bestow some favour. Weinfeld pointed to the similarity of the 'covenant of grant' and the covenants with Abraham and David: 'the grants to Abraham, Caleb, David, Aaron and the Levites have much in common with the grants from Alalah, Nuzi, the Hittites, Ugarit, and Middle-Babylonian *kudurru*s, i.e. mainly in documents from the second half of the second millennium BC.'[12]

BIBLICAL USAGE

Again one must emphasize that the biblical documents must be allowed to speak for themselves. Yet the work done on covenant in the ancient world has drawn attention to variations in the use of the word *berith* in scripture. There is good reason to think that biblical examples of covenant fall into three categories which must be radically differentiated. The three must be studied within their own framework and the resemblances to extra-biblical material must not be used so as to distort the biblical material itself. Despite this caveat, it can be seen that the three categories strikingly correspond to treaties, parity covenants and covenants of grant. A brief survey of the biblical material will help our interpretation in the following pages of this study.

The term 'covenant' occurs 284 times in the Old Testament (as *berith*) and 33 times in the New Testament (as *diatheke*). As suggested above, these occurrences fall into three groups which I may designate parity-covenants, law-covenants and generosity-covenants. Each of the three is found in human relationships but only the latter two are used metaphorically of the relationship between God and his people. We also find *berith* used figuratively of relationship to non-personal entities. Ignoring the last-mentioned figurative uses, we have five groups to consider.

(I) PARITY-COVENANTS IN HUMAN RELATIONSHIPS

The Old Testament contains at least eleven examples of explicit secular[12] parity covenants.[13] Others are alluded to. Thus one is said to be profaned (Ps.55:20), and one maliciously intended against God (Ps.83:5). Isaiah refers to covenants of peace being broken (Is.33:8) It is also possible that the 'prince of a covenant' in Dan.11:22 refers to 'some prince who had been in covenant relationship with Antiochus'[14]. Hos.10:4 ('swearing falsely in cutting a covenant') is possibly a general allusion to disloyalty in parity covenants. Marriage is such a mutual contract according to Prov.2:17; Ez.16:8; Mal.2:14. Amos 1:9 and Obad.7 seem to refer to political parity-covenants between two brother nations.

(II) THE COVENANT OF GRANT WITHIN HUMAN RELATIONSHIPS

There seems to be only one Old Testament reference to a 'covenant of grant' among human relationships, where the term *berith* is actually used, and that is Jer.34:8–22.[15] The allusion here is to a covenanted proclamation of emancipation for slaves (Jer.34:8,10,15). (This is compared with God's covenant in keeping the Sinai covenant. Such a comparison prevents one from entirely dissevering the different kinds of covenant; they have something in common.)

(III) COVENANTS OF IMPOSED OBLIGATION IN HUMAN RELATIONSHIPS

When the Israelites are forbidden to make covenants with surrounding nations what is in view is especially a covenant of imposed obligation. Israel must not prescribe lenient terms for the Canaanites, imposing on them oaths of loyalty and submission. 'You shall not make a covenant with them', said the Mosaic law (Ex.23:32; see also 34:12,15; Dt.7:2; Jdg.2:2). It is clear that in the envisaged covenant Israel would have been the senior partner, prescribing conditions of relationship and showing mercy to a defeated enemy (Dt.7:2). This is what happens in the deception of the Gibeonites where the note of Gibeonite inferiority is clear and the Israelites are tricked into making a covenant with them (Jos.9;6,7,11,15,16). The Gibeonites come as those seeking protection, putting themselves under Israel as overlord. The relation of junior and senior partner is clear also when the citizens of Jabesh say to Saul, 'Make a treaty with us and we will be subject to you.'[16]

This kind of treaty was made also when a king received an oath of allegiance from subjects. When Abner's kingdom was insecure he sought such a covenant with David (2 Sa.3:21). It was eventually ratified at Hebron (2 Sa.5:3; 1 Chr.11:3). Similarly Jehoiada is recorded as making such a covenant (2 Ki.11:7; 2 Chr.23:3). This kind of covenant might be made between a king and his soldiers, as in the case of Jehoiada (2 Ki.11:4; 2 Chr.23:1). The king of Babylon imposed such a covenant upon the royal seed of Israel according to Ezekiel

17:13–16,18, and possibly v.19 also. (However v.19 could refer to Sinai.)[17] It is possible, although not certain, that the oath taken by the priests in Neh.13:29 relates to a covenant of imposed obligation. Fensham argues that 'the covenant of priesthood' is a sworn promise not to marry foreign women.[18] A preferable view is that the covenant here is the 'covenant with Levi'.[19] Hos.12:1 seems to be another allusion to such a covenant, in this case one in which Israel submits to the demands of Assyria.

It is noticeable that in each of these instances the covenant is imposed by the senior partner or entered into by way of voluntary submission on the part of the junior. The oath-taking is performed by the junior partner.

(IV) THE SINAI COVENANT

In the instances mentioned so far both partners are human beings; if God is mentioned at all it is as a witness. But *berith* is also used metaphorically to denote relationships between God and men. Such a metaphorical use of the term appears unique to Israel. In cases where *berith* is used to denote God's relationship to men, which type of covenant is being metaphorically transferred?

There appears to be no example where a parity covenant is envisaged as existing between God and men. The nearest to this would be instances where the marriage relationship denotes metaphorically God's relationship with his people. However although marriage is used this way it is not clear that the term 'covenant' is used in this connection, despite its use with reference to marriage on the ordinary level (Pr.2:17; Ezk.16:8; Mal.2:14).

My view is that the Sinai covenant (and its renewals) closely resembles the format of a typical covenant of imposed obligation but all other covenants in which God is involved follow the analogy of the covenant of grant.[20] The Sinai covenant is, in terms of verbal statistics, the covenant most frequently mentioned in the Old Testament. Although covenants with Abraham and David might outstrip it in ultimate importance, yet it is the Sinai covenant which receives the most frequent mention of all covenants in the Old Testament. It is mentioned for the first time in Ex.19:5. From its earliest inception the notes of human obligation are heavily underscored. The people respond to it with promises of obedience (Ex.19:8). After the rebellion of the people, the covenant is taken up again (Ex.34:10). Frequently its conditionality is underlined (e.g. Dt.7:12). God will look on the people with favour (Lev.26:9) only if the people will listen and carry out his commands (Lev.26:14). There are threats for disobedience (Lev.26:15). If the people disobey, the 'vengeance of the covenant' will be executed (Lev.26:25).

The covenant at Sinai involved documentation from its inception. A 'book of the covenant' is coeval with the covenant itself (Ex.24:7; 2 Ki.23:2,21). Sacrifice is also involved, hence the phrase 'the blood of the covenant' (Ex.24:8; Zc.9:11).

As with any covenant of imposed obligation, there is heavy emphasis on what is required by the senior partner, in this case Yahweh. After the statements of God's prevenient graciousness in redeeming Israel and bringing the nation to Sinai (Ex.19:1–4), the covenant is introduced (Ex.19:5,6) and its conditionality is forthwith announced: ' . . . if you will indeed hear my voice and keep my covenant you shall be to me a special possession above (or among) all peoples, for all the earth belongs to me. And you will be to me a kingdom of priests and a holy nation.' Three privileges are promised to the nation: special possession by God, priestly ministry[21], and 'life . . . commensurate with the holiness of the covenant God'.[22] They are dependent on obedience to the covenant, which as Exodus 19–24 unfolds, is shown to be obedience to codified law. One notes the contrasts with the Abraham story. The demand for obedience is not at all a later development within a covenant relationship. Rather it is of the essence of the Sinai covenant from its earliest mention. There is no equivalent to the divinely induced sleep which put Abraham into a position of sheer passivity. Instead, from the earliest mention of the Mosaic covenant the people are summoned to obedience and the oath of allegiance is demanded of them.

Thus there is a very close connection between the Sinai covenant and law.[23] Often covenant and law are identified (Ps.78:10; 103:18; Jer.11:8) but this is never the case with any covenant other than Sinai. God tells Moses: 'Write down these words, for in accordance with these words I have made a covenant' (Ex.34:27). One notices the close connection of law, covenant and codification. At times law and covenant are totally identified. Dt 4:13 speaks of 'his covenant, his ten words'. To disobey the commands is to forget the covenant (Dt.4:23; see also 2 Ki.17:35,38). To recite the law is to take the covenant on one's lips (Ps.50:16). The ten words are the 'words of the covenant' (Ex.34:28) and the tablets of stone are sometimes called 'the covenant' (1 Ki.8:2; 2 Chr.6:11; see also Dt.29:1,9; 2 Ki.23:3). The law was kept in the ark, and the ark is therefore known as the 'box of the covenant'[24] We have reference to the 'tablets' of the covenant (Dt.9:9,11,15). Such a covenant of law is distinguished from that of the patriarchs. It is said at Sinai: 'Yahweh made not this covenant with our fathers' (Dt.5:3).

Obedience to commands results in the covenant's being 'established' (Dt.8:18). Disobedience results in the people's perishing (Dt.8:19f.). Breaking a command is called 'transgressing the covenant' (Dt.29:25; Jer.22:9) or 'breaking the covenant' (Dt.31:16,20; Jer.11:10; 31:32 (x2)). To break the covenant commandments is to ignore God's wrath and the curses (Dt.29:1) or penalties (Jer.11:8).

Although the people may break the Sinai covenant, there are statements to the effect that God keeps his covenant (Jdg.2:1; Dn.9:4). However conditionality is still in view when it is said: 'God keeps covenant . . . with your servants that walk before you' (1 Ki.8:23). There are also references to 'keeping (or not keeping) the covenant', where it is the people who are in view, and their obeying the law (Ps.25:10; 44:17) or disobeying it (Ps.78:10,37). Observing God's word and keeping his command are identical (Dt.33:9). The point is made that God keeps his side of the covenant relationship (Ne.9:32 and Ps.111:5,9, where one notes the reference to 'precepts' in 111:7). Yet the implied conditionality remains in qualifying statements (see 2 Chr.6:14; Neh.1:5).

A covenant to seek God or put away pagan wives (as in Ezr.10:3) may come in a different category, yet it is similar to law-covenant, for the junior partner in the relationship gives promises to the overlord.

God's response in keeping the covenant (for which see Ps.25:14) may be made a matter of prayer. A psalmist prays that God will have regard for his covenant (Ps.74:20). Psalm 106:45 speaks of God's hearing such a prayer. These passages refer to the promise in the Sinai covenant that where repentance is shown God will respond with deliverance (see also 1 Ki.8:50–53).

It is the Sinai covenant that is in view when mention is made of the 'salt of the covenant' (Lev.2:13; Nu.18:19) and the bread before Yahweh is an 'everlasting covenant' according to Lev.24:8[25]. The Sabbath also plays a significant part in the Sinai covenant. It is given as an 'everlasting covenant'.[26]

There are times when the Sinai-covenant and the covenant with Abraham are mentioned together. The contextual background to Dt.7:9 is that of the Sinai covenant. Dt.7:12 makes this clear ('Because you keep these judgements . . . God shall keep the mercy that he swore . . . '). Yet we have reference here also to the oath to Abraham (Dt.7:22; cf. Gn.22:16 cited also in Ex.32:13). The argument linking the two covenants is that: God did not choose Israel because of inherent merit (Dt.7:7); rather he was keeping the oath to Abraham (Dt.7:8). The Israelites must learn of God's ability to keep a covenant. God will keep the Sinai covenant if they are obedient (Dt.7:9, referring to the Sinai covenant). If they are obedient God will keep with that particular generation the promise to Abraham which will in any case be kept with one generation or another. The oath to Abraham will be kept. The generation which keeps the Mosaic covenant will find that it enjoys the land, the fruit of the Abrahamic covenant. Thus Deuteronomy 7 weaves together themes that derive from the two covenants.

(v) COVENANTS OF GRANT GIVEN BY GOD TO INDIVIDUALS

Other covenants involving God's relationship towards individuals are not covenants of law but rather covenants of grant. The explicitly mentioned covenants of this nature are as follows. There is the covenant with Noah (Gn.6:18; 9:9,11–17) which is unilateral, universal and requires no duties on Noah's side to be fulfilled. The covenant with Abraham and the patriarchs (Gn.15:18; 17:2, 4, 7(x2), 9–11, 13(x2), 14, 19(x2), 21) is said sometimes to be with Abraham but also

with Abraham, Isaac and Jacob (Ex.2:24; 6:4,f.). It is mentioned in
1Ki.13:23 and (as though it were three covenants) in Lev.26:44f. It is
explicitly mentioned in Dt.4:31; 1 Chron.16:15,17; Neh.9:8; Ps.105:
8,10; Ez.30:5.

Third, there is evidently a covenant with Phineas (Nu.25:12f.) and,
fourth, with David (2 Sa.23:5; 2 Chr.13:5; 21:7; Ps.89:3,28,34,39;
132:12; Is.55:3; Jer.33:21).[27] A fifth individual covenant is that
embodied in the servant of the Lord (Is.42:6; 49:8) which is compared
with the covenant with Noah (Is.54:10) and with the Davidic covenant
(Is.55:3). It is related to the gift of the Spirit in Is.59:21. Leupold[28]
thinks that Is.61:8 refers to Sinai but I prefer to link it with the
previous Isaianic references to a new covenant. Sixth, a new covenant
is on the horizon of thinking in Jer.31:31,33; 32:40; 50:5; Ez.16:60–62;
34:25; 37:26; Dan.9:27 and Hos.2:18.

Seventh, a covenant with Levi is mentioned in Mal.2:4,5,8 and
possibly in Neh.13:29; it is presupposed in Jer.33:21. This is never
mentioned explicitly in Ex.32:26–29; Dt.33:8–11.

In none of these seven 'covenants of grant' is there the impression of
imposed command that we have noted in connection with Sinai.[29]

A vital matter, and one which points to at least two radically
divergent types of covenant, is the question of who takes the oath. In
the Sinai covenant the oath is taken by the people (Ex.24); in the other
covenants, by God. M.Kline emphasizes this: 'Notice must be taken of
a feature which law and promise covenants have in common but
which, nevertheless, being more closely analysed, serves to distinguish
between the two . . . *It is the swearing of the ratificatory oath that
provides an identification mark* . . . '.[30] It is this crucial fact that
warrants our treating the Sinai covenant as a different kind of
covenant compared to all other covenants involving Yahweh as a
participant.

THE ABRAHAMIC AND SINAI COVENANTS CONTRASTED

These radical divergences between Abrahamic and Sinaitic covenants
have considerable implications. An innovative note was struck when
the Sinai covenant was introduced. It was a covenant that had law
within it from its earliest mention. When Abraham was in covenant
with God, it was God who swore to bring about its potential and
Abraham's needful obedience was only slowly made explicit. By
contrast, the relationship between God and Israel at Sinai was such
that the vow of obedience was coeval with the covenant itself and
constituted its central ingredient. The auto-imprecation (self-curse)
for breach of oath in Gen.15 could not materialize because God would
not fail in faithfulness to his oath, once it was sworn (i.e after the
occasion of Gen.22). The situation was very different in the case of the
Sinai covenant. Its central element was always explicit, codified,
national, law. The curse could fall at any time the people were

disobedient to their sworn loyalty. The story of failure (Ex.32:1–8) and threatened curse (Ex.32:9–10) follows immediately upon the first mention of the giving of the covenant (Ex.19–24), and its worship (Ex.25–31). The conjunction of Ex.31:18 and the next sentences in Ex.32:1 points to the immediate breach of the covenant, immediate liability to wrath.

One may thus also contrast the type of obedience required by the Abrahamic and Sinai covenants. The obedience required from Abraham was that of person-to-person response to God, who had promised to bless Abraham. Instructions came in the context of one-to-one fellowship with God. The relationship of God and Abraham was not totally suspended upon obedience, for Abraham had long been in fellowship with God without there being any mention of required obedience. True, the Sinai covenant is rooted in God's kindness, and in an established relationship as a result of redemption from Egypt. There was never any question of redemption being achieved by obedience. Yet the obedience required is national, external, secured by threat of curses. It is good within its own framework of reference, but one can see why Paul regarded it as an interim measure, and why he regarded the Abraham level of relationship with God as higher than the Sinaitic mode of relating to God, and why he viewed Abraham not Moses as the model for the Christian.

DEFECTS OF THE SINAI COVENANT

Another major issue is the relationship between Mosaic law and nationhood. In addition to the comparatively late origin of the Mosaic law within the history of redemption, and its treaty-like nature, certain other characteristics of the Sinai covenant are important for the argument that is being developed. One of them is the connection between the law and the origin of the nation of Israel. The Pentateuch represents the law as coming in at the point where Israel becomes a distinct nation, outside of the domination of Egypt, and responsible for its own national life. God takes a nation to himself, redeems them from bondage and takes steps to bring them to their own territory. At such a time they are given the law.[31] Several aspects of this may be emphasized.

(I) THE LAW WAS GIVEN TO ISRAEL ALONE[32]

In Christian theology the law – especially the approximately one per cent of it that constitutes the decalogue – has often been generalized and turned into external principles for the guidance of the Christian. This however requires more exegetical and theological argumentation than is normally given. The Old Testament shows the Torah as being given to Israel alone of the nations and specific reasons are required if one is to justify universalizing it. In the Old Testament the nations are accused on grounds of conscience (to use a modern term) rather than on grounds of law. This is conspicuous in Amos 1:1–2:16.[33] When Amos addresses the nations (Damascus, Gaza, Tyre, Ammon, Moab) he accuses them without reference to the law, which is never mentioned. Yet when he turns to Judah the law is immediately referred to (2:4). Similarly when he addresses Israel (2:6–16) the institutions (2:11f.) and the history (2:9) of the nation are mentioned and allusion is made to the law (2:8; cf. Ex.22:25f.). The Old Testament makes much of the point that Israel alone was redeemed, Israel alone was chosen, of all the nations of the earth (Amos 3:2). To Israel alone God gave a covenant of law, a point emphasized by the opening words of the decalogue itself (Ex.20:2).

(ii) NATIONALISTIC AND DISCRIMINATORY ELEMENTS

The giving of the law introduced nationalistic and discriminatory elements into the Old Testament that were not present in God's promise to Abraham. The theme of the Abrahamic promise was that 'all nations' would be blessed through Abraham's seed. The law was not for 'all nations'; it was for Israel alone. In this respect it was a divergent trend compared to what had preceded it. There was in it an element of discrimination. Conversely to Paul's statement in Galatians, there was distinction between slave and free, Israelite and gentile, between male and female.

(iii) LARGE SEGMENTS OF THE LAW FUNCTION AS CRIMINAL CODE

A.Phillips claims indeed that even the decalogue was no more than Israel's criminal code.[34] I shall argue that the tenth commandment is an exception in this respect. Furthermore, some sections of the law are clearly not related to crime, such as the tabernacle arrangements. Yet many aspects of the legislation of Israel do function as criminal code for the protection of societal life. C.J.H.Wright disagrees with Phillips, yet he also sees the decalogue as 'very deeply rooted in the concrete circumstances of Israel – social, economic and political'. He contends that the fifth, seventh, eighth and tenth commandments should be seen as designed to protect the household-plus-land units upon which the covenant relationship, humanly speaking, rested.[35]

Many expositions of the decalogue move from crime to 'deeper applications'. Under various headings of the decalogue, they discuss personality cults within Christendom, excessive veneration of church buildings, indulgence in bad language, care for one's health by taking a day's rest per week, honouring those who led us to faith (our 'spiritual fathers and spiritual mothers'), controlling one's temper, the 'look that springs from lust', helping the underprivileged, careless criticism of others, and so on. But it must be remembered that the decalogue itself did not deal with such matters. We need not discuss at this point whether 'spiritualization' of the law is justified. (The danger is that one will fail to notice the way Jesus took authority away from the

decalogue and on to himself. The higher 'fulfilment' of the law
proceeds from a relationship with Jesus that is not mediated by the
Sinai arrangements.)

Ignoring exegetical minutiae, it is significant that all the commands
except the tenth relate to society, to external visible morality, to cultic
arrangements, or to crime. Much of the legislation of Israel seems to
exercise the same function in the Hebrew world that the similar laws
did in surrounding cultures. One need only review (for example) the
Old Babylonian Laws of Eshnunna (early second millennium BC) to
see regulations similar to those of the Old Testament, such as
compensation for injury, regulations concerning marriage and the
rights of slaves.[36] The same areas of life are touched upon as in much
of Exodus-Deuteronomy, especially the 'Covenant Code'. One sees
similarities also in the Middle Assyrian laws (late second millenium)
edited by Driver and Miles.[37] When Resnick compares Akkadian
codes, not only with the Old Testament but also with the Qur'an, he
finds 'striking resemblances of terminology and wording.[38] The significant point here is a simple one: the Old Testament legislation, like
those of all ancient near eastern legal collections, deals in public life,
as befits legislation for a nation. Its main concerns are regulation of
public matters: property, ownership, contract, barter, debt, distress,
partnerships, hire, the father's house, matrilocal marriage, concubin-
age, polygyny, endogamy, widowhood, nuptials, divorce, *patris potes-
tas*, adoption, legal succession and the like.[39] Since the Torah provided
a standard of national morality, to be kept by individuals but with the
interests of the nation in view, and since such a law was administered
by public officials, it is appropriate that externality and concreteness
should characterize the legislation. Inward purity of heart cannot
easily be the subject of legislation and cannot be regulated by
magistrates. It was largely left alone by the Pentateuchal requirements.

We have not yet reached the exposition of any sections of the New
Testament. Yet already one may begin to ask: are aspects of Israel's
law which function as criminal code adequate to guide and rule
Christians who possess the Spirit in post-Pentecostal fulness? Will it
not be too low a standard for them to live by?

(IV) THE LAW AND THE HARDNESS OF THE HEART

The law takes into account the hardness of people's hearts. It will be
obvious that such an observation stems from Mt.19:8; so far as I know
it is never made explicit in the Torah itself. Yet it is a point that could
have been deduced from the movement from the Abraham-type to the
Sinai-type of relationship to God. One observes the happy relationship
between God and Abraham, with its trustful responsiveness to God
(Gn.12:4), its magnanimity (Gn.13:8), its spontaneous generosity
(Gn.14:20), its prayerfulness and concern for the righteous (Gn.18),
its willingness to go to any lengths in pleasing God (Gn.22).

Then we observe that even after the nation's redemption Israel is characterized by bitter complaining (Ex.15:23f.), once (Ex.15:21–27) and again (Ex.16:1–36) and again (Ex.17:1–7). One observes discontent (Ex.15:23), rejection of God's leader (Ex.15:24; 16:2), self-pity, concern for physical comfort, longing to abandon God and return to Egypt (Ex.16:3), continued disobedience despite explicit instructions (Ex.16:26–28), testing God's goodness (Ex.17:2), violent hostility to Moses (Ex.17:4), large numbers of internal complaints and quarrels (Ex.17:13–18). In asking Paul's question, 'Why then the law?' the narrative itself suggests Paul's answer, 'On account of transgressions' or, 'Because of their hardness of heart'.

Again one may be forgiven for jumping ahead and asking: are the standards of the Torah adequate for the individual Christian? In view of its nationalistic elements, one might also ask: are its standards adequate for Christians who wish their faith to be brought to bear upon his nation? Even here one has doubts. Should the Old Testament view of divorce be regulative for a nation heavily influenced by Christian people or making a national claim to Christian faith? Should slavery be tolerated, even encouraged in such a nation, given certain provisos to make it humane? Should the death penalty be mandatory for at least five areas of crime?[40]

Another aspect of the Mosaic law connected with its use at a national level is the fact that

(v) THE LAW MAKES USE OF FEAR AS A MODE OF CONTROL

C.R.Williams points out that 'penological philosophy has been shaped by one or more of the following four purposes: retribution, deterrence, restraint, and rehabilitation'. He goes on to consider the 'teleology' of Mosaic law. He suggests four reasons why God's expectation (Dt.13:11; 17:13; 19:20; 31:31) concerning 'crime prevention through fear of punishment' is comparatively rare in modern penological literature. He surmizes that it may be because the penalties of Mosaic law were more unpleasant, more public, swifter and more certain than modern penal institutions.[41] What Williams does not discuss, presumably because it is so conspicuous that it hardly needs discussion, is the assumption that fear of punishment was indeed a mode of control and demotivation in Mosaic legislation.

Certainly the introduction of the Sinai covenant was awe-inspiring. The people must not approach the mountain (Ex.19:14) nor even its edge (Ex.19:14). On the crucial third day thunder, lightning and cloud emphasize the unapproachability of God. The remedy for the peoples' terror was the mediatorship of Moses (Ex.20:19). Under the law, the people have no direct access to God. His unapproachability is embodied in the structure of the tabernacle where the people have no way into his presence and the only contact with God is via mediators, the priests. Even the mediators are denied full access to God. The once-a-year entry into God's presence by the one-and-only high priest

serves to emphasize the continued inaccessibility of God throughout
the duration of the Sinai covenant – a point made by the author of
Hebrews (Heb.9:8f.).

The effect in the narrative is to heighten the awe and terror. Later
mention of the 'fear of God . . . to keep you from sinning' (Ex.20:20)
seems to refer back to the terrors of the Sinai-event (Ex.19:7–25).
There the 'fear of God' involved the inaccessibility of God via the law-
covenant.

Of course the theme of the 'fear of God' is found throughout the
Bible. Yet there are different kinds of fear. There is the 'creaturely
awe which made the very seraphim hide their faces', seen in the
immense reverence with which Abraham confesses himself 'dust and
ashes' as he prays (Gn.18:27). Even under the New Covenant one has
the expression 'the fear of Christ'. The New Testament intensifies this
motif when it warns of the 'worse punishment' (as compared with
Sinaitic penalties) that falls upon one who profanes the blood of the
covenant (Heb.10:29). Yet as one considers the Sinai covenant there
are aspects to its terrors which do not characterize the New Covenant.
The vision of God's majesty so arouses terror that the people will be
inclined to keep the Sinai code because of the fearful majesty of God
that they have witnessed.

All this is distinctive of the introduction of the Sinai code, and is
probably what the author of Hebrews had in mind when, although not
dismissing fear of God altogether (Heb.4:1; 12:28), he yet could say:
'You have not come to a mountain that may be touched . . . and to a
blazing fire, and to darkness and gloom and whirlwind', to a covenant
that provides no access to God (Heb.12:19) and where even the
covenant mediator is gripped with alarm (Heb.12:21; see Dt.9:19). We
must avoid a false antithesis, as if sheer fear characterized Sinai but
total absence of fear characterizes the New Covenant, yet there is a
contrast that is rightly drawn by Heb.12:19–21. The 'fear of Christ' in
the New Testament is surely fear of loss of reward, fear of chastening,
fear of loss at the judgement seat of Christ. It is not the sheer terror of
Exodus 19; it is certainly not fear of magisterially administered
penalties.

A significant association of fear, inaccessibility and the Sinai
covenant is found in Exodus 34. Paul's midrashic exposition of the
chapter is well known. However one may assess the details of Paul's
interpretation, the theme of terror is clear. Yet Paul associates this
with the receiving of the law and contrasts it with the liberty of the
Holy Spirit. In doing so he builds upon the Old Testament itself, for
Exodus 34 portrays the resumed giving of the law after the great
rebellion of Exodus 32.

(VI) THE SINAI COVENANT WAS CHARACTERIZED BY TEMPORAL PENALTIES

We have already mentioned these temporal penalties. There was the
death penalty for premeditated murder (Ex.21:12ff; Nu.35; Dt.19),

kidnapping (Ex.21:16; Dt.24:7), disobedience to authorities and parents (Dt.17:12; 21:18ff), adultery (Lev.20:10; Dt.22:22), homosexuality (Lev.20:13), one form of incest (Lev.20:11f), false prophecy (Dt.13:1ff), profanation of the Sabbath (Nu.15:32ff), blasphemy (Lev.24:13ff), idolatry (Lev.20:2ff), magic and divination (Ex.22:18). In some respects the requirements were not as severe as those of the laws of Mesopotamia. Crimes against property did not attract the death penalty; rather the death penalty was required for crimes against life and against the structure of the family.[43]

Another threat was that of the offender's being 'cut off' (Ex.30:33; Lev.7:20ff; 20:17ff). This has generally been taken to mean that God directly punishes the offender with premature death.[44] Others think the phrase is another way of referring to the death penalty[45] or that it means expulsion from the nation.[46]

A third type of penalty was corporal punishment for certain offences, such as a fight between two persons (Dt.25:1–3; see also 22:18). It was apparently administered by striking the culprit's back with a stick (Prov.10:13; 19:29, etc). A fourth type of punishment was compulsory restitution. This was required in cases of theft or misappropriation. If penitent the thief had to restore the goods stolen plus a fifth (Lev.6:15). A thief caught still in possession of the property would have to repay double. If the goods had been disposed of, their restoration would have to be fourfold or fivefold.[47]

There are also the 'curses of the covenant', described by Wenham as 'a horrendous list of curses containing some of the most spine-chilling passages in the whole Old Testament'.[48] These are explicitly said to be designed to motivate by fear ('If you do not obey . . . these curses shall come upon you', Dt.28:15).

(VII) LIMITED EFFICACY OF SACRIFICE

The sins for which sacrificial expiation was available were relatively insignificant. Provision was made for the expiation of certain sins, but it must be noted that there is no reason to think that any sin could be expiated by sacrifice. T.H.Gaster thinks the sins that could be expiated were contact with impurity, physical or moral, infringement of taboos, violating of cultic laws, refusing to testify, the 'contagion' of childbirth, and 'leprosy'.[49] There is no reason to think that serious moral faults, such as breach of the decalogue, could be expiated. Rowley comments: 'Much is said in the law of unwitting sin in connection with the sin-offering and the guilt-offering, and it would seem that only unwitting sins were capable of being cleansed by sacrifice.'[50] The fact that sins could be punishable by death or by being 'cut off' means that there was a limitation upon the sins affected by this merciful provision. Also we find mention of sins committed 'with a high hand'. It is not easy to see precisely what this phrase means. Lev.6:1–7 allows sacrificial atonement in the case of deliberate sin, if the sinner confesses his fault and makes restitution. Allusions to sinning with a high hand in Exodus 4:8, Num.15:27–31, 32–36, 33:3, suggest that advance planning was involved. Whether a man is killed *bishegagah* or not distinguishes murder from manslaughter. Rowley is correct in saying 'For murder and adultery the Law provided no means of atonement, and only demanded the execution of the murderer.'[51] It is surely with these limited Mosaic provisions in mind that the author of Hebrews can say that the priestly system catered for the 'ignorant and wayward' (only!). Only with the new covenant did he see provision for sin and iniquity being 'remembered no more' (Heb.5:2; 8:12). Likewise it is a step beyond the Mosaic covenant for the gospels to say 'All sins and blasphemies shall be forgiven the sons of men' (Mk.3:28; cf.Mt.12:31).

(VIII) THE LAW AND MAGISTRACY

There is a connection between the law and magistracy. It is in accord with the points made above that the Torah is specifically tailor-made for judges. This is characteristic of all ancient near Eastern laws. M.R.Lehmann rightly says of the ancient near East: 'The existence of legal order on earth was entrusted to human judges and their judicial systems, but the right and power to supervise man's strict compliance with his commandments and obligations was retained by the divine powers.'[52] In the composition of Exodus the introduction of the law follows immediately after the introduction of the eldership. The latter is brought in to assist Moses' handling 'cases' of dispute or crime. At certain points one can see that the law was designed for elders. Within the Decalogue itself, 'You shall not bear false witness' is not a statement about general truth-telling. Rather its setting is that of a law-court.

In the ancient near East 'judges' over civic life are known from great antiquity. The *sapitum* (equivalent to the Hebrew *shopet*) is now known in texts from Ebla dating to ca.2300 BC. The texts from Mari (ca.1800 BC) also give glimpses of 'governors' or 'judges' maintaining social order. In Israelite society the judge appears as the one who dispenses justice, punishes the evil-doer and vindicates the innocent. According to the biblical testimony Moses was a 'judge' of Israel and 'cases' were brought to him. Thus the 'judges' of Israel were initially Moses' deputies (Ex.18:13–27; Dt.1:9–18). Although a distinct meaning of the term *shopet* operates in Judges (where the meaning 'saviour' prevails rather than 'judicial official') the old meaning evidently continued into the post-exilic period, for Ezra is portrayed as setting up judges to administer justice in his day (Ez.7:25). This is of significance in one's understanding of the Christian and his relationship to the Torah. The law was designed for a nation and was therefore administered by the magistracy for the purpose of maintaining social order, religious conformity and national stability. Although it had to be kept by the individual Israelite it was not designed to be central in a one-to-one personal relationship to God, a relationship of faith, guided by the Spirit.

Again it is natural, in view of the points previously made, that the law should be codified. Indeed in the representation of Exodus 24, there never was a Mosaic covenant without codified law. The 'book of the law' is written and is used in the very origin of the covenant; codification is of its essence. In this respect the late origin of the New Testament within the new covenant community forms a striking contrast to the Mosaic covenant. In the Mosaic covenant the written word of law was the covenant. This forms a contrast to the Abraham stories where, as has been seen, the commands of God that came to Abraham came mystically, 'in the Spirit', and without codification.

We have already referred to the relatively late origins of legal language in the unfolding story of the Bible. It is Mosaic not patriarchal. The same is true of the vocabulary of writing. Although writing was well established as a hallmark of civilization from 3500 BC onwards, long before any conceivable date for the patriarchal period, and masses of *siprim* (books, documents, writings) are known from the fourth millenium onwards, yet the verb *katab* never occurs in connection with the patriarchs. It first occurs in an isolated incident recorded in Exodus 17, and thereafter is used supremely in connection with the law (Ex.24:4,12, etc.). After the clearly editorial reference to *seper* (book) in Genesis 5:1 (dating a document rather than the events it narrates), and the solitary mention of *seper* in Exodus 17:14, the first mention of a 'book' is Exodus 24:7 with its reference to the 'book of the covenant'.

It was in the Mosaic covenant that the principles of righteousness were first codified. There are numerous references to Moses' recording the Torah. He 'wrote the words of this law in a book' (Dt.32:24) which was deposited (31:26) in Israel's sanctuary. Provision is made for its periodical reading (Dt.31:11). The king should possess a copy (Dt.17:18f.). As a result documented law would be available as the object of meditation (Jos.1:8).[53] E.J.Young believed that these statements refer to the whole Pentateuch[54]. Yet Deuteronomy has a character of its own and is a distinct unity; the commands concerning writing within Deuteronomy need not refer to the whole Pentateuch but rather to the matters mentioned in Deuteronomy. However in the Exodus account also we find repeated emphasis on the documentation of the parts of the *Torah*. Moses must write 'all the words of Yahweh' (Ex.24:4 referring to Ex.21:2–23:33 and possibly to Exodus 19 and 20 also). The 'second' law (Ex.34:10–26) is also the subject of commands concerning documentation. It is to be noted that nothing like this characterized either the patriarchal period or the ministry of Jesus. The origin of the new covenant is connected with the Christ event, not with anything written or codified initially. Although there may have been records from earliest days, these receive no central position in the new covenant. Although the apostolate had crucial significance, the 'apostles' teaching' of Acts 2:42 was initially living oral ministry. It took some years before anything written had 'canonical' significance. The Mosaic covenant was immediately codified; the codified law was the covenant. But in this respect there is a disjunction between covenant and writing in the new covenant.

THE SANCTITY OF THE LAW

In spite of everything that has been written above, the entire Mosaic law is holy, righteous and good. The preceding pages may seem to present a highly negative approach to the law as it appears in Exodus. Certainly what emerges from these narratives will mean that I must be somewhat hostile to a misuse of the law, and that I must conceive of it as an interim measure in God's purpose. However it must be emphasized that the Old Testament does not present the law as in any way evil or demonic. When Paul says that the law is 'holy, righteous and good' he is entirely in accord with the impression given by the Old Testament itself. Nowhere in the Old Testament is it even implied that the law comes from any source other than God himself. Some have interpreted Paul as implying a demonic origin for the law, and as holding a view of the law approximating to those of later gnosticism and Marcionism. Whatever Paul may have believed, no hint of demonic origin for the law is found in the Old Testament. Nor is the law ever presented as evil.

The reader may be wondering how an author can highly value the law and yet use such negative language concerning it as appears in previous pages. The answer is that negative language (as found not only above but also in Galatians) is appropriate when considering the matter from the viewpoint of the new covenant and the person-to-person relationship that the Christian has with God. The law is not for the righteous person. It does not control the Christian's person-to-person relationship with God. It does not justify (cf. Rom.3:20). It does not sanctify or enable any kind of fruitfulness (cf.Rom.7:4). It does not regenerate or give life (cf.Gal.3:21). Yet, taken upon its own terms and in its particular location in salvation-history, the law is entirely good, entirely beneficent, and in no way against the promises of God (cf.Gal.3:21). Its weakness arises from sinful human nature (cf. 'through the flesh', Rom.8:3) not from its own inherent evil. Its abolition – as we shall see – comes not by negation but by its fulfilment. For the ungodly it retains relevance (cf.1 Tim.1:9). In such a way it may be 'used lawfully' (cf.1 Tim.1:8).

In the previous paragraphs it has been necessary to adopt prematurely a New Testament standpoint. So far as the Old Testament itself is concerned we merely note that nowhere is the Law described as evil. Even the angelic mediation of the law mentioned in Acts 7, Galatians 3, and Hebrews 2, is not heavily underlined, although the presence of theophany in Exodus 19–24 is noticeable (the source of the later view, presumably).[55] Several aspects of its holy character may be noted.

(i) The law is given in an atmosphere of sanctity. The precepts of God are altogether good. Despite the impression of inadequacy which one may glean from the Old Testament and which has been high-lighted in previous sections, the law is never portrayed in any terms other than good ones. It is inherently good; its purpose is altogether beneficent.

(ii) The law is God's law. Although it is 'Mosaic' (the term has here been used rather frequently as a protest against generalizing concepts of the 'moral law'), yet within the Pentateuch its divine origin is emphasized.

(iii) It is 'good' for what it is designed to do. Although the New Testament criticizes its use in certain respects, it may be 'used lawfully' in accordance with its divine purpose.

(iv) It is 'sacred'. Its origin in the setting of purification and theophanic manifestation suggests its sacredness in nature and in content. There seems to be no occasion in the Old Testament where the Mosaic law is directly criticized. Even the New Covenant promises of Jeremiah find fault with the people of Israel rather than with the old covenant itself ('which covenant . . . they broke', Jer.31:32).[56] It must be remembered however that when one describes the law as 'holy, righteous and good' what is in mind is the totality of the Mosaic covenant. This includes the ceremonial, punitive and ritual aspects of the law. Often defences of the sanctity of the Mosaic law have in mind primarily or even exclusively the moral element. I am not however making such a restriction. The whole law is presented as divine.

OLD TESTAMENT CRITICISMS OF THE LAW

The nearest approach the Old Testament makes to criticism of the Mosaic covenant is found in certain statements which reflect adversely upon the sacrificial system: Ps.40:6–8, Jer.7:22, Amos 5:21. Admittedly one may interpret these statements not as indicating disapproval of the sacrificial system but as disapproval of its use by insincere worshippers. This explanation is more convincing in some cases than in others. In the three texts cited the language is very strong and seems to point not only to misuse of the sacrificial system but to the fact that the system itself is not God's ultimate ideal. Nevertheless, apart from these possibly adverse reflections upon the sacrificial system, the Old Testament contains no hint of an origin of the law other than in the will of God. Yet it must be said that even if these verses reflect more upon the misuse of the sacrificial system than the system in itself, this is not really important. For if the system is capable of being misused then its inadequacy is revealed. This is the point of Heb.8:8 and 10:5–10.

A more striking anomaly is the fact that God can be portrayed as hating a particular provision found within the Torah. Malachi portrays God as saying 'I hate divorce', yet the Torah permits divorce. A few verses later Malachi – or his editor – brings the work to a close with a section in which he urges his readers to 'Remember the Torah . . . its statutes and judgements' (Mal.4:4, Heb.3:22). Here a tension exists between something entirely divine ('the Torah of Moses . . . which I

commanded') and something within it which God hates. One can draw
no conclusion except that in the circumstances of its origin the Torah is
thought to be wholly of God and wholly good, yet it is at points
recognized as less than ideal and its necessity arises not because it is a
perfect expression of God's will for all time but because taken as a
whole it is an accommodating expression of God's will. Nothing in the
Old Testament itself would justify a neo-Marcionistic approach. Yet
one can see how the negative statements of Paul and the positive
assessment of Romans 7:12 can both have justification.

KEEPING THE LAW

Not only is the law good in itself, the records of the origin of the
Mosaic law constantly assume that the law may be kept. In Christian
theology, especially in the Lutheran and Reformed traditions, one is
used to the idea that it is quite impossible to keep the Mosaic law. This
concept owes much to the tenth commandment, which will be
considered below. Yet if one leaves aside the tenth commandment, the
law constantly postulates that it may be kept. Blessing follows when it
is obeyed: 'the man who obeys them will live by them' (Lev.18:5; cf.
Ezk.20:11,21; Ne.9:29). Although the 'life' that is promised must not
be equated with the 'eternal life' of the New Testament and refers
more to national stability, longevity and prosperity than to the fulness
of the Spirit and the expectation of heaven, nevertheless blessing is
promised through the keeping of the law. Only by concentrating on
the tenth commandment is there introduced an element of radicalization and internalization such that it becomes impossible to keep the
law.

To put the same point in New Testament language: an unregenerate
person without faith may keep the law to a certain extent. This seems
to be the point of Paul's remark in Phil.3:6. Paul, before his Damascus
road experience, kept the law. Reflecting upon his Pharisaic experience does not make him speak of his inability to keep the law; rather
he speaks of his ability to keep the law. One notices in this connection
the absence of any 'change of name' motif in the Sinai stories. While
too much weight cannot be placed upon an omission, yet it is
noticeable that whereas Abram, Jacob and Sarai have to become new
people with a new name in order with the help of 'El Shaddai' to
receive the promises, no such enabling is involved in the Mosaic
covenant. All of this means that the law may be kept without faith.
'The law is not of faith', says Paul.

THE TENTH COMMANDMENT

Among the verses of direct legislation mentioned in Exodus, there
seems to be not a single verse which focuses on purity of heart other
than the tenth commandment. (Deuteronomy is a different matter but

one must remember that Deuteronomy claims to be a Mosaic exhortation based upon the law rather than the law itself; I have dealt with this matter briefly elsewhere.[57])

In Exodus the tenth commandment reads: 'You shall not covet your neighbour's house . . . wife . . . male or female slave . . . ox . . . ass . . . or anything that is your neighbour's.' The version in Deuteronomy is virtually the same but reverses the order of 'house' and 'wife', and uses the verb *tit'awweh* instead of *tachmod*. The form of the tenth commandment has features which distinguish it from all the preceding commandments'. The repetition of the verb ('You shall not covet . . . You shall not covet . . . ') is without precedent in the previous nine commands. There is an overlapping of categories, for the tenth command touches upon the sexual category ('your neighbour's wife') mentioned in the seventh command, and upon the sanctity of property ('anything that is his') mentioned in the eighth command.

A crucial matter, if it be allowed, is that the tenth command also looks inward to the desire rather than to the external sins mentioned in the previous nine. The latter point is not undisputed; it has been argued that *chamad* refers to a deed as well as to an emotion and thus, like the previous nine commands refers to an externally evident crime. The point is an important one and warrants further consideration.

In 1927 J.Herrmann argued that the verb *chamad* referred not only to an inward appetite but also to an action.[58] If his argument is correct, it would add further weight to the points made above. It would intensify the contrast between law and grace which forms the bulk of the present work. Yet in my opinion it is more likely that the tenth command is the single exception to the point argued above and, unlike every other part of the Pentateuchal legislation, only considers the heart. Herrmann argued that in such passages as Exodus 34:24 and Psalm 68:17 the verb included an act as well as an emotion. Alt based a similar thesis on the presence of *ch-m-d* in the Karetepe inscriptions.[59] The arguments of Herrmann and Alt were accepted by Kohler and Stamm.[60] They were opposed by Proksch and Colz, and were severely criticized by W.Moran.[61] Moran pointed to occasions when the verb does not seem to refer to any deed, and urged that it was a mistake to see any contrast between the verbs *ch-m-d* and the hiphil of *'-w-h*.

For the following reasons I reject Herrmann's thesis and follow Moran.

(i) The verb *ch-m-d* is closely linked with *chemdah* which clearly means 'desirable thing' and not 'desired-and-appropriated thing'. The noun focuses upon an appetite not a deed. The same is true of *chemed* in Is.32:12; Ezek.23:6,12,23, Amos 5:11 (leaving aside Isaiah 27:2). The Ugaritic *chmd* is also linked with pleasurableness and the beauty that stimulates desire.[62]

(ii) The *niphal* of the verb seems to mean 'pleasing' or 'desirable' (Gn.2:9; 3:6; Ps.19:10(11); Ps.21:20). It is difficult to see anything other than stimulated desire in the verses that use it.

(iii) In several passages where *chamad* is used, there seems to be a distinction between the desire and the deed. Thus Micah 2:2 reads 'They desire houses and seize them.' There would be no need to say 'and seize them' if *hamad* itself included the idea of such seizure. A similar phenomenon is even more evident in Jos.7:21 where the three verbs *wa'er'eh . . . wa'echmedem . . . wa'eqqahem* give a clear sequence. What can they mean but 'I saw . . . I desired . . . I took'? There may be an allusion to Deut.7:21: 'Do not desire . . . and do not take.' In these passages there seems to be a very clear distinction between desire and deed.

(iv) In Ex.20:17 there is a repetition of the same verb (*chamad . . . chamad*). In Deut.5:21 there is a repetition using a similar verb (*tit'awweh . . . chamad*). Whatever the critical history of the two recensions it seems unlikely that an intensifying repetition in the one case should (as Herrmann implies) become a contrast in a variant recension. As in two other closely parallel passages (Ps.68:19; 132:13f.) the two verbs are surely used interchangeably.

(v) In Prov.6:25 the reference to the heart is surely implicit. The whole surrounding context gives the impression of stimulation of desire, in this case sexual appetite. The link between beauty and desire is also present in Isaiah 53:2.

(vi) In three places (Jb.20:20; Ps.19:10; Pr.21:20) where the *qal* participle is used, the idea seems to be that of desirable beauty. The single use of the *piel* in Cant.2:3 again makes good sense if it speaks of great desire or delight.

(vii) In only two passages (Ps.68:17; Ex.34:24), upon which Herrmann leans heavily, the drift of the sense would be more forceful if a deed is included rather than a desire only. Yet in view of the total usage it is unlikely that the central denotation of *chamad* refers to deed and desire rather than desire only. It is surely more likely that Ps.68:17 and Ex.34:24 are cases where there is a pregnant usage of the verb. One might compare *zakar* ('remember', cf. *zikron* 'remembrance') where generally a simple act of memory is in view, but where (as I have argued elsewhere[63]) the verb may be extended and mean 'remember and so act'. The fact that such verbs may receive extension of meaning on certain occasions does not mean that they always or primarily denote acts rather than mental / emotional states. In the case of *chamad* the bulk of evidence favours the central meaning 'desire'. To read its occasional wider sense back into Exodus 20:17 would in my opinion be a mistake.

We have discussed *chamad* since our primary focus is on Genesis and Exodus. It is however universally agreed that the verb in Deuteronomy 5:21 (*tit'awweh*) undoubtedly refer to the craving of the appetite. It has not been suggested that the *hithpael* of '-w-h refers to a deed. The point would still stand that there is a deeper probing into the inner life in the tenth commandment. This means that the tenth commandment is not a mere repetition of the eighth as has sometimes been suggested. It is rather a deliberate deepening of requirement in the final lines of the decalogue.

THE COVENANTS CONTRASTED

The exegetical conclusions must by now be obvious. There is a striking contrast between the two covenants, the Abrahamic and the Mosaic, in at least the following respects: (i) the implementing party (i.e. the one who swears to undertake fulfilment), (ii) personal promise versus national promise, (iii) orientation to crime, public worship, national stability versus orientation to a 'seed' for Abraham, (iv) requirement of faith versus the possible absence of faith, (v) personal renovation versus human ability.

Although influenced by Galatians, I am not seeking to draw heavily upon Galatians at this stage. Yet as one reflects upon the Torah itself one cannot but remember the statements of Romans and Galatians. The law itself reveals its inadequacy when considered in detail. It is not of faith. It focuses very largely on nationhood. We would not discern human need from the decalogue if it were not for the tenth commandment. The stage is set for a radical rejection of Mosaism, because although good in itself it is inadequate for the Christian. It is weak and useless (one might suggest) not because of any evil within itself but because of the 'weakness of the flesh' (Rom.8:3). If it is to be 'fulfilled' the mode of its 'fulfilment' will not come from the law itself. The question of conditionality and unconditionality, and unilaterality and bilaterality, has often been discussed. These terms have been avoided, since they encourage too simplistic views of the covenants. A simple contrast (conditional versus unconditional) is too unsophisticated. It is better to think of two altogether different types of covenant, both in some sense conditional. Yet the conditionality comes in in a different way. The Abrahamic covenant is unconditional in its beginnings and unconditional in its security, yet it does not come to complete fruition till it meets in Abraham a response of radical obedience. Although rooted in God's initiative and goodness, the Sinai covenant is conditional at every point from the moment of its inauguration.

9

Freedom from the Law in the
Epistle to the Galatians

The contrast between the story of Abraham and the inauguration of the covenant with Israel via Moses is taken up by the apostle Paul and powerfully argued in the epistle to the Galatians. [1] The Galatians did not have the advantage of reading Romans alongside their own letter but had to take it as it was presented to them as a statement of Paul's teaching. There would be other things that Paul could have said but we must take it that he would regard Galatians as in and of itself not a confusing statement of his view of the Mosaic law. At any rate there is a limit to what can be presented within the limits of one book and I focus on Galatians. My exposition of Romans is being presented elsewhere and my study of Romans 7 is already available. [2]

To discuss in detail the historical-critical questions that surround the epistle would require a monograph. [3] All that is possible here is to state the presuppositions that form the basis of the following pages.

The earliest gentiles to become Christians, so far as we know, were Cornelius and his friends (Ac.10–11). Even in those 'early days' (Ac.15:7) this raised difficulties with Jewish Christians (Ac.11:2). Not long afterwards (AD 45?) [4] large numbers of gentiles began to profess faith in Antioch where there were also a large number of Jews. The news reached Jerusalem (Ac.11:22) and Barnabas was sent to Antioch (AD 45/46?). Under his influence there were further evangelistic successes (Ac.11:24). Barnabas knew Saul of Tarsus and his early preaching (Ac.9:20) and perhaps in AD 46 went to Tarsus to find him and involve him in the work. They returned together and spent a year preaching in Antioch (Ac.11:26, AD 46–47?). After a prophetic prediction of famine, the Antiochene Christians sent a gift to the Jerusalem church, asking Paul and Barnabas to take it (Ac.11:30). It is likely that Galatians 2:1–10 tells of a meeting that Paul had with the Jerusalem leaders at this time (AD 47?) [5]. A serious rift could have arisen if their approach to gentile Christians were the subject of disagreement. In the event, despite conservative complaints (Gal.2:4), all went well and Paul and Barnabas were commended. It was recognized that gentiles could become Christians without becoming Jews first.

Paul and Barnabas returned to Antioch and then after a while set out on their first missionary expedition, in which churches were founded in Cyprus and southern Galatia (summer AD 47?) Either just before or just after this mission Peter paid a visit to Antioch as recorded in Gal.2:11–14. For a while he had free fellowship with the gentile Christians. However the news of Peter's behaviour was causing a strong reaction from the conservative Christians at Jerusalem. Peter's well-known about-turn took place and Paul rebuked Peter in words summarized in Gal.2:11–14. We do not know precisely how Peter responded but the wording of Ac.15:10–11 is very Pauline and may suggest that Peter took Paul's point.

At about this time (AD 48?) the conservatives at Jerusalem began to agitate more than ever. They had reached southern Galatia and were troubling the churches that had been founded only a year previously. The successes of the gentile mission were scandalizing the conservative quasi-Christian Jews, and they were visiting gentile Christians to propagate their teaching. The Galatians had listened and had become suspicious of Paul, doubting his apostleship and suspecting that he was (as the Judaizers said) a corrupter of the original Jerusalem gospel. So in about AD 48 or early 49 Paul writes Galatians and in conjunction with the church at Antioch he goes with others to Jerusalem to confer with the apostles concerning the matter. The result is the well-known decisions of Ac.15:19–21.

The one major theological enemy that Paul confronted were the Judaizers. It is likely that they were ultra-conservative Jewish Christians whose Pharisaic background made it difficult for them to allow any laxity with regard to the keeping of the Torah. It would be helpful if we were able to totally reconstruct the argument of Paul's critics and enemies. Yet the only source of information concerning them derives from Paul's words; they are all we have to use as a basis for reconstruction. It is possible that major aspects of his critics' arguments received no comment from Paul. 'Mirror reading' rests on the assumption that Paul's autobiographical remarks are invariably defensive. Paul's autobiographical section in Galatians resembles the practice of autobiography in antiquity and sets forth a positive view of the nature and origin of his gospel.[6] We must therefore be wary not to simply invert every statement Paul makes. However, if we proceed with due caution we may still detect something of the charges of his enemies. The threefold structure of the letter, suggested below, indicates that the three key issues were (i) apostolic authority, (ii) the truthfulness of his gospel, and (iii) the danger of his gospel, as insufficiently securing the life of godliness. Despite Lyons's warning, the negative emphasis of Paul's remarks ('*not from men*', Gal.1:1) suggests that the Judaizers were arguing that Paul's apostleship was merely derived from Jerusalem. He had not been an original follower of Jesus and was altogether a late arrival on the scene of what had been a Jerusalem-based Christianity. It is likely that he was regarded as a corrupter of the original gospel.

A number of personal accusations are overheard in the letter. Paul had been a persecutor of Christians. It is possible that this was used by Paul's opponents to discredit him. The defensive tone of Gal.1:10 and 2:17 suggests that he was accused of having a loose attitude towards sin. It could be urged that his converts no longer trusted him (4:15). Apparently he was accused of contradicting what he secretly knew to be true, for it was said that he had actually practised circumcision but had reduced the message of Jerusalem-Christianity in order to ingratiate himself with gentile converts. Is this the point of Galatians 5:11? Above all the Judaizers obviously had a different gospel in which the keeping of the Mosaic law was essential for salvation (see 2:16), for fellowship (see 2:11–14) and for maturity (being 'perfected', 3:1).

The fact that Paul found it necessary to outline the moral implications of the gospel in Galatians 5:13–6:10 seems to imply that critics of Paul urged that his view of the law was dangerous and would lead to licentiousness. We may assume that actual charges lay behind the exposition of 5:13–6:10.

It appears also that although the Judaizers and their sympathizers were eager to impose many aspects of Mosaism, including the keeping of days (4:10) and submission to circumcision (5:2), there was some carelessness about the law of love. If we may judge from passing statements, those influenced by the Judaizers were fearful and insincere (2:12f.), lacking straightforwardness (2:14). They had become hostile to Paul himself (4:16). The Judaizers themselves had devious motives (4:17). Paul hints at conceit and mutual provocation amidst the controversial situation at Galatia (5:26). Apparently some had been 'overtaken' in a sin (6:1). Paul felt it necessary to speak concerning pride (6:3) and neglect of Christian zeal (6:9f.). Apparently the insurgence of Mosaism had in no way heightened love among the Galatian Christians.

AN OVERVIEW OF GALATIANS

After a preliminary greeting (Gal.1:1–5) and protest (1:6–10), the letter to the Galatians falls into three main sections, which take up three main problems. Gal.1:11–2:21 are largely concerned with a statement of Paul's apostolic authority. Gal.3:1–5:12 restate his gospel in the light of the current controversy. Gal.5:13–6:10 take up the question of the implications of his teaching, with reference to life and godliness.

We now consider the main argument of Galatians, seeking to bring out Paul's teaching with regard to the law.

Galatians 1:1–5 Paul's introductory remarks touch upon the same three issues. After a strong statement of his apostolic authority ('Paul an apostle . . .'), he states the heart of his gospel concerning Christ ('who gave himself for us . . .'), but expands his statement in order to indicate the consequences of the death of Jesus for Christian living ('in order to rescue us . . .'). Paul has thus already touched upon the three issues that will be clarified: authority, atonement and sanctification. These are the three central matters in 1:11–2:21; 3:1–5:12 and 5:13–6:10 respectively.

Galatians 1:6–10 Paul omits his customary thanksgiving and plunges into the theme of his letter. His opponents' 'gospel' is no gospel at all; Paul severely announces the judgement of God against it. Verse 10 is probably a comment on the language of vv.6–9. What is it that makes Paul use such strong language? Is he persuading God? Does he have his eye on a group whom he is seeking to please by using such strong language? He replies that he is not seeking to persuade God nor to please men; he is seeking to persuade men; he is seeking to please God.

Galatians 1:11–2:14 Paul affirms his apostolic authority. He feels a need simply to state the facts as he sees them. His message is not human (1:11) but divine (1:12). He has not corrupted an original gospel which he had picked up in Jerusalem. In fact in his early post-conversion years he had little contact with Jerusalem. He admits he was a persecutor of Christians but that was in his pre-Christian years when he *was* a Judaizer. He certainly did not get his message from the apostles during that time (1:13f.). His conversion was independent of the apostles (1:15–16a); nor did he consult any apostle at the time (1:16b-17). It was not until the third year after his conversion that he finally met the Jerusalem leaders. At that time he became personally acquainted with Cephas and met James but he did not derive the main shape of his message from them (1:18–20). At the time he was comparatively little known and had received no commission from Jerusalem, but he was already preaching and the basic content of his message was settled – independently of Jerusalem (1:21–24).

If *Galatians 2:1–10* is to be linked with Ac.11, then Paul proceeds to tell of the next occasion he visited Jerusalem. (If however 2:1–10 links with Ac.15 then a major change in the nature of his argument takes place. Gal.1 had told the story *up to the point where it was known what he was preaching*; Gal.2:1–10 jumps to another matter altogether.) At this time he did see something of the apostles. Paul went to secure first-hand confirmation that the apostles approved of what he was doing. There was a danger that his ministry should be needlessly damaged by rumours of Paul's disagreement with the earlier apostles. He took Titus as a test case (Gal.2:1f.). All went well for Paul's work. Titus was not circumcised (2:3). (Later on that occasion however pseudo-Christians pressed for the circumcision of Titus, but the apostles would not yield). The exegesis of vv.3–5 is difficult but it may be literalistically translated:[7]

'But even Titus, who was with me, though he was a Greek [phrase of concession], was not pressurized to be circumcised – but [this matter arose] on account of the infiltrated false brethren who slipped in to spy on our freedom which we have in Christ Jesus, in order that they might enslave us

– to whom we did not yield submission even for an hour in order that the truth of the gospel might continue with you.'

No one yielded to 'false brethren'. Paul was accepted by the apostles. Their spheres of ministry differed but not the central message (2:6–8). Paul was welcomed as in fellowship with Jerusalem-based Christianity (2:9). The one request concerning the poor he had already acceded to (2:10).

Galatians 2:11–14 describes the occasion of Paul's conflict with Peter. It did not arise out of disagreement concerning the teaching of the gospel but from Peter's not practising the gospel he believed in out of fear of Judaizers. Peter acted insincerely and Paul rebuked him publicly. It is at Gal.2:15 that Paul plunges into a defence of his gospel and thus into the matters that more directly concern us.

Galatians 2:15–21 is a bridge between the section dealing with independent apostolic authority (1:11–2:14) and the restatement of his gospel (3:1–5:12). What Paul said then to Peter is what Paul wishes to say now to the Galatians. Paul nowhere describes Peter's response to his rebuke. The Galatians knew the outcome and the 'bridge section' in 2:15–21 leads Paul simply to proceed with the theological argumentation with the Galatian Christians.

In verses 15f., Paul distinguishes between 'Jews' and 'sinners'. Clearly 'sinners' is being used relatively to refer to the degradation of the gentile world. Yet he says (v.16) that even Jewish Christians know they are not justified by works of the law, but by the faith(fulness) of Christ.[8] They have put their faith in Christ so as to be justified by the faith(fulness) of Christ. Justification by the law is impossible.

Three matters are of importance here: the meaning of 'works of the law', the 'faith of Christ' and 'justification'. The 'faith of Christ' is considered below, where it is argued that the translation here assumed is indeed correct. Similarly I assume the correctness of a forensic interpretation of *dikaioo* and the basic correctness of the Lutheran-Protestant doctrine of justification. (Some modifications will be presented later.) The linguistic evidence concerning *dikaioo* seems clear [9] The point here (in connection with 2:16) is that a person's standing before God is settled by faith alone.

The more vital question at this point is: what is the meaning of 'works of the law'? Three possibilities merit consideration. (i) For some the phrase refers to the 'ceremonial law'. This is the basis of E.D.Burton's major commentary.[10] and it has recently been adopted by J.D.G.Dunn.[11] (ii) For D.Fuller, C.H.Cosgrove, C.E.B.Cranfield, C.F.D.Moule and others, *nomos* in this phrase and elsewhere in Galatians refers not to the Torah but to the wrong use of the Torah, and *ta erga tou nomou* refers to a legalistic use of the Torah rather than the Torah itself.[12] (iii) The older view is that the phrase refers to sincere keeping of the Torah. This last-mentioned approach seems to be warranted by the following evidence. (Other interpretations will be assessed after we have considered Gal.3:1–14.)

There are several reasons why *ta erga tou nomou* must be taken to refer to works which conscientiously seek to obey the demands of the Torah:

(i) The Hebrew equivalent occurs in 4QFlor 1:7 where *ma'asei torah* clearly refers to sincere obedience to the Torah. Closely similar phrases occur in 1QS 5:21; 6:18 (*ma'asaio batorah*), 1QH 1:26; 4:31 (*ma'asei hatsedaqah*) and 'works of the commandments' in 2 Apoc. Bar.57:2 (where the Hebrew is lacking). In these occurrences it is clear from the surrounding contexts – and is widely agreed – that these phrases refer to conscientious law-keeping and *mitswot* refers to concrete demands of the Torah. To take one example, *ma'asaio batorah* in 1QS 5:21 simply alludes to the rule that the scroll has just mentioned that members of the community 'cling to all his commandments according to his will' (1Q 5:1) and 'return with all his heart and soul to the law of Moses, according to all that he has commanded' (1QS 5:8). Paul's phrase participates in the usage of his day and unless there is strong evidence to the contrary should be interpreted similarly.[13]

(ii) It is worth noting that when Paul addresses Jews or those influenced by Judaizers he speaks of the 'works of the law'. However when he (or his disciples) are referring to pre-Mosaic times or to gentiles the word used is 'works' (see Ro.4 and 9:4–10 referring to pre-Mosaic times, and Eph.2:9; 2 Tim.1:9; Tit.3:5 where gentiles are being considered). Moo points out the essential similarity in the way *ta erga tou nomou* and simply *erga* are used.[14] When addressing the Romans directly (3:20,28) Paul uses the phrase 'works of the law'. When making the same points from the story of Abraham (Ro.4) it would be inappropriate and contrary to Paul's thought to refer precisely to the Law and he uses simply 'works'. This suggests the essential identity of the two terms and suggests also that *ta erga tou nomou* refers to works done in sincere obedience.

(iii) Although Paul was very concerned with the issue of circumcision and table-fellowship he explicitly makes the point in Gal.5:3 that one cannot pick and choose between parts of the Mosaic covenant. One must take it that the Christians' relationship to the 'whole law' has been in mind all along. There may be some uncertainty about the main concern of the Judaizers but what concerns Paul is the 'whole law'.

(iv) Paul puts the matter in epochal terms. In Gal.4:21 he explicitly refers to the whole covenant of Moses. In the light of 4:21–31 one must say that in Galatians *nomos* refers primarily to the entire arrangement that came into the world through Moses.

In *Galatians 2:17–21* Paul develops what he has said in Gal.2:15f. Six points are noteworthy:

(i) *Freedom from the law may lead to the charge of antinomianism (2:17)* Verse 17 is difficult. The question deals, as Paul's uniform use of *me genoito* indicates, with a false conclusion from correct premises.[15] Paul's teaching ('seeking to be justified in Christ') involves the discovery that one's status before God is no different from that of the gentiles ('we ourselves . . . no less than the gentiles'). If the law is not brought in as a mode of justification and as a rule of life, is that not acknowledging sin, tolerating it and sinking to the level of the gentiles? Is not Christ, in that case, a minister of sin?[16] Although there are other interpretations,[17] yet on most exegeses it is the charge of antinomianism that is being raised. I understand Paul to mean that restoring the law is transgression. This gives excellent sense to the following verse (see the paragraph below). Not to abandon the law is itself to transgress the law. This is not always understood and a true doctrine of justification leads to the charge of antinomianism. It is this charge Paul considers in v.17.

(ii) *Returning to Mosaism leads to transgression (2:18)* I take it that v.18 explains the end of v.17. Christ is not a minister of sin, because if I build up again what I broke down (subservience to Mosaism), I show myself a transgressor because it is not God's will that the law should be rebuilt. (A subsidiary thought might be that inevitably the law will be broken and 'transgression' occur in another way.) Restoring the law is the transgression Paul mentions in v.18. This interpretation gives excellent sense to the line of thought as it moves into the following verse: 'because I *through the law* died to the law'. If it is *through the law* that one dies to the law, then *to resist dying to the law is itself a transgression of the law.*

(iii) *It is the law itself that leads to the Christian's dying to the law (2:19)* This phrase has been interpreted in several main ways. Is it that Paul's experience of despair under the law leads him to abandon the attempt to find peace by its means? This seems too psychologizing, and reflects a psychologizing interpretation of Ro.7. A better interpretation is that objectively Christ has fulfilled the law and objectively has met its demands. The believer is therefore legally released from its curse. The thought is compact but statements concerning the law in Gal.3:13 and 4:4 suggest that it should be taken in this way.

(iv) *Freedom from the law leads to 'living unto God' (2:19)* It is important to note that Galatians 2:19 deals with godliness not with imputed righteousness. This is often overlooked. C.K.Barrett can write: 'The law is not dead . . . as a means of justification it is dead, but as a guide to the life of obedience it is not.' But Paul is dealing here with the charge of antinomianism. His concern is the life of obedience and it is in such a context that he says, 'I died to the law' not ' . . . in order to be justified' (although he could have said that) but ' . . . in order to live unto God.' Barrett's remarks reflect the longstanding Reformation theology in which the law is null with regard to justification but not with regard to sanctification. But Paul's statement is more radical. Release from the Torah enables sanctification – 'living unto God'.[18]

(v) *Justification coheres with union with Christ (2:20)* This is Paul's refutation of the antinomian charge. Justification is not *identified* with sanctification but it is an aspect of union with Christ and so leads to the godly life. Admittedly, justification does not violently force sanctification but it does correlate with it. Justification is an aspect of a wider union with Christ which secures that the godly life is possible.

(vi) *Paul's view of justification without the works of the law coheres with grace and does not nullify grace (2:21)* It is in fact the Judaizers' moralism and nationalism that nullifies grace.

Galatians 3:1–5 draws attention to the circumstances in which the Galatian Christians had received the Spirit. Paul had 'placarded' Jesus's death, and as they had trusted Jesus the Spirit had been given. The appeal is to vibrant experience. Paul refers to 'manifestations' of the Spirit. C.Osiek believes he has in mind 'external manifestations of prophecy, tongues, and other spiritual gifts'.[19] Ramsay (from a South Galatian viewpoint) refers to the striking events mentioned in Ac.13:52; 14:3,9; 15:8f.,12[20]. Paul thinks the experiential argument in itself is sufficient to prove his point ('This only . . . .'.) Apparently he refers to an occasion when the Spirit was received experientially, corporately, and in connection with simple preaching about Jesus. What was being preached on the occasion when the Galatians received the Spirit and thereafter experienced so much blessing,[21] including miraculous manifestations (3:5) was a message concerning Jesus and his death and had nothing to do with the Torah. Paul argues from this that a doctrine of justification by simple faith in Jesus without Mosaism is implied by their past experience.

A significant matter is the question of the meaning of *akoes pisteos*. Since *akoe* has two main meanings and *pistis* may be taken in more than one way, there are four possibilities. Does it refer to (i) the message of the faith,[22] (ii) the message about faith,[23] (iii) hearing the faith[24] or (iv) hearing with faith? I think the last-mentioned is the most likely.[25] It would seem that human faith is here contrasted with human works. This would mean that trust is in view rather than 'the' faith, and this coheres with Paul's argument as a whole. He is concerned about the *reality* of faith rather than its formal articulation. Whichever interpretation is adopted there is emphasis on faith (for even if 'faith' means the 'message' it is still the message-*believed*).[26]

Many scholars write as though the only issue in Galatians concerned *initial* salvation or one's *status* before God. Thus Schmithals discusses the law as 'the ground of salvation' or as 'necessary to salvation'.[27] Popular evangelicalism has tended to say Paul resists justification by the law but is happy with the law as a rule of life in Christian sanctification. Yet it must be noticed that Galatians is not concerned with initial salvation only. It is also about practical godliness. It refers to 'being completed' (*epiteleisthe*, present tense, 3:3) and the ongoing experience of freedom (5:1). It is concerned with the continuing easy burden of love instead of the heavy burden of the Torah (5:1). It refers to service (5:13) and continuing in love (5:14). It focuses upon spiritual admonition (5:25) and the actual life we live (5:26; 6:2–6). These matters clearly lie in the area of sanctification rather than justification. The Galatians have already received the Spirit, but they are turning to the Torah both as an aid to godliness and as a needful ingredient in maintaining acceptable status before God. Paul explicitly refers to how they are 'being completed'. With regard to godliness as well as justification (to use the Protestant distinction) the Christian must be free from the Torah in order to live unto God.

Galatians 3:6–9 presents a fresh argument, this time from the Old Testament. How was Abraham justified? Jewish scholars of Paul's day were accustomed to the idea that Abraham kept the Torah.[28] Such a viewpoint goes back at least to the days of Sirach which says 'Abraham . . . kept the law of the Most High' (Sir.44:19–21). Paul however disjoins Abraham from the Torah. 'He denies the existence of the Torah at the time of Abraham on the ground that the Torah was revealed only 430 years later' (Gal.3:17).[29] Arguing from Gen.15:6, Paul points to the fact that in the early stages of the story of Abraham we have only promises given to Abraham (Gen.12:1–3; 13:15–17; 15:4f.) and a statement of Abraham's faith (Gen.15:6). No mention of any kind of torah is found in the account of Abraham's 'righteousness' mentioned in Gen.15. Circumcision does not come into it; Israelite nationality does not come into it (Gen.15 is before the origin of Israel). Justification is open to gentiles (nothing distinctively Israelite is found at this stage of Abraham's life). *Simple* faith led to Abraham's being justified without his having any of the qualifications and conditions the Judaizers are pressing upon the Galatians. If Abraham is the prototype for all believers then simple faith is the way of salvation. Gentiles such as the Galatians need no further qualifications or preparations for justification.

Galatians 3:10–14 apparently depends on a missing but understood sentence ('Cursed is everyone who does not obey the Torah'; *no one obeys the Torah*; therefore all are cursed). This would imply a spiritual interpretation of the Torah (parallel to Rom.7:7 rather than to Phil.3:6).

Paul *expounds* (rather than simply quotes) Deut.27:26 in an expanded version. The LXX had expanded the MT by twice adding *pas*. Paul further expands the LXX by adding *tois gegrammenois*. It would not be difficult to defend the expansions.[30] The additions emphasize (i) the totality of obedience required in all the nation, (ii) the totality of obedience for all the commands, and (iii) the *written* (as opposed to oral?) nature of the law that must be obeyed.

Verses 11f. go on to contrast the principle of Deut.27:26 (Gal.3:10) with that of Hab.2:4. On most interpretations[31] faith is contrasted with doing. What is involved in faith is trusting and waiting for God's action. The law does not require faith (v.12a, a striking assertion!). Life was gained by obedience whether such obedience arose from faith or not. Paul uses Lev.18:5b to make his point. The 'living' refers to continued national prosperity. It is probably a mistake to think the promise of life is hypothetical (as in traditional reformed thinking following Calvin[32]) or a way of salvation valid for a dispensation of salvation-by-law.[33] Bruce is right to say that 'the promise of life is a genuine promise'.[34] It is at this point that the 'New Perspective' on

Paul is helpful. Since Stendahl's article on 'Paul and the Introspective Conscience' (originally delivered as a paper in 1961), [35] it has been increasingly argued that Paul's doctrine of justification does not concern introspection or 'seeking a gracious God'. The background to Paul's doctrine has a societal aspect to it. Dunn treats Paul *wholly* along these lines.[36] Yet there is no need to posit an *antithesis* between personal justification and its societal implications. The two are connected; one generates the other. Paul's doctrine of justification includes individual justification. For Abraham the prototype believer was – in Paul's reading of the Old Testament – an individual. To have the kind of faith he had is to become his seed. The 'seed of Abraham' is not generated by membership of the earthly nation of Israel (Paul's point in Rom.9:6–13). The fact that justification is by faith only and is the solution to one's quest for a gracious God *implies* that justification is not by nationality, not even the nationality of those 'to whom were entrusted the oracles of God' (Rom.3:1f.). So Paul's view of justification has societal implications. If salvation is by faith there can ultimately be 'neither Jew nor gentile'. Issues of national identity *were* at stake at Antioch, as J.Dunn argues. Yet surely Dunn has gone too far in interpreting Paul exclusively along these lines.

However the social/nationalistic aspect of the matter *is* prominent in Paul's thinking and is part of his law / gospel contrast (as Gal.3:28, 'neither Jew nor Greek', suggests). It is for this reason that one can understand Paul's dissatisfaction with Lev.18:5 *as a mode of personal justification*. Lev.18:5 was part of regulation for a nation. It was largely administered by magistrates. It gave 'life'. But the kind of 'life' that Paul is interested in is not conveyed by the law. The law brought a certain measure of blessing for Israel; Paul is not denying it. However the 'living' mentioned in the fifth commandment was explicitly 'living long in the land'. This was not an adequate principle for Paul's preaching to gentiles. Whatever 'life' was promised by the law, it was not eternal life since it did not necessitate faith. Of course the law can be interpreted as calling for faith – or at least for a new heart. But the magisterial aspects of the law render it inadequate as a personal way of salvation. Paul will shortly explain (3:19) that it was 'added' on account of Israel's transgression and was quite distinct from the earlier example of faith seen in Abraham.

Verse 13 speaks of the removal of the 'curse of the law' by the death of Jesus. The Spirit is received by such faith in Jesus not by obedience to the Torah (v.14). Much of this is widely acknowledged as a correct exposition of Galatians. The only point which differs from the commonplace evangelical exposition is the view of 'life' adopted here.

'THE LAW'

However several writers do not see in Galatians a radical rejection of Mosaic law, since they think *nomos* has an altogether different nuance. Thus D.Fuller argues that since in Gal.3:10 the statements as traditionally interpreted hinge upon a clause which is not present but which is understood, the traditional interpretation is unlikely. He prefers to treat *nomos* as referring not to the Mosaic law but to a legalistic interpretation of it. *Ergon nomou* then refers to something sinful but not to the law itself. Paul is not opposed (thinks Fuller) to a faithful law-keeping but only to works of self-confident law-keeping.[37] Others argue similarly, notably C.E.B.Cranfield and F.Flückiger.[38]

Yet there are major objections to this approach. It is true that Paul's use of the term *nomos* has various nuances. Nevertheless there are objections to viewing *nomos* in, e.g.Gal.3:10 as meaning 'legalism'. (i) Fuller and Cranfield seem not to take seriously the attested meaning of the phrase outside of the New Testament. We have mentioned this matter above. (ii) Fuller and Cranfield neglect the flow of thought in Galatians. For the term *nomos* first occurs in Galatians in Gal.2:15–21. By that stage of the letter Paul has already said a good deal, so that the contextual flow of the argument reveals what he means by *erga nomou* when he first uses the term. He has referred to Jewish institutions, mentioning life in Judaism (1:13f.), the 'traditions of my fathers' (1:14), circumcision (2:3), Jewish food laws (2:12). In sentence preceding Gal.2:15f. Paul has used the phrase *Ioudikos ze(i)s* and *Ioudaizein* (2:14). In the flow of argument then, *ergon nomou* must allude to the totality of Mosaic institutions. It is this meaning that is demanded by the references to the law in 1;13f.; 2:3,12,14. The reference in 2:15–21 must surely retain this meaning. When Paul says that righteousness cannot be attained *dia nomou*, why should we now take *nomos* to refer to anything other than what he has been referring to all along? There is nothing in Galatians 1:1–2:14 to suggest any duality in the use of *nomos*. While it is possible to *impose* this meaning on *nomos*, nothing *requires* us to take it this way.

Paul sets up a contrast between *ergon nomou* and *akoue pisteos*. What exactly is the nature of the contrast? It concerns hearing concerning Christ versus law-keeping. It is not a contrast between two different ways of keeping the law. It is not (to coin some terms Paul could have used) *ergon nomou en pistei* versus *ergon nomou en sarki*. He is discussing whether or not *ergon nomou* should be rejected altogether. The fact that it is possible to coin such phrases as *ergon nomou en pistei* and *en sarki* is itself a refutation of the idea that there was no convenient phrase Paul could use to designate legalism.

(iii) Such arguments neglect the use that Paul makes of Abraham. The point in Gal.4:17 is that Abraham was justified and lived a godly life in the total absence of Mosaic institutions. Abraham is not a model of one who keeps the Mosaic law in the right spirit, but a model of one who was justified without the law at all.

(iv) Fuller especially struggles with Gal.3:18, and has an extra note to deal with it. It is clear that in 3:17 'the law' refers to everything that was introduced into Israel through Moses. Does the meaning change when in the next verse 'law' and 'promise' are contrasted? Surely v.18 continues to use the word as in v.17. It is difficult to see a contrast between *nomos*, the law, and *nomos*, legalism, in the movement from one verse to the next.

Fuller has two arguments against this. One is that the Judaizers would never have agreed to a contrast between Abraham and Moses, and would have argued that Abraham was righteous on the basis of keeping the law before it was given. Paul must therefore (argues Fuller) be using *nomos* in the Judaizers' sense in v.17. But surely Paul is *disputing* the Judaizers' viewpoint by insisting that there is epochal significance in the fact that there was a lengthy period in which the law had not been given. He is not so much arguing from particular texts as arguing from epochs of time in Old Testament history. To see a change in meaning in the movement between v.17 and v.18 would require at least a definite indication that such a change is required. No such indication is to be found.

Fuller also argues that 3:21 prevents us from seeing a sharp contrast between law and promise. However if it is true that 3:18 must not contradict 3:21, it is also true that 3:21 must not contradict 3:18! It is true that ultimately the introduction of the Mosaic epoch does not militate against the Abrahamic promise but rather contributes to it. The question is: how does the law aid the gospel? In Fuller's view it is because there is really no contrast between them at all; the contrast is simply between the misuse and the true use of the law. 3:21 could mean this if taken in isolation, but this does not do justice to 3:17f. or to the total thrust of Galatians. It is preferable to view Gal.3:21 as asserting that in restraining Israel's sinfulness by the imposition of the law, the Mosaic institutions were protecting Israel and thus securing the arrival of Jesus, the seed of Abraham. The two verses, 3:18 and 3:21, must be given full weight and neither should be allowed to cancel out the other. Gal.3:21 cannot be used to negate the natural reading of 3:17f.

It ought to be noticed that in speaking of 'the Law', Fuller and others are in effect taking the word 'law' to refer to the 'moral law' familiar in Western theology. It was Thomas Aquinas, especially, who popularized in theological circles the habit of using the phrase 'the law' to designate a moral code extrapolated from the Ten Commandments.[39] Paul's use of *nomos* generally keeps in view the totality of Mosaic institutions. When Cranfield, for example, defends the law, he is defending not Mosaism but 'the Law' in the modern sense of a code extrapolated from the Decalogue. It is doubtful whether this is at all legitimate; it certainly would require stronger argument before 'the law' could be viewed in this way in Galatians.

Another way in which the force of Paul's thesis has been reduced is to argue that the *ergon nomou* refers only to the ceremonial aspects of the law. This is a stronger argument than the previous one since it is true that Paul has mentioned largely ritualistic aspects of the law (circumcision, food-laws, the traditions of the fathers), rather than the decalogue. In the particular situation in Galatia these clearly were at issue. Even so, to reduce *ergon nomou* to something entirely ceremonial cannot be justified. When Paul does turn to the love-command and the need of godliness (5:12–6:10) he does not revert to the decalogue. He rather says that walking in the Spirit releases from Mosaism (5:18). In Gal.3:17f. he thinks in terms of epochs of time. So again it must be insisted that what he has in mind is the totality of the Mosaic epoch. Although in this particular conflict heavy emphasis was being placed on the distinctively national and cultural aspects of the law yet the term *nomos* denotes a total epoch of time and a total system, including the decalogue. The decalogue receives no special treatment in Galatians (although it does in Rom.13:8–10) because it does not seems to have been the subject of dispute as much as the cultural aspects of the law, notably circumcision. Yet Paul's dismissal of the law in the interests of life in the Spirit evidently involved an end to direct preoccupation with the decalogue. He expects that the decalogue – with the whole law – will be indirectly fulfilled by walking in the Spirit.

I conclude then that *ergon nomou* meant for Paul precisely what it meant in contemporary usage: it refers to a sincere attempt to live a righteous life by obedience to all of the institutions of the Torah. The best interpretation of Gal.3:10–14 is (*pace* Fuller) to take it that there is indeed a missing clause which is taken for granted ('No one can keep the law with regard to seeking a righteous standing before God'). Deut.27:26 referred to public life in Israel but the principle cannot be applied to personal relationship to God. The argument is compressed but it is the understood clause that provides the missing link between 3:10a and 3:10b. The link is not altogether missing because it is provided by Gal.3:11f.. Habakkuk spoke of the individual pursuing a relationship with God by faith (Gal.3:11). Lev.18 spoke of 'living' *at a national level* by obedience. With regard to justification before God it is the former not the latter that applies.

An important question concerns the precise identity of the 1st person plural pronoun Paul uses in Gal.3:13f.,23–25. The 'we' is generally taken to refer to include Jewish and gentile Christians.[40] Yet there are indications that this is an exclusive   e' and refers only to the people of Israel. In Gal.2:15 Paul used emphatic language: 'We, being by nature Jews . . .'. This indicates that it is at least possible he is using exclusive 1st person plural pronouns in 3:13f.,23–25 also. Fung argues that since the statement 'We are no longer under a custodian' (v.25b) is explained by 'you are all sons of God' (v.26), the 'we' must include the 'you'.[41] But Fung's argument is weak. The two statements are not identical. Galatians contains some 1st person pronouns which are clearly exclusive (2:15) and some that are clearly inclusive (e.g. 1:3–5). T.L.Donaldson shows[42] that among the various statements in Galatians 3–4 there are four stages in the statements concerning redemption. Following Donaldson we may lay them out as follows. There is reference to:

1. *The group ('We') and its plight*
    'We' were under the curse of the law (3:10,13).
    'We' were confined under law; the law was 'our' pedagogue (3:23f.).
    'We' were under law, slaves of the *stoicheia* (4:3,5).

2. *Identification of Christ with the plight of the group*
    Jesus became a curse for 'us' (3:13).
    Faith/Christ came (3:23–25).
    Jesus was born under the law (4:4).

3. *Redemption of the group*
    Christ redeemed 'us'.
    Now that faith has come 'we' are no longer under a guardian (3:25).
    'To redeem those under the law' (4:3).

4. *Saving blessings for all believers*
    'So that the blessing of Abraham might come upon the gentiles
    . . .so that we [Jews and gentiles] might receive the promise of the Spirit (3:14);

    'for in Christ Jesus you are all [Jews and gentiles] sons of God through faith' (3:26);

    'so that we [Jews and gentiles] might receive adoption (4:5).

Paul's argument deals with how the gentiles come to be included in God's people. The passages referred to all *conclude* with a reference to blessings available to all Christians. But the shifts in the pronouns are surely significant. The 'we' in 2:15 is emphatically stated over against the 'Gentile sinners', and leads into the 'no one' of 2:16. ('Even *we* know . . . for no one is justified . . .'). It cannot be accidental that Paul moves from 'us' to 'gentiles' in 3:13f., and then moves from 'us' to 'you' in 3:23–29. It cannot be coincidental that he consistently uses 1st person plural pronouns when speaking of those who are under the law. This corresponds to Rom.2:12,14; 7:1; 9:4 and 1 Cor.9:20 where the giving of the law is related only to Israel. A crucial preliminary in blessing coming to gentiles was the removing of the barrier of the law. The argument in Gal.3:1–14 is reminiscent of Eph.2:11–22. Redemption from the law that was Israel's distinctive had to be achieved before the gentiles could be 'fellow citizens with the saints'. Donaldson rightly puts the point: 'Due to the very nature of Israel's special role, the redemption of Israel is at the same time and on the same terms the redemption of the Gentiles.'[43]

Galatians 3:15–18 puts the same point in terms of an illustration. It is an illustration more than an argument. Paul compares the two covenants (Abrahamic and Sinaitic) to two similar human arrangements in law. First a general principle is adduced. Once ratified, a covenant is not lightly abrogated.[44] Then the principle is applied. Genesis relates a covenant concerning the coming of a 'seed' to Abraham. Torah was not involved. 'Seed' is a conveniently ambiguous term which may be singular or collective.[45] If Genesis had used the plural it would not have been possible to refer it to Jesus. The fact that the term used is singular *or* collective means that the word may be applied to Christ. The 'seed' of Abraham is Jesus. Only by being incorporated in Christ are others part of the 'seed'.[46] All this was promised to Abraham, to be sought by faith.

Four centuries later a further covenant was brought into being, with the nation of Israel via Moses. The fact that an addition was made cannot nullify or abrogate the original promise of universal blessing for all nations through the seed of Abraham. Abraham received blessing without the law. Abraham was the model for justification. How could the Mosaic law be needful for justification if it had not been given in the days of the prototype believer, Abraham?

God came to Abraham with sheer promise (Gen.12;15). Abraham was said to be justified (Gen.15:6) when he had done no more than act on God's mere word. No Torah had been given. When 430 years later the law was added it was not sheer promise. What Paul has said has made the law totally irrelevant. The inevitable question is already looming up in the reader's mind. Verse 19 follows inevitably from vv.15–18. If one's interpretation of 3:6–18 does not inevitably give rise to the question, 'Why then the law?', the correct line of thought has not been found. Gal.3:6–18, as understood above, implies that the law is entirely irrelevant to salvation, It thus leads naturally to the next question: why then the law?

Galatians 3:19a takes up the questions that arise. The law is *not* a means of justification (2:16); it is *not* a means of sanctification (2:17–19). What then was the law designed for? Paul's answer is that it is an *interim* measure. In this, he implicitly disagrees with those writers of his day who maintained that the law was eternal;[47] rather, its functions were temporary. Paul's phrase 'added . . . until' is to be interpreted as designating an epoch of time during which the law functioned. The point that the law is transitory is made five times in Gal.3:19–25 (vv.19c, 23a and c, 24a, 25). It was given 'because of transgressions'. The majority view concerning this phrase takes it to express purpose ('for the purpose of'), not antecedent cause ('on account of')[48]. The word *charin* in itself could be taken either way. The majority view is heavily influenced by Rom.3:20; 4:15; 5:13,20; 7:5 and 1 Cor.15:56.[49] Yet within the context of Galatians there is something to be said for taking it differently. (i) The view that *charin* expresses antecedent cause is much simpler. It is not immediately apparent in Galatians what 'for the purpose of transgression' means. It requires the introduction of passages from Romans to give it meaning. (ii) On the other hand Paul is about to speak of the law's having a restraining effect (3:23) and of being a *paidagogos* (3:24f.) with the Galatians compared to children under guardians and stewards (*epitropoi, oikonomoi*, 4:2). The idea that Israel's transgression had been so great that the Torah was needed to restrain them until the fulness of the gospel was introduced fits perfectly with the flow of argument. The point is not so subtle as those made in Romans. This means that the Torah was added to an already adequate gospel-of-promise because the greatness of Israel's sin required restraint. When it is remembered that the law was magisterially administered, it is all the more likely that this is what is in Paul's mind. The Mosaic system was an interim measure, given to keep Israel moral by means of fear of punishment until 'the seed' should come.

Galatians 3:19b–20 are difficult to interpret but would seem to imply (as in the similar reference to angels in Ac.7:53 and Heb.2:3) that angelic mediation of the Law[50] implies its inferiority. God sent angels to bring in the Mosaic epoch; he sent Jesus to provide salvation. The point seems to be that two mediatorial stages were involved in the giving of the law. Far from coming directly from God, it came through a line of transmission: God – angels – Moses – people. The enigmatic sentence *ho de mesites henos ouk estin, ho de theos heis estin* is said to have over 300 interpretations[51]. If (as seems likely) the 'one' of the two parts of the sentence both refer to God, then the mediator Paul refers to is not God's mediator. Whose mediator is he, and who is he? Bruce and Vanhoye are likely to be right in saying the mediator is Moses and he was mediating for the people in receiving the law from the angels.[52]

Galatians 3:21f. argue that the Law is therefore in harmony with the promise. It keeps Israel in existence and so paves the way for the coming of 'the seed'. Though it could not 'give life' (3:21b) yet it encloses the world under the judgement of sin, leaving only one door open, the door for the coming of Jesus.[53] Since Paul has so far referred to the Law only as given to Israel, one might ask why he mentions the world at this point. In line with the contrast of 2:15, the point seems to be that if the Jews are condemned by the law, gentiles are equally condemned for they are in a worse state than Israel.

Galatians 3:23–4:7 consistently emphasizes a clear time-contrast. We read of the time from 'before this faith . . . until faith' (3:23). We have the time-phrase, 'Now that faith has come' (3:25). We see a contrast between infancy and maturity (4:1) and between two epochs 'when we were children' and 'when the time had fully come' (4:3f.). We read of what 'we were' and of what is 'no longer' (4:7). The contrast that flows through this section refers to epochs of world history before and after the coming of Jesus. The law is an interim measure until the coming of Jesus.

A crucial question is: who exactly are 'we' in Galatians 3:23ff? The pronoun seems to refer to Israel. We note (i) that Paul makes an explicit distinction between 'we who are Jews by birth' as opposed to 'gentile sinners'. The 'we' of 3:23–4:7 corresponds to the 'we' of 2:15. (ii) Paul refers to Mosaic institutions including circumcision (5:2) and Jewish festivals (4:10). There is no reason to think that gentiles were ever placed under these obligations in pre-Christian times. 'We' must refer to Jews. (iii) Throughout 3:23–4:7 'we' is used at points that refer to Israel; 'you' at points where full sonship of Jews and gentiles is in view.[54]

When Paul says that 'we' were redeemed from being under the law he is referring to the passing of the old covenant believers into full maturity. Gentiles receive that full sonship without going through the period of infancy that Israel experienced. For Paul the law is only an interim measure and the total Mosaic covenant is abrogated. The Christian church is in a state of adulthood and full multinational maturity over against the infancy of the pre-Christian people of God, Israel.

Galatians 4:8–20 Here Paul expresses his distress at the change among the Galatians (4:8–11), reminds them of the past in which they had been so happy (4:12–16) and warns them against current Judaistic influences (4:17–21).

Galatians 4:21–5:1 This sub-unit is often disparaged. Even Calvin judged that 'as an argument it is not very strong'.[55] Paul takes the story of Abraham and Hagar and draws from it a principle which he applies to the Galatians. The fact that Abraham's inheritance went to his circumcised son could be used against Paul's gospel. Paul replies: 'But Abraham had *two* sons, one of whom did not get the inheritance – the one born in accord with the mere human resources and not according to faith.'

Verse 21 seems to mean two things: (i) The legalists have never seen what the law demands. If the Galatians could see the law truly they would never want to be under it. People who think they can be Christians by the law have never seen what the law says. (ii) Paul is about to quote from Genesis. The Torah contains other things beside legislation. Paul says: 'I want to put something else to you, also from the law.' [56]

Verse 22 recalls the story. God gave Abraham the promise of a 'seed'. The inheriting of the promise was to come about through persistent faith. After long delay Abraham made a major mistake. He took Hagar and 'got' (*eschen* – aorist) a child through her. He was seeking to get the promise fulfilled himself and thus Ishmael was 'acquired'. But the Genesis account does not portray this as the right way to achieve fulfilment of the promise. It was an expression of unbelief. Paul is about to use the story as an illustration. Turning to Hagar will illustrate turning to the law.

The birth of Isaac (v.23) was a step forward in the fulfilment of the promise. Isaac was a wonder-child. His birth aroused amazed incredulity. Whereas Ishmael was born *kata sarka* ('in the course of nature', NAB) Isaac's birth came from the Spirit's working (involving of course normal conception) as Abraham was again relying on the promises. In the former instance Abraham had lapsed from faith, turning to a human expedient in seeking to get the promises fulfilled. Paul is repeating the argument of Gal.3:3. To turn from faith to law-keeping is to move from the Spirit to the flesh. It is relying on human ability and adopting an unbelieving expedient. In v.24 Paul maintains that this analogously expresses[57] the same principle that is at work in two covenants – for he regards the Mosaic covenant and the Abrahamic faith as two covenants. He does not, in the manner of Calvin,[58] integrate them into one overarching covenant under different administrations.

Verse 25 is beset with problems of interpretation. The longer reading (*To de Hagar Sina oros en te(i) Arabia(i)*) is probably preferable.[59] The statement is a statement concerning interpretation. It is in the analogy that Hagar 'is' Mount Sinai and all it stands for.

Paul reminds his readers of the consequences of the lapse of faith. Hagar 'corresponds to the present Jerusalem, for she serves as a slave with her children' (v.25). Since Hagar was a slave her child was a slave also (as was generally the case in the ancient world). This illustrates the working of the Sinai-covenant and the new-covenant. This illustrates what happens when the Galatians turn to the law. To turn to the law only produces more bondage. Slavery begets slavery. Present-day Jerusalem (the Judaizers claiming Jerusalem as their authority), says Paul, only bears children for slavery – the Judaized converts. To turn to the law will always lead to bondage and reliance on the flesh. It means thinking that *simple* faith in Jesus is inadequate to justify, inadequate to sanctify. One turns to a system rather than to a person, and the result is always bondage.

What are Paul's governing principles here? (i) Faith in Jesus is adequate for the living of the Christian life without submission to Mosaism. (ii) Turning to the law is really a form of panic. Abraham was momentarily, fearful that merely by trusting the promise concerning the seed, the seed would not come. Something similar happens when one turns to the law. It means turning away from a simple trust in Jesus to self-justification and self-sanctification by the flesh. (iii) To turn to the law can only produce bondage. Ishmael was not one of the children of the house. He was only a servant-child.

But, says Paul (v.26), the Jerusalem above is free. 'Jerusalem above' is not the church but the heavenly metropolis from which the life of the church comes.[60] The Judaizers wish to bind the church to the Torah coming from an earthly Jerusalem. They are preoccupied with the authority of what they conceive to be an original Jerusalem-based law-bound gospel. But Paul thinks of another capital city: the Jerusalem above. In the Old Testament Jerusalem was the centre of God's people, but there is also a heavenly metropolis. The Jerusalem above is what counts. No one gains life by listening to the instructions from the Jerusalem below. Life comes from heaven. C.H.Cosgrove points out that Paul's argument here deals not with status (justification, sonship) but with whether life in the Spirit depends on law-keeping.[61] The earthly centre of legalism will never help. The heavenly seat of power will help with life and freedom. She is our mother.

Spiritual life is not by the keeping of the Torah but by life from above. It is God's giving new life by the Spirit in response to faith. Gal.4:27 quotes Isa.54:1, where the new heavenly Jerusalem is blessed with many children. The numerical increase of Gentile believers is due to the power of the Spirit coming from heaven. At the same time Paul alludes to the barren Sarah. Abraham had to go on believing despite the impossibility to human sight of any fulfilment. He had to go on believing God, not trusting to human resources. He did so and (despite the lapse in connection with Hagar) the promise came to pass and Isaac was born. This is the way of life for the Christian.

Verse 28 bluntly states the similarity of the situations. Believers in Galatia are like the miracle child; they are not to be like the product of fleshly resort to human expedients. An extremely negative view of the law is visible here.

Verse 29 recalls the fact that in the Genesis account, according to one interpretation of Gen.21:9,[62] Ishmael 'persecuted' Isaac; so it is now. The Judaizers want to impose law. They do not like simple faith. They will attack; they will criticize; they will slander.

Verse 30 recalls the instruction of Gen.21:10: 'Get rid of the slave woman. The slave will not inherit.' In Paul's terms this means 'Get rid of legalism. Eschew bondage. Reject the teaching of the Judaizers. Rely upon Jesus with a simple faith.'

Verse 31 concludes Paul's argumentation. The Galatian Christians should think of themselves as successors to Isaac, and the Jerusalem-based visitors as successors to Ishmael.

Several conclusions may be adduced at this point. (1) Evidently for Paul the law given at Sinai and the Abrahamic gospel represent two covenants not one. Systematic theologies are often centred around 'the covenant' (Barth, H.Berkhof and others) but Paul speaks of covenants in the plural (Rom.9:4; Eph.2:12); and never of 'the covenant' as an entity overarching and including the Mosaic epoch. There is a contrast between Moses and Abraham. The language of biblical theology and the language of systematic theology sometimes diverge and it is not necessarily wrong for them to do so. Yet the very extensive use of the singular has overshadowed the significance of Paul's use of the plural. While the Mosaic covenant is a *forward* step in the sense of carrying forward the purpose of God which moves towards the seed of Abraham, yet it is also an *intrusive* step. The two covenants are not assimilated.

(2) The thrust of the argument throughout Gal.4:21–5:1 is that turning back to Mosaism rather than *sheer* recourse to God's promise is to make the same mistake that Abraham made in having recourse to Hagar in order to bring about the purpose of God. Abraham had been given the promise of a 'seed' but the extreme delay led to his turning to 'the flesh' to promote the arrival of the seed. Similarly the Galatians are eager to see the promises of God fulfilled in their lives. They have rejoiced in the experience of the Spirit and wish to continue to do so. Yet they are having recourse to Mosaism to bring about the fulfilment of the promises of God.

(3) A consideration of Gal.3:19 alongside Gal.4:21–5:1 makes one realize that for Paul the law should not have been needed at all. It is only the sin of Israel that necessitated it in the first place. After the

coming of Jesus it is 'no longer' needed as a guardian and pedagogue . To have recourse to it is trusting to the ability of the flesh to bring God's will to fruition. In all of this Paul never suggests that it is a misinterpreted Torah that he has in mind. Within this section his first mention of 'the law' (4:21) referred to the Torah not to a perverted version or use of it. The Torah itself is no longer the 'guardian' of God's Israel, the international Christian community.

Galatians 5:1 completes 4:21–31 and calls upon the Galatians to stand in the freedom Christ has given them. The 'freedom' Paul has in mind is freedom from Mosaic ritual, freedom from loss of blessedness (4:15), from bondage to nationalistic ambitions expressed in the rite of circumcision, from bondage to a system-centred mode of growth in 'grace' – which Paul would not call growth in 'grace' at all!

Galatians 5:2–11 begins with a warning: to receive circumcision implies lack of faith in Christ's sufficiency and therefore amounts to turning from Christ (5:2). It implies an acceptance of the total Mosaic covenant (5:3). It will negate the Christian's experience of grace (5:4). Verse 5 is difficult to interpret and could be taken in two ways according to whether the emphasis is on hope or upon righteousness. If the emphasis is on 'hope of righteousness' it will mean that our eschatological vindication comes not by Mosaism but by the Spirit. If the emphasis is on 'righteousness', understood as day-by-day ethical righteousness, it will mean that godly living is not produced by law but by the Spirit.

At v.6, for the first time in the letter, the focus is on love. It is notable that the contrast between law and Spirit and Paul has been sketching corresponds to a contrast between preoccupation with circumcision (either for or against) over against love. If the Mosaic covenant (represented in the Judaizers' eyes by circumcision) is not the answer, then neither is hostility to the law! The law is relatively insignificant; what matters is love. Paul contrasts love as much with uncircumcision as with circumcision.

Verses 7–12 show Paul remonstrating with the Galatians and denouncing the Judaizers.

Galatians 5:13–6:10 At 5:13 Paul sounds a new note. He repeats his summons to freedom but now for the first time adds that it is not 'freedom for an opportunity for the flesh' (*me ten eleutherian eis te sarki*). Why does Paul turn to a different aspect of the matter at this point? Is it because there is an 'antinomian' party at Galatia? Or have some Christians taken his doctrine of freedom from Mosaism so seriously that major moral breaches have occurred? Or are some Galatian legalists in some respects but antinomian in others? There seem to be two reasons why Paul introduces another aspect of his teaching here.

He needs to reply to accusations concerning moral licentiousness. 2:17 seems to imply that there were such accusations. We have no glimpses, in this section, of any specific group of opponents who are infiltrating the Galatian Christians. It is likely therefore that Paul turns to the matter of godly living not because he is facing a party of libertines but because he must *as a good teacher* give the 'other side of the coin' in respect of the teaching given so far. He must show that his doctrine of freedom is not libertinism, that freedom from Mosaism leads in fact to *fulfilment* of Mosaism.

This is why he now warns against the 'flesh' and points to general requirements of service in love, which are not a matter of legislation (5:13). This love, which evidently has no need of Mosaic guidance in fact 'fulfils' all that the law was pointing to. Thus the law is 'fulfilled' without legalism (5:14). Paradoxically the law-obsessed Galatians show little love. This in itself should be a hint that recourse to Mosaism carries no guarantee of love. The Judaizers evidently believe that Mosaism will restrain the flesh. Paul, who regards the law as an adjunct of 'flesh' (3:3), says it is the *Spirit* who restrains the flesh (5:16). There is, he says, a battle between the Spirit and the flesh so that believers do not do completely what they want in either direction (5:17). But if the Spirit is thus present, the very fact of his leading is one aspect of and a proof of the fact that the believer is in a new realm altogether and has finished with a direct relationship to the law (5:18).

One might ask: how does the believer receive guidance concerning the life of the flesh? How, in the absence of Mosaism, can one know what is sin? Paul replies that 'the works of the flesh are *phaneros* – obvious'. He believes that the presence of the Spirit ought to make one immediately and directly aware that sins such as are mentioned in 5:19–21a are indeed works of the flesh. It is unnecessary to consult the Torah to discover whether a fit of rage (for example) is a work of the flesh. Nor would it be helpful, for many of the items in these verses receive no treatment in the Torah. If the Christian indulges in such sins he will forfeit his *inheritance* of the kingdom (5:21b). This 'inheritance' is not 'justification', for the two are distinct. If, as is clear in at least one place, [63] 'inheritance' has both present and future dimensions, the warning of 5:21 means *either* that one's present experience of God's blessing is lost *or* that one is in danger of being 'saved through fire' (Paul's phrase in 1 Cor.3:15).

The fruit of the Spirit (5:22f.) has love as its first aspect. If one focuses on love the remaining aspects of the (unitary) fruit of the Spirit will follow. 'Against such there is no law' is a litotes comparable to Ac.21:39 ('not a citizen of an unimportant city') and Rom.1:16 ('not ashamed of the gospel'). It is an emphatic way of saying: this fulfils all that Mosaism required. A person free of the sins of 5:19–21a and characterized by the traits of 5:22f. has fulfilled the Torah. Those who are in fellowship with Christ (*hoi . . . tou Christou*) are in such fellowship because they have resisted their sinful inclinations.

It is generally thought that v.24 refers to all Christians. If so, it will mean that a transfer from the kingdom of darkness has taken place (see Rom.5:12–21; Col.1:13) such that *in principle* the power of sin is broken. However, since not all Christians actually and inexorably crucify sin, (see Gal.6:1) it is possible that *hoi . . . tou Christou* refers to those who are actually and currently in living fellowship with Jesus. The first part of the sentence then refers to a section of the Christian community, not all of it. The latter part of the sentence refers to the result: they alone actually mortify sin.

Paul appeals to the Christian to obey the Spirit (5:25) and itemizes some aspects of what this will mean. It will involve avoiding mutual provocation (5:26) – a sin evidently rife among the Galatian Christians despite their attachment to the law. It will involve restoration of the fallen (6:1), bearing the burdens of others (6:2). Here, in an almost casual manner, Paul uses the phrase 'law of Christ'. His meaning must be taken from the total thrust of all that he has said in Galatians, especially 5:13–6:1. This 'law' refers not to the sayings of Jesus (which are not mentioned in Galatians), nor to a spiritualized version of the Mosaic law (this would militate against everything he has said) but to the two things Paul has mentioned thus far: the primacy of love and deliberate step-by-step obedience to the Spirit (5:25). One aspect will be burden-bearing. This *is* the law of Christ.

The phrase is ironical. It is as though Paul were saying: 'Do you want to be under a law? I will give you one: practise love and keep in step with the Spirit. This is the law – of Christ and not of the Mosaic covenant.' In the light of the total thrust of Galatians the force of the phrase must be in *antithesis* to Mosaic law.[64]

Paul continues to focus on 'life in the Spirit' when he comments briefly on one's attitude to oneself (6:3–5) and to the needs of the 'instructor' (6:6). Verses 6:7f are important. The Christian must sow to the Spirit. His concern is not so much with the Torah but with the direct leading of the Spirit in the pathway of love. The Spirit's leading will always be along the pathway of love. His leading will not *contradict* the moral aspects of the Torah although it will go beyond them. Much depends on whether or not the Christian will 'sow' to the Spirit or to the flesh. 'Reaping eternal life' refers to the actual enjoyment of the powers of the kingdom (cf.5:21). 'Destruction' is Paul's term for forfeiting the enjoyment of the kingdom (5:21) and (it may be suggested) for the loss that takes place at the judgement seat of Christ when such a Christian is 'saved through fire' (1 Cor.3:15).

This interpretation differs from the usual interpretation of Gal.6:8. Its justification depends on the whole line of interpretation of the letter thus far. There is a hermeneutical circle here. If one consistently confines oneself to interpreting the warnings of Scripture as references to apostasy or proven non-genuineness of salvation then one will follow the same line here. But the thesis of this work is that a third approach is possible, and that the warnings of Scripture may be taken to refer to lack of reward (near and far, this-life and beyond this life). One's overall approach to this matter will determine how one reads passages such as these. Certainly Paul is addressing Christians here. Tracing the thread of argument in the various warning passages will inevitably follow one of the three routes I mention. The most likely understanding is that Paul does not refer to apostasy, does not invite introspection, but warns nevertheless against severe loss here and hereafter.

Two concluding exhortations (6:9f.) bring this section to a close.

Galatians 6:11–18 need not detain us overmuch. Paul takes up the pen himself (6:11) as he brings his letter to a close. He still cannot resist resuming his central concern. Still he must warn against the Judaizers. He points to the outwardness of circumcision (6:12). Does v.13 refer to gross sins of the Judaizers or to the fact that the law cannot be perfectly and internally fulfilled when it is directly approached? If this letter were Romans the latter would be a correct interpretation (compare Rom.7). In Galatians one cannot be sure that the thought is always running parallel to Romans, yet probably the reasoning here is comparable to Rom.7:7–25 and 2:21–29. In Gal.6:13b Paul is still concerned with Mosaism versus the 'law of Christ'. The legalist is inclined to boast of an external obedience (6:13b, see Lk.18:9,11f.). Paul will boast only in Christ (6:14). The direct 'new creation' of God in the heart is *all* that matters to him (6:15). It is only this 'rule' – again the word is ironical – that receives his benediction (6:16). He hopes his letter will deal with those who think otherwise, and that he will receive no further distraction (6:17). Upon this note his letter closes with a final benediction (6:18).

CONCLUSION: THE LAW IN GALATIANS

We may summarize Paul's view of the law as it appears in Galatians in a number of propositions.

I. PAUL'S CONCERN IN GALATIANS IS WITH THE ENTIRE CORPUS OF MOSAIC INSTITUTIONS

His argument generally implies this. There are references to circumcision (2:3; 5:2f.,6,11; 6:12f.), to food laws (2:12), calendrical regulations (4:10). Yet the ritual and ceremonial aspects of the law are not his only concerns. 'Works of the law' refers to the totality of Mosaic institutions. The word *nomos* also generally refers in Paul to the totality of Mosaism. This is clear when he uses the term in speaking of an epoch of time (Gal.3:17,23,24) or when he speaks of the whole law (5:3,14). I have argued that it is what is in view when he speaks of the 'works of the law' (2:16; 3:2,5,10). In Gal.3:10 the 'book of the law' clearly refers to written Torah with its many institutions. Other uses of the term in the same contexts generally retain the same meaning and refer to the totality of Mosaic institutions looked at as a whole (2:19,21; 3:11f.,18f.,21; 4:4f.;5,21; 5:4,18). In one instance (4:21) reflection on the Torah includes the book of Genesis. In Gal.5:23 we have a negative statement ('against such there is no law') which reflects upon the Torah. The 'law of Christ' is mentioned only in Gal.6:2 and here there is antithesis to the law of Moses. Thus in virtually every instance in Galatians *nomos* directly refers to or reflects upon the totality of Mosaic institutions. When Gal.3:10 cites Deut.27 the moral element is included, for the twelve curses of Deut.27:15–26 mention such matters as idolatry (27:15), dishonouring parents (27:16), fraud (27:17). The curses are not confined to ceremonial matters.

2. PAUL MAINTAINS THAT MOSAISM FAILS AS A MEANS OF JUSTIFICATION OR OF SANCTIFICATION

It does not help in justification (2:16; 3:11). It fails to sanctify (2:19). It fails to give righteousness (3:21). It fails to give the Spirit (3:2–5). It cannot lead to inheritance (4:18). It cannot give life (3:21). It cannot give freedom (4:21–31) but only brings bondage (4:21–5:1).

3. PAUL ASSERTS THE TOTAL ABOLITION OF THE LAW FOR THE CHRISTIAN

Paul does not envisage that such an abrogation will result in a consequent diminishing of godliness. He denounces licentiousness but the righteousness he envisages for the Christian is not derived from the Torah although it fulfils the Torah. Paul's assertion of freedom from the Torah is radical. Salvation neither begins with nor continues by any part of the Mosaic law. Justification functions without the law. The law should not be brought back in for the purposes of sanctification. The Spirit is received without the law. The Galatian Christians must radically reject those who would re-impose Mosaism. The Hagar allegory implies that when recourse is had to the law it is only the 'flesh' that is at work. Just as Ishmael was the product not of Abraham's faith but of his temporary disbelief in the promise, so the law (which is 'not of faith') was brought into salvation history on account of the sins and disbelief of Israel. It was thus an interim measure. It tyrannised over the nation during the period between Moses and Jesus. It had now however been removed and the Christian should need no direct recourse to it. It is ignored in justification (2:16); it must not be turned back to for sanctification (being 'perfected', 3:1); the 'hope of righteousness' similarly is unrelated to the Mosaic law.

4. RECOURSE TO THE LAW RESULTS ONLY IN DIMINISHED SPIRITUALITY

This fact is not directly asserted by Paul but it is implied in his descriptions of events. In Paul's view the Judaizers were guilty of much sin despite their legalism. They perverted the gospel (1:8f.) and spied out liberty (2:4). This could be a matter of simple conviction. Yet Paul also portrays the life of the Judaizers as characterized by insincerity (4:17) and avoidance of suffering (6:12). Paul describes his own pre-Christian life in similar terms (1:13). Under the influence of the Judaizers even the greatest of Christians became infected with fear (2:12). Thus Barnabas allowed a breach of fellowship (2:13) and was inconsistent in his living out the gospel (2:14). The Galatian Christians lost their joy (4:15). Christ needed to be formed in them again (4:19). Paul hints at loss of love among the Galatians (5:6) and damage to their fellowship (5:9,26; 6:1). Evidently in his view increased preoccupation with Mosaism did not heighten spirituality but lessened it.

5. THE MOSAIC LAW WAS INTENDED TO RESTRAIN SIN IN ISRAEL AND SO FURTHER GOD'S SAVING PURPOSE

For the apostle the Torah is no longer a 'rule of life' for the Christian. Nor does it persuade of sinfulness.

6. PAUL USES A NUMBER OF DIFFERENT ARGUMENTS TO SUPPORT HIS POSITION

His arguments may be listed as: (a) Scriptural – 3:10–14; 4:21–5:1, (b) Scriptural-historical – 3:6–9, 15, (c) Pragmatic-expediential – 3:28f., (d) Christological – Christ replaces Torah, 2:16, (e) Personal,4:11,12–20; 5:10–12, (f) Practical – law fails, 2:16, (g) Experiential – freedom from the law yields positive results, 3:1–5; 4:6–7; submission to the law induces bondage, 4:8–10; 4:15; 5:1,4.

7. PAUL'S TEACHING CONCERNING FREEDOM FROM MOSAISM CORRELATES WITH A HIGH DOCTRINE OF THE SPIRIT

In Gal.3:1–5 Paul speaks of an experiential 'receiving' of the Spirit which could be recalled as a memorable event. In 5:19 the works of the flesh are not said to be 'revealed' by the law; rather they are 'obvious'. One who 'walks in the Spirit' should not need Mosaism to detect immorality, impurity, licentiousness, and so on. Meditation upon a codified document is unnecessary. The characteristics of the fruit of the Spirit do not include any reintroduction of the law. In the Torah the love-requirement is found amidst lists of ritual requirements; yet the Spirit will lead into love as a first priority. Paul puts love first in the list of the various aspects of the fruit of the Spirit. The remainder of the list are aspects of the life of the Spirit that will follow once Christian love is practised. By living in such a way the Christian 'fulfils the law' without directly focusing upon the law.

When one does focus on Mosaism this does not lead to the fulfilling of the law. Rather, legalists lose their joy (4:15), struggle to find sanctification by the flesh (3:1–5), forget the way they received the Spirit (3:6–9), fall into bondage and produce only slaves as converts (4:21–31). They cease to run well (5:7). Life becomes burdensome and the 'easy burden' of love is forgotten (6:2).

8. THE ALTERNATIVE TO RIGHTEOUSNESS BY LAW IS RIGHTEOUSNESS BY THE SPIRIT

The Spirit is present in the Christian. He enables love. It is through love that faith serves God. God requires the obedience of 'sowing to the Spirit'. The works of the flesh are (presumably again through the

Spirit) obvious to the Christian. The Christian 'keeps in step with' the Spirit and thus fulfils the law. This kind of life is freedom. It motivates the Christian because it is presently and eschatologically rewarding.

9. THE LAW IS FULFILLED INDIRECTLY BY WALKING IN THE SPIRIT AND THE PRACTICE OF CHRISTIAN LOVE

There is striking paradox at this point. Although not 'under' the law, the Christian fulfils it. Looking solely to the power of the Spirit, believers thus fulfil that which they were not attending to, the Mosaic law. By focusing on the Spirit they keep and more-than-keep the lower level, the Torah the original purpose of which was to restrain the sins of Israel. The Christian fulfils the Torah, but not by being 'under' it. To 'fulfil' the law means to more-than-keep it. It is to live at such a level that the Mosaic law is outclassed.

PAUL, THE LAW AND LEGALISM

It will be seen that I am not wholly convinced by the 'paradigm shift'[65] that has taken place in recent years, largely due to the work of H.Räisänen and E.P.Sanders[66]. The two have a good deal in common (and each had access to the other's manuscript). Both work with only six letters of the Pauline corpus (Romans, 1 and 2 Corinthians, Galatians, Philippians and 1 Thessalonians). Both build on Sanders's 1963 article, 'The Apostle Paul and the Introspective Conscience . . .' . Both consciously oppose what is often called the 'Lutheran orthodox' approach to Paul's view of the law. Sanders's earlier work, *Paul and Palestinian Judaism*, had urged that Paul was not struggling to 'find a gracious God'; in the contemporary setting Paul would see the Israelite's good works as the response by one already in covenant with God, maintaining his position within the covenant relationship.

Räisänen and Sanders argue that Paul does not have a unified and coherent view of the law. Räisänen points to five areas in which he believes Paul says conflicting things concerning the law. (i) Paul is said to work with differing concepts of the law at different points. Thus while he generally believes that the law was given to Israel alone, at other points he argues that the gentiles also come within its embrace. Also while he sometimes seems to postulate no divisions within the law yet in practice he focuses upon its ethical aspects. (ii) While Paul seems at times to abrogate the law he elsewhere seems to envisage a continuing role for it. (iii) Paul both argues that the law can be fulfilled yet also teaches that to do so is impossible. (iv) At some points Paul denies that the law can 'give life' while saying elsewhere that it has a life-giving purpose (Rom.7:10). (v) Paul utterly denies that the law is a gateway to salvation yet in Romans 9–11 refers to Israel's continuing significance as an elect nation.

Sanders maintains much the same viewpoint with regard to the first, second and fourth items mentioned.

There is not space to survey all the issues involved or offer a detailed reply. Brief comments must suffice.

(i) Sanders is surely right to see that Paul's view of justification involves not only a rejection of legalism but also a rejection of the Mosaic covenant. The argument of Gal.3:15–4:7 and 2 Co.3 imply as much.

(ii) I think Räisänen is right to argue that in Rom.9–11 Paul sees a future for the nation of Israel (although in the light of 9:6 not all would agree), and that this may be in tension with Galatians 3–4. Yet the tension is not as great as Räisänen suggests. The argument in Rom.9–11 does not generally (outside 9:4) go back to Moses; rather it goes back to 'the fathers'. Paul views Israel as having a hope based not on the Torah but on God's faithfulness to Abraham.

(iii) Räisänen contends (against Sanders) that Paul assumes a more 'legalistic' religion than is visible in the Jewish documents of the same period. One may question however whether popular religion of Paul's day was as free from legalism as the written works of the age. Is Paul's polemic aimed at erudite, intelligent, contemporary theology? Paul's polemic targets *sin* in whatever form it comes. If his life's work involved popular evangelism, his written works were likely to be countering something popular rather than something academically respected by the rabbis. It is arguable that by Paul's standards contemporary Judaism was legalistic, as indeed is every religion in human history, including some deviant versions of the Christian faith, which Paul would have regarded as 'another gospel'. 'Covenantal nomism' is still a form of religion that Paul would have called 'being perfected by the flesh'.

(iv) A major question concerns the exegesis of Rom.2:12–16,25–29. Räisänen thinks non-Christian gentiles are in view. Possibly, yet there is much to be said for the alternative view that the focus is on Christian gentiles. If Räisänen's exegesis of Rom.2 is not correct the problem of Paul's consistency is not so great.

(v) My own view is that Paul's statements concerning freedom from, yet fulfilment of, the Torah are consistent. *The Christian who walks in the Spirit deliberately fulfils the Torah accidentally*. A consideration of this proposition will go far to resolve the tensions in Paul's statements concerning the law. The law is 'established' but *not* by the Christian's being *under* it. Paul seems to have antinomian leanings in that he teaches the abolition of the Mosaic covenant, but then he has a surprising twist of thought in which the law is fulfilled, despite its abolition, by the Christian's walking in the Spirit.

(vi) The tensions that Räisänen and Sanders point to would perhaps be resolved if it were accepted that Paul can view the law on two levels. He can look at it simplistically. Viewed thus, the law restrained sin by means of fear of punishment. It was tagged on to the gospel, but was no part of the gospel. It was never 'of faith' but was given to define *visible*, *public* sin and so restrain it until the Seed should come. Yet (in Romans) the last of the ten commandments suggested a deeper way of viewing the law. Thus there can be a duality in Paul's view of the law. Looked at simplistically the law held no terrors for him. He had been a moral, upright Pharisee. No one could 'blame' him for any transgression. Yet he knew also of a deeper way of looking at it.

These brief and sketchy comments are not intended as a complete statement of my position concerning Romans and other Pauline material, but as a hint that suggests the task of finding harmony in Paul has perhaps not been carried forward as far as it could in the works of Sanders and Räisänen.

(vii) One matter seems to be of special importance. When discussing Paul's view of the law, Reformation traditionalists – and many others also – assume that Paul is arguing against justification by law-keeping. However it seems that too little consideration has been given to the fact that many of Paul's statements concerning the law are linked not with his doctrine of *justification* but with his doctrine concerning *godliness*. In Rom.7:5f. (for example) freedom from the law results in *fruitfulness*. Phil.3 is concerned not simply with justification but with experiencing Christ's power, reaching the *exanastasis*, receiving the prize for one's labours. Paul focuses as much if not more on *life over the course of many years* than upon the mode of entry into the Christian community. This suggests that Paul is much more 'antinomian' than is often thought. For him, Mosaism hinders not only justification but every aspect of the Christian life. This radical combination of quasi-antinomianism combined with fulfilment of the law indirectly is an insufficiently explored paradox in Paul's teaching. While Sanders's and Räisänen's works contain much interesting exegesis, it appears that they have not grasped Paul's view of freedom from the law in all of its aspects. R.G.Gundry makes a similar point. Where Sanders thinks the subject of Galatians is the condition on which Gentiles enter the people of God and not how one stays in the people of God, Gundry takes a contrary view and rightly says that 'the question of staying in is the issue, at least the primary one in Galatians'.[67] Our interpretation above has confined itself largely to Galatians, and these barest hints concerning a wider perspective must suffice.

SOME OBJECTIONS CONSIDERED

Since I have assumed that Paul's view is to be taken as a norm for the Christian, it is well that some objections to Paul's view be considered – or at least to my exposition of his views. One obvious question is: *does not Christian godliness require definition and content?* What will define the nature of Christian godliness if not the Mosaic law or an ethical code derived from it? Is not 'obedience to the Spirit' altogether too vague a concept? Might not the Mosaic law define what that obedience actually is? J.B.Webster comments: 'Any talk about human obligation remains very abstract and formal if it does not actually specify the shape that human life takes in entering into God's revealed purpose'.[68] One might answer as follows:

1. However troubled one might be about the 'vagueness' in the concept of 'obedience to the Spirit', it is a problem which Paul did not seem to have. Paul did believe that the Spirit's ministry is adequate to lead and to motivate. He did not make much use of Mosaic law in giving structure to Christian godliness.

2. This does not mean, however, that Christian godliness is beyond verbal discussion. One can put into words the way the Spirit leads, as the admonitory passages of the New Testament make clear.

3. On the other hand it is doubtful whether decisions concerning particular problems may be resolved by casuistry. L.B.Smedes asks us to

> consider an armed man trapped in a bank. He takes everyone in the bank hostage and threatens to kill them all. You tell him that he will be allowed to go free if he puts down his guns and surrenders.You lie, you know he will be arrested.

Smedes goes on to say that this is a case of 'justified lying'.[69] But where in this is there room for the direct leading of the Spirit? A simple moralistic decision concerning whether or not a lie is justified in this situation ignores the possibility that 'at that time you will given what to say'. I do not suggest that the moral issue is unimportant; I merely observe that Smedes gives no scope for the leading of the Spirit. Yet it is precisely this unusual help that was promised the disciples in a critical situation (Mt.10:19). Smedes is concerned about casuistry. The New Testament makes more of the direct help of the Spirit. This leads to another question: might not different Christians be led differently amidst the crises of life? Might not the same Christian be led differently in different but similar situations? This would not be the case if it were simply a matter of finding the correct sub-sub-section of a moral code to apply, (which might in any case be difficult in the life situation that Smedes envisages).

4. The fact that the leading of the Spirit transcends the Torah does not mean that the leading of the Spirit produces anything less than the morality of the Torah. There is therefore an *a posteriori* check on anything claimed to be the leading of the Spirit. If the morality of the Torah was breached, then the leading of the Spirit was not being followed. In the last analysis the righteousness of the law *is* fulfilled. Paul dies to the law in order to live unto God by the Spirit. But living unto God by the power of the Spirit will fulfil the law – and *a posteriori* may be seen to have done so.

5. No doubt it will be said that there may be much self-deception about the leading of the Spirit. Agreed! But there is also much self-deception concerning obedience to the law! One only has to consider

the New Testament presentation concerning the scribes and Pharisees
to note that high legalism may be combined with self-deception. For
example, amidst the hatred and deceit involved in the trials of Jesus his
enemies stay outside the palace of Pontius Pilate to ensure they keep
the regulations concerning ceremonial uncleanness (Jn.18:28)! Here
surely is *moral* antinomianism, *law-abiding* sin. Why should it be
thought that only a doctrine of 'obedience to the Spirit' leads to self-
deception but that the law will do otherwise? Is it not the most
grotesque self-deception when men say of Jesus 'we have a law and by
that law he ought to die'?

   6. It may be suggested that Paul does use the law in exhortation.
The fact, however, is that such a paraenetic use is rare. Of course
much depends on what one means by 'the law'. One finds a variety of
contradictory statements about this. C.F.H.Henry thinks for example
that 'The first commandment is everywhere interwoven in the New
Testament' and goes through each command of the decalogue seeking
to show its presence in the New Testament.[70] Other writers can
maintain that the decalogue is conspicuously not present in the New
Testament. How can there be such a vast contradiction? Determining
whether the New Testament does or does not use the decalogue should
surely be a simple matter. The reason for the disagreement is failure to
note how the content of the decalogue overlaps with the righteousness
of the New Testament *without* any citation of the decalogue. Henry
succeeds in demonstrating a large *overlapping of content* in the
commands of the New Testament and the Decalogue.[71] (He is weak
however in his comments concerning the Sabbath, where an overlapping of content is difficult to find.) But to accept that there is an
overlapping of content[72] and to assert that the decalogue is cited,
expounded or urged are two different things. The righteousness of the
New Testament fulfils the Torah. One may therefore expect the
admonitions and discussions concerning obedience to overlap in
content with the decalogue. With the exception of the Sabbath this is
precisely what one finds and one may in this sense accept all that
Henry writes. Yet he does not note that of the many references he
cites in five compactly written pages[73] few are in any way citations of
the decalogue. In other words he demonstrates an overlapping of
content, a proof that New Testament righteousness fulfils the decalogue. But he does not show that the New Testament urges the direct
authority of the decalogue. The only significant reference out of
almost fifty is Eph.6:1–4 (discussed below).

   When we examine seven Pauline epistles (although nothing different is found in the other six) we find that explicit use of the Pentateuch
in this way is conspicuous by its absence. *Romans* contains an appeal
for presentation of one's faculties to God (6:12f.,19), mystical union
with Jesus in order to become fruitful for God (7:4), appeals to resist
the flesh (Ro.8:12–13), to walk by the Spirit (8:13f.), to be sensitive to
the demands of love (ch.4). There are statements to the effect that the
leading of the Spirit will lead to the fulfilment of the law (Ro.13:8–10;

Gal.5). It is precisely by virtue of having died to the law that this is made possible. Yet there is no direct application of Pentateuchal demands in this. Where is the law cited in the many admonitions of Romans 12:1–15:13?

In *1 Corinthians* we find direct rebuke of the pride of the Corinthians and their glorying in wisdom, but the law is not brought in. One half expects citation of the law in the case of the immorality handled in ch.5 but it is not mentioned here, nor in chs.5 and 7, concerning marriage. One would not be surprised to find mention of the first three commandments in the section dealing with things offered to idols but they are absent. In the middle of the section Paul instead seems to treat the Mosaic law as an adiaphoron, and says (9:21) he is *ennomos to(i) Jesou*. I do not think this is a reference to any Pentateuchal demand.

Nor is Mosaism found in *2 Corinthians*. The section in 2 Cor.6:14–7:1 might well have mentioned the first three commandments but does not.

In *Galatians* the works of the flesh are 'obvious' (*phaneros*), not to be identified by meditating upon the Torah. Paul does not think it requires a codified document for us to know what 'love' is; he appears to believe that this primary requirement speaks for itself. One recalls Matt.7:12 where love means no more – and no less – than imaginatively reversing one's position in one's relationship to others and acting accordingly. Of course, Paul's letters contain discussions of conduct. Love is not beyond discussion in propositional terms.

In *1 Thessalonians* Paul has to comment on weaknesses and misdemeanours among the Thessalonians. He refers to sexual immorality (4:3), fraudulence (4:6), and idleness (4:11). One almost expects him to cite: 'Six days you shall labour', but he prefers to appeal to the Thessalonians *directly*, taking it for granted that they know he is right in what he says. In the past *his* words – not Pentateuchal words – had come to them 'with the Holy Spirit and with deep conviction' (1:5). He expects that his *direct* exhortations, still without specific reference to the law, will carry the same kind of authority, conveyed by the Spirit.

We find much the same in *Philippians*. Where are the Pentateuchal citations here? They do not exist. There is rivalry and disunity at Philippi, but Paul handles the matter directly and appeals to the story of Jesus without pressing the law upon them.

In point of fact there are very few references to the law in Paul's appeals for Christian godliness. The most important passage in this connection is *Ephesians 6:1–4*. Yet in this case the total flow of argument must be noted. A turn of thought begins at 5:18 or perhaps even earlier. Paul appeals first for the fulness of the Spirit (5:18), then in a series of participial clauses describes the lordship of the Spirit. It will involve song (5:19) and fellowship (5:19), heartfelt thankfulness (5:20) and mutual submission (5:21). From this point – without even using a main verb in 5:22 – Paul flows into a section concerning three different sets of relationship (5:22–.33; 6:1–4; 6:5–9). In this context the law is mentioned (6:2). Is the apostle doing anything more than arguing that to be filled with the Spirit will lead to the fulfilling of the law? Here too, however, he does approach the matter of the law *directly* but via the mention of the fulness of the Spirit. Is this at all different from Rom.8:1–4 ('What the law could not do . . . God did . . . in order that the righteous requirements of the law might be fulfilled')? To be sure, Paul mentions the law: in the long run the ten commandments *are* fulfilled by those who obey the Spirit. The question is: how does this come about? Not, apparently, by putting oneself *directly* under the law but by being full of the Spirit. If one walks by the Spirit deliberately one fulfils the law accidentally. Paul scarcely mentions the Torah. When he does so in Eph.6:2 it is in the context of Eph.5:18–6:9. It is linked to the outworking of life in the Holy Spirit.

Our conclusions stand. For Paul, Mosaism fails whether as a means of justification or of sanctification. While he does not envisage a diminished spirituality he asserts the abolition of the law as the focus for the Christian. Recourse to the law results only in diminished spirituality. The law was a temporary measure to restrain sin. In the post-Pentecostal epoch a greater measure of the experience of the Spirit has replaced the function of the law in the life of God's people. The Spirit will lead into love as a first priority. The law is fulfilled indirectly by walking in the Spirit.

10

Matthew's Gospel and the Mosaic Law

We now consider our theme in the context of the Gospel of Matthew, the gospel that has been considered emphatic in its treatment of 'law'. I am inclined to date the Gospel in the AD 60s and assume that it was redacted in a situation of sensitivity to the break between Israel and the church. I think it likely that Matthew's milieu is Palestinian and that the Gospel does in fact go back to the apostle Matthew, either as being himself the editor-author of the tradition, or as a main contributor to it.

More important is the question of whether Matthew is writing against a background of antinomianism. Some have thought that (in R.H. Smith's words) 'he was deeply disturbed by a permissive or antinomian trend apparent among some charismatics.'[1] Others disagree.[2] My view, the basis of which will appear, is that Matthew is arguing on two fronts. He is concerned about licentiousness. Yet the kind of righteousness he looks for is not legalist, far less Pharisaic legalism. If we find him taking a balanced position which is neither licentious nor legalist we shall know he was aware of the two dangers.

The question of historical authenticity seriously affects our interpretation. If, for example, Jesus' words concerning flight on a sabbath (Mt.24:20) reflect something that Jesus himself actually said or something in the ministry of Jesus, there is no need to see at that point a reflection of the sabbatarianism of the Matthean church. Travel on the sabbath would be restricted in the time of Jesus. If however this saying is exclusively a Matthean invention then we are seeing Matthew's view of the law rather than a glimpse of the days of Jesus' ministry. J.P.Meier can say that the anti-Jewish statements in Matthew 'are aimed at possible abuse within the church'.[3] This approach may lead us to interpret Matthew as more legalistic than he really is. The question is a large one. I believe Matthew has compiled his own material in his own way but the traditional material he is using is basically reliable. This means that the picture of Jesus' ministry around AD 30 is not merely a reflection of the 'Matthean church'.

In stating any thesis with regard to the teaching of any of the gospels it is easy for a slanted approach to be maintained 'if the author is free to choose which sections of the gospel will be treated to verify his point.'[4] I shall heed Meier's warning by considering the unfolding of the gospel. My presentation differs in this respect from that of scholars such as Bornkamm.[5]

MATTHEW 1:1–4:11

Here Matthew presents the royal Messiah.[6] Jesus is the fulfilment of the promises to Abraham and David (1:1–17), miraculously introduced into the world by virginal conception, also in fulfilment of Davidic promises (1:18–25).Chapter 2 also revolves around the theme of the kingship of Jesus (2:2). The unresponsiveness of Israel is revealed, for although the Jerusalem leaders are well informed (2:4–6) their ruler is hostile toward Jesus. Instead, gentiles are present to welcome him (2:1f., 9–12).

The next theme is the kingly rule of the Davidic messiah. John preaches the imminent arrival of the kingdom (3:1–6), revealing that membership of the kingdom comes not through Abrahamic descent (3:9) but through the fruit that befits repentance and the bestowal of the Spirit by Jesus (3:1–12). Membership of the nation does not suffice for experience of the kingdom. In 3:13–17 Jesus submits to John's baptism, which is needed if he is 'to fulfil all righteousness'. He receives the endowment of the Spirit and the voice from heaven (combining Ps.42 with Is.42) reaffirms his sonship and commissions him to be the suffering servant of Is.40–66.

Jesus' sonship is the object of Satanic temptation ('If you are the Son . . . . If you are the Son . . . .', Mt.4:3,6), inciting Jesus to proceed to glory without fulfilling the call to suffering that was implicit in 3:17.

Thus five themes have been introduced in Mt.1:1–4:11: (i) the Davidic messiahship, (ii) Jesus' sonship in relation to God, (iii) fulfilment of the Old Testament, (iv) the attainment of glory only through suffering, (v) reception of Jesus by gentiles rather that by Israel. Although Matthew wished to adopt a particular stance with regard to the Torah, yet the Torah is not central in his opening and programmatic section.

MATTHEW 4:12–9:34

This section describes Jesus' preaching at Nazareth (4:1–17) and the call of the disciples (4:18–22). Matthew adds a summary statement concerning Jesus' public ministry (4:23–25), a sample of Jesus' teaching (5:1–8:1), and a section that revolves almost entirely around Jesus' miracles (8:2–9:34).

The main focus is on Jesus' relation to the kingdom. His preaching is the gospel of the kingdom (4:23). His teaching (5:1–8:1) unfolds around the same theme. Jesus first describes the characteristics of the members of the kingdom (5:1–12); their effect on the world will be to preserve (5:13) and illuminate (5:14–16).

Matthew 5:17–20 (considered more fully below) is primarily concerned with the mission of Jesus. In relation to the Old Testament the purpose is not destructive but consummatory. No status or prestige in his kingdom comes to anyone who does not act and teach in accordance with such a Messianic mission.

Matthew 5:21–48 take up the point of 5:17–20. In the six well-known antitheses we find Jesus relating to the Torah as expounded by the rabbinical thought of his day. 5:21 (liability to the council) and 5:43 (hating one's enemy) allude to developments of the law. Jesus radicalizes the law, interpreting murder as anger (5:21–26), lust as something that begins in the heart (5:27–30), divorce as something that generally should not occur at all (5:31–32), vows as something to be left aside because the disciple's speech is to be characterized by simplicity and truthfulness (5:33–37). The magisterial instructions concerning revenge are replaced by the requirement of humble non-vindictive kindness towards personal enemies (5:38–42) and the qualified love of the rabbis replaced by the unqualified love of Jesus, a love which is called 'perfection' (5:43–48).

Matthew 6:1–33 are about the practical and religious side of life. Ostentation is to be shunned, else reward will be lost (6:1). This principle is elucidated in three contexts (6:2–4; 6:5–15; 6:16–18). The member of the kingdom is to be characterized neither by covetousness (6:19–24) nor anxiety (6:25–34). The kingdom is involved in all these. The model prayer includes prayer for the kingdom (6:10); the cure for both covetousness and anxiety is the seeking of the kingdom (6:33).

Matthew 7:1–27 introduces the theme of judgement. One kind of judgement is to be avoided (7:1–5), another is to be practised (7:6). Any needs within the kingdom may be sought by asking, knocking, seeking. God will give all that is needed (7:7–11). The basic rule is to treat others by reversing positions and seeing how one would wish oneself to be treated. This puts in a nutshell the gist of 5:3–7:11. This is the fulfilling of the Old Testament.

This sub-section of Matthew concludes with an appeal to enter such a kingdom (7:13f), and a warning against those who would deceive (7:15–20) and who are not concerned to do God's will (7:21–23). The parable about heeding or not heeding Jesus' words comes in here (7:24–27), and the section concludes with a note concerning the crowd's reaction (7:28f.) and the departure of the disciples with Jesus (8:1).

NOT TO DESTROY BUT TO FULFIL (5:17–20)

Matthew 5:17–20 is of the first importance in any study of Jesus' attitude to the law. The verses deserve to be studied as a whole but have often been regarded as a series of distinct units, each of which may be studied with a view to discerning its 'setting in life'.[7] Matthew, however, presents this material with connecting words. 'Therefore' (5:19) looks back to vv.17f.; 'for' (5:20) brings the small unit to a conclusion.

Matthew 5:17 The opening words, 'Do not suppose . . . ', seem to envisage that the mission of Jesus might be misunderstood. The aorist has the force of 'Do not begin to think . . . '. Jesus' friendship with 'sinners' could give rise to misunderstanding. To understand the phrase as mere rhetoric is surely a weak interpretation. The two occurrences of the phrase in this gospel (5:17; 10:34) reflect upon the possibility that the nature of Jesus' mission might be misunderstood.

It has been debated whether *ton nomon he tous prophetas* is to be understood conjunctively (referring to the totality of Scripture) or disjunctively (referring to the Torah on the one hand and the prophetic expectation or interpretation on the other). Nothing much hinges on the difference. Our main concern must be with the precise force of the antithesis between *katalusai* and *pleroo*.

1. It has been taken as pointing a contrast between abrogating the law in its totality and continuing the law *in its totality*. A.M. Honeyman speaks of 'unqualified acceptance and approval . . . .The Law is eternal and its most minute prescriptions retain its validity.'[8]

2. G. Bahnsen thinks it refers to 'the abiding validity of the law in exhaustive detail'.[9] However, he in fact allows for some parts of the law to be abrogated.

3. R. Alderson apparently thinks it implies that the moral law continues to be a rule of life.[10]

4. Others understand *pleroo* to mean 'supplements'; Jesus enlarges or 'fills out' the moral law.[11]

5. Some think the two contrasting verbs focus mainly on Jesus' obedience.[12]

6. E.Kevan believed the main point was that Jesus came to expound the law in a deeper way.[13]

7. J.A.Alexander and B.B.Warfield thought the main point was that Jesus would cause the law to be kept.[14]

A convincing exegesis must satisfy several conditions.

(i) The meanings attributed to *katalusai* and *pleroo* must be adequately attested.

(ii) The interpretation of *pleroo* must be applicable both to the law and to the prophets.

(iii) Any view that finds Jesus asserting the normativity of only a part of the Torah is suspect.

(iv) Our interpretation should conform to the whole thrust of Matthew's gospel. The programmatic statement in 5:17–20 must cohere with vv.21–48 and Matthew's gospel in its totality.

(v) We must accept H.Ljungman's evidence that *plerosai* is not necessarily the equivalent of Hebrew *qum* and that there may at times be a difference between *plerosai* (where the emphasis may at times be of utter completeness) and *telein* or *teleioun* (which often means 'terminate' without the note of distinctive completeness). In other words the matter cannot be dismissed simply by equating *plerosa(i)* and *telein / qum*.[15]

The central emphasis of Matthew 5:17 is likely, in my opinion, to focus on Jesus' personal keeping of the law, in fulfilment of the forward-looking character of the Torah and the prophets. Other interpretations seem less convincing.

The first opinion mentioned above does not seem to take seriously the indications within Matthew that the law, although upheld and fulfilled, is fulfilled *not* by mere continuation of its traditional force but by some reorientation in the light of the coming of Jesus. However this approach is to be much commended in that it does take seriously the fact that Matthew is referring to every part and every aspect of the Torah.

The second and third do not take seriously the fact that it is the whole Torah that is in view. It is not possible to leave out the ritual element (*pace* Bahnsen) and it is not possible to leave out both the ceremonial and the civil aspects (*pace* Wenham, Alderson, and others). Although some distinction is made within the law (v.41),[16] the tripartite division into ceremonial, civil and moral law characteristic of Thomas's *Summa Theologiae* cannot be used to restrict the meaning of 'the law . . . one yodh . . . one projection'.

The fourth view takes *pleroo* in a way that does not correspond to the use of the verb in Matthew's gospel, and neglects the fact that Jesus came to 'fulfil . . .the prophets'. Although it might be argued that Jesus 'supplements' the prophets yet that is not the way the verb is used in the well-known 'fulfilment quotations' of this gospel.[17]

Kevan's view, the sixth of those mentioned, is inadequate in that the verb *pleroo* does not mean 'expound'. Nor has Kevan done justice to the Christ-centred nature of the instructions in Matthew 5:21–48.

It seems that the most satisfactory way of understanding Matthew 5:17 is to take it to refer to Jesus' personal keeping of the law, in fulfilment of the forward-looking character of the Torah and the prophets, for the following reasons:

1. It takes *plerosai* in the sense that is common throughout Matthew's gospel. It is well-known that one of the distinctives of the first gospel is its concern for the fulfilment of the Old Testament. It is likely that *plerosai* will have the meaning in 5:17 that it has constantly throughout the first gospel.

2. It allows *plerosai* to have the same meaning both with reference to the law and the prophets.

3. Such a meaning of *plerosai* is well attested.

4. It coheres with the exposition of Matthew as a whole, as we shall see. If Matthew's teaching is *not* coherent the interpretation of Matthew 5:17 must remain largely a matter of guesswork. Matthew must be allowed to show us what he means.

Matthew 5:18 The two time references in Mt.5:18, both of which commence with *heos*, imply that the law has a task to perform, and that the law will continue, more stable than the fabric of the world, until its task is completed.

Do 'until heaven and earth pass away' and 'until all things come to pass' refer to the same time when the law reaches its terminus? Or is 'until all things come to pass' an open-ended phrase suggesting that the requirements of the law might come to pass at some stage within world history, but without suggesting that the *eschaton* is the occasion of such fulfilment? Could it be that different aspects of the law might come to be fulfilled at different times and that emphasis is to be placed upon *panta*? In which case could it be that *some* things might 'come to pass' before the *eschaton* but 'all things' will not be fulfilled before the end of the age?

There are thus three possibilities concerning the terminus of the law. (i) Jesus himself is the occasion of its being fulfilled. (ii) The *eschaton* or end of the age (see Mt.28:20) is the terminus of the law. (ii) Some aspects of the law could be fulfilled at the coming of Jesus, but not until the end of the age are 'all things' fulfilled. The last-mentioned possibility is itself capable of being taken in more than one way. Is it that some parts of the law are fulfilled but the whole is not fulfilled until the end? Or is it that the law is totally fulfilled by Jesus but it will continue until 'all things' are fulfilled, i.e. until disciples fulfil it and the law-breakers or law-disparagers (see v.19) are judged by it? If the former is the case this leaves us with a further question: what are the aspects that are fulfilled or unfulfilled at any given point?

An exegesis of 5:17 is more likely if it avoids contradiction with 5:21–48. No one who studies the careful composition of 5:17–20 can imagine that Matthew's view of the law has not been thought through. Any interpretation that allows no modification in the law at all is unlikely in view of 5:21–48 where, at the very least, there is a change in viewpoint between what 'you have heard' and what 'I (Jesus) say unto you'.

Verse 18a uses the language of strong affirmation in explanation of v.17. The verse has four parts: *amen gar lego humin,* / *heos an parelthe(i) ho ouranos kai he ge/ iota hen e mia keraia ou me parelthe(i) apo tou nomou* / *heos an panta genetai.*18a is evidently explaining why the law must not be disparaged but must be fulfilled. It is unsatisfactory to give a weakened meaning to 'For'. Particles and seams are important in interpretation. The introductory formula gives christological heightening and prepares the way for the 'I say unto you' of 5:21–48. Jesus draws attention to himself as well as making a statement concerning the Old Testament scriptures.

In v.18b the associations of the verb in the Bible (Ps.148:6 LXX; Mt.24:35; Mk.13:31; Lk.16:17), in rabbinic writings[18], and elsewhere (1 Clement 27:5) all suggest that the *eschaton* is in view. Verse 18c shows that every minute part of the law is involved. This warns the modern Christian off any interpretations of 5:17–20 which see only the 'moral' parts of the law being affirmed.

Verse 18c is the crucial clause ('until all things take place'). *Two*
time clauses (5:18a, 18d, occur alongside one another. There is a
parallel in Mt.24:34f., where a further allusion to heaven and earth
(24:35) immediately follows a time clause when the time involved is
not the *eschaton* but takes place within a generation. (I assume here
the exegesis of Mt.24 presented below.) This should caution us that
the interpretation of v.18c is not determined by v.18b.

The natural meaning of *ginomai* is 'happen'. This coheres with
plerosai in v.17. It resembles the usage elsewhere in Matthew
(1:22;21:4; 26:54,56). Apparently we once again have a statement
that the law – every minute part of it – has a destiny to fulfil. The
fulfilment of its destiny is certain, more settled than the fabric of the
universe.

If *ginomai* means 'happen', ta *panta* must refer to events. There is
no antecedent to the phrase. When do 'all things . . . happen'? The
very structure and proportioning of the gospel puts heavy emphasis on
the events of Jesus' final entry into Jerusalem, his death and resurrection. Yet it becomes clear that the death and resurrection of Jesus do
not immediately usher in the end of the epoch. Jesus will be with his
disciples until the 'end of the age'. 'All things' must refer to events that
Matthew envisages must take place before 'the end' comes. This will
involve at least the following: the fulfilment of predictions concerning
Jesus' death and resurrection (Mt.16:21; 17:9,12,22f.; 20:17–19;
20:28), the removal of the kingdom of God from the leaders of Israel
(21:43), the fall of Jerusalem (21:44; 24:2) and in preliminaries
(24:28),[19] the undated 'coming of the Son of Man' (24:36–25:46), as
well as the climactic events of Mt.26–28. Matthew is referring to *events*
that *must* happen. The 'all things' must surely refer to the totality of
the events that he has in view.

What then is the total impact of Matthew 5:18? Its phrasing is
probably intended. to be enigmatic. It strongly affirms the validity of
the law, as part of the Scriptures, until the end of the epoch and
subject to the further qualification 'until all things happen'. Matthew
does not use simply *heos* (which could imply that the terminus is fixed
and known, but *heos an*, which implies that the terminus is dependent
on some circumstance or condition.[20] It could be translated 'until
whatever time'. If 'the end' comes in stages the fulfilment of the law
may come in stages also. If v.17 has referred to the *personal* fulfilment
of the law by Jesus it will also focus on the gospel events in the life,
death and resurrection of Jesus. Yet the reference to the end of the
eschaton (as it seems to be) suggests that a fuller fulfilment of the law is
yet to come.

The fact that verses 17f. move into verses 19–20 with the *disciples* in
view suggests that the law is initially fulfilled in the ministry of Jesus
(cf. v.17) but will be further fulfilled by Jesus' disciples. The law will
abide 'until *whatever* time all things happen' – a phrase that allows for
variation in the time that things happen. The fact that the disciples
'fulfil' the law does not necessarily mean (and 5:21–48 will suggest it

does not mean) that they are simplistically 'under' the Torah. Rather it means that *a posteriori* their manner of living will be seen to have fulfilled the Torah. Their righteousness will outstrip that of scribes and Pharisees. Then at the *eschaton* the law will cease altogether.

Matthew 5:19 brings a change of viewpoint. In v.17 the emphasis was on Jesus himself ('I have come to fulfil'). In v.18 the emphasis was on the details of the law but the solemn affirmation of Jesus ('Truly I say to you') kept the person of Jesus in view. Now v.19 builds upon what has been said ('Whoever therefore') and focuses not upon Jesus' fulfilling of the law but upon the disciple and the Christian teacher, who must not disparage or loosen any detail of the law, but rather honour it. The word *therefore* indicates the connection between Jesus' honouring the law and the honour accorded it by others.

Again what is in view is the totality of the law. Even the least command must not be disparaged. Also in view is the Christian teacher; anyone who slackens (*luse(i)*) in their personal life or Christian ministry will suffer a reduced status in the kingdom. Conversely the person who practises the total law and recommends such in their teaching will gain a position of eminence in the kingdom. There is a 'dispensational' element in this; *before* the law has been fulfilled it retains total validity.

Matthew 5:20 brings the sayings in 5:17–20 to a climax. The opening words, 'I say to you', sound like a conclusion. The introductory particle *gar* shows that the verse continues to explain what has been asserted is vv.17–19. At this point three questions tease the expositor: (i) What is the implied 'righteousness of the scribes and Pharisees' that is being excelled? (ii) In what way does Matthew envisage its being excelled? (iii) What is it to 'enter the kingdom'?

THE RIGHTEOUSNESS OF THE SCRIBES AND PHARISEES

The 'scribes' are the prestigious students of theological and juridical knowledge, held in high esteem by the majority of the people. In Matthew's Gospel they appear as closely allied with the priesthood (Mt.2:4; 16:21; 20:18; 21:15; 26:3), with the elders (the other 'lay' members of the Sanhedrin, Mt.16:21; 26:57) and with the Pharisees (Mt.5:20; 12:38; 15:1; 23:1–29).

The scribes are mentioned 24 times in this gospel. They are portrayed as well-informed concerning the birth-place of the Messiah (2:4). Mt.5:20 implies that they are righteous in *some* sense. Their manner of teaching lacks authority (7:29). One scribe is portrayed as zealous in his support of Jesus and yet unaware of the suffering involved (8:1:-20). The clause following Mt.8:1f. ('*another* of the disciples', 8:21) implies that this scribe was a disciple of Jesus.

More often the scribes are depicted as hostile to Jesus. Some of them are shown inwardly accusing Jesus of blasphemy (9:3). They are associated with the Pharisees in 12:38, where they crave an external proof of Messiahship, a craving which Jesus condemns as 'evil and adulterous' (12:38f.). Yet Matthew is not invariably hostile to the scribes, and can envisage some as disciples of the kingdom of heaven (12:52).

Matthew 15:1 is important as showing how Matthew envisages their 'righteousness'. This includes zeal for the traditions of the elders, yet may be combined with evasion of greater matters of obedience (fulfilment of the fifth commandment) and is portrayed by Jesus as external ('their heart is far away') and of human origin ('precepts of men') only. Their 'righteousness' is compatible with non-recognition of Jesus and the perpetration of the injustice of Jesus' trial (16:21). In 17:10 they are again (see 2:4) viewed as erudite in the text of the Old Testament yet unaware of its significance and fulfilment (17:11f.). Mt.20:18f. is similar to 16:2 but goes further in defining the precise mode of suffering imposed by scribes and their associates. The preliminary mental ('mock') and physical ('scourge') cruelty is also mentioned.

In the Matthean description of the events of Palm Sunday the scribes appear as hostile to the authority Jesus has claimed and the adulation he has received (21:15).

The fullest treatment of the scribes in Matthew occurs at Mt.23: 1–39. They are presented as expositors – even as accurate expositors – of the law (23:2f.) yet as living in a manner inconsistent with their own expository gifts (v.3), imposing a strain on the common people (v.4a), lacking compassion (v:4b), concerned to receive praise (v.12), and about externalities (v.5), and about titles of prestige (vv.23ff.). They are zealous, yet their zeal is not the fruit of compassion but self-oriented proselytism (v.15). They are casuists, expert in subtle but evasive distinctions (vv.16–22).

Thus the 'righteousness' of the scribes appears as involving intense loyalty to the minutiae of the Torah, yet relating to external matters only ('the outside of the cup'). It involved gross inconsistency ('You strain out a gnat and swallow a camel'). Mt.23:28 defines the 'righteousness of the scribes'; they are 'outwardly righteous'.

References to the scribes in Matthew's passion narrative accord with the description of the scribes earlier in the gospel. They participate in Jesus' arrest (26:57) and join the chief priests and elders in mocking him (27:41).

Matthew presents the 'righteousness' of the scribes as marked by three characteristics: externality; scriptural expertise combined with spiritual unperceptiveness; and lack of compassion despite external legality.

The association of 'scribes and Pharisees' tells us that in Matthew's view the two groups were closely allied. The Pharisees are mentioned thirty times in Matthew's Gospel. In eleven instances they appear in association with the scribes and share the portrayal considered above. In the remaining nineteen instances we learn more. We are introduced to them when Matthew mentions their response to the ministry of John the Baptist. They are eager to participate in the new movement (3:7) but unwilling to bring forth ethical fruit (3:8), and rely on their ancestry for acceptance with God (3:9). Along with the Sadducees (see 3:7; 16:1), they face the imminent judgement of God (3:10–12). They object to Jesus' sympathy with ruthless tax-collectors and outcast 'sinners'. The latter would include not only those living a flagrantly immoral life (murderers, robbers, deceivers, etc.), but also the common people who did not endorse the Pharisaic interpretation of the law, and who might follow a disapproved vocation.

A significant statement concerning the Pharisees occurs in 21:45, where the imminent judgement of God is predicted and the Pharisees rightly perceive that Jesus includes them among those whose destruction is near.

At one point in Mt.23:1–39 the Pharisees are singled out for combining external righteousness with inner impurity (23:36). Matthew's last mention of them shows them maintaining their malice towards Jesus after his death (27:62). The 'righteousness' of the Pharisees is a term that can only be used with sarcasm.

In what way, then, should the righteousness of the scribe and Pharisee be exceeded? The immediate context (5:21–48) and the wider context (Mt.1–28) would suggest that Matthew saw this in terms of (i) internality as opposed to externality, and (ii) orientation to Jesus as opposed to orientation to the Mosaic law in itself. The fivefold 'I say unto you' of 5:21–48, together with other occasions when Jesus directed attention to himself, require us to see the greater righteousness as focusing on Jesus directly. Thus within the Sermon on the Mount Jesus speaks of suffering not for the law's sake but for his (5:11). Mt.5:17–20 itself primarily draws attention to Jesus ('I came to fulfil . . . I say to you'). Later Jesus will present himself as the one who speaks authoritatively concerning reward ('I say. . . They have their reward', 6:2, 5, 16), and concerning anxiety (6:25,29). More forcefully still, Jesus is the one who determines judgement. Jesus says to some, 'I never knew you' and allocates final sentence (7:23).

It is this radical change in orientation that enables us to say that in Matthew's view the Christian fulfils the law but does so not by focusing on the law but by focusing on Jesus directly. The point is not that the Christian does not keep the law but that his central interest is direct obedience to Jesus himself.

(iii) Another aspect of the righteousness that exceeds the righteousness of scribes and Pharisees must be sought in the love command. The crucial deficiency in scribes and Pharisees was that despite familiarity with the law they conspicuously lacked compassion.

Our third question concerning Matthew 5:20 must be: what does is mean to 'enter the kingdom of heaven'? (i) It may refer, in McNeile's words, to 'attaining to final bliss'.[21] (ii) It is possible to interpret the phrase of initial experience of salvation.[22] (iii) A third and preferable view takes the phrase to refer to one's ongoing experience of the powers of the kingdom of God. On this view it concerns something continuing and progressive.

Without jumping to final conclusions about Matthew's Gospel, we may say that five points are highlighted here.

(i) The law is greatly honoured. Every minute detail of the entire Torah is treated with reverence. On the basis of Mt.5:17–20 no reader could possibly say that Jesus wished to *disparage* the law or neglect the question of its fulfilment.

(ii) Every minute part of the law is revered. The Matthean Jesus honours the ritual of the law, the sabbath observances, the festivals. The Jesus of this pericope would have tithed dill and cummin.

(iii) The law has a task to fulfil in the history of the world. Through the law something had to 'happen' (*ginomai*). Like the prophetic ministry of the Old Testament, it has a forward look.

(iv) The events for which the law is designed and to which it points will be fulfilled. It will accomplish its goal.

(v) In some undefined manner the law is to be fulfilled in such a way that its most ardent supporters (scribes and Pharisees) will find their 'righteousness' exceeded.

' . . . BUT I SAY' (5:21–48)

The six units of this section lead us to ask: how is the Mosaic law being handled here? Is it being intensified so that the Mosaic requirement stands but is taken further? Is it being negated at any point? Is it being internalized? How do the requirements of Mt.5:21–48 compare with those of the Torah?

The first antithesis deals with murder versus the Spirit of reconciliation. Here the first part of the contrast combines a prohibition from the decalogue with an added phrase ('liable to the council') which summarizes judicial proceedings in the Old Testament (see Nu.35:12; Dt.17:8–13).[23]

In Jesus' counter-statement the law is radicalized, internalized, and reorientated to Jesus himself. It is radicalized in that much more is required of the disciple than merely abstaining from the crime of murder; also the judgement is heightened. It is internalized in that what it requires alludes to words, memory and attitudes as well as the actual deed of murder. It is reorientated in that Jesus' requirement mentions only himself. It does not involve abrogation in every respect; permission for murder is not given!

The second antithesis, which deals with adultery versus inner purity, also contains a prohibition from the decalogue. Jesus' counter-statement again radicalizes, internalizes and reorientates the command. It is radicalized in that the requirement goes further than the decalogue. It is heightened in that the judgement mentioned is Gehenna. It is internalized in that what it requires concerns the 'heart' rather than the magistrates. It is again reorientated to Jesus alone.

The third antithesis, which contrasts the permission of divorce in the Torah with Jesus' approach to marriage, contains a citation from Deuteronomy. It modifies the Torah in that a permission conceded in what was allowed as part of a civic code for Israel is altogether withdrawn. The focus of the passage is not on divorce as such but upon a subsequent remarriage. Dt.24:1–4: treats divorce as a practice already known and permits its continuance. The main point of the legislation is that a divorced woman who has contracted a second marriage must never remarry her first husband. The second marriage is regarded as legal. Contrary to some exegetical opinion, the reason for prohibiting remarrying the first partner seems to be that the first marriage set up a relationship that still exists and it would be a kind of 'incest' to go back to it after a second marriage. The first divorce does not put the partners back into their pre-marriage situation.

Over against the Torah, Jesus withdraws the regulation altogether. The exceptive clause is interpreted in widely different ways. I concur with the view that the exceptive clause allows divorce but does not permit remarriage.[24] However, the precise interpretation of the exceptive clause does not affect our particular concern. On any view the law's requirement is changed. The law is obviously viewed as less than ideal in its implications concerning marriage. But we need not postulate a criticism of the law. Its weakness may be viewed (as in Mt.19:3–9) as arising out of *human* weakness rather than from any defect in the law itself. Nevertheless here is a clear instance where the Mosaic requirement is considered inadequate for the member of the kingdom of God under the rule of Jesus.

It is notable however that what Jesus requires is not *less* than the law but something *higher* than the law. In this sense one cannot say that the standard of the law is actually abrogated, as though sin were given more scope. This is a forward step, not a retrograde lessening of the standard of the Torah.

The fourth antithesis, which deals with oaths versus simplicity of speech, may contain an allusion to the third command of the decalogue but it is more likely that the allusion is to Lev.19:12 and such passages as Num.30:2ff; Dt.23:22–24; Ps.50:14. Jesus calls for withdrawal of a provision of the Torah, radicalization and reorientation to himself. The Torah is contradicted since in it oaths are at times positively demanded. Jesus does not refer to *false* oaths. Although casuistry is in view (see 23:1:-26), yet the demand of Jesus does not restrict oaths to the serious oaths of the law but requires general abstention from all oaths.

The addition of the intensifying *holos* seems to sweep away *all* oaths, in the interests of simplicity of speech. This does involve alteration of the Torah. However it seems that Matthew would not envisage an oath being refused if it was demanded, for Jesus himself responded to the request for an oath according to Mt.26:64. Jesus' reply is: 'You said it.'

In the fifth antithesis, which concerns the restriction of justice as opposed to the danger of a vindictive spirit is the disciples, Jesus refers to the principle of Ex.21:24, Dt.19:21 and Lv.24:20; then over against the Torah, Jesus radicalizes the requirement and again reorientates it to himself.[25]

In the sixth antithesis, which concerns selective love over against universal love, Jesus refers to an expanded version of Lv.19:18, where the words *kai miseseis ton echthron sou* are added. Banks points out that some Old Testament passages approach the spirit of Mt.5:43 (Dt.7:5; 20:16–18) and the command concerning the slaughter of the Canaanites may be tersely summarized in the clause concerning hatred.[26] In a number of antitheses it is difficult to know whether Jesus alludes exclusively to the Old Testament or to the Old Testament as mediated through changes of emphasis current in his own day. Since there are places in the Old Testament where kindness to an enemy is urged (Ex.23:4; Lv.19:34; Jb.31:29; Pr.24:17; 25:21) it seems likely that the Old Testament is being viewed in the form of its first century exposition. Yet it would be an exaggeration to say Jesus is rejecting only Jewish perversion of the law. The slight changes in the six antitheses point to the first century setting, yet (unlike the Corban passages) *perversion* is not in view. Jesus says nothing here about perversion of the law.

Thus in 5:21–48 (i) Jesus' requirement at certain points intensifies the law. (ii) At certain points the intensification is also an abrogation of the precisely Mosaic form of the law. (iii) This involves a transfer of authority from the law to Jesus himself. (iv) The requirements of Jesus are seen to be internalized when compared to requirements of the Torah. (v) The placing of love and the requirement of 'perfection' at the end of the section seems to imply that love is the climax of all the requirement of Jesus. This impression is confirmed by 7:12b.

Matthew 7:12 puts in a nutshell the thrust of the whole of 5:3–7:11. We shall return to the 'love command' in connection with Mt.22:3–40. *Oun* has a summarizing force. The 'higher righteousness' of 5:11–45, the avoidance of ostentation (6:1–18) of over-concern about possessions (6:19–34), the unjudgemental (7:1–5) yet discerning (7:6) spirit that have been mentioned – all will be characteristic of the person who pursues love.

MATTHEW 8:2–9:3

Here the words of Jesus are followed by the works of Jesus. Just as in 5:1–8:1 Matthew presented his readers with a block of teaching, so Matthew 8:2–9:3 is grouped around a number of Jesus' miracles. The first three show Jesus' concern for those ostracized by the rabbinic community (8:2–4, 5–13, 14f.). Jesus puts compassion above ritual requirements in touching the leper (despite Lv.5:3). However, despite this implicit gradation of the law, Jesus shows himself willing to keep the law when the demands of compassion were not affected, for he follows the requirement of the law in telling the cleansed man to present himself to a priest in Jerusalem with the offering prescribed in such cases (Mt.8:4; see Lv.14:10ff). From Mt.8:11 it is apparent that Jesus envisages that one day ritual requirements will be transcended. A Jew sitting at table with a gentile would normally contract ritual defilement but Jesus envisages that this will happen without defilement in the Messianic banquet.

This section contains comparatively little dealing directly with the Torah. One simply notes that Jesus puts compassion above ritual demands and does not scruple to break the oral developments of the law when compassion makes this necessary. His table fellowship with the ostracized involved disregarding the rabbinic requirements.[27] Matthew relates this to Hos.6:6, used here with a christological emphasis (for we have there an *elthon* saying just as in 5:17) and the introduction of the love command, which implies a criticism of the Pharisees' developing the Torah in such a way that mercy is excluded. Yet Jesus' obedience to the law is seen in 8:4.

MATTHEW 9:35:–16:12

Here we see the authority of Jesus in word (5:1–8:1) and deed (8:2–9:34) being extended to his disciples. The section commences with a summary statement comparable to that of 4:23–25. Again Jesus is engaged in a teaching and healing ministry. A new note is heard at 9:36f. where compassion is shown to lie behind Jesus' concern for a ministry to the people. This prepares the way for a lengthy discourse concerning the mission of the Twelve. They are commissioned (10:1–4) and in an orderly manner Matthew shows us Jesus giving them instructions. As Jesus commends the apostles to their work, so he continues with his own (11:1).

The following sub-sections of the gospel (11:2–30; 12:1–50; 13:1–52; 13:53–14:36; 15:1–16:12) build on the basis set forth in 9:3–11:1. How will this nation-wide mission be received? The following sections offer a glimpse of misunderstanding and rejection (11:2–30), and of rising Pharisaic opposition (12:1–50).

In *Matthew11:2–30* even the Baptist falls into doubt concerning Jesus (11:2–15), yet he receives encouragement (11:4–6) and his ministry is affirmed (11:1–15). 11:11–13 teaches that (i) the law has a forward-looking function and points to the Messianic age (ii) it is part of the corpus of the total Old Testament, and (iii) it has a terminus of some kind in the ministry of Jesus.

John and Jesus are alike in being rejected (11:16–19); the theme of Jesus' rejection forms the context of the upbraiding of the cities of Israel (11:20–24). Yet over against such rejection Jesus is thankful for those to whom the kingdom is revealed (11:25–27) and an offer is made to the weary (11:28–30). Here the 'yoke' is not the law (as in Sirach 51) but that of Jesus himself.

Healing on the sabbath rouses Pharisaic wrath (12:1–14). In Mt.12:1–9 we note that Jesus sits loose to Pharisaic scrupulosity concerning the sabbath. He is unconcerned when his disciples pick heads of grain (12:1) and interprets David as putting human need above the Torah itself (12:4). Priestly 'breaking' of the fourth commandment is regarded as innocent (12:5); the requirement of mercy comes above the Pharisees' *halakah*. This seems far from any legalism. It is no accident that the pericope immediately following (12:9–14) also relates to sabbath breaking. Both incidents deal with the law and the Pharisees' opposition to Jesus. The offence committed is that of harvesting and preparing food on the sabbath. Carson rightly observes: 'Ransack the Torah as you will, and it remains difficult to see what law was broken by the disciples.'[28] It is the Pharisaic *halakah* that has been transgressed.

Matthew 12:9–14 concerns the *halakah*. No part of the Torah forbade healing on the sabbath but the Pharisees clearly place an exaggerated emphasis on inactivity as being inherently good on the sabbath. But for Jesus inactivity is not 'good' in the presence of a sick man. What is 'good' is to heal him. The Pharisees' *halakah* is disregarded. In the two units (12:1–8,9–14) no breach of the Torah is actually committed. Yet at one point in Jesus' reply a negative stance even with regard to the Torah is implied. For Jesus points to a scriptural incident which reflects upon the Torah itself. By interpreting David's action as putting human need above a ritual requirement of the Torah (12:4), he has allowed that even a requirement of the written Torah may be disregarded in a situation of need.[29]

At this point we note (i) that Jesus is indifferent to the Pharisaic *halakah* and (ii) that within the Torah he differentiates between the demands of compassion and the demands of ritual. The former may override the latter, notwithstanding the great authority of the Torah. Jesus has thus allowed a gradation of commands within the Torah.

Matthew now presents Jesus as withdrawing from the area where conflict has arisen in order to continue his Messianic ministry elsewhere (12:15–21). An exorcism elicits further criticism from the Pharisees (12:22–37). A request for a sign is the occasion of a statement concerning the 'evil and adulterous' condition of the generation whose leaders are the Pharisees and scribes (Mt.12:38–45). Over against such a generation and over against the misunderstandings even of his family, Jesus speaks of his true family, those who do the Father's will (12:46–50).

Matthew 13:1–53, with the parables of the kingdom, is placed at this juncture. They show the varying reception accorded to the preaching of the kingdom and a significant statement in 13:52 points to a different kind of scribe. Matthew has so far portrayed 'scribes' as hostile to Jesus. But here those who have understood the parables (13:51a) and who *know* that they understand them (13:51b) are by that very fact ('therefore', v.52) trained for the kingdom. The new kind of scribe will have a place in the kingdom that comes in the person of Jesus. 'What is new' is added to his now greater understanding of the law and the prophets. The kingdom has arrived, yet comes gently, resistibly, 'in a mystery'.

Matthew 13:53–14:3 contains further descriptions of misunderstanding and rejection. Jesus is rejected by Nazareth (13:53–58) and John is finally rejected by Herod (14:1–12). Despite the claim of 13:51b, the disciples are revealed as still immature. A further miracle (14:13–21) brings out a contrast between the disciples and Jesus. In view of the previous miracles, they could be expected to feed the five thousand ('*You give them to eat*', 14:16), but they are conscious only of insufficiency (14:17) and it is Jesus who feeds the crowds. Again, they might have been expected (in view of 8:24–27) no longer to fear storms, yet the incident of 14:22–33: reveals that they are still fearful. Even Peter, the leader of the twelve, is 'a man of little faith' (14:31). Nevertheless, the miracles of Jesus continue (14:34–36).

Matthew 15:1–16:12 contains a further incident of conflict. The Pharisees criticize Jesus for not obeying the traditional law; in return Jesus criticizes them for making void the law (15:1–20). The unit in Mt.15:1–20 brings us to the fourth of the eight sections of Matthew where there is heavy focus upon the Christian and the Torah.[30]

The controversy arises because the disciples break the developed Torah of the Pharisees and the closely associated scribes (15:1). The specific incident giving rise to the debate (15:2) is failure of the disciples to observe ritual washing before eating. Matthew's account discloses some distinct interests. He is concerned only about the oral tradition of the Pharisees and makes no reference to the law in its undeveloped pentateuchal form.

Jesus responds to the question by powerfully attacking Pharisaic legalism, contrasting the Scripture with their tradition. References to 'you' are set against the 'command of God' (15:3); 'God said' contrasts with 'you say' (15:4f.). Thus Jesus relates the matter to his view of Scripture. The Torah is 'the command of God'; Pharisaic tradition arises from human opinion alone. Matthew stresses the authority of the Torah more than Mark for he has 'God says' where Mk.7:10 has 'Moses said'.

Secondly, Jesus attacks the Pharisees' hypocrisy and lack of compassion, portraying their religion as external. The tradition nullifies the Torah (15:6) and thus betrays insincerity (*hupokritai*, Mt.15:7).

Thirdly, Jesus maintains that the Pharisees' legalism implies something about the nature of their worship. It is external, a matter of lip rather than heart (15:8).

The attack on Pharisaic tradition leads Jesus to speak about the nature of sin. Sin derives from within; it has no relation to any food placed in the mouth.

A reference to the offence caused by Jesus' teaching (15:12–14), is followed by further development of the teaching about sin and food (15:15–20). The Pharisaic tradition is explicitly rejected: eating with unwashed hands does not make a person 'unclean' .

Thus Jesus appears as (i) strongly critical of the Pharisaic *halakah*, yet (ii) upholding the authority of the Torah and in no way criticizing it.

Matthew 15:1–20 has thus shown Matthew's readers more conclusively than ever how great a gulf exists between Jesus and the

Pharisees. The Pharisees indeed will shortly come under divine judgement (15:12) and the disciples are to leave them alone (15:13).

Accordingly, Jesus withdraws to a largely gentile region, Tyre and Sidon (15: 21) and shows his willingness to minister, although secondarily, to gentiles (15: 22–28).Then he proceeds to Galilee (15: 29) and works Messianic signs there (15:29–31). Despite this contact with gentiles, the concluding line is: 'they glorified the God of *Israel* (15:31). Here, as in 2:1–12 and 8:5–13, Matthew shows that despite opposition from the representatives of Israel (15:1–20), gentiles are open to his ministry (15:21–31).

Another feeding of the crowds (15:32–39) occasions a further request from Pharisees and Sadducees that he will perform a sign. Jesus refuses (16:1–4) and again warns the disciples, this time about the 'leaven' of the Pharisees' teaching (16:5–12). Aware of the rising opposition of the Jewish authority, Matthew's readers are now ready for a step forward in his account and the introduction of the word 'church'.

As one surveys the multiplicity of events in this section (9:25–16:12), one cannot but notice the absence of any emphasis on the law. Matthew could evidently deal with numerous units of tradition while saying relatively little about the Torah.

MATTHEW 16:13–20:28

The rising opposition of the Pharisees leads to one of the turning points of the gospel (16:13–20). In the revelation at Caesarea Philippi we discover that despite the disciples' weaknesses and stumbling misunderstandings Peter speaks on behalf of the group as a whole[31] when he confesses his faith in Jesus as the Christ, the Son of the living God. In this context Jesus introduces the word 'church' and speaks of 'his' church being built despite the opposition of the powers of Hades. Pharisaic opposition has mounted to a head. The evangelist presents the revelation at Caesarea Philippi as a crucial turning point in the life of Jesus; a new section of Matthew commences here with the words, 'From that time . . . ' (16:21).

Matthew 16:21–20:28 continues, in narrative form, a progressive development as definite as in any Pauline epistle, though more subtle. We have seen Jesus' basic character as the Messianic king predicted by Scripture, welcomed by gentiles but largely rejected by Israel (1:1–4:22). We have seen samples of his teaching and of his miraculous power (4:23–9:34). We have seen steadily mounting opposition from Israel and misunderstanding in the disciples (9:35–16:12). Yet the disciples have reached a breakthrough in the revelation at Caesarea Philippi and the future of Jesus' ministry will lie with them (16:13–20). Matthew now shows Jesus concentrating on giving further instruction to his disciples. There are sections concerning the cross (16:21–23), discipleship (16:24–28) and a revelation of the glory of Jesus, which will eventually sustain and illuminate Peter, James and John after the resurrection (17:1–13).

In the story of the transfiguration it is possible that Moses and Elijah are meant to be the greatest representatives of the law and the prophets respectively. If so then one aspect of the story is the fact that both law and prophets are seen as testifying to Jesus, who however ultimately outstrips both. The heavenly voice does not say, 'Listen to the law and the prophets', but draws attention to the supremacy of Jesus ('This is my Son') and invites us to 'Listen to him!'

The teaching continues, as the healing of an epileptic boy supplies an occasion for Jesus to stress the significance of faith. In Galilee Jesus again predicts his death and resurrection and teaches about the temple-tax (17:24–27) and true greatness (18:1–35). The question of the temple tax throws light upon Jesus' attitude to the oral law.

THE TEMPLE TAX (17:24–27)

The duty of paying the temple-tax was not directly ordained in the written Torah and at the time of Jesus was a *halakah* that had arisen towards the end of or after Hasmonean times. The Sadducees were offended by it; the Qumran community paid its levy once but not regularly[32]. Jesus (i) argues that he is under no *compulsion* to obey this requirement (17:25b–26) but (ii) says there is no sin in paying the tax and expresses willingness to pay it (17:27). Evidently the keeping of the *oral* law, as opposed to the more authoritative written law, is an *adiaphoron*, a matter of indifference. Payment or non-payment is determined by what is expedient in the light of Jesus' mission. To pay is expedient because not paying will cause needless stumbling among some who are not antagonistic to Jesus' mission. ('Them' in 17:2 probably refers to the 'others' of Mt.17:25f.). The story illustrates Jesus' 'willingness to comply with the conventions of the society to which he belonged'.[33].

The narrative continues to move towards Jerusalem and a third prediction indicates the significance of the direction of travel (20:17–19). Jesus continues his teaching and the request by the mother of James and John (20:20–23) prompts a statement of the need for servant-like service (20:24–28) in accordance with Jesus' own mission (20:28).

Two sections especially bear upon our theme: those concerning divorce (19:3–12) and the rich young man (19:16–22).

DIVORCE (19:3–12)

Scribal debates about divorce revolved around the interpretation of Deut.24:1–4, the main point of which was that a divorced woman who had remarried could never again return to her first husband. The school of Shammai restricted 'some indecency' to sexual sin authenticated by witnesses, but the dominant practice of the day, governed by the school of Hillel, is said to have understood this as any cause of complaint, even poor cooking.[34]

In 19:3–12 the Pharisees seek to involve Jesus in this debate. In response, (i) Jesus points to an ideal higher than the Torah. In going back to Gen.1:27 and 2:24 Jesus implicitly indicates that the Torah is – in respect of divorce – less .than ideal (19:4–7). (ii) However the Pharisees press the question .of the authority of the law (24:7), which leads Jesus to bring forward a further principle. The law is less than ideal since it caters for human hardness of heart (19:8a). Again Jesus reiterates its low standard compared to the original ideal (19:8b). (iii) Going even further, he introduces his own requirement which is altogether higher than that of the Torah. Verse 9 is notoriously controversial, being similar to Mt.5:31.

The Pharisees begin (v.3) with a question. Wishing to entangle Jesus in the Herod-Herodias affair, they ask whether divorce is permitted 'for any and every reason?'[35]. We recall that (i) Qumran forbade divorce altogether, (ii) Hillel permitted a husband to divorce for trivial reasons, and (iii) Shammai permitted the husband to divorce on grounds of grave indecency. In vv 4–6 Jesus argues from the story of creation that divorce is entirely wrong.

In v.7 the Pharisees raise the question of the Mosaic law. They slightly distort it by using the word 'command', which is not quite the point of Deuteronomy 24.

In vv.8f. Jesus (i) speaks of *permission not command*, (ii) argues that this permission is grounded in man's hardness, (iii) urges that such a permission was less than ideal and was a lapse from God's original requirement, and (iv) bans divorce altogether for his disciples except with one proviso. (Possible interpretations of this exceptive clause have already been mentioned. My own view is that an exception is made on grounds of adultery but that the exception does not allow for remarriage while the partner is alive. However my argument here is not affected by the precise interpretation of the exceptive clause.)

The next sub-unit (vv.10–12) has been taken to refer to the preferability of singleness[36] or to the need to remain continent after divorce (for example by Dupont[37]). The decision does not affect our enquiry.

To sum up: in this passage we note (i) presentation of a higher standard than the Mosaic law, (ii) indication of weakness in the Mosaic law, and (iii) reorientation to Jesus himself with the recurrence of the familiar phrase, 'I say to you.'

THE RICH YOUNG MAN (19:16–26)

A common interpretation has been that Jesus used the law to 'convict of sin' (19:17–19). When the young man moralistically and simplistically claims to have kept the law (19:20) the commandment is intensified and radicalized so as to reveal the spiritual nature of the law in connection with covetousness (19:21). This view has predominated in the evangelical literature.[38]

Yet much of the traditional exposition appears to be built on false premises. It assumes (i) that the young man was 'seeking salvation' in the sense that Martin Luther was 'seeking a gracious God', and (ii) that Jesus' purpose in bringing in the law was to prepare for the gospel by convicting him of sin. On.this view, the young man is seeking forgiveness of sins or (to use a Pauline term) justification. However this approach is too Pauline. It is as though the young man were asking the question, 'What must I do to be saved?' in the same sense as the Philippian jailer. There are reasons however to suggest that the issue is not justification or *initial* salvation, but concerns something richer and fuller.

Matthew's version shows a number of redactional differences in comparison with Mark's (Mk.10:17–31). Three major ones are: the change in the ascription of goodness ('What good thing?' instead of 'Good master') and removal of the phrase 'Why do you call me good?' (Mk.10:18); the addition of Lev.19:18 in Mt.19:19; and the reference to perfection in 19:21. The changes seem to be motivated by (i) a desire to remove distracting christological questions; (ii) introduction of the love command, which is one of Matthew's special interests; (iii) a heightened emphasis on the question of the role of the law, which is another of Matthew's special interests.

There is emphasis on the young man's being *one* of the crowd (v.16). This may be intended to save the reader from thinking that the command to forsake all wealth is a *generalized* command. From the outset Matthew has stressed that Jesus is dealing with an individual. The group of disciples in 19:13 are explicitly not the recipients of the instruction of 19:21.

The young man's quest for 'eternal life' raises some important questions. The traditional Protestant interpretation is that 'eternal life' means conversion and initial salvation. However, there are good reasons for thinking that the focus of the phrase 'eternal life' is different, referring more to reaping the blessings of salvation and its consequent reward. This is suggested by the following considerations:

(i) In the Marcan account, to some form of which Matthew probably had access, the young man uses the term 'inherit' (Mk.10:17). The verb 'inherit' never refers to initial salvation. While we are dealing with Matthew not Mark, yet there is no reason to think that Matthew's 'have' (*scho*,19:16) implies anything different here. Matthew has not altered his Marcan source in *this* respect, and he uses the term 'inherit' in 19:29. 'Inheritance' always speaks of reward. Abraham was 'justified' in Genesis 12 or 15 (see 15:6) but his 'inheritance' was not secured until Gen.22 when he had reached a high level of obedience. The ultimate possession of the inheritance is beyond the grave. 'Inheritance' language goes back to the Old Testament and is typologically analogous to Canaan. Obedience is rewarded by inheritance; disobedience results in disinheritance.

(ii) 'Entering the kingdom' does not in Matthew refer to initial salvation but is generally connected to one's regular manner of living.

It comes about by poverty of spirit (5:3), enduring persecutions (5:10), living in a way that fulfils the law and outstrips the righteousness of the scribes and Pharisees (5:19f.). It is not a matter of an initial act of faith but of seeking (6:33), of doing Jesus' will (7:21). All this suggests that we are not dealing with 'conversion' in the traditional evangelical sense but with reaping the benefits of the kingdom by the way one lives. This is Matthew's concern more than that of conversion. He deals with excelling *in* kingdom (18:1). Even the phrase 'entering the kingdom' apparently refers not to 'conversion' but to the experience of blessings within the kingdom.

(iii) There is no clear example in the synoptic gospels of *initial* conversion being referred to in terms of 'entering the kingdom'. Matthew's language of the kingdom either refers to ongoing daily living (as in the references cited) or (as in 8:11; 25:34) to something future.

(iv) The general thrust of the entire section in 19:1:-20:1 clearly refers to reward. The 'eternal life' referred to must concern reaping the blessings of the kingdom or eschatological reward (or, quite likely, both) because Jesus refers to 'treasure in heaven' (19:21). The apostles' response to Jesus' words are, 'Then what shall we have?' (19:27). B.B.Warfield rightly notes that the section 'is succeeded by the parable of the workmen in the vineyard who were surprised that their rewards were not nicely adjusted to what they deemed their relative services'.[39] The question of the young man does not refer to justification (to use the Pauline term) or initial coming to discipleship; rather it concerns the experience of eternal life and reward, an 'inheritance' resulting from a life of discipleship. The traditional interpretation of Mt.19:16–22 has focused on Pauline justification instead of inheritance (although in Paul too 'inheritance' is reward, as Col.3:24 makes explicit). B.B.Warfield rightly complained about 'habits of thought derived from a Lutheran inheritance'.[40]

Eternal life is more than justification-forgiveness. It is the *experience* of life, the 'life of the age to come' which is known even in this world. For the Jewish young man it would traditionally be the Torah that gave such life. ('The Torah is great, because it gives to those who practise it life in this age and in the age to come' (*Pirqe Aboth* 6:7).

Jesus questions the man concerning his view of goodness. Goodness is defined in terms of God ('There is One who is good'). It is likeness to God that is the true mark of goodness. (One may compare Mt.5:45–48, where also likeness to God and 'perfection' are linked.) The Matthean wording leaves aside the christological issue but still asserts the unworthiness of humankind and the unique goodness of God alone. An exact scrutiny of the text reveals that God's goodness is not *defined* in terms of the law. (Mt.19:8 is only a few lines back and has acknowledged weakness in the law.) Jesus merely moves on to make use of the law.

The question concerns what the young man must *do* to have eternal life. He is concerned about specific good works. In v.17 Jesus' reply starts from where the young man is. He asked about doing. Jesus' reply concerns doing. Yet it must be noted that Pauline interests must not be brought in at this point. The basis of first entry into God's kingdom is not the issue. The young man is not enquiring about 'justification' or about initial entrance into the kingdom of God. In Mt.9:9 Matthew's *first* becoming Jesus' disciple apparently requires no preparatory return to the law. Following Jesus is enough for salvation: 'Levi' was accepted immediately. Rather the passage here deals with the level of godliness that secures blessing, what may be called 'getting eternal life'.

Jesus' reply points to the keeping of the commandments. The young man's question, 'Which ones?' assumes there is a gradation within the law (v.18a). In vv.18f Jesus accepts that assumption and points him to the sixth, seventh, eighth and ninth and fifth commandments in that order. The law is *not* given a spiritualized exposition. Hendriksen's remark about 'deeply spiritual and penetrating interpretation'[41] of the law corresponds to nothing in the text.

Why were the first, second, third, fourth and tenth omitted? Even the religious externalism of the average first century Jew could be regarded as keeping the first three commands. The fourth concerned ritual and is not on a level with the others. The tenth is altogether in a different category. It Is perhaps reflected on in the further progress of the conversation. The addition of the love command in Matthew corresponds to the importance the evangelist attaches to this aspect of the law. Yet at the same time it must be said that even the love command receives no detailed exposition and the young man's claim to have kept even this command is not questioned by Jesus. Evidently he felt that he had shown love to others. *Indirect* refutation of the young man's claim will come in the test of his willingness to give to the poor (Mt.19:21).

Although claiming to have kept the commands (v.20), the man still feels something is missing in spite of his consciousness of total law-keeping. Now Jesus goes higher. No longer does he directly quote the law although his demand could be based on the tenth command. Instead Jesus first gives a *particularized* instruction. The young man says he is willing to keep the generalized laws of the Torah and even to do something (*ti*, 19:16) outstanding. Is he willing to follow a personal, particularized, instruction from Jesus himself? Second, Jesus tests his willingness to show outstanding love: if Jesus *in his case and in a specific instruction* requires outstanding generosity, will he follow this particular instruction? Finally Jesus asks the young man to join him in the radical commitment of companionship among his disciples who 'follow' him. The 'following' must not be spiritualized. It is not a reference to general loyalty to Jesus but involves literally becoming one of the team who accompany Jesus.

At this point we see Jesus leaving aside all talk about the Torah and focusing on radical commitment to himself and his particularized commands to individual disciples. As in Mt.5:20,48 and 19:16–22, a righteousness beyond that of scribes and Pharisees is needed.

Two further points deserve notice. (i) This kind of radical commitment to a life of love and obedience to Jesus' particularized commands is called 'perfection'. (ii) The result of such a life is reward: 'You shall have treasure in heaven.' We have come full circle to where the questioner started. From the very beginning he was concerned about experience of life and reward. This focus is confirmed in the following verses, where the disciples refer to what they have done and their literally accompanying Jesus (19:27). They ask: 'What then shall we have?' (19:27) Jesus replies by talking of reward (19:29) but the term he uses is 'inherit'. The following parable (20:1–16) deals with the remarkable surprises of grace displayed when a householder at the end of the day allocates reward for work done. The whole section from Mt.19:16 – 20:16 has focused upon reward.

The only possible query concerning this interpretation arises from the use of the word 'salvation' in 19:25. This is not a weighty objection. The young man uses the term 'eternal life' (19:16); Jesus similarly speaks of 'entering life' (19:17). In talking to the disciples Jesus later refers to the 'kingdom of heaven' (19:53); the term 'inherit' is used in 19:29. It seems likely that at some points in the New Testament 'reward' and 'salvation' are so closely linked that a futuristic usage of the word 'salvation' actually refers to reward[42]. In any case it should be noted that the term does not occur on the lips of Jesus in Matthew's presentation. We could have here, as elsewhere in Matthew,[43] an error of the disciples which Jesus implicitly corrects.

What view is taken here of the Mosaic law? One notes (i) the law is not in any way disparaged. (ii) The life Jesus requires is not less than the law. (iii) Yet there is a level of godliness that outstrips the law. (iv) Jesus asks for obedience to particularized commands that may go further than the Torah. (v) Jesus requires radical reorientation to himself. He puts himself in the place of the Torah. (vi) This is called 'perfection' and one is encouraged to believe that the result will be an experience of eternal life now and reward hereafter.

The passage does not contain a two-tier ethic, as if the law represented a level of godliness for 'ordinary' disciples with 'perfection' available for an elite. Nor is it a two-stage way of leading a person to initial salvation, with the law preparing the way for submission to Jesus. Rather it is a two-stage way of reaching the higher level required for all disciples. 'Perfection' is required of all Jesus' disciples (see also 5:48).

MATTHEW 20:29 – 25:46

This resembles other sections in that miracle stories are interwoven with sections pursuing dominant themes. But the emphasis here is on Jesus' final entry into Jerusalem and upon the rejection of Israel.

The healing of the blind men (20:29–34) significantly shows them using a Messianic title ('Son of David'). Jesus does not reject the title; the healing asked for is given. Entering Jerusalem (21:1–11), he fulfils prophecy (vv.4f) and performs a sign that implicitly claims the temple is subject to his lordship (vv.12–17). The miracle of the cursing of the fig-tree functions as an acted parable concerning the barrenness and unproductiveness of Israel (vv.18–22). Israel's unbelief is underscored in the question concerning authority (vv.23–27) and the parables of the two sons (vv.28–32) and of the vineyard (vv.33–41) further emphasize the same point. A programmatic statement follows (vv.42f.), concerning the rejection of Israel, and the reaction of the chief priests and Pharisees is noted (vv.45f.). A further parable on the same theme is found in Mt.22:1–14.

In Mt.22:15–26 the malice of Jesus' opponents is seen in several controversies which potentially entrap Jesus. The debates concern taxation (22:15–22), resurrection (22:23–33), the greatest command (22:33–40) and Psalm 110 (22:41–45). This leads into an extended denunciation of the scribes and Pharisees (23:1–39), and a prediction of the fall of Jerusalem and the parousia (24:1–25:46). The initial emphasis on Jerusalem is followed by descriptions of judgement day.

Little of this has any heavy emphasis on the Torah. However, two sections call for detailed comment.

THE GREATEST COMMANDMENT (22:34–40)

The setting is one of controversy. Mt.22:15 sets the tone of Mt.22:15–46. It is Jesus' enemies who raise a question about the law, as is usually the case in Matthew. (See 12:2;15:2;17:24;19:7,16). When Jesus is speaking on his own initiative he rarely raises questions of Torah. In Mt 5:17–48 he is replying to a possible misunderstanding. ('Think not . . . ', Mt.5:17) At a few places he freely makes the point that he fulfils the law (Mt.7:12) and that the epoch of the law centres upon him (11:13). In Mt.23 Jesus raises the issue of the law himself but does so immediately after 22:15–46 and in order to denounce the legalists. Thus it is Jesus' enemies who love to raise issues – sometimes quite minor ones – concerning the Torah. Great interest in the righteousness of the law may apparently coexist with great hostility to Jesus. We note that preoccupation with the Torah does not lead to faith in Jesus and does not necessarily convict of sin.

The question put in 22:35 reflects contemporary attempts to reduce the law to a few items. One finds such discussions in the sayings of the rabbi Hillel ('What is hateful to you, do not do to thy neighbour. This is the whole law.')[44]. Rabbi Aqiba (fl.AD 110–135) said that Lev.19:18 was *kelal gadol battorah* ('the great principle in the law'). Rabbi Ben Azzai, from approximately the same period, uses the same phrase. A *kelal* is a general or basic command from which all the other commands could be deduced. Although these sources are generally somewhat later than Jesus they obviously go back to earlier days

(Tobit 4:15, which echoes Hillel's saying, goes back to pre-Christian times). It seems from Mt.22 and its parallels that such discussion already occurred in Jesus' day and that Jesus was invited to give his answer to such questions.

However friendly or unfriendly to Jesus the man may have been (note Mk 12:32–34), Matthew wishes to present his question as one generally asked in hostility. But that does not prevent Jesus from answering it. As with the two previous questions (Mt.22:15–22,23–33), Jesus takes the question at face value and replies.

His response links Dt.6:5 with Lev.19:18. Perhaps such a linkage had been made before. (There are similar sayings, possibly pre-Christian, in *The Testament of the Twelve Patriarchs* – T.Issa.5:2; 7:6; T.Dan.5:3). Jesus' answer again urges the need of love. The love-command is presented in its two aspects, love towards God and love towards humankind. The message to hostile Jewish questioners is that the law abides in its validity and its greatest aspects concern love. If this were all, we might think that Jesus was simply teaching a spiritualized and heightened version of the law. However, the matter is *not* left there and one must notice the connection between 22:15–40 and vv.41–45. Having replied to a series of hostile questions (22:15–40) Jesus asks some questions of his own (22:41–45). The hostile questions have dealt with relationship to Caesar (22:15–22), with the miraculous (22:23–33) and with the law (22:34–40). Jesus' questions concern himself (22:41–45). This conclusion means that the protracted debate does *not* leave the impression that the Jews merely face the heightened morality of the love-command. Certainly the love-command is mentioned in the Torah and is its greatest aspect. Yet the matter does not stop there. A christological emphasis is also intro-duced. Again we meet the same twofold emphasis we have noted in 19:16–22 and elsewhere. Jesus ranks love as the greatest aspect of the Torah and all else 'hangs' upon the love command. Yet the love-command is not presented in a vacuum but in the context of submission to Jesus as the Son of God. The legalists' question in itself would have left the matter wholly in the realm of law. In vv.14–45 Jesus faces them not with a legal question but a christological challenge. Love is God's supreme 'law' – but can it be legislated? Can there be love if Jesus is not received as Son of God? This is the challenge left with the legalists. Matthew's gospel says nothing more about law. The next few verses will pronounce condemnation upon the very people who asked about the greatest command of the law.

Jesus also adds something else not mentioned by the Pharisees: 'On these hang the law and the prophets.' What does it mean to say that the whole Old Testament 'hangs' (*krematai*) upon the double com-mand of love? The phrase (Mt.22:40), which is distinctive to Matthew, resembles 7:12. The verb used, like its late Hebrew equivalent (*talah* or *tala'*) may express dependence, (as in the rabbinic saying *hm'so tlwy btlmwd w'yn tlmwd bm'wh*, 'Conduct depends on teaching not teaching on conduct')[45]. But what is the precise nature of the dependence? (i) Is the idea that of *derivation*: the law and the prophets depend on love in the sense that they derive from it?[46] (ii) Or is the idea that of *summation*, such that the love-command summarizes and puts in a nutshell all that the Torah and the prophets require? (The rabbinic question, 'What is the smallest section of Scripture on which all the essential provisions of the Torah depend (*tlwyyn*)[47] uses *talah* when seeking to expresses the varied stipulations of the Torah in the smallest form). (iii) Is the idea that of the *indispensability* of the love-command such that the law and the prophets have no validity unless they express or are combined with love? (iv) Is *coherence* the main point, such that love is the 'decisive expression' of the Old Testament or that the commandments 'find their coherence in the overriding principle of the double commandment to love'?

Two principles must guide us. (i) Since the saying here relates to the law and the prophets one must interpret *kremannumi* in a way that suits both. (ii) A convincing exegesis must understand *kremannumi* in a way that is attested (or that is attested for *talah*).

It is not likely that the idea is derivation, for it is not easy to see how the prophetic message can be wholly derived from the love-command. Nor is it likely that the thought is of love replacing the law. Replacement is not involved in *kremannumi* or *talah*. Nor does this thought make sense in the case of the prophets.

Taking account of the meaning of *kremannumi* and of the context it seems likely that the idea is that the law and the prophets serve the interests of love and depend on it in that they have no significance except to bring about love. ('Love' will of course be understood christologically and within the context of Christ's will; Matthew does not refer to an undefined moralism). On this understanding (i) the attested meaning of *kremannumi* is followed, (ii) both law and prophets contain indications that they are intended to further the cause of love,[48] (iii) the commands concerning love therefore sum up all that law and prophets are seeking to bring about, (iv) this view does justice to the salvation-historical perspective. As in Mt.5:17–20, the law and the prophets are seen to have a goal within history. They depend on the principle of love in that this is the purpose that lies behind them.[49]

So is it possible that where love is operating the legislation of the Torah is no longer directly and immediately needed? E.Schweizer affirms this in an extreme manner: 'Righteousness as a whole depends on the fulfilment of these two commands . . . they are the *only* ones that need be obeyed.'[50] However, this is not compatible with Matthew's gospel as a whole. Yet for Matthew the Torah is fully valid during the ministry of Jesus. 'Matthew' (whoever he may be) is presenting his version of the Jesus story, using the material he has at his disposal. If the redaction of Matthew exclusively reveals his church it is a rather legalistic church that we glimpse. If however Matthew is presenting historical material, as I think he is, then Mt.22:40 says no more than that the total corpus of the Old Testament was furthering

the cause of love (understood, as we have said, christologically).[51] The
question must be asked in a more nuanced way: Does the law directly
lead to love? Does love arise by preoccupation with the law? Could it
be that the law takes society a step in the direction of love but the
'fulfilment' of it cannot arise from law alone? Mt.24:40 says no more
than that the need of love was the underlying reason for the giving of
the Torah and the total corpus of prophetic ministry. In *this* verse he
does not say what carries the cause of love to its fulfilment. Yet the fact
that he now presents a section (22:41–46) dealing with the claims of
Jesus will give us a hint. The final sentence of the gospel (28:20b) will
offer the possibility of fellowship with the risen Jesus. There is more
than one way in which the love commands may be 'the only ones that
need be obeyed'. It is unlikely (despite Schweizer) that they are the
'only ones that need be obeyed' in the sense that the Torah may be dis-
obeyed. But in conjunction with Matthew's last word (Mt.28:20b) it
could be said that they may suffice as the Christian's central focus (to
change Schweizer's wording). Only thus will the law be 'fulfilled'.

What then is the view of the law taught in Mt.22:34–40? (i) The
greatest aspect of the law, it says, is found in a phrase that does not
occur at all in the central aspects of the Torah. Instead of quoting
words from the decalogue which might have been candidates for
selection as the greatest command, Jesus goes to an obscure section of
the Torah and selects a mention of love (Lev.19:18). (ii) He accepts
the notion of gradations within the law. (iii) The validity of the law
abides unabridged for hostile Israelites, to whom it was originally
given. (iv) The unabridged validity of the law leads to questions
concerning the one to whom it pointed, or the one whom it 'proph-
esied' (Mt.11:13). This leaves unanswered questions. According to
Matthew, Jesus was not concerned to say everything that could have
been said to these hostile Israelites. He points them to the need for
love, questions them with regard to himself – and leaves the matter
there.

The fact that Mt.22:41–46 follows immediately after the section
concerning the greatest command suggests that Matthew is not content
to leave a statement concerning law except in connection with a
statement concerning the person of Jesus.

OBEYING THE SCRIBES AND PHARISEES (23:3)

We have already surveyed Matthew's view of the scribes and Pharisees. At this point we must consider 23:3 more fully. The saying is
rather startling when read alongside Matthew's denunciation of the
two groups. We may identify several approaches to it.

1. At one end of the spectrum of opinion is the view that 23:3
simply indicates the high value ascribed to the Torah in Matthew's
teaching. For Bornkamm it shows that Matthew held to the
'unabridged validity' of the Torah[52]. This takes seriously the fact that
Matthew is dealing with the whole law.

2. The theonomy school also draws attention to Mt.23:3 but fails to explain how there can be any exception to the total validity of all aspects of the Torah if 23:3 is taken at face value. Bahnsen thinks that it is 'to the extent that they legitimately sit in Moses' seat' that the Pharisees' teaching should be obeyed. Yet if one takes the text at face value this does not seem precisely the distinction being made. Matthew is surely distinguishing between practice and teaching. The scribal and Pharisaic teaching is to be followed but not their practice. If one interprets the text along these lines, the scribes and Pharisees are hypocritical yet accurate expositors. Mt.23:3 does not question their expository skills. Having taken Mt 23:3 at face value, by what right can the theonomy school introduce any qualification or reduction of this statement?[53]

3. Reformed theologians commonly say that Mt.3:23 affirms the law but seek to limit the extent of the law envisaged. Thus N.B.Stonehouse thinks that in spite of a *prima facie* impression that the law is affirmed here, the contradiction with the rest of the chapter prevents us from interpreting the saying as totally approving scribal and Pharisaic teaching, since these verses 'go to the extreme of acknowledging the authority of the teaching of the scribes and Pharisees'. For Stonehouse, 23:3 means that the scribes and Pharisees 'were to be honoured in their affirmation of the law of Moses'. What this signifies is not altogether clear; apparently that the scribes and Pharisees were to be honoured in their general affirmation of the law, but not heeded in their detailed convictions.[54]

4. J.P.Meier offers a 'dispensational' understanding.[55] Jesus' statement affirmed the Pharisees' and scribes' role but not their teaching, and this affirmation extended only to the time of the resurrection. However it is precisely their *teaching* (as opposed to their conduct) that Jesus does apparently affirm. Jesus has criticized *contemporary* Pharisaic teaching (Mt.5:21–48; 15:3f.; 16:12) and does so again in this very passage (23:16–36). He has just denounced their ignorance (22:41–46).

5. Garland[56] is so impressed by the contradiction between 23:3 and the rest of Matthew that he discerns incoherent editorial work at this point.

6. Another approach is to take 23:3 as a concessive and gentle approach to Jewish law-keeping at a time when the breach between church and synagogue is not yet final.[57]

7. More satisfactory is the exegesis of Jeremias, France and Carson. France thinks 23:3 cannot be taken at face value; it was spoken 'with an ironical, tongue-in-cheek tone'. D.Carson believes that what we have here is 'biting irony, bordering on sarcasm'[58]. This is surely correct. It is quite impossible to take 23:3 as a positive or concessionary remark. For Matthew does *not* handle the scribes and Pharisees with gentleness. In the light of Matthew's treatment of the scribes elsewhere (chapters 5;14; the bulk of 23) it is impossible to think that he approves of the total teaching of the scribes and Pharisees. Yet it is

the *total* teaching including the oral developments of the law that are in view.

It is possible, however, to go even further than Carson. What we seem to have here is an *ad hominem* argument. Jesus is speaking with strong irony, but with a reasoned purpose. It is as if he were saying: 'You want to keep the law? Well, do that! Let us see you actually achieve it. Even the experts in the law cannot keep it, but you go ahead and do so!' If this correctly reproduces the thrust of 23:3, then the argument resembles that in Gal.4:21 and 5:3f. Does anyone wish to keep the scribal and Pharisaic law, traditions and all? Then let them do so! But let them not imagine that even the scribes and Pharisees themselves are capable of keeping their own teaching.

It has been argued[59] that Mt.23:23 also indicates Matthew's conservative view of the role of the law. Although he knows there are distinctions and gradations within the law, nevertheless even the most meticulous tithing will not be abrogated in Jesus' kingdom. The law, it is argued, will retain total validity.

FULFILMENT AND THE ESCHATON

At this point I think a 'dispensational' element *does* enter. Carson points out that Jesus is not at all dealing with the relationship between the Mosaic epoch and his own reign of Jesus. 'Jesus describes what *the Pharisees* should have done'[60]. In Matthew we have allusions to the pre-AD70 situation of the temple altar (23:16–22), the sacrificial system (5:23f.), and the Sabbath (24:20) without any necessary implication that such Mosaic institutions retain their validity. One need not read into this Matthew's view of the law. The central point in Mt.23:23 is that it would not be right for the Pharisee to brush aside the law or to disregard its requirements. He is commended for his meticulous observance of one of the details of the Torah. However to see here a 'rule of life' for the post-resurrection believer is to read too much into Mt.23:23. The last few verses of Matthew's Gospel, as we shall see, leave us with a picture of believers under the commands of Jesus and the authority that derives from his resurrection. The law of tithing was given in the Torah (Lv.27:30; Dt.14:22). Jesus claims according to Matthew that he has come to fulfil the law, but his life is not finished and the law has not yet received its lifelong fulfilment in the life of Jesus. It would certainly not be right for Jesus to say that a Jew who is *not* one of his disciples should *not* keep the law. When addressing his disciples and the relatively sympathetic crowds (5:2; 7:28) Jesus has portrayed himself as the new authority to which disciples must submit. But it would not be right for Jesus to imply that a Jew who has not transferred allegiance from the Torah to the more-than-Torah found in Jesus' authority is in any way released from the Torah.

What we have in Mt.23:23 is a concession. A teacher of the law who is not a disciple of Jesus is quite right to be utterly scrupulous in submission to the Torah. Jesus is in process of fulfilling the law; at such a stage in salvation history even its smallest demands must be scrupulously observed.[61]

Chapter 24, although saying little about the Torah, requires comment because of the distinction I have drawn between an immediate 'fulfilment' of the Old Testament scriptures and a more distant *eschaton*. Mt.24:3 introduces the disciples' three-part request for further information concerning (i) the fall of Jerusalem, (ii) the sign of the fall of the city, and (iii) the sign of Jesus' parousia. They take it for granted that these coincide.

Jesus' reply initially focuses wholly on the fall of Jerusalem. Everything in 24:4–27 has local reference. There are allusions to Judea (24:16) and the restrictions of the sabbath (24:20) A contrast is specifically drawn between 'these things' and 'the end' (24:6).

The crucial verses are 29–31. They have been interpreted of the parousia occurring either immediately, within one generation, or after the inter-adventual period between the two comings of Christ[62]. R.T. France develops an old line of thought when he argues that they refer to the fall of Jerusalem described in apocalyptic language.[63] I basically agree, but would add one further point: the reason the verses apply parousia language to the fall of Jerusalem may be that the fall of Jerusalem is seen as a foretaste of the parousia. The language is itself appropriate to the parousia. The 'coming' of Dan.7:13 is seen in the events of the fall of the city; the parousia is experienced *by way of foretaste* within one generation. The proof that Dan.7:13 is fulfilled will be experienced by the disciples themselves.

It is thus the events connected with the fall of Jerusalem which are experienced within one generation. Mt.24:36 introduces a contrast (*de*, 'But . . . '). 'These things' (24:3,34) are to take place soon, '*but* of *that* day no one knows the day or the hour . . .'. None of this involves the Torah (except 24:20 incidentally) but it is relevant for the understanding of Mt.5:17–20 above. One could say that a *two-stage eschaton* is envisaged, one prefiguring the other, one near, one undated.

MATTHEW 26:1–28:20

This section describe the death and resurrection of the Christ. We are shown certain preliminaries, the approach of the Passover (26:1–5), his prior anointing for burial (26:6–13), the plans of Judas (26:14–16). The last supper takes place with its significant symbolism and predictions (26:17–30). The Mosaic legislation regarding the Passover is to be kept, yet in the midst of a Passover-like supper it is dramatically transformed. Henceforth not the passover laws but the institution of Jesus concerning the Lord's Supper are to be authoritative. Peter is warned of his weakness (26:31–35). Jesus prays in Gethsemane but is disappointed by the disciples' weakness (26:36–46). There follow the betrayal and arrest (26:47–56), the trial before Caiaphas (26:57–68), Peter's denial (26:69–75), the deliberation next morning (27:1f.), Judas' regrets (27:3–10), the interview with Pilate (27:11–14), the release of Barabbas (27:15–23), the condemnation of Jesus (27:24–26), the soldiers' mockery (27:27–32), the incident concerning Simon (27:33), the details of the crucifixion (27:34–54), the involvement of the followers of Jesus (27:55f.) including Joseph of Arimathea (27:57–60), and the setting of a guard over the tomb (27:61–66).

Chapter 28 portrays the visit of Mary Magdalene to the sepulchre (28:1–8), Jesus' meeting with the disciples (28:9–10), and the tale of the guards (28:11–15). The concluding commissioning of the disciples[64] brings the gospel to a close, mentioning the setting of the occasion (28:1–17) and Jesus' final words (28:1–20). The closing words of the gospel again stress Jesus' personal authority and lordship over his disciples. The requirements of the Torah have given way altogether to the requirements of Jesus. The risen Lord of the church continues to have direct authority over his disciples till the end of the age. If R.H.Smith is right in thinking that the end of the gospel explicitly addresses the issue of legalism and antinomianism[65] then it is significant that Matthew's Gospel presents us with the risen Lord exercising authority over the church, an authority exercised in the interests of righteousness. For Matthew, no written document represents ultimate authority. The assumption is that leadership over his disciples belongs to the risen Jesus alone. Reference to the 'end of the age' implies the continuance of his presence and power. The authority under which the apostles will place their converts is not a law-code but that of Jesus himself, directly. Hubbard points out that in a number of commissionings in the Hebrew bible people are put under the authority of the Mosaic law (see Jos.1:7; 1 Chr.22:13). The gospel is not dominated by Mosaism. The 'I' of Jesus replaces the Mosaic law that is the supreme authority in the commissioning of Joshua. (Jos.1:7) and Solomon (1 Chr.22:13). In the final commission law is not mentioned. Jesus alone fills the horizon.[66] .

CONCLUSION

Finally, we are able to draw some conclusions about Matthew's view of the law and about how his contribution might help in constructing a systematic theology.

1. The term 'law' in Matthew seems always to refer to the total Torah.

2. Matthew does not disparage the Torah; he does not envisage that it will be despised or abrogated by direct disobedience.

3. Law is analogous to prophecy in that both point forward to events in history.

4. Jesus has no great concern to submit to the oral developments of the Torah. He disregards requirements that law-abiding Jews shall not

eat with gentiles (9:9–13) and explicitly puts the requirement of mercy over against the Pharisaic custom (9:13, citing Ho.6:6). A similar disregard for the extension of requirements concerning the Sabbath is buttressed by the same citation (12:7, also citing Ho.6:6). The Pharisees' query (9:11), although it does not use the word 'law', clearly derives from their legal tradition. Matthew alone has the citation of Ho.6:6. Matthew is interested in showing that Jesus put mercy above the Pharisaic extension of the law.

The high view of the sanctity of the Mosaic law does not always include its oral developments. In 15:3ff the teaching of the scribes is called the 'precepts of men' (15:6,9,14, cf.16:6,11). For Matthew the sin of the Pharisees includes content of teaching as well as hypocrisy

Thus Matthew shows Jesus in 'fellowship' with 'sinners' (9:10) to the vexation of the Pharisees (9:11). In their eyes at least Jesus does what is 'not lawful' (15:2), a charge he does not deny, but dismisses their traditions as 'of men' (15:9) rather than commandments of God (15:3) or the word of God (15:6). His reason for paying the temple tax was 'lest we cause then to stumble' (17:27); in principle 'the sons are free' (17:26).

5. In interpreting the law Jesus ranked moral above ceremonial requirements. This implies a gradation in the law. Compassion outstrips ritual requirements. Jesus' only citation of the demand of the law singles out the demand for love, and its concomitants, justice, mercy and faithfulness. This does not mean that Jesus was not concerned at all about ceremonial requirements. Mt.8:4 suggests otherwise.

6. Jesus came to fulfil the law (5:17). When tempted he has recourse to Deuteronomy (4:1–11). When he cleanses a leper he is concerned that the law be observed (8:4).

7. The fulfilment of the law by Jesus results in a change of epoch. The law and the prophets prophesy until – and only until – John (11:13). The consequent change in the applicability of the law is defined by the coming of an epoch which takes the kingdom of God a step further than anything known in the day of John (11:11).

8. Implicit in the previous point is the important fact that the governing principle of the Christian life is not, simplistically, domination by the Torah.

9. Christian godliness, although it will not simplistically continue Mosaism, will nevertheless fulfil the law since this is fulfilled by the disciple (5:17; see also 1:19). John speaks to Herod of what is 'not lawful' (14.4) Stature in the kingdom is measured by the extent to which the law is fulfilled. The Christian outstrips those who live under Torah legislation.

10. At points Matthew's Gospel is strikingly un-Mosaic. The opening paragraphs revolve around Abraham and David but have no concern with anything distinctively Mosaic .

11. Becoming a Christian entails a change in one's 'rule of life'. This change is christologically determined and involves a transfer of

dominion. The position formerly occupied by the law is now occupied by Jesus and life becomes Christ-centred not law-centred. In no place where Christ's demand is explained is the law actually cited, except for the love-command. The law is not cited in the demands of John the Baptist (3:7–12) nor in the description of the life of the kingdom in 5:3–16, nor in the second half of the antitheses (5:21–48) concerned with it. The remainder of the Sermon on the Mount focuses on being directly beneath God's eye (6:1–18) avoiding covetousness (6:19–24) or anxiety (6:25–34). Judgement is based on Jesus' words (7:1–11,13–27; 7:12 concerns the *indirect* fulfilment of the law). The disciple's yoke is that of Jesus (11:29). Jesus' breaking of the Sabbath (12:6) is justified because he himself is 'greater than the temple' (12:6).

Throughout, Jesus addresses the disciples *directly*, laying *his* demands on them without citing the Torah. This is frequent throughout the gospel (note also the Christ-centredness of 4:19–22; 5:11,21–48; 6:16,25,29; 7:22–27).

12. If we seek to discover Matthew's view on the present use of the law, we shall find that he does not think like this. 'Fulfilling' the law is not the same as 'using' it. Matthew does not want Christians to be preoccupied with the law. Preoccupation with Jesus and his requirements, without the mediation of the Torah, will nurture Christian godliness. Directly, the law is not 'used' at all. (Whether Matthew would object to the use of a Christianized version of the Torah to promote social order in a modern state is hardly within the purview of his gospel.) Although 'conviction of sin' is the theme in Mt.3, the law is not mentioned at all.

13. If Matthew were asked to define the *purpose* of the Torah he would apparently reply: (i) to point to Jesus and (ii) to provide a temporary and somewhat defective delineation of a level of godliness needful to serve the interests of love in Israel. It was a guide to morality in Israel before the coming of Jesus.

14. Christian godliness goes higher than the law. Jesus' demand is more radical. Often the commands of Jesus do not contradict the law but heighten it. One enters the kingdom via a spirituality that is higher than the law.

15. Because Christian godliness goes higher than the law it dispenses with parts of the law. When the demands of Jesus are compared with those of the law there is a change at certain points. Occasionally the demands of Jesus contradict or abrogate the law, not in the interests of a lesser spirituality but to promote a heightened spirituality (e.g. 19:3–12). The legal requirement to keep the Passover is abandoned and the requirement laid upon the disciples is to observe the Lord's Supper (Mt.26).

16. Christian fulfilment of the law derives indirectly from submitting to the lordship of the risen Jesus.

17. Christian godliness is numerically simpler than the complexity of the law, since love reduce commands to a 'rule of thumb'. The 'rule of life' focuses on a single point. While this is summarized in the love

command of 22:34–40, even this is Jesus' response to a question, not delivered on his own initiative.

18. Righteousness consists of life under Jesus, life under the eye of God.

19. The command to love one's neighbour is for Matthew the key that opens understanding of the law. It is stressed in 22:39 and added to 19:9b in Matthew's redaction. It twice expresses Jesus' attitude to the law (9:13; 12:7). In 24:12 'lawlessness' equals lack of love. Thus love is seen to be the goal of the law and the prophets (13:39f.; 7:12). Jesus may put forward the demand of love without mentioning the Torah.

20. There is gradation within the law. Mercy is above sacrifice (9:13ff; 12:7).

21. Thus Mosaism is 'swallowed up' by the demands of Jesus. If we ask whether the Torah continues to have authority, the Matthean answer is: Yes, but only as transformed, heightened and mediated through the person of Jesus. In practice this will mean that the focus of interest is Jesus not the Torah. It is possible to incite godliness without mentioning the Torah.

22. Matthew's theology of Christian obedience is thus non-legalistic. It is person-centred, fellowship-centred. It is higher than the Torah in its Old Testament form.

23. The emphasis of Matthew's Gospel is that the entire Old Testament, including the Mosaic law, has been fulfilled in Jesus. Matthew's approach to the Torah is positive. He will not allow any disparagement of the law, although he *does* disparage those who think the law enables them to be adequately righteous. Jesus did not disparage the law; rather he fulfilled it. On the other hand Matthew does not view Christian godliness as mere law-keeping. The authority governing the Christian is Jesus.

It is in this way that the Christian 'fulfils' the law. Any kind of life that leads to the disparagement of Scripture will be a mark of sin, and of a lower status in the kingdom of God. Obedience to Jesus will fulfil the law.

Matthew regards this as different from being directly under the Mosaic law. The strong contrasts in the antitheses of 5:41–48 indicate a strong contrast between living under Jesus and living under the law. It is *not* by living under the law that one *fulfils* the law. For the life into which the risen Jesus would lead us (Mt.28:18–20) is a fulfilment of all that God has in mind in the ancient Scriptures.

In essence, Matthew's teaching (i) is non-legalistic (ii) is Christ-centred, (iii) fulfils the law, but (iv) looks for a level of godliness that goes higher than the law.

Despite the reputation for legalism attributed to Matthew in modern scholarship and despite the differences of emphasis, Matthew and Galatians are easily compatible and are even mutually supportive. Matthew portrays a Jesus who kept the law and refuses to disparage it. Galatians portrays a Jesus who was 'born under the law'. Despite numerous negative statements, Paul falls short of ever disparaging the law.

. Although Matthew indicates that there is a way in which the law is to be fulfilled at a higher level than anything known among the Pharisees and in scribal circles he does not define how this will come about. We are left at the end of the gospel with ongoing experience of the risen Jesus. His disciples are under the leading of his teaching and continue in fellowship with him. When we move from Matthew to Paul, we discover that Paul says much the same in terms of the Holy Spirit. Both writers insist that Christians *fulfil* the Law. Matthew puts this in terms of fellowship with the risen Jesus, Paul in terms of the Holy Spirit. If therefore we ask, 'What must I believe?' and seek to incorporate into our thinking the teaching of both Matthew and Paul we may indeed be conscious of slight differences of emphasis between them but we need have no difficulty in incorporating the emphases of both into our own lives. Anyone heeding the teaching of both Matthew and Paul in thought and life will regard the law as divinely given, will not wish to disparage it, but neither will they feel themselves directly under it. They will seek continued fellowship with the risen Jesus. They will want to walk in the Spirit. Because they are not interested in a direct relationship with the Law, they are likely to be labelled antinomian. Yet it is along such lines that they will 'fulfil' the law.

11

The Faith of Christ

There are three reasons for including a consideration of the 'faith of Christ' at this point. (i) Historically, it has been regarded as important by certain so-called 'antinomians'[1] and is thus part of my theme. (ii) I think the theological 'antinomians' who took such a view were insightful. Such a theme is indeed part of the basis of the Christian's assurance. (iii) I am now seeking to outline the contours of a revised 'Reformed' theology, and this would be a major aspect of it.

It is worth pondering the New Testament data. There are eleven occasions in the New Testament where the term 'faith' is followed by a genitive referring to Jesus (Ro.3:22,26; Gal.2:16,16,20; 3:22; Eph.3:12; Phil.3:9; Jm.2:1; Rev.2;13; 14:12). Their interpretation is disputed. Does 'the faith of Jesus' refer to faith in Jesus exercised by those who trust in him, or possibly the faith about Jesus which they hold (the so-called 'objective genitive')? Or does it refer to the faith that Jesus himself exercised (the so-called 'subjective genitive')?. Apart from these allusions to the 'faith of Jesus', Jesus is clearly presented as a man of faith, one who depended on his Father and upon the Old Testament scriptures. In Hebrews 2, where the writer is unfolding the theme of Jesus' humanity and ability to sympathise with humankind since he too is flesh and blood, part of his humanity is his exercising faith. He is portrayed as saying of the Father: 'I will put my trust in him'. The miracle of the cursing of the fig-tree is attributed to Jesus' faith.

The first scholar in post-Reformation times to have seriously urged that *pistis christou* refers to Jesus' personal faith was apparently J.Hausleiter of Greifswald[2]. The suggestion appears not to have been taken seriously, but in 1955 G.Hebert also argued that the phrase was a subjective genitive[3] and something similar was maintained by T.F.Torrance in 1957 and received support from Barth and others[4]. Some replies were issued[5]. Debate has continued however and recent writers have been more open to the possibility that *pistis christou* in the New Testament at least includes ideas involved in a subjective genitive[6].

There are reasons for thinking that the New Testament *pistis christou*, and the like, refers to the faith of Christ.

1. No indisputable case of *pistis* with an objective genitive exists. No example is cited in the 9th edition of Liddell and Scott's *Dictionary* (two mentioned in the 8th edition were reclassified in the 9th edition). Nor is any example mentioned by Moulton and Milligan's *Vocabulary*.[7] Thus the natural first reading of *pistis Iesou* is 'faith that Jesus has'. It is this reading of the phrase that is suggested by the vast majority of occasions where *pistis* is found with a genitive.

2. Several statements in the New Testament are tautologous if translated as an objective genitive. Is it likely that Paul meant to say, 'Knowing that a man is justified through faith in Jesus even we have put faith in Jesus in order to be justified by faith in Jesus' (Gal.2:16)? Surely this is repetitive and tautologous.[8] Is it likely that Paul meant to refer to the righteousness 'through belief in Jesus Christ upon all who believe'(Ro.3:22)? Is the repetition not rather odd? Another curious repetition is Gal.3:22: 'the promise by belief in Jesus Christ to whose who believe'. A similar double reference is found in Phil.3:9. Paul might use the occasional odd expression, but here are four occasions where there is (on a objective-genitive view) a rather eccentric double reference to faith. It is more likely that the expressions concerned should mean, 'We have put faith in Jesus to be justified by the faith of Jesus' (Gal.2:16) and ' . . . righteousness through the faith of Jesus for all who have faith' (Ro.3:22) and so on.

3. The phrase for 'faith in Christ' is *pistin eis* (Ac.20:21, etc), *pistis en* (Ro.3:25,etc) and *pistis epi* (Hb.6:1, etc.). In such cases, where the expression used indisputably refers to faith in Christ there is never a double reference to faith (as in Ro.3:22, Gal.2:16; 3:22; Phil.3:9).

4. Then there is the matter of New Testament usage. Leaving aside some debatable occurrences, there are 60 places in the Greek New Testament where the noun *pistis* is clearly followed by a genitive. In at least 44 of them the genitive is clearly subjective[9]. In the remaining 16 instances the interpretation of the genitive is more open to discussion[10]. It could indeed be argued that no example of an objective genitive with *pistis* exists in the New Testament. Mark 11:22 could refer to the 'faithfulness of God'; Ac.3:16 could mean 'the faith that his name inspires'; there may be good reasons for taking Ro.3:22,26, Gal.2:16,16,20; 3:22, Eph.3:12, Phil.3:9, Jas.2:1, Rev.2:13 and 14:12 to refer to the personal faith of Jesus. Phil.1:27 may refer to the 'faith that the gospel inspires' rather than 'faith in the gospel. Col.2:7 may refer to the 'faith wrought by the working of God' rather than faith 'in' the working of God. 2 Thess.2:13 could refer to faith inspired by the truth or brought about by the truth. Thus there is no indisputable objective genitive using *pistis* anywhere in the New Testament. These observations accord with those of G.Howard, who observes that of the 24 instances of *pistis* followed by a genitive of a person in the Pauline corpus (ignoring the disputed references to Christ), on 20 occasions the faith refers to that of a Christian, one refers to the faithfulness of God (Ro.3:3), two to the faith of Abraham (Ro.4:12,16), and one to

anyone who has their faith reckoned to them as righteousness (Ro.4:5). Thus in all cases the faith referred to is the faith *of* a person not faith *in* a person.[11]

5. Then there is the phenomenon of identical constructions in Ro.3:22; 3:26; and 4:16. There is a noticeable similarity between the phrase *ek pisteos Abraam* (Ro.4:16) and the phrase *ton ek pisteos Iesou* (Ro.3:26). Why should one be translated as an objective genitive and the other as a subjective genitive? The natural assumption is that if one refers to the faith(fulness) of Abraham, and another to the faith(fulness) of God, then the third will refer to the faith(fulness) of Jesus. Robinson rightly says that Paul 'is confusing his readers unless he intends the same grammatical construction'.[12]

6. In some texts the genitive looks more subjective than objective. It seems less likely that Eph.3:12 bases our assurance of access in prayer upon our faith than upon his faith (or faithfulness). Paul surely bases boldness upon something in Jesus, rather than in the human believer? Phil.3:9 refers to 'a righteousness not my own'. Is it not more likely that Paul will go on to refer to Jesus' faith(fulness) rather than to something which is my own, i.e. my faith? In Rev.2:13 the risen Christ refers to 'my name' and 'my faith'. Is not the *mou* in *to onoma mou . . . ten pistin mou* likely to be the same kind of genitive on both occasions? If the former is possessive, can the latter be anything but possessive? Are not the genitives of Rev.14:12 (*tas entolas tou theou kai ten pistin Iesou*) likely to be of the same nature?

In short, there is good reason to think that several if not all of the allusions to a *pistis Iesou* include reference to Jesus' personal faith, and that there is considerable significance in the fact that the Christian's faith is anchored to Jesus' faith. The phrase *pistis christou* considered in itself could be taken in many ways. (i) It may mean the faith that Jesus had. (ii) It is conceivable that it could mean 'faith in Jesus', although this is not as natural a way of taking it as is often supposed. (iii) It could mean 'faithfulness of Jesus'. (iv) Conceivably it could mean 'faithfulness towards Jesus'. Yet other possibilities have been canvassed.

At the very least a subjective genitive is included in the meaning of the expression and the New Testament relates the personal faith of Jesus to his humanity, his sympathy, and his substitutionary work as a Saviour.

In Reformed theology the work of Jesus has often been portrayed as substitutionary sin-bearing. A second aspect of Jesus' work has been his positively fulfilling the law and living a godly life. This has caused more controversy: in Arminian circles the 'active obedience' of Christ has generally held less significance. In fact, many who have been happy to say that Jesus died for them have been less happy to say that he lived for them.[13] Yet there is biblical ground for the idea of Christ's righteousness being given to us.[14] Christ's obedience was 'for us' just as his death was 'for us'. We are 'righteous' in Christ as well as forgiven.

But the substitutionary work of Christ has a significant third aspect. Jesus not only lived for us and died for us but also believed for us. (This does not dispense with the need for individual faith any more than Christ's righteousness dispenses with the need for individual righteousness.) This also relates to the theme of freedom from condemnation and assurance of salvation.

(i) If a person faces judgement because of their sins and the inadequacy of their life, do they not face judgement also because of the inadequacy of their faith? Human faith is never perfect. We do not exercise faith in every situation. Even the greatest Christian knows lapses of faith. The writer to the Hebrews warns believers against unbelief. The disciples can be asked 'Where is your faith?' as though they had misplaced their faith in a crisis (Lk.8:25).

(ii) Just as Jesus' death may be viewed as substitutionary sin-bearing, and just as Jesus' life and resurrection may be viewed as substitutionary righteousness, so Jesus' faith may be viewed as substitutionary faith. Part of human godliness is the practice of faith in every situation. Unbelief is treated as reprehensible and incurs judgement. If Jesus is to be viewed as sinless he must be viewed as a man of faith. The temptations in the wilderness were, amongst other things, temptations to unbelief ('If you are the Son of God . . .'). His being tempted at all points includes temptation to doubt. His sinless life includes his exhibiting a life of faith. If both his sin-bearing death and his sinless life relate to human need, so also does his perfect faith relate to human need.

(iii) Faith has as its object the person of Jesus (Ac.16:31), the name of Jesus (Ac.3:16), the blood of Jesus (Ro.3:25, assuming that the 'faith' is the believer's faith). Gal.2:16 and comparable texts show that it also has as its object the *faith* of Jesus.

A particular point of interest is the way in which the faith of Christ relates to assurance of salvation. It is not unusual for Christians to have anxieties concerning their sins. In such a situation pastoral counsel may offer assurance by pointing to Jesus as sin-bearer, the one who has achieved what he cannot achieve, perfect compensation for sin, perfect righteousness. If a Christian feels the inadequacy of their life they may be comforted by the thought of being 'righteous in Christ'. Luther advised a monk in distress: 'Learn to know Christ . . . and say "Lord Jesus Christ, you are my righteousness, I am your sin. You took on you what was mine; yet set on me what was yours. You became what you were not, that I might become what I was not" '.[15] As Toplady wrote:

> My Saviour's obedience and blood
> Hide all my transgression from view.

This highlights the twin themes in evangelical substitutionary theology: 'obedience and blood'. But there is a third locus of anxiety which may be the most destructive of all: doubt about the adequacy of one's faith. It is the adequacy of Jesus' faith which provides assurance at this point also. This is the point of Paul's referring to 'putting faith in Jesus' faith(fulness)'. Our sins are expiated by Jesus' blood; failures in life are covered by Jesus' obedience; lapses in faith are covered in that our faith is anchored to Jesus' perfect faith. Just as Jesus was 'not spared' (Ro.8:32) anything of the agony of the cross, and was totally righteous in his life, so he was totally believing, totally faith-full. Paul says 'I live by the faith of Christ.' Few things take us totally out of ourselves, out of our self-concern, out of every doubt and fear, as does the knowledge that the faith of Jesus was and is at work on our behalf. If Paul says 'I live by the faith of Christ' should not Christians today say the same?

The words 'I believe; help my unbelief' (Mk.9:24) express a feeling widespread among Christians. Is there no objective ground of assurance by which we may know that our weaknesses of faith need not cause despair and condemnation? Freedom from the law could be viewed as a negative matter. Is there nothing positive which might be both liberating and exhilarating? There is: the fact that our faith is faith in Jesus' faith.

Somebody may ask whether the Christian really needs more 'assurance'. Do we need to think of more as having been 'earned' for us by Christ? I reply: (i) If the New Testament does indeed point to the 'faith of Christ' as a significant theme it is the pathway of faith to incorporate it into our theological thinking. (ii) There can be no doubt that some Christians are just as concerned about the inadequacy of their faith as they are by their sinfulness and their sense of a low level of godliness. A Christian may feel that a sin that once characterized their life is now long forgotten but a perennial sense of weakness of faith cannot (at least by some Christians) be dismissed so easily. (iii) If personal experience may be brought into the matter, then my own experience of having lived for some years with this theme of the 'faith of Christ' suggests that is *par excellence* the remedy to introspection. I am not surprised that it excites the opposition of more law-centred Christians. It virtually prevents introspection altogether. Those who wish to encourage more self-examination are right (from their own standpoint) to be hostile to the theme of the faith of Christ. But if the theme has a New Testament basis, what shall we say of such introspection? Our faith may be small and defective. Jesus' faith is all-embracing. If our small faith looks to his great faith, how can we fail?

12

Justification in a Non-Legalistic Theology

The first name that occurs to many people in connection with justification is that of Luther. There is good reason for this; although it has been claimed that the early church anticipated the teaching of Luther,[1] no clear statement of New Testament teaching concerning forensic justification is found before him.[2] After Paul and before Augustine the Christian life was generally not conceived in terms of 'justification'. Augustine himself did not hold to a sharp distinction between justification and sanctification. A forensic doctrine of justification was slow to emerge and owes much to Melanchthon as well as Luther.[3] A clear distinction between justification and sanctification is not to be found in Luther's early works,[4] and it seems to have been Melanchthon's greater expertise in Greek that led to a more sharply forensic doctrine. Article IV of the Apology for the Augsburg Confession was written by Melanchthon. Luther was the pathfinder, but Melanchthon brought the matter to sharper definition. One must however also point to early developments of Lutheranism as well as Luther's own teaching.[5]

While some might question how far Luther himself was aligned with the New Testament, most evangelical Christians would at least maintain that he was closer to the New Testament than his predecessors. Certainly he was influenced by some elements of the contemporary situation; his teaching was an adaptation of Paul's teaching to the needs of the 16th century. Paul was concerned with Jewish-gentile relationships; Luther with conscience. However when the differences are taken into account Luther remains remarkably faithful to Paul. Intra-evangelical controversies since the 16th century have largely taken the Lutheran doctrine as a starting point and have not really dissented from the central contentions of Luther's view of justification. Evangelical studies of justification have largely been repetitions of the four hundred year old tradition. Arminians have emphasized works and perseverance more than Luther did.[6] High Calvinists have correlated it with their predestinarianism.[7] 'Antinomians' (as they are tendentiously nicknamed) have quoted his more extreme statements.[8] Opponents of Protestant doctrine took the trouble to refute him, but sometimes did not read him well.[9] Yet all have made use of Luther.

IMPLICATIONS OF NON-LEGALISM

In modern times justification has been neglected; many works of Christian doctrine ignore it altogether. However the studies of Küng and Käsemann[10] and some intra-confessional discussions have saved it from total extinction as a topic of interest. Its neglect is the greatest weakness in many modern charismatic movements. My purpose here is simply to underline the distinctive emphases of a non-legalistic doctrine of justification. While taking for granted the exposition of the doctrine that has been presented by mainstream evangelicalism,[11] I shall note some distinctive implications brought about by acceptance of radical freedom from Mosaism. I also assume that the forensic and declarative force of *dikaioo* may be taken as more or less agreed. Although the overall interpretation of justification is by no means settled, the Lutheran interpretation of the verb *dikaioo* has been vindicated by further study. An emphasis on being 'made righteous' generally speaks of what accompanies justification rather than what the word itself entails.[12] I shall not attempt to present a fresh case for evangelical theology but to consider in what ways a non-legalistic interpretation of Scripture will modify one's view of justification.

(i) In a non-legalistic theology the doctrine of assurance is heightened and protected. We have seen that both Arminanism and high Calvinism tended to have a weak doctrine of perseverance, the one because of its views concerning loss of salvation, the other because of its introspection. Freedom from Mosaic law will lead to a heightened doctrine of assurance. It releases the believer from doing works as a means of salvation (not of course from the doing of works altogether). It releases the believer from the need of self-examination, with a view to assessing one's salvation. The ground of salvation is at one and the same time the ground for assurance. Faith is an assurance about Jesus. Its immediate consequence ought to be an assurance about oneself. To counsel the doubter will involve no more than drawing out what is implicit in his assurance concerning Jesus.

(ii) A non-legalistic theology will modify the traditionally tight link between justification and sanctification. Historically, evangelical Christians have heavily emphasized the close connection between the two. At this point I am using the word 'sanctification' in the sense of progressive growth in godliness, becoming more and more like Jesus. J.Murray is right to note that 'it would be . . . a deflection from biblical patterns of language and conception to think of sanctification exclusively in terms of a progressive work'.[13] Sanctification is both indicative ('I am sanctified') and imperative ('I must become sanctified'). This is an instance where systematic theological language is not as close as it might be to the vocabulary of the Bible. At present I use the term 'sanctification' exclusively in its progressive sense. This is an important matter when considering such topics as the *ordo salutis*, the 'order of salvation', where what is true of sanctification in one sense might not be true of sanctification in another sense.

Paul's words, 'Is Christ divided?' have been reapplied. The modern evangelical asks the question, 'Can Christ as saviour be divided from Christ as sanctifier?' and answers 'No'.[14]

THE ACCUSATION OF LICENTIOUSNESS

Underlying this is fear of being open to the charge of licentiousness. Since the days of the Protestant Reformation this has haunted evangelical theology. J.R.W.Stott focuses on it quite explicitly. The Roman Catholic questions, he says, need to be taken seriously:

'We need . . . to respond to their pressures upon us. The chief might be a series of questions like the following. 'Do you still insist that when God justifies sinners he 'pronounces' but does not 'make' them righteous? that justification is a legal declaration, not a moral transformation? that righteousnesss is 'imputed' to us, but neither 'infused' in us nor even 'imparted' to us? that we put on Christ's righteousness like a cloak, which conceals our continuing sinfulness, that justification, while changing our status, leaves our character and conduct unchanged? that every justified Christian, as the reformers taught, is *simul justus et peccator* . . . ? If so, is not justification a legal fiction, even a giant hoax, a phoney transaction external to yourself, which leaves you inwardly unrenewed? Are you not claiming to be changed when in fact you are not changed? Is not your doctrine of 'justification by faith alone' a thinly disguised free licence to go on sinning'.

Stott strongly emphasizes the inseparability of justification and regeneration. 'Once we hold fast that the work of the Son for us and the work of the Spirit in us, that is to say, justification and regeneration, are inseparable twins, it is quite safe to go on insisting that justification is an external, legal declaration that the sinner has been put right with God, forgiven and reinstated.'[15]

What is significant about Stott's remarks is that his statement of the inseparability of regeneration and justification is specifically a reaction to Roman Catholicism, and that he talks about 'responding to pressure'. In this respect he is following a path trodden by many evangelical theologians since the days of Reformation conflicts.

One may agree with Stott's remarks about the inseparability of regeneration and justification. However I question whether evangelical traditional theology has rightly stated the inseparability of justification and sanctification. The impression is given that justification-regeneration forces inexorable and inevitable godliness. There is some truth in this. Regeneration will certainly lead powerfully in the direction of godliness. I myself have written something similar,[16] commenting on Romans 6.

'The Christian has been enslaved to God. This is a very powerful and strong word. It is a very great and mighty thing that has happened to the Christian. It is a great change, a complete change. He is utterly removed from the dominion of sin and put under the dominion of grace. God's grace has also taken up residence in his life and rules powerfully from within. It is not an ambition or something the apostle hopes will be true one day. It is already true; it has already happened. We have been poured into the mould of the gospel and are internally propelled towards righteousness (6:17); we are the servants of righteousness which governs and controls us (6:18). We are internally driven by God's ruling and reigning grace.'

Regeneration is a powerful event. It changes us radically and makes us new people. Only gross ignorance would ever make a Christian think they can lightly sin. Righteousness has enslaved us, taken hold of us with great power. This is greatly encouraging. It tells us that we can live a godly life, and that there are powerful reasons for doing so. The grace of God is working where sin once abounded. Paul says, 'You are the slaves of the one whom you obey' (Rom.6:16). But none of this must be exaggerated to the point where it virtually says a Christian cannot sin at all! Or that grace 'forces' godliness. A non-legalistic theology will put it differently. It is not biblically or theologically correct to give the impression that justification automatically brings about godliness.

In the history of theology, to tie justification and sanctification too closely invariably produces a moralistic trend. This is precisely what happened during the seventeen and eighteenth centuries. Within the predominant Anglicanism before 1642, Anglican theologians, influenced by continental theologians, sharply distinguished justification and sanctification; whereas after the restoration of kingship (that is, after 1660) Anglican theologians linked the two together. The result was the well-known moralism of late seventeenth and early eighteenth century Anglicanism.[17]

JUSTIFICATION AND SANCTIFICATION

However a number of biblical considerations ought to make us hesitate before we integrate too closely justification and sanctification (in the Protestant sense of those terms).

(i) In the New Testament Christian living is urged upon the Christian readers. Such exhortation would not be needed if godliness were inevitable.

(ii) The New Testament contains solemn warnings to the Christian who lapses from godliness. It says that if we do not mortify the flesh we shall die and that if we sow to the flesh we shall from the flesh reap corruption. It envisages a person's so grieving their conscience that, despite being a 'brother', they are ruined in their relationship to God. There is surely no implication here that Christian status is inseparably and inexorably linked to the godly life as though godliness and Christian conversion were like Siamese twins.

(iii) The New Testament mentions Christians who were guilty of sin. The incestuous man of 1 Cor.5 was apparently viewed with complacency by the Corinthians (1 Cor.5:2). Some at Thessalonica clearly were defrauding their fellow Christians and Paul has to repeat a solemn warning to the effect that God would avenge such sin (1 Thess.4:6–8). This widespread New Testament phenomenon is surely not compatible with Protestant statements concerning the inseparability of justification and sanctification.

(iv) 1 Corinthians contains a clear statement that a Christian may be 'carnal'. This might appear a contradiction in terms. The concept is certainly incompatible with any doctrine of the inseparability of justification and sanctification since a 'carnal' Christian must be someone who is justified but whose sanctification is sadly defective.

(v) That such inconsistency might be found in the Christian even at life's end is made clear by 1 Cor.3:15.

It follows that the relationship between justification and sanctification needs to be restated. Justification and regeneration are indeed Siamese twins (or perhaps the same baby viewed from different angles). Where one is, the other is. The same could be said of justification and definitive sanctification. But if by 'sanctification' one means progressive growth in holiness and godly living, surely the right way to state the relationship is to say that one's justified-regenerate position in Christ enables progress in godly living, demands such progress, inspires it, and has a tendency which leads powerfully in that direction. That it inexorably and invariably produces godliness however must be questioned. Although the Christian is called upon to live a godly life, the New Testament takes seriously the possibility that God's people may be rebellious and inconsistent. Grace makes godliness possible. It is not easy to imagine a person's becoming a Christian without its affecting their manner of life. Yet the New Testament doctrine of justification seems to take the possibility of severe sin in the Christian much more seriously than is common in the traditional doctrine of justification.

We must allow for the fact that genuine salvation may be accompanied by severe inconsistency. There is scarcely a passage in the New Testament which queries the genuineness of the salvation of anyone who professes faith in Jesus. One passage that could be taken that way (Ja.2:14) and the one invitation to self-examination (2 Cor.13:5) need not be read introspectively. What we find in the New Testament is a very serious realization that genuine Christians whose salvation is not in doubt may fall badly. Much space is given to motivate them not to fall, but to work out their salvation in practical living. Their position in Christ is secure; but godliness is not an automatic by-product. Justification-regeneration-adoption are all part of the transfer to a kingdom of grace (Rom.5:12–21). It should not be misused (Rom.6:1–12). After our settled and secure salvation we are called upon to work at something which is not automatic – the practicalities of Christian living. Yet the appeal is non-legalistic because it affirms that assurance of salvation is inherent in faith without and before good works. Distinct attention is given towards motivating the Christian to godliness after his salvation is sure. Justification and sanctification are connected not by being tightly integrated but by a distinction. Justification prepares for sancification but does not (as both Arminianism and Calvinism have suggested) force sanctification.

Evangelical theologians have sometimes linked justification and godliness so tightly as to threaten assurance of salvation.At this point non-legalistic theology calls for a further step of radicalization in the traditional evangelical approach, a more-Lutheran-than-Luther realization of the freedom of salvation. Basing itself on a high assurance of salvation, it calls for godliness without legalism or introspection.

We have seen that there is indeed a link between justification and sanctification; the former produces a strong impulse in the direction of the latter. The love of Christ 'constrains'. But it appears that justification does not inexorably secure practical godliness, that the salvation of the inconsistent Christian need not be threatened, that justification does no violence to the personality (a point in which all would agree, although its implication is not always noted).

Actually it may be argued that it is the traditional doctrine of high Calvinism which is 'antinomian'. For if one presses the point that justification produces sanctification inexorably, then anyone with an assurance of salvation has no need to concern themselves with their spirituality because implicit in such a doctrine is an assurance of practical sanctification! I do not know that anyone argues in this manner, but if justification-sanctification are indivisible (even though distinct) then an assurance about one is an assurance about the other. Those who do attain assurance of salvation have also assurance (if they are consistent) about their actual sanctification, like the Pharisee of Luke 18; if they doubt their actual sanctification this must challenge their assurance of salvation. The latter has happened more often than the former. But the dilemma casts doubt upon the original assumption. Justification-sanctification should not be so tightly integrated. The non-legalist view sees justification as preparing the way for a godly life, and as enabling such godly life, but insists that the life of godliness does require distinct attention. The Christian with an assurance of salvation must consciously and deliberately walk in the Spirit. If he walks in the Spirit deliberately and practises Christian love deliberately (two phrases for one reality) he will fulfil the law accidentally. Practical sanctification will have followed justification – but not inexorably.

It follows that a non-legalistic theology will view the 'threatening' aspect of the New Testament in a distinctive manner. Roman Catholic and Arminian theologies associate the threats of the New Testament with loss of grace and apostasy. Christians are told to 'work with anxious concern to achieve your salvation' (as the Roman Catholic

NAB translates Phil.2:13). In Calvinist theology admonitory passages
of Scripture tend to be interpreted introspectively. However in a non-
legalistic theology they will be correlated with promises and admonitions concerning reward or loss of reward. A non-legalistic theology
will allow for teaching concerning reward or loss of reward without
tightly integrating such teaching with the doctrine of justfication. In
this Luther has already pioneered the way – although his progress is
marred by the continuing influence of the pre-Reformation view of the
law. Heinz's remark is significant: 'Luther's unambiguous rejection of
the doctrine of merit must not deceive us into thinking that the
reformer does not hold fast to the biblical sayings about reward.'[18]
This aspect of the matter is a major motivating force in Christian
godliness.

The priority of justification-faith over practical sanctification is to be
taken with great seriousness. A clear *ordo salutis* must be upheld. The
scholastic Protestant teaching concerning an *ordo salutis* is widely
disparaged today. This is understandable since it has often become
introspective and hair-splitting. Preoccupation with the stages of
salvation has distracted from the way of faith. The 'preparationism' of
the English and American Puritans is generally rejected. Yet one
aspect of the matter must be maintained: the priority of faith and
justification over other aspects of salvation.

It is a curious fact that while Roman Catholic theologians may be
found who affirm the distinctness of justification and sanctification and
who assert the priority of the former over the latter,[19] yet some
Protestant evangelicals have moved closer to the traditional Roman
Catholic view. Thus P.Toon presents justification and sanctification as
'complementary models whose truth should not be pressed into a
logical or chronological relationship'.[20] Similarly, Rahner asserts that
'according to Trent and its ordinary interpretation in Catholic theology
and also according to the Scripture, one must speak of two sides of one
and the same process, not of two phases one after another'.[21]

While I have no interest in constructing a complex and introspective
ordo salutis yet the priority of faith (i.e. of believing the testimony of
God concerning Jesus) as the entrance to all spiritual blessings is
prominent in the New Testament, including, for example, Romans
and Galatians.

In the structure of Romans justification is presented before the
appeal for godly living, which is introduced with the word 'therefore'
because it is built upon the doctrine of justification. The first
exhortation in Romans is 6:11, which concerns only the grasping of
one's position in Christ. It is followed in 6:12 by the first exhortation
concerning practical godliness. This clearly invites the Christian to
build upon what has already been said in 3:21–6:10, a passage
containing no exhortation at all. Paul is virtually saying, 'In the light of
what is true of you and your position in Christ I am asking you not to
let sin rule . . . '. There is a clear *ordo* here. The Christian's position in
Christ must be established before any ethical appeal is made. As the

epistle continues to expound the believer's position in Christ a similar pattern in followed in 8:1–13. Verses 12–13 build upon 8:1–10. A sustained ethical appeal (12:1–15:13) is reserved until Paul has spoken at length about the believer's position in Christ.

Galatians shows a similar structure. Only after establishing freedom from the law does Paul commence ethical appeal (Gal.5:13ff). It would be difficult to deny the intentionality of all this. The basis of ethical appeal is one's position in Christ. One implication is that justification has priority – even chronological priority – over the appeal for practical godliness. After the 'mercies of God' and the 'therefore' have been grasped, one is ready for the 'I beseech you' (Rom.12:1–2).[22]

Any law-centred theology is likely to integrate justification and sanctification too closely. Its doctrine of assurance is likely to be weak or non-existent. It may even regard assurance as a sinful claim. Such assurance of salvation as it may offer is likely to be based (like that of the Pharisee in Luke 18) on an assurance of the individual's own sanctity.

Part 3

Motivation

13

Inheritance

Two questions arise at this point. The first is: what motivates and admonishes the believer to the godly life? The second may be seen as an alternative form of the first: how should we interpret the reprimands and warnings of Scripture?

A full reponse would be many-faceted. Here we shall concentrate on one of them only: the idea of 'inheritance' in the Bible. The two theologies we have surveyed (evangelical Arminianism and developed Calvinism) are alike in that they tightly integrate justification and sanctification. Another aspect of this is that they tightly integrate heaven and reward. In both theologies heaven is the reward. Fletcher denounced the maxim, 'Good works shall be rewarded in heaven and eternal life, although not with eternal life and heaven', although he had once held it himself. He labelled it an 'antinomian error'. For the Arminian Fletcher, getting to heaven is the reward. Salvation and reward are tightly integrated.[1] Yet developed Calvinism is at this point little different. Calvinist expositors assume that 'inheritance' is 'getting to heaven'. The very term 'reward' tends to be associated with 'working for heaven'. Accordingly some Calvinist writers dislike the concept, while others are eager to stress that reward is by grace and assume that all Christians will inexorably achieve their inheritance. Once more, salvation and reward are tightly integrated. A.A.Hoekema urges that although the sins of Christians are revealed on judgement day this gives no cause for alarm since 'the sins and shortcomings of believers will be revealed in the judgement as *forgiven sins* . . . believers have nothing to fear from the judgement'.[2] The same integration of salvation and inheritance is implicit here: the believer, being justified, has therefore 'nothing to fear from the judgement'.

I would maintain that salvation and reward are not so tightly integrated as Arminian and Calvinist theologies both assume. The Arminian need not be so legalistic; the Calvinist need not be so secure *with regard to reward*.

'INHERITANCE' IN THE OLD TESTAMENT

In the Old Testament seven words are translated 'inheritance' or 'inherit'.[3] 'Inheritance' is explicitly mentioned about 650 times in the

Old Testament, and in the New Testament contains 48 verses which mention being an 'heir' or 'inheriting'. We may consider the biblical material in three sections.

The first biblical reference to inheritance is Gn.15:7–8. Here the inheritance is land. 'I brought you out . . . to give you this land . . . to inherit it', says God to Abraham. The inheritance is not Abraham's justification, which he already has. The land which God wants to give as a gift will be 'inherited' in the future. It is natural to ask: what does its actual possession depend on?

Abraham, already justified (15:6), is offered inheritance and is reassured by the offer of God's covenant. The covenant-making ceremony (15:9–11) brings attached promises (15:12–21); the inheritance is the land (15:18, echoing 15:7–8).

Genesis 21:10 contains a passing mention of the inheritance but the next significant mention is in 22:17, following the oath of 22:16. Abraham is told that his seed will inherit the gate (or territory) of his enemies (Canaan). Actual possession of the inheritance remains in the future. Confirmed by oath, *it will be given to him by oath as a reward for the obedience of Genesis 22*. Even at this early stage, *inheritance is reward for obedience, given by oath*.

When Sarah dies (23:2), Abraham, who all his life has been promised land, has nowhere to bury her! He has to go as a landless alien to a resident Hittite to plead for a small plot (23:4). By 24:1 Abraham knows he is about to die and arranges Isaac's marriage in order to ensure that he will have a physical seed, but when he dies (25:8) he has still received no land other than a patch of burial ground. Surely it is these events – going beyond Genesis 22 – that are the background to Heb.11:13–16. The final discovery of Abraham's life is the realization that inheritance cannot consist merely of territory in this life and that the 'territory' must be beyond the grave.

'Inheritance' is mentioned again in 28:4. Isaac is praying for Jacob that what happened to Abraham his father might happen to Jacob his son, and that Jacob might come into the 'blessing of Abraham'. The point seems to be that since God's oath is irrevocable the land must be given to someone. But God did not specify in detail to whom the inheritance would come. If Jacob is blessed he will 'take possession'. Apparently in Scripture something which is promised by oath can be lost to one person and fulfilled for someone else. The promise will be fulfilled but the question of who will benefit remains open. Exodus 13:5,11; 32:13 mention that God swore to bring the Israelites to Canaan (alluding to Gn.22:16,17) but despite the oath the first generation did not reach Canaan. Yet the fulfilment of the oath is certain.(One recalls Heb.4:6, 'It remains for some to enter . . .) Numbers 14 mentions an oath of wrath (v.21) and an oath of mercy (v.23). God swears that someone will get the inheritance; he swears that the first generation will not get it. All of this is surely background to Heb.6:4–6, to which we come below.

During the period of Mosaic law territory was allocated to Israel, but this had to be taken. The territory was lost because of sin (the Exile) but reovered following repentance (the Restoration). These events all illustrate the principles affecting inheritance. The basic principles of inheritance continue but certain legal ingredients are 'added' or 'come in alongside' (cf. Rom.5:20; Gal.3:19). We may identify certain major principles.

(i) The inheritance is both given and taken. As Leviticus 20:24 puts it clearly. 'You shall take their land, and I will give it to you to possess it. The verb (*yarash*) often means 'to take possession, especially by force'.[4] When the spies of Numbers 13 come back to Moses, Caleb says 'Let us go up at once and seize it' (NAB, Nu.13:30).

(ii) This means that there is a difference between the allocation of the inheritance and the possession of the inheritance. The Mosaic law stipulated that once the inheritance was allocated it was illegal to sell the family-land. At most it could be leased for up to seven years. One could say that it was 'predestined', but this did not mean that every Israelite enjoyed his inheritance. One could have inheritance allocated but not get it. It could be that it was never attained because the necessary conflict was avoided. The exile from 586 to 538 BC was the greatest example of Israel's being disinherited because of sin.

It is this fact that gives rise to double expressions that one finds in connection with inheritance. When one reads of 'possessing one's possessions' (Ob.17) or of 'the inheritance which you shall inherit' (Dt.19:14) one reason for the double expression is that it was possible for there to be a 'possession' which was not 'possessed'.

(iii) The Levites had no territorial inheritance. No portion of the land was appointed for their exclusive use (Nu.18:23; Dt.12:12). They were a standing lesson to the nation that all Israelites were to be a people utterly dependent upon and totally surrendered to God. There is such a thing as inheritance directly received from God himself without territorial acquisition. The Levites had no share or inheritance. Yahweh was their inheritance. This means (a) their material provision would come through tithes and the Levites were thus dependent on the level of godliness among the people for their material well-being, and (b) they would have the privilege others did not have of ministry in the tabernacle (Nu.18:5–7). When God said 'I am your share and your inheritance' (Nu.17:20), he was promising to directly bless them, independently of territorial acquisitions. The institution of the Levites thus prepared the way for an 'inheritance' conferred directly by God himself rather than mediated through the legislative arrangements concerning Israelite territory.

(iv) Under the law enjoying the inheritance depended on obeying the Mosaic law (Dt.4:1; 6:18). The Israelites would lose their inheritance if they were disobedient (Dt.28:58,63). They could possibly get it back if they could be renewed unto repentance (Dt.30). When the people of Judah were exiled to Babylon because of idolatry, God kept their inheritance for them. When they repented of their breach of the covenant God brought them back.

(v) There appears to be a connection between the Israelites' having an inheritance and God's having an inheritance in Israel. In Dt.4:20 God is said to have an inheritance in his people; then in 4:21 the land is said to be the people's inheritance. The close juxtaposition of the two uses of the inheritance idea is striking. If the people will be an inheritance for God's delight, he will give them their inheritance for their delight.

(vi) Getting to one's inheritance is allied to 'entering into rest'. Shortly before the conflict that would bring them into Canaan, Moses told the people: 'You have not as yet come to the rest and the inheritance which Yahweh your God is in the process of giving to you' (Dt.12:9). 'Rest' is the first phase of 'inheritance'.

'INHERITANCE' IN THE NEW TESTAMENT

Thirdly, we consider the New Testament material concerning inheritance. The main points include at least the following:

(i) Nowhere in the New Testament is 'inheritance' dependent merely on justification. It is not received by faith only. It is rather the reward for meekness (Mt.5:5), suffering in the form of 'leaving everything' (Mt.19:27–20:16), suffering with Christ (Ro.8:17). It comes by being built up by the word of grace (Ac.20:32). It is the result of diligent faith (Ac.26:18),[5] and of serving the Lord from the heart (Col.3:23–24). It is attained by faith and patience (Hb.6:12), and could be affected by the way one relates to one's husband or wife (1 Pe.3:7). It comes by overcoming sin (Rev.21:7,8). Matthew 25:34 immediately relates inheritance to what has been done unto the least of Jesus' brothers.

(ii) The territorial aspect of inheritance, so prominent in the Old Testament, is not found in nationalistic form. It is present as 'the earth' (Mt.5:5), 'the world' (Ro.4:3). The same theme is present in Ro.8:18–25 if one is right in linking this to v.17.

(iii) An important point is that Jesus lived for inheritance. He is the 'heir' of the gospel parables (Mt.21:38; Mk.12:7; Lk.20:14). The author to the Hebrews introduces the theme in his opening sentence, describing Jesus as having been appointed heir – a reference to the resurrection/reward of his obedience to the point of death.

(iv) Inheritance has both present and future phases. It is the enjoyment of the kingdom of God in this life. 'Inheriting the promises' clearly refers in Hebrews to what is achieved in this life by diligent faith. Yet there is also an eschatological aspect: one 'inherits the kingdom' on a judgement day (Mt.25:35). Presumably Mt.5:5 has a mainly eschatological reference. The new heavens and new earth fulfil the territorial promise to Abraham (Ro.4:13). There is a resurrection to be 'inherited' which is distinct from the resurrection to condemnation of Jn.5:29b and Dan.12:2b. The dual aspect is clear in Mk 10:30: 'now in this time . . . and in the world to come'

(v) There is a connection between resurrection and reward. They are linked in Phil.3:11 and 1 Cor.15:50, which speaks of 'inheriting' resurrection. There is little point in verse 58 if the resurrection reward is inexorable and automatic. How can resurrection motivate one's labours if every Christian gets it regardless of works or their absence? I suspect that 1 Cor.15:41–42 means more than one may think at first sight ('One star differs from another star in glory. So also is the resurrection . . .') and indicates variation in level of glory. Certainly there must be differentiation within resurrection if 1 Cor.15:58 is to make any sense.

(vi) Abrahamic obedience is specifically contrasted with obedience to the Mosaic institutions. Territorial inheritance was attained in Israel by the law. It was external, material, physical, nationalistic and could be attained by any Israelite, regenerate or unregenerate, who was externally obedient to the Mosaic law. There is an analogous but contrasting equivalent to this in the New Testament, where the starting-point of receiving inheritance is justification but what is required is obedience to the Spirit. Romans 4 begins by emphasizing the starting-point (justification by faith, 4:1–12), then goes on to deal with how inheritance is attained (by persistent faith, 4:13–21). Subsequently Paul will introduce an 'if' (Rom.8:17). A similar point is made in Gal.3:18,29; 4:1,7,30, where (because of the particular controversy at Galatia) the subject matter is largely our standing before God. In a later section (5:12–6:18) where the theme is actual godliness, he warns that inheritance can be blocked (5:21).

(vii) We come now to the main point: inheritance is reward. This is the central motivating theme in the New Testament. Consider, for example, Mt.19:29. This is part of a section that includes 19:23–20:16 and vv 27, 29 show that the main point is reward. In answer to the question 'What . . . shall we have?' Jesus speaks of inheritance. Verse 30 makes the point that there will be some surprises, and the following and connected parable continues to deal with reward (20:16 repeats 19:30). The main point is not that all rewards are equal but that the priorities ('first . . . last') are not what would generally be regarded as 'lawful' (20:15). Other gospel passages make the same point.[6]

In the epistles, Col.1:12 and 3:24 treat inheritance as reward. The phrase *antapodosin tes kleronomias* is a genitive of definition and means 'recompense consisting of inheritance'.[7] *Hikanosant* means 'qualify' or 'authorize'. Paul thinks of reward as something that is open to the Christian, but is dependent on works of faith.

Romans 4:13,14; 8:17; Gal.3:18, 29; 4:1, Tit.3:7 and 1 Pet.1:4 come in sections of the epistles where the writer may be thought to be not dealing with reward so much as the Christian's basic position. The

main theme of Galatians 3–4 is how one may stand before God
'justified' and so be in a position to live for God. In such places reward
does not receive heavy emphasis, although it is still present. 1 Pet.1:4
means 'in order to obtain an inheritance' (note NASV) and it refers to
an inheritance 'in' heaven, not heaven as inheritance.[8]

In Ro.4:13,14 Paul expands the land-promises given to Abraham.
The fact that land/inheritance was so obviously reward in Genesis
makes it likely that this is in view here. Paul is deliberately repudiating
the nationalistic-legalistic approach to inheritance within the Mosaic
covenant, and pointing to faith alone as the starting-point of an
ongoing faith which will receive the inheritance. 'The promise' in
Ro.4:13 does not concern justification (since it looks to the new
heavens and earth) but it comes about through righteousness-by-faith,
i.e. it is open only to those who are justified by faith. This contrasts
totally with inheritance by legalistic obedience. Ephesians 1:3–14 does
not stress justification but again it could refer more to the possibility of
inheritance than to its irresistible security.[9]

ROMANS 4

These passages are occasionally thought to prove that reward and
salvation are synonymous, so we shall look more closely at one of
them.[10] Following a fearful yet realistic description of sin in Rom.1:18
to 3:20, Paul moves ('But now!') into an account of the gospel. Verses
21 and 22a contain his basic description of salvation. The coming of
Jesus inaugurated a new epoch for the human race. Salvation consists
of being given a righteousness. It is a righteousness of wholly of God.
It is without the law. It comes through the faithfulness of Jesus Christ,
was witnessed to by the Old Testament, has to be received by faith,
and is appropriate to every member of the human race.

Now Paul begins to argue his case. He returns to his point that
everyone needs this salvation (3:22b-23). He emphasizes its freedom,
and explains this is so because it comes through what Jesus achieved
on the cross. The cross was a propitiation, by means of Jesus blood, to
be received in faith (3:24–26). This way of salvation excludes boasting
(3:27–28), is appropriate for everyone (3:29–30) and fulfils the law
(Rom.3:21).

Romans 4 Paul continues this exposition. The way of salvation he
has described is precisely how both Abraham (4:1–5) and David (4:6–
8) were saved. The gospel fulfilled the Old Testament; in 4:9–12 Paul
shows how it relates to circumcision.

At this point that we reach Paul's mention of 'inheritance'. The
passage is often interpreted as though there were no change of
thought, and some Reformed and evangelical expositors find it
somewhat difficult. It is interesting that Dr Lloyd-Jones's mammoth
series of 372 sermons on Romans 1:1–14:17 included only two on 4:9–
17, in which he takes for granted that inheritance and justification are
virtually identical themes. Yet, in my own thinking, it has become

quite certain that in 4:13 Paul develops his argument and goes on to make a slightly different point. His point is that the goal of salvation, the reward that salvation makes possible, is reached not through law-keeping but through the 'righteousness of faith' he has already referred to. There are at least four reasons for taking it this way.

Firstly, Paul is developing his argument from the story of Abraham where, as I have tried to show, a distinction is made between justification and inheritance. Abraham was justified at the point mentioned in Genesis 15:6, or even earlier. The inheritance is something he will receive later.

Inheritance is certainly not justification. Is inheritance 'getting to heaven', then? No, for in Paul's thinking certainty of reaching glory is correlated with justification. Having been justified, we rejoice in expectation of glory (Ro.5:2), 'those whom God justified he glorified' (Ro.8:30). Dr Lloyd-Jones made much of this and rightly says that 'the Apostle jumps from justification to glorification . . . we should all learn to make this jump'.[11] Later (expounding 8:28–30) he urges that justification and glorification are so tightly linked that if you have the one you have the other.[12] All of this is absolutely right, but it means that if one is pursuing inheritance it is not precisely 'glorification' one is pursuing. That is obtained implicitly in being justified. What then is inheritance? In the case of Abraham it was land, a seed, honour, the experience of the oath of God. Justification and inheritance are distinct and it is that story Paul is explicating in Romans 4.

A second reason for distinguishing one's status in salvation from inheritance is that they are obtained in slightly different ways. We are saved – initially justified and given the pledge of glory – by faith alone. In Romans 3 and 4 Paul persistently makes this very point (3:22,25, 28; 4:3,5, etc). He has argued it in the case of Abraham (4:1–5) and David (4:6–8), and insisted that it is not a matter of circumcision or Israelite nationality (4:9–12). Earlier (3:28) he has said it is not a matter of keeping the Mosaic law. He makes that same point again in 4:9–12 since obedience to the law is supremely indicated by obedience to the command concerning circumcision.

Nor is heaven obtained by works. That too is by faith alone and is secure for us the moment we believe. This is clear in 5:1–2. Being justified we have peace with God. If we are justified we are as good as in heaven already. We are seated in the heavenly places. Those whom God has justified he has already glorified in plan and purpose and position.

But inheritance is different. Inheritance comes not by initial faith alone but by persistence in faith, and all that that involves by way of works of faith. Whenever inheritance is the theme – anywhere in the New Testament including Romans 4 – the surrounding context always mentions persistent faith or godly character or works of faith as opposed to works of Mosaic legislation. Simple faith brings justification. Simple faith brings assurance of heaven. Persistent faith brings inheritance.

Thirdly, Romans 4:13 talks of righteousness and inheritance as two things, not one thing. The promise that Abraham and his seed would inherit the world came (not through the law but) through the righteousness of faith. If 'A' comes through 'B' then 'A' and 'B' are different. Justification and glorification are so correlated in Paul's thought that if 'inheritance' meant justification – glorification Paul would in effect be saying: 'The promise *that Abraham would get justified* was not through the law but through justification'! This would not make sense. Inheritance is not justification. Rather inheritance comes through justfication.

Abraham believed God and that – simply his believing – was reckoned to him for righteousness. But it was not by this initial faith that Abraham immediately received the inheritance. He had to continue in faith for a long time before his inheritance began to come to him. It was by faith and patience that Abraham inherited the promise of Isaac. This is the language of Heb.6:12 but the principle is clear in Genesis, even if Hebrews had never been written. Only persistent and ongoing faith brought the birth of Isaac. Justification took no time; inheritance required time. Justification did not require patience; inheritance did.

It is true that the final phase of 'inheritance' is beyond the grave and Paul mentions that point by refering to 'the world'. Yet there is a difference between 'getting to heaven' (to use popular language) and reward in heaven. Abraham was justified, fitted for heaven, early in the Abraham story. Inheritance in the Abraham story is the direction Abraham is moving in, the goal that he is striving for.

My fourth reason for distinguishing justification and inheritance arises out of my own experience of preaching. Over twenty years ago in Lusaka I was occupied with a four-year series of expositions of Romans. I learnt a lot through wrestling with Paul's great epistle. At that time I took for granted the Puritan approach to heaven-inheritance as one and the same thing. But I got into difficulties trying to build my life on it and trying to preach it to ordinary people. My problem was that Paul obviously regards Abraham's experience, described in 4:18–21, as a great struggle. 'Against all hope' Abraham exercised faith (4:18). When I came to preach through these verses I found this very difficult. Is faith a great struggle? Is assurance of justification a matter of long-term endeavour, so that even after many years one may not have arrived at it? My difficulty is apparent in my two volumes of bound notes. 'Why does Paul use this illustration of saving faith?' I wrote – taking it for granted that it was saving faith that was being illustrated! 'Is believing in the Lord Jesus so staggering? Why does Paul describe faith as though it were extremely difficult? Is not faith a simple and easy thing?' Working along typical Puritan lines I could arrive at only one answer – in the 1970s. 'The difficulty comes', I concluded, 'because of conviction of sin.' As I saw it, 'Paul is describing Abraham's faith – the faith that saved him . . . [but there were] . . . tremendous difficulties in the way . . . specially in connection with conviction of sin.' At that time I was trying to do justice to the great struggle Paul describes as being 'in hope against hope' but I assumed that the theme was assurance of heaven.

I repent in sackcloth and ashes!

Romans 4 makes it clear that Abraham did have a struggle of faith. But the conflict was not about assurance of heaven. He was not 'in hope against hope' about justification! Rather the conflict concerned the birth of Isaac which was part of his promised inheritance. That matter involved an 'if' (as in Ro.8:17). The inheritance could involve trusting God and his word over a long period of time, 'without weakening in faith', contemplating one's weaknesses (4:19) but not collapsing in unbelief, growing strong in faith, maintaining one's assured faith. The end-product of this process is not justification; nor is it heaven, which can be a matter of assurance immediately because it correlates with justification. Rather, the end-product of this experience is inheritance, obtaining the promises concerning how God will use us in this life, experiencing God's, 'Well done'.

So Paul argues that the goal of our salvation ('inheritance') is reached not through law-keeping but through this 'righteousness of faith' which he has referred to. He explains this in a section extending from 4:13 till about the middle of v.17. At this point Paul begins to decribe what this faith was actually like as it worked out in Abraham's life and laid hold of the inheritance that God had promised him. This is his subject until the end of v.21, where he proceeds to explain that the faith which inherited was the very same faith which brought Abraham's justification in the first place (4:22). It is this kind of powerful faith in a risen Jesus which brings justification (4:23–25).

As I understand it, 4:13–21 shows that saving faith, when persisted in, becomes inheriting faith, without any use of the Mosaic law. The same point appears conversely in 4:22–25. The faith that inherits without any use of the Mosaic law is not other than the faith that saved us in the first place. The difference between the two is simply a matter of persistence!

LOSS OF INHERITANCE

At this point we leave Romans 4 and return to consider 'inheritance' more generally and in particular an eighth aspect of New Testament teaching about inheritance.

(viii) Inheritance may be lost. This is suggested by Ro.8:17, but is more explicit in 1 Cor.6:9,10, Gal.5:21 and Eph.5:5, where Paul lists the sins that block the way to inheritance, here and hereafter, if a Christian is tolerant of them.

A difficult related question concerns the Christian's experience of God's wrath in the *eschaton*. It will already have become clear that I hold a high doctrine of the Christian's security of salvation. Yet the temporary 'fire' of 1 Cor.3:15 that does not destroy justification – salvation challenges further exploration. Ephesians 5:5, for example, comes in a section dealing with the outworking of faith, and warns that serious sins will be an impediment in the way of present-enjoyment and future-reward in the kingdom. (There appears to be a double focus here of present and future 'inheritance'.) It also warns that God's final wrath, although intended for the 'sons of disobedience', may nevertheless touch the disobedient Christian. There is little point in Paul's words otherwise. It is possible for a Christian, although intended to be a *syn-metochos* ('fellow-sharer') in inheritance (Eph.3:6, cf 5:7), to be – anomalously and grotesquely – a *metochos* ('sharer') in wrath. I do not believe this implies loss of justification, but the significance of being a 'sharer' in wrath must not be explained away. I concede that much of this is provocative. I can only ask however that my unusual combination of theological points – total security combined with serious judgement of Christian sins – be seriously considered. It would at least explain matters that have given both 'Arminians' and 'Calvinists' much difficulty.

Evangelical Arminianism	*Developed Calvinism*	*Further Developed Calvinism (M.Eaton)*
Universal atonement	Limited atonement	Universal atonement
Irrestible integration of justification and sanctification	Irrestible integration of justification and sanctification	A resistible link between justification and sanctification
Integrates salvation – inheritance	Integrates salvation – inheritance	Sharply distingushes salvation – inheritance
Disobedience = loss of salvation, loss of inheritance	Disobedience = proved unreality of salvation, no inheritance	Disobedience = loss of inheritance but not loss of justification
Legalistic, in that salvation is by works	Introspective, in that proved-salvation is by works	Neither legalistic nor introspective, in that justification is by faith alone
Motivating yet discouraging. Present-salvation may be certain. Yet it could be lost since final salvation is by obedience.	Doubly discouraging, in that assurance of salvation is conditioned by the demand that good works be adequate	Doubly encouraging in that present and future salvation is sure. Motivating in that upon a secure base one may reach for inheritance.
Legalistic in that it maintains the continuing relevance of the Mosaic law	Legalistic in that it maintains the continuing relevance of the Mosaic law	Liberating in that the experience of the Spirit occupies the place once occupied by the Torah.

What I am urging, on the basis of this biblical material, is that there may be an approach to security and admonitition that does not imply justification by works and yet which does not have the in-built legalism and introspection of developed Calvinism. It may be represented by the following diagram.[13]

Part 4

Admonition in the New Testament

14

Security and the Interpretation of Warnings

I believe the New Testament teaches that a true Christian will never lose their justification, their faith, their regeneration.[1] They do not lose what God has given them, although they may lose further blessings that God wishes to give them. In this sense they cannot lose their salvation. It is true that the word 'salvation' may be used to refer to the reward that comes at the final stage of one's 'salvation'. The Christian may indeed lose 'salvation' in this sense.[2]

There seem to be two main reasons why many Christians find difficulty in accepting the eternal security of a Christian's justification. Firstly, there is the phenomenon of 'falling away' (as it is generally called) among those who seem to have been Christians. Many of us know individuals who seemed at one time to be Christians but who have subsequently shown no sign of their former commitment. In addition to personal experience, a second reason is awareness of scriptures which seem to suggest that the Christian's security should not be understood so unconditionally.

In response to the first objection it must be acknowledge that our ability to discern who truly is regenerated by the Spirit may not be as great as we sometimes think. This is at least a partial answer.

But for any Bible-believing Christian the second is the more weighty objection. A key factor in a theology of obedience and grace must be how it interprets the warnings of Scripture. The two areas of Scripture considered in this chapter (Romans and John's Gospel) affirm Christian security. After examining them we will survey the warnings of Scripture and put forward several guiding principles of interpretation. The position outlined here differs from both developed Calvinism and evangelical Arminianism.

It must be first said that there are passages of Scripture which (unless one has very good reason to take them differently) do seem to teach quite clearly and lucidly that a Christian cannot and does not lose salvation. They are not particularly obscure or difficult. They are not passages dealing with something else and awkwardly dragged in to prove a controversial point. There may be difficulty in believing them but there is no great problem about understanding them – and the two types of difficulty ought to be distinguished.

SECURITY IN ROMANS

Consider first of all the thread of argument in the letter to the Romans.[3] Early in the letter Paul argues at length that all people everywhere are sinful and need a righteousness that comes from God. He concludes: 'Every mouth is stopped and the whole world is held guilty before God' (Rom.1:18–3:20). Then he presents the way of salvation. God has put forward Jesus to be the sacrifice for our sins. Jesus is to be received by faith. He argues this extensively from the Old Testament (Rom.3:21–4:31).

In chapters 5–8 Paul describes the results of salvation, and it is in the course of this argument that he makes clear the utter and total security of the Christian and the sheer impossibility that he or she could ever 'lose salvation', if by that phrase is meant loss of justification, loss of the imputed righteousness of Jesus, loss of regeneration.

Romans 5:1–11 lists the immediate results of being justified by faith. Christians are at peace in their relationship to God (5:1). They have received (past tense) an introduction into grace in which they stand. They have not simply 'decided for Christ'; they have transferred into a realm of grace and have gained a 'standing' there. Paul does not give the slightest hint that there is anything insecure or conditional about this but immediately goes on to describe believers as rejoicing in their expectation of getting to glory. Paul does not qualify this expectation by hinting at any other possibility. Simply, believers will get to glory.

Romans 5:12–21 goes further. Not only do Christians possess these immediate blessings because they are 'justified' – having formerly been 'in Adam', they are now 'in Christ'. Paul's argument is not yet complete but already the reader might ask, 'How can someone who is joined to Christ ever fall out of the kingdom of God? Can Christ fall out of the kingdom of God?' Then Paul goes further. An important difference between the old position 'in Adam', before coming to faith, and the present position 'in Christ', is that grace is much stronger than sin ever was. In their pre-Christian days believers experienced sin as a powerful tyrant holding them in its grasp.But grace is so much stronger; believers are 'in Christ', in a kingdom of grace; grace rules over them. How can they be insecure?

In chapters 6 and 7 Paul points out that Christians have 'died' to sin, and that sin shall not rule over them. Paul does not say they are trying to die to sin, or that they shall one day die to sin. It is an accomplished event: they have died to sin. The point is not that they can never sin again but that sin can never rule over them again. Romans 6:9 is explicit. Jesus has risen 'never to die again' (NASV). But we are 'in Christ'. Just as he died and was released from this realm of sin 'once for ever', so we died and sin shall not have dominion over us. The powers of sin can never again get at Jesus, so it can never establish its dominion over believers. They are under the dominion and rule of God's grace.

All this is an expansion of what Paul has said about having acquired a standing in a kingdom of grace. He does not say that it depends in any way on how well a person's Christian life is proceeding, or how successful they are in defeating sin. A death has taken place in the Christian, a radical and eternal transfer from one realm to another, from the dominion of sin to the dominion of grace. The point is explicitly made that Jesus does not go back to the realm of sin. Since we actually are 'in Christ', how can we go back to the realm of sin? The Christians at Rome may have experienced temptation and fallen to it; the strong exhortations later in the letter suggest their battle with sin is real and that there is a real possibility of falling. But before he approaches any exhortation about godly living Paul wants to make it clear that Christians do not and cannot go back to the realm and dominion of sin. The letter contains no exhortation until 6:11 and then it is not about *doing* something but about *reckoning* something. Only after his hearers have taken a firm hold on the fact of their secure position of freedom from the rule of sin will Paul produce the first command of the epistle concerning sin: His argument is: 'Jesus has died to the realm of sin for ever. You have died to the realm of sin for ever. So therefore do not let sin reign in your mortal body.'

Nowhere here does Paul take into account the possibility that any Christian might not respond to the appeal of 6:12–13. He simply says, 'Sin shall not have dominion over you, because you are not under law but under grace.' Later in the chapter (vv.16–23) he appeals to them to willingly and voluntarily present their members to God. The only hints of warning occur in 6:21, 23. 'The outcome of those things is death . . . .The wages of sin is death'. What do these hints of warning mean? Is Paul taking back what he has said and warning that death could have dominion over the Christian after all? Verse 22 disproves any such conclusion. Here, between the two warnings of 21,23, is yet another statement that Christians have been 'freed from sin and enslaved to God'. True, they will suffer if they turn back even to taste the shame (6:21) from which they have been delivered. Elsewhere Paul warns of how one may 'reap' if one sows to the flesh, and may lose reward so as to be 'saved through fire' (1 Cor.3:15). But nowhere does he retract the radical assertions of Romans 6 about total and eternal release from the dominion of sin. At no point does he suspend our security in the kingdom of grace upon our faithfulness.

In Romans 7 Paul applies his 'reign of grace' theme to the matter of 'the law', that is, to the Mosaic arrangements of legislation and worship given to Israel in the exodus period. Christians, he says, have 'died' to the law. How can they ever be condemned? What is there to condemn them? Since the law has once and for ever been dealt with, how could a Christian ever be condemned or sent to hell? For any

Christian to lose their salvation would prove Paul wrong in everything he has said in Romans 5–7.

Romans 8 goes even higher. The Christian, Paul says, cannot be condemned. He introduces no conditions or qualifications so far as security in grace is concerned. Christians are 'in the Spirit'. A conditional note is introduced in 8:17. We shall be 'heirs with Christ if indeed we suffer with [him] in order order that we may also be glorified with [him]'. (The word 'him' is not in the Greek, but the verbs mean 'suffer-with' and 'be-glorified-with'. The NASV rightly adds the word 'him' to bring out the meaning.) The question of precisely how to interpret these warnings is discussed below; at this point it must suffice to say that there is a difference between a conditioned initial salvation and a conditioned reward. When Paul is dealing with initial salvation and our standing before God he nowhere hints at the possibility of any condition other than the saving faith which he takes for granted. He mentions union with Christ, which is already a fact, and introduces no further condition when claiming that 'there is no condemnation for those who are in Christ'. But when Paul writes about being recompensed in glory, a condition is introduced. However the themes of (i) justification and (ii) the rewards that accompany our being glorifed are quite different. Salvation is by 'faith only'; reward is most certainly not by 'faith only'. Salvation is received by faith with no further condition (i.e. apart from faith); reward is suspended on how we live. *It* depends on the works of faith. The two matters are distinct. When a statement is conditonal it is vital to take note of what it is that is conditioned.

At 8:28–30 – and not until this point – Paul invokes his doctrine of predestination. He has not mentioned it when writing about sin (1:18–3:20) and justification (3:21–4:25), nor even, so far, in explaining the Christian's position in grace (5:1–8:26). It appears only only now, as a concluding and conclusive argument to complete the case he has been building up: that the Christian can never be condemned.

'For those whom he foreknew, he also predestined to be conformed to the image of his Son, that he might be the first-born among many brothers. And those whom he predestined, he also called. And those whom he called, he also justified. And those whom he justified he also glorified.'

This is not the place for a detailed exposition of 8:28–30. Paul's argument seems to run like this: – Predestination to salvation, however mysterious it may be, is a fact. The word 'foreknow' – as is widely agreed by all shades of opinion – means to set one's love on someone in advance.[4] Of course God 'knows' about every individual in the human race but this is not the point of 'foreknow' in 8:28, where it means to fore-love more than fore-know. It is about fore-loving the person, not fore-knowing the faith. Those whom God has 'loved in advance' in this way, he has predestined to be like Jesus. Those people he 'calls', that is, he powerfully brings them to a knowledge of Jesus. Those people he justifies. Those people he glorifies.

Let us imagine there are a hundred people God has 'loved in advance'. ('A hundred', rather than 'millions' is something we can think about.) How many of them has he determined will be conformed to Jesus? One hundred! How many of them are summoned to Jesus Christ? One hundred! (The word 'call' always means something effective in passages in Paul concerning salvation.) How many of those called to faith in Christ are actually justified? One hundred! How many of those justified actually get to glory? One hundred! 'Those whom he has justified he has glorified.' It is so certain that Paul uses the past tense. It is as good as done in the mind of God. How many are lost along the way? None.

At this point Paul seems to pause and asks, *'What then shall we say to these things*? Now what do you think of all this? Do you believe it? Can you accept it? Is it too good to be true?' He knows his readers might still be staggered at such amazing security, so he goes on to deal with the questions they might have in their mind.[5]

Might there be some force somewhere which would drag the Christian down into such sin and failure that salvation would be lost? Paul answers: *'If God be for us* – and obviously he is – *who can be against us?'* What is this mysterious foe that can overthrow the Christian? Put a name to it! It does not exist. Perhaps I may need something that I lack and I will fail as a result? Might I not fall into sin? Might God's love to me not be diminished through my weakness and failures? Paul answers: 'He who did not spare his own Son, but delivered him up for us all, how will he not, with him, also freely, give us all things'. Every need will be met. Will we need further forgiveness? It will be given. Will we need restoration? It will be given. What will it take for us to have such needs met? They come 'with him'. God gave us Jesus freely; he will give us everything else we need 'also freely'.

Thirdly, is it possible that somehow the Christians at Rome could fall and be finally condemned? Paul answers the implicit query. 'It is God who justifies. Who can condemn?' There is no possibility of God's decision concerning our acquittal being overthrown. Jesus has died for all sins; there is no possibility of his death being ineffective for the believer. It is Jesus who intercedes; there is no possibilty of his intercession being ineffective.

There is a fourth possible anxiety: might not the trials and tribulations of life somehow overcome us? Paul answers: 'Who can separate us from the love of Christ . . .?'

Paul's final affirmation (in this part of his letter) is comprehensive. Verses 38f. begin, 'I am persuaded that neither death, nor life . . .'. Here Paul includes *everything*! Everything that happens to us is connected either to our dying or to our living. He continues, ' . . . nor angels, nor principalities, nor things present, nor things to come . . .'. Here again – *everything*. Everything that we might worry about is either a present problem or is about to come. ' . . . nor height, nor depth . . . ' also amounts to *everything*; everything is somewhere

between the heights and the depths. ' . . . nor any other created thing
. . .' – here also, *everything*; everything in this universe has been
created by God, including ourselves. None of these ' . . . shall be able
to separate us from the love of God, which is in Christ Jesus our Lord'.
God, says Paul, is determined to get us to glory and nothing in all
creation can stop him. What stronger statement of the Christian's
absolute security could there be? It is futile to say, 'But we ourselves
could stop ourselves from getting to glory.' Could not Paul have
thought of that? Was it sheer incompetence on his part that he forgot?
Are not we ourselves included in 'all creation'? Would it not completely nullify everything Paul has said in Romans 8 if there were after all
a possibility that something should separate us from God's love to us in
Jesus?

This explains why I believe that the Christian cannot lose his or her
salvation. It will not do to argue that although nothing outside of us
can overthrow our salvation we ourselves are responsible to keep
ourselves from doing this by rebellion and unbelief. Paul was not so
superficial that he did not think of that. When he said, 'Nothing in all
creation can separate us from the love of Christ . . . ', he had surely
not forgotten that we ourselves might do so. Paul was making an
absolute statement. When he dealt with the fear that we might, after
all, be finally condemned by some sin, was it not this very anxiety he
had in mind? In any case he has already said that grace reigns over us
and that sin shall not have dominion over us. How could he virtually
deny in Romans 8 what he had said so clearly in Romans 5 and 6? How
can he envisage a Christian who ceases to be under a reign of grace
when he has already said that the Christian can never again be ruled
over by sin or law or judgement?

Paul's statements in Romans 8 are absolute: nothing in all creation is
able to separate the Christians in Rome from the love of God in Christ
Jesus. One might have difficulties about other verses or about
application, in particular Christians who seem to 'fall away'. But if we
were simply taking Romans at its face value we should surely say: the
Christian cannot lose his or her salvation.

SECURITY IN JOHN

Much the same conclusions arise from a study of John's Gospel. We
need not work through every detail of the gospel,[6] but it will be
helpful to note the setting of John 6, which is important for our theme.
At this point a steadily increasing opposition towards Jesus is gaining
momentum. After the prologue (1:1–18) comes the record of seven
significant days when Jesus gathered some disciples who saw his glory
in his first miracle (1:19–2:11). There follow samples of his ministry in
Jerusalem (2:13–3:26), Samaria (4:1–42) and Galilee (4:43–54). In
chapter 5 Jesus is again in Jerusalem, where his ministry is arousing
conflict. A miracle (5:1–9a) leads to controversy with the Jewish

leaders (5:9b–18), and to a major discourse of Jesus (5:19–47). In chapter 6 two further miracles (6:1–15, 16–21) lead into another major discourse, a context including teaching about the security of the believer.

It is the day after the feeding of the five thousand (6:22). The people follow Jesus from the 'other side of the sea' to Capernaum (6:22–24), but when they find him (6:25), Jesus points to their wrong motive: 'You seek me . . . because you ate your fill of the loaves and were filled' (6:26). He urges them to believe in him, the one God has sent (6:29). But they want a sign (6:30). Apparently the feeding of the five thousand was not sign enough! They want – at their demand – something analogous to the manna from heaven (6:31).

In reply Jesus points out their mistake in thinking that Moses worked a sign in order to establish his credentials. Their asking Jesus to be like Moses shows they have not understood the story concerning Moses, let alone the greatness of Jesus (6:32). Actually there is 'bread from heaven' before their very eyes if only they could see it (6:32b–33). When they ask for this 'bread from heaven' (6:34), Jesus offers himself: 'I am the bread of life.' Anyone may come to him. Whoever does so will never hunger or thirst. When they had their 'fill of the loaves' it was only a sign pointing to something richer and deeper. Yet they refuse to believe. The people as a whole are characterized by unbelief. The miracle which has taken place before their very eyes has prompted eagerness to fill their stomachs rather than than to trust in Jesus as the bread of life.

Yet over against their unbelief Jesus says something that is greatly encouraging; God's purpose is going forward despite the unbelief of the majority of the crowd.

JOHN 6:37–48

'All that the Father gives to me will come to me, and the one who comes to me I will by no means cast out. This is the will of him who sent me, that of all that he has given me I should lose nothing, but raise it up at the last day . . . .This is the will of him who sent me, that everyone who sees the Son and believes in him may have everlasting life; and I will raise him up at the last day' (6:37–40).

We may notice three implications in these words of Jesus.

1. The vast majority of the crowd do not exercise faith. Despite the miracle they have witnessed they do not believe. Yet they have seen the miracle and God's sign from heaven stands before them, Jesus himself. Such is the power of unbelief.

2. Despite the unbelief of many God has a people that he has 'given' to Jesus. However difficult it may be and however many questions we may want to ask, we clearly have here a doctrine of predestination. Some, not all, are given to Jesus by the Father. Those people will believe. Behind the 'coming' of those who believe is a work of God the Father, who has determined that a specific people will

believe. The guarantee that those people will come to faith is found in the fact of God's prior plan that Jesus will be given a people.

3. Such is the Father's determination that these people will belong to Jesus that he has also determined that not one of them shall be lost. It is in this context that Jesus says 'I shall never cast him out.'

It must be noted that this means more than simply that Jesus will not send away the one who comes to him. Jesus will receive bring the believer into the community of those who are given to him, and having done this will never cast him out.

The verb also occurs in John 9:34,35. In John 9, because the man born blind defends Jesus, the authorities 'put him out', i.e. they remove him from the circle of synagogue adherents of which he had formed part. Jesus however comes to comfort and help him. What the Pharisees did to the blind man (9:34f) is precisely what Jesus will never do to the one who comes to him (6:37).

Another example is found in 2:15. Here Jesus 'drove out' the traders who misused the temple – the very thing Jesus says he will not do to anyone of those given to him. Similarly Jesus says that in the cross the prince of this world is 'cast out' (12:31). The same word is used. Jesus, who 'cast out' the devil from his position, will never 'cast out' the one who has come to him.

The statement in 6:37 is clear: those who are given by the Father to Jesus will come to Jesus, and will be Jesus' people, and that having come to be Jesus' people they will never be put out of that community. It is notable that these words of Jesus refer to the individual. Of every person who comes to Jesus it is said 'I will raise him up at the last day.' (The resurrection involved here is clearly the resurrection to glory.)

Much the same thought recurs in John 6:44. 'No one can come to me unless the Father who sent me draws him; and I will raise him up at the last day.' The unbelief of the crowd who witnessed the feeding of the five thousand is not in the least surprising but precisely what anyone would expect who knows anything of the power of unbelief. Unbelief is so engrained in humankind that no one ever would believe if there were not a people given to Jesus. Those people are drawn by the Father; those people do believe. No act of force takes place. It is simply that in a hidden and gentle way the Father wins them to faith. He does it effectively. He does not fail in his purpose. Those that the Father has given to Jesus will come to him. Such are raised up at the last day in the resurrection to glory.

The thought is repeated in 6:54f. Whoever comes to Jesus already has eternal life. They will not be lost but will be raised to glory (6:54). The drawing of the Father has been exercised; otherwise he or she never would have come to Jesus (6:55). At the end of the chapter some 'disciples' 'draw back'. Over against these Peter says, 'We have come to believe.' The 'disciples' who draw back might be understood as genuine believers who had become fearful of following Jesus: alternatively these 'disciples' were simply people who had joined the group following Jesus from place to place although they did not believe in him. The twelve have however persisted in following Jesus. Jesus comments: 'Did I myself not choose you, the twelve, and yet one of you is [not 'will be'] a devil' (v.70). One of those that Jesus has earlier chosen as disciples will be lost. Although chosen as a disciple, he is in himself – at that very moment – a devil. He will be lost because although chosen by Jesus as a disciple he was not one of those 'given' by the Father to Jesus.

SECURITY IN JOHN 10

As John's Gospel continues the conflict between Jesus and his enemies intensifies. In chapter 7 Jesus is the centre of intense debate. This is followed in chapter 8 by a discourse about Jesus as the light of the world. Chapter 9 sees the conflict growing more acute. Jesus heals a blind man (vv.1–12) and the Pharisees complain that the healing has taken place on the sabbath (vv.13–34). This leads Jesus to comment on their spiritual blindness: 'If you were blind, you would have no sin; but now you say "We see" your sin remains.' There is a connection between these events and the parable in chapter 10. The one who 'does not enter by the door', the 'thief and a robber', represents the Pharisees of John 9 who have cast out the blind man. In 10:1–9 Jesus speaks of himself as a door; in verses 11–18 he is like a shepherd. Jesus secures the life of his people (v.10). He is a good shepherd (v.11). The false shepherd – the Pharisee who will 'put out' a healed disciple of Jesus – does not really care for the sheep (v.12), but is concerned only for himself (v.13). There is a close and intimate union between Jesus and his people (v.14), like that between a shepherd and the sheep whom he knows and who know him. He lays down his life to secure their safety (v.15). Verses 16f. refer to the incorporation of gentiles into this 'sheepfold', and Jesus' great willingness to lose his life in order to fulfil the Father's purpose (v.18).

John 10:19–24 describes the controversy and varied reaction caused by the parable. Verses 25–30, where he takes up the matter again, are vital for our theme. 'You do not believe because you are not of my sheep. My sheep hear my voice and I know them, and they follow me; and I give them eternal life and they shall never perish; and no one shall snatch them out of my Father's hand.'

The approach is identical with that in chapter 6. Referring to the fact that many do not believe, Jesus says not, 'You are not my sheep because you do not believe', but – putting it the other way around – 'You do not believe because you are not of my sheep.' It is not faith that leads to God's election; it is God's prior election that leads to faith. Once again we find a doctrine of predestination. We must resist the temptation to speculate beyond what is revealed in this matter. Yet however baffling our questions may be, one thing is clear. There is a doctrine of predestination here. We find the same three implications here as in chapter 6.

1. Faith does not characterize the vast majority of people. The Pharisees do not see who Jesus is.

2. Despite the unbelief of many, God has a people that he has 'given' to Jesus. They are called here his 'sheep'. It is some, not all, who are thus given to Jesus by the Father. Those people will believe. Behind the 'coming' of those who believe lies a work of God the Father, who has determined that a specific people will believe.

3. Not one of these will be lost from among God's people. Jesus says 'I give them eternal life, and they shall never perish'. The second half of the sentence ('they shall never perish') throws light on what is meant by 'I give them eternal life.' The reference is surely not only to something that happens at one's first faith and can then be lost. When Jesus says, 'I give them eternal life' he is speaking of a gift, something that is theirs for ever. Because the gift is permanent Jesus can continue, 'They shall never perish.' The next statement goes further: 'No one shall snatch them out of my hand.' Here is a clear statement of the Christian's eternal security. It will not suffice to 'balance' responsibility and security and say 'Neither is absolute, i.e. accomplished apart from man's decision.'[7] This is not how John puts it. Human decision would, to John's mind, always lead to apostasy. But Jesus' sheep do hear God's voice, they do follow. This is the nature of God's keeping them.

The 'balance' is the same as that predicted by Jeremiah as an aspect of the 'new covenant'. The promise of the 'old covenant' could be broken, says Jeremiah, but he goes on to contrast this covenant that couild be broken with a different unbreakable covenant. 'I will make an everlasting covenant with them that I will not turn away from them, away from doing them good; and I will put the fear of me in their hearts so that they will not turn away from me' (Jer.32:40). God promised to bring in a more effective covenant than the covenant of law. The new covenant would be unbreakable. The Christian is in an unbreakable covenant – unlike the Sinai covenant. God will not turn away from us, and however low we sink we shall not turn away from him. At our worst we shall still know the gospel is true. We shall still have faith.

John also teaches this 'balance' between responsibility and security.

Jesus' words receive varied reaction. Some wish to stone him (Jn.10:31); others come to faith (10:32).

SECURITY IN JOHN 15

The story continues wtih the climactic 'sign' of the raising of Lazarus, which becomes a major contributing factor in the plot to kill Jesus (11:45–57). Events move swiftly now: Jesus is anointed by Mary of Bethany (12:1–8), enters Jerusalem (12:9–50). Soon John is telling us of his actions and teaching in the upper room (13–14), and while walking to Gethsemane (15–16).

Two points may be made concerning 15:6. Firstly, it is part of the extended illustration depicting Jesus as the 'true vine', and it is doubtful interpretation to press the details of parabolic or illustrative teaching. Secondly, the chapter does not deal in any way with initial salvation. It is concerned with fruitfulness (v.2). The disciples are already 'clean' with what might be called their 'initial salvation'. Jesus is concerned about what lies ahead and what they will do for him (v.5). Without him they cannot achieve anything. Before them is a life of fulfilling God's will (v.5), entering into a life of love (v.12). They are chosen in order to have a lasting impact upon this world (v.16) and the Spirit will enable their future ministry.

None of this refers to justification by faith or new birth or anything that could be designated 'initial salvation'. Rather it deals with service and ministry and achievement for God. Pressing the details in v.6 into clear teaching about security or apostasy is a doubtful procedure. Calvinists say the verse refers to false conversion. Judas had real contact with Jesus but was 'a devil' all along.[8] Arminians refer it to apostasy. But in the context it surely refers to the uselessness that results when a Christian does not abide in Christ. E.A.Blum[9] mentions all three possibilities but thinks it alludes to Judas. One can get more out of the passage only by relating it to other Scriptures, and this can be done along three routes as mentioned by Blum (see below).

SECURITY IN JOHN 17

The lengthy discourse in John 14–16 flows into the prayer of chapter 17. This is followed by the account of Jesus' death and resurrection (18–20) and the epilogue to the book (21).

John 17 is closely linked with 14–16 as v.1 ('After Jesus said this . . .') suggests. Teaching (14–16) and prayer (17) are a conscious combination. The praying of Jesus was evidently intended to be overheard; we are reminded of 11:42 ('I said this because of the people standing around').

John 17 demands our attention because of its strongly predestinarian statements and its contribution to the teaching concerning 'eternal security'. It is much loved by Calvinists. Jesus first prays for his own glorification (vv.1–5). The phraseology used ('giving eternal life to all whom you have given to him') roots the salvation of the disciples in the will of God more than in the faith of the disciples. It is not that their faith and faithfulness are needless (vv.6,8 refer to keeping and receiving) but the more ultimate truth is that of Jesus' donation of grace to them. Jesus has authority over 'all mankind' (v.2) but that authority is exercised in bestowing eternal life on a group of people who are said to be 'given' to Jesus (v.2). Having brought about their salvation Jesus now asks that he may return to his pre-incarnational glory.

Next (vv 6–19) Jesus prays for the group of disciples who have worked with and in obedience to him. His prayer is limited to this group, who are an 'elect' (if one may borrow Paul's term) given out of the world to Jesus. In some sense they – rather than the entire human race – belonged to the Father before Jesus' ministry ('They were yours', v.6).

A vital statement for our present concern is found in v.12: 'I was keeping them . . . . I guarded them, and not one of them has perished *ei me ho huios tes apoleias* . . . .'. There are two ways of translating this last phrase, and the difference is vital because one translation teaches very clearly the possibility of an exception to Jesus' keeping power. If *ei me* has its meaning of 'except' the sense is, 'Not one of them has perished except the son of perdition but one of them I was unable to keep!'

'EI ME', 'EXCEPT' AND 'HOWEVER'

However we have already seen in connection with Gal.2:16 that *ei me* or *ean me* is sometimes used to introduce an exception to something more general than what has been previously mentioned. There are other examples.

Gal.2:16 is not to be translated 'No human being is justified by the works of the law except through the faith of Jesus' – which would imply we are justified by the works of the law upon one proviso.

Matt.12:4 is not to be translated 'what it was not lawful for David to eat, nor for those who were with him except for the priests' since this would imply there were priests with David.

Gal.1:6f. does not speak of 'a different gospel, which is not another except certain men trouble you' – this suggests Paul believed there is another gospel.

Luke 4:26f.should not be translated, 'There were many widows in Israel . . . . Elijah was sent to none of them except to Zarephath.' This sounds as if Zarephath was in Israel, which is the opposite of the point Jesus is making.

Rev.21:27 should not be translated, 'Nothing unclean shall come into it except those whose names are written in the Lamb's book of life' – which would imply that those in the book of life are unclean!

Neither is John 17:12 to be translated, 'Not one of them has perished except the son of perdition' – which implies that one of the elect has perished.

The clearest way to express this usage of *ei me* is to use a full-stop and then restart the sentence.

Gal.2:16 is to be translated, 'No human being is justified by the works of the law. They are justified only through the faith of Jesus.'

Matthew 12:4 is to be translated, ' . . . what it was not lawful for David to eat, nor for those who were with him. It was lawful for the priests.'

Gal.1:6f. speaks of 'a different gospel, which is not another. However certain men are troubling you.'

Luke 4:26–27 should be translated, 'There were many widows in Israel . . . Elijah was sent to none of them. He was sent to Zarephath.'

Rev.21:27 should be translated 'Nothing unclean shall come into it. Those whose names are written in the Lamb's book of life will enter in.'

And Jn 17:12 is to be translated 'Not one of them has perished. However the son of perdition has perished . . .'

LOVINGKINDNESS WILL NOT FAIL

If the word in Jn 17:12 means 'except' and refers to apostasy, then it could be argued the word in Rev.21:27 means 'except' and implies extreme antinomianism! Actually in both cases the word is to be expressed by a stop and a fresh start with the word 'However'. This is the English way of expressing this usage of *ei me*.

Clearly *ei me* may have this force. That this is the correct way of translating Jn 17:12 is suggested by two further points. Interpreted thus 17:12 runs parallel to what we have already seen in chapters 6 and 10. It is yet another statement of the security of the believer. This translation coheres with John 6 and 10, unlike translating by 'except'.

This interpretation agrees with the Fourth Gospel's presentation of Judas. At 6:64 he is specifically placed among those who did not believe. The second sentence of 6:64 ('For Jesus knew who they were who did not believe and who it was who would betray him') is an exposition of the first sentence ('There are some of you who do not believe.') Unbelievers in general and the betrayer in particular are placed in the category of 'some . . . who do not believe'. Judas was chosen as a disciple but Jesus' knowledge that Judas 'is' (present tense) a devil precedes his choice of him. Jn 6:70 thus says that one chosen as a worker with Jesus is at that point a devil. Jn 13:10f. explicitly describes the disciples as 'clean' with the cleanness of spiritual cleansing and new birth, and explicitly dissociates such cleansing from Judas. Jn 13:18 differentiates the 'chosen' from Judas, using 'choose' in a different way from Jn.6:70. Evidently John thinks of Judas as 'chosen' to ministry but not 'chosen' in the sense that would be determined by the thought of 17:9.

The same thought is apparent in John 9:12. Carson is right in saying – he could have made the point even more strongly – 'Jesus' prayer for his disciples . . . excludes Judas.'[10] We need not discuss whether 'son of perdition' denotes character or destiny. Understood in either way, John 17:12 is a powerful statement. Jesus loses no one. His people do not perish in the sense of losing their basic and foundational possession of eternal life.

Jesus' prayer that his disciples be kept from the evil one (17:15) prompts a further thought. Earlier in the gospel Jesus has said, 'You hear me always' (11:42). It is not conceivable, the gospel implies, that any prayer of Jesus should fail. If he prays for his people to be protected from the devil, they will be protected from the devil. It is futile to interject, 'But they may fail to keep themselves.' Is not their failure to keep themselves a victory for the devil? If Jesus prays it will not happen, can we say that it might?

We have said enough about John's Gospel. It seems plain that, if it were not for the two stumbling blocks we have mentioned, anyone taking these passages at face value (and we have glanced only at Romans and John) and submitting to Scripture, would say that a Christian can never lose his or her salvation. The oath concerning Jesus as the one who always lives to bring us to glory will be as secure as the unbreakable covenant God made with David. 'My lovingkindness I shall keep . . . for ever . . . . If his sons forsake my law . . . I will visit their transgression with the rod . . . But I will not break off my lovingkindness . . . .' While Psalm 89 refers not directly to Christian experience but to the covenant with the house of David, it illustrates the workings of God's covenants of grace. Lovingkindness will not fail.

If we sin we shall fall and we shall suffer, but we shall not fall utterly. No one shall take us from his hand.

CONDITIONALITY, REWARD AND LOSS

A straightforward reading of the passages we have referred to will lead the Christian to say, 'I know I believe in Jesus. I also know that I cannot be lost.' But the New Testament contains many severe warnings addressed to Christians; how should we integrate them with our understanding of the believer's security? Paul warns about the loss of the prize (1 Cor.9:24–27, cf 2 Tim.2:5). There are other sayings that mention a reward and the possibility of losing it (e.g. Mt.6:2). There are warnings about the fire of God in John 15:6 and 1 Cor.3:15. There is implicit warning in the reference to conditional presentation before the Father in judgement (Col.1:23), conditional promises concerning seeing the Lord (Mt.5:8; Heb.12:14), promises making heirship with Christ conditional on suffering with him (Rom.8:17), conditional promises concerning reigning with Christ (2 Tim.2:12). The conditional promises of Revelation concerning overcoming are well known (Rev.2:7,11,17,26; 3:5,12,21) as are the warnings to the seven churches (Rev.2:5; 2:16,22–23; 3:3,19). Some promises are attached to exhortations about how we live (e.g. Mt.5:5); indeed, the word 'reward' may be used in a promise attached to a statement about how we live (Mt.5:12; 6:1,4,5,6,16,18). We find references to conditional forgiveness (Mt.18:21–35, esp.v.35; 6:12,15) and conditional promises about safety (Mk.13:13).

Communities are warned they may lose their communal position in God's kingdom if they do not continue in faith. Romans 11:20–22 is a striking example. A church may cease to have a testimony. Revelation 2:5 envisages a lampstand being removed from its place. In this connection, we mention the story of the cursing of the fig-tree (esp. Mk.11:14) since it parabolically applies to Israel. Special attention needs to be given to the warnings of Hebrews (Heb.2:1–3; 3:7–4:13;

6:3–8; 10:26–31; 12:14–17; 12:25). There are verses that speak of one's name being removed from the book of life (Rev.17:8; 20:12,15; 21:27) or from the tree of life, and the holy city (Rev.22:19), verses that challenge Christians with talk about Gehenna or the lake of fire (Matt.5:21–26; 5:27–30; 10:22,28,33) and seem to warn them of serious consequences that will follow if Christ is denied. Matthew 10:38 speaks of a person's being unworthy of Jesus, and verse 39 speaks of losing one's life. This is the opposite of reward (Mt.10:41–42; see also Matt.18:8,9; 25:41; Mk.9:43–49; Rev.20:15).

Similar to such warnings are those linked with the parousia (Mt.24:35–51; 25:1–13, esp.v.13; 25:14–30, esp.29–30; 25:31–46) and warnings about great loss in the day of judgement (Mt.7:26–27). In 2 Timothy 4:1 Paul charges Timothy to fulfil his ministry in the light of judgement day. What is the point of doing this unless something can be gained or lost in the judgement day? Mark 8:35–38 mentions 'losing one's life' (Mk.8:35–38); the context is the second coming of Jesus. Some New Testament admonitions use the word 'destruction' when addressing Christians, or speak of a disciple 'perishing' (e.g. Mt.7:13–14). Jude 5 speaks of those who were once saved, then 'destroyed'. Mt.18:14 assumes the possibility (in the light of 18:7–13) of a little one perishing. Rom.14:15 uses similar language. Other Scriptures use the word 'death' (e.g.Rom.8:12–14). Judgement is threatened against particular sins (e.g.Mt.7:1–2) and believers may share in the judgement that will fall upon the world's sins. (Although Mk.12:40 is about a judgement that will fall upon unsaved teachers of the law, the point is that we must not share in their sins. If we do, we share their judgement.) Christians must take care to avoid experiencing God's wrath (Eph.5:6–7). Those who are already disciples are urged to enter the kingdom (Mt.18:3; Ac.14) and not lose it (Mt.5:20; 1 Cor.6:8–11; Gal.5:21; Eph.5:5). There are warnings about loss of honour in this life (Mt.5:13) and thereafter (1 Jn.2:28). Even for the Christian death is better than causing others to stumble (Mt.18:6–7, Mk.9:42).

'He that endures to the end shall be saved' is often cited in popular discussions about 'falling away'. Matthew 10:22 refers to the sending out of the twelve and the persecution they will experience. It is likely that it means that the person who endures in the ministry of witnessing under these dificult circumstances will be kept safe. But one notes verse 28. It might seem to be a statement that backsliding will result in loss of salvation or proof of non-salvation. (See also Mt.24:13, Mk.13:13). Other miscellaneous statements could be noted. Judas fell away from his ministry (Ac.1:25, ASV). In the parable of the sower the second type of person 'falls away', and the third is entangled in things that choke God's word. The result is unfruitfulness (Mt.13: Mk.4). One may be last or least in the kingdom (Mt.19:30; 5:19) and Jesus predicts that all the disciples will 'fall away' – a term that is explained as disowning Jesus (14:27,30).

INTERPRETING THE WARNINGS

Enough has been said of warnings addressed to the Christian to make it plain that any theology of grace may be evaluated by the way it treats such passages.

There are three main lines of interpretation. Two of them have already been touched upon, but there is another line of approach, less frequently considered.

(i) Some refer the warnings to loss of salvation. Arminius said one cannot have assurance of final salvation, and that it is better to be in fear concerning final salvation.[11]

(ii) Some take the warnings to refer to an unreal salvation. They believe that what seems to be salvation turns out not to be salvation after all. This is exceedingly introspective and totally destructive of any assurance.

(iii) A more perceptive and discriminating approach is based on the fact that the New Testament warnings are generally connected with (i) present usefulness to God, (ii) experience of the powers of the kingdom, (iii) inheriting God's promises in this life, (iv) experiencing reward, (v) salvation through fire.

GUIDELINES FOR INTERPRETATION

The following interpretative guidelines summarize my understanding of the admonitions of the New Testament:

1. Warnings of apostasy that relate to communities do not touch the doctrine of perseverance. The use made of Rom.11:22–24 by Shank, Marshall, Duty,[12] and others does not meet the point at issue. Romans 11 deals with the problem that the community of Israel as a whole has lapsed from a position of blessing in God's dealings with the world. Paul responds by pointing to (a) a distinction within Israel (9:6), (b) Israel's unbelief (ch.10), (c) the principle of the remnant and the fact that he himself is a Jew (ch.11:1–10), and (d) the possibility that the nation as a whole will not abide in unbelief. In the story of a community an epoch may occur when the bulk of the people do not have the faith of their ancestors; this is the principle of Ro.9:6. Here Paul warns that in the march of history a people may arise who although physically descended from gentile Christians do not share their faith, and thus repeat the tragedy of Israel. In such a case, he says to the gentile Christians at Rome, they too 'will be cut off'. None of this impinges upon the security of an individual believer.[13] A similar point could be made with regard to Revelation 2:5 where the church of Ephesus as a whole is being addressed.

2. The possibility should be considered that certain passages of Scripture deal neither with initial conversion nor with eschatological salvation but with present experience of salvation.

Consider Gal.5:21 and its companion-passages in 1 Cor.6:9 and Eph.5:5. Paul warns: 'Those who do such things will not inherit the kingdom of God' (*hoi ta toiauta prassontes basileian theou ou klerono-mesousin*). Arminians tend to cite this as proving the possibility of apostasy on the grounds of lack of godliness. Some Calvinists understand it as referring to loss of an 'imitation' salvation because such sin proves faith was never present. But there is a wider range of possibilities.

(i) Is the meaning that those who ever have committed such things cannot reach salvation? No one takes it that way, so far as I know, and the present tense *prassontes* is against it.

(ii) Is it that those who commit such things once lose their salvation? Surely not.

(iii) Does it mean that those who frequently commit such sins lose their salvation or are proved not to be Christians? Or – as I once thought myself – that those who are under the dominion of such sins prove themselves not truly Christian? Some rather 'ordinary' sins are mentioned. Paul includes *thumoi*, outbursts of wrath. Yet Calvin confessed shortly before his death that he was prone to impatience and bad temper which, he said, was part of his nature but concerning which he was ashamed.[14] Had he lost his salvation? Paul includes *dichostasiai*, dissensions, and *eritheiai*, rivalries. Yet A.Dallimore entitled a chapter of his biography of George Whitefield 'Dissensions and Rivalries in England'.[15] Were Whitefield and John Wesley not Christians after all? One remembers also that Luke records a 'sharp disagreement' (*paroxusmos*) between Paul and Barnabas on one occasion (Ac.15:39). Did Paul fall prey to his own warning? Was he in danger of losing – or falsifying – his salvation?

(iv) Does it mean that those who are guilty of such things but do not repent do not inherit God's kingdom? Yet do not some Christians remain blind to their weaknesses all their lives? Was not Luther quite blind to the sinfulness of his hostility to fellow reformers? Does not his story indicate that he never did repent of his attitude to Zwingli and others?[16] Was not Melanchthon nervous even of letting him see Calvin's letter to him because he feared a violent reaction?[17] Is not the attitude of some Calvinists towards what they think is 'antinomian' itself not rather antinomian?[18] What does this mean? Do such people lose – or falsify – their salvation?

There is however another way of approaching Gal.5:21. 'Inheriting the kingdom' does not have to refer either to initial conversion-justification or to eschatological 'getting to heaven'. A more reasonable interpretation (certainly one that is pastorally practical) takes it to mean that the Christian who tolerates such sins in his life fails to experience in the here-and-now the blessings of God's kingdom. Surely Calvin lost something at that very point of his life when he lost his temper. Surely the rivalry between Wesley and Whitefield did damage to the kingdom of God and brought blessing to neither of them at that stage of their life. Neither Arminian apostasy nor Calvinist introspection is involved in Gal.5:21. On this view the future tense refers to what will immediately happen in the life of any believer at the point where he or she tolerates 'such things'. Other passages may be interpreted similarly.

3. It is important to distinguish between justification and reward. Consider for example 1 Cor.9:27. For G.B.Wilson it deals with 'imitation' salvation. 'A preacher of salvation may yet miss it. He may show others the way to heaven, and never get thither himself'.[19] Yet in the entire section (1 Cor.9:1–27) there is no discussion of salvation. Rather what is mentioned is ministry, preaching, service to God in gaining disciples both from the Jews and from the gentiles. In 9:24–27 the point is explicitly that of 'gaining a prize'. G.Fee's exegesis of the passage is persuasive, and pin-points the reward-theme of these verses. Yet he seems to take it for granted that the reward is salvation. 'Paul keeps warning and assurance in tension', he says.[20] But what if assurance and warning are not in tension? If there is real assurance it is difficult to take warnings of loss of salvation seriously. If there is real warning of loss of salvation it is difficult to have any real assurance for the future. This is not tension but contradiction; the two negate each other. But Paul does not equate salvation and reward; he explicitly distinguishes them in the same epistle (3:15). I suggest it is worthwhile considering the two matters distinctly. A warning concerning the one need not be a warning concerning the other.

4. We must take seriously the severity of loss of reward as a terminal chastening of the recalcitrant Christian. The warnings of the New Testament show that there can be very great loss for the Christian at the judgement-seat of Christ. Thus it is possible to be ashamed at the parousia (1 Jn.2:28ff), to lose honour. It seems to be possible for the Christian not to reign with Christ. Yet the combination in 1 Cor.3:15 ('He shall suffer loss . . . he shall be saved') should warn us not to assume lightly that loss of reward is loss of salvation. Is there a 'ruination' at the judgement seat which is not a removal of what one had previously been granted?

5. We should also take seriously the absence from the New Testament of any reference to reversal of justification-regeneration. If loss of salvation in the Arminian sense of the phrase were an authentic biblical concept then one ought to find somewhere a clear statement of reversal of justification or reversal of regeneration. Yet it seems that this concept is absent from the New Testament and indeed is specifically denied.

6. The concept of 'tasting Gehenna' needs to be pondered. There are clear statements in the New Testament that warn the Christian away from Gehenna. Is it possible – I ask – that 'Gehenna' and similar phraseology do not always refer to what in traditional thinking is called eternal punishment? However difficult the concept may be, it seems that what the New Testament teaches is the traditional doctrine of eternal punishment. The temporary fire of 1 Cor.3:15 is a theme that ought to be considered more thoroughly than has traditionally been the case. In New Testament times 'gehenna' could have 'purgatorial'

overtones. I realize that 1 Cor.3:15 is the verse that has been cited more than any other in support of the idea of purgatory. There are major differences between what I have in mind and the Roman Catholic concept.[21] The bath water (purgatory) can be thrown out; but the baby (1 Cor.3:15) must be held tight.

15

'Falling Away' in the Epistle to the Hebrews

Among all the warnings of the New Testament, two in Hebrews have been much quoted as supporting a doctrine of apostasy, and consequent loss of salvation: Among those who write controversially on the subject Hebrews 6:1–8 and 10:26–31 are often cited as the clearest passages of Scripture asserting the possibility of apostasy. Yet one has the impression that these passages actually present a problem to Calvinist and Arminian alike. The Calvinist dislikes the notion of 'falling away' but the Arminian dislikes the thought of restoration being impossible.[1]

SOME INTERPRETATIONS OF HEBREWS 6:4–6

There are some sixteen basic ways of interpreting Hebrews 6:4–6.

1. The dominant view in modern scholarly writings sees here a reference to apostasy for which there is no forgiveness.[2]

2. Tertullian and others have thought the passage teaches that certain serious sins, notably adultery, are beyond forgiveness.[3]

3. The *Shepherd* of Hermas teaches that remission of serious sins may be allowed at baptism-conversion, and once more after that, but not a third time.[4] Presumably Hermas's view rests upon Heb. 6:6 which warns that it is impossible to renew again (*palin anakainizein*) the one guilty of 'falling aside' (*parapipton*). Although Hermas cited visionary experience he seems also to have deduced from 6:6 that one could be renewed once. This view was apparently accepted teaching in Alexandria at the beginning of the third century. After the Decian persecution both the rigorist view of Tertullian and the semi-rigorist view of Hermas lapsed altogether until modern times.[5]

4. Following the Decian persecution Heb. 6:4–6 was taken to refer to the impossibility of a second baptism.[6] This remained a common view and was maintained in the middle ages.[7]

5. Calvinists have generally understood the writer to be referring to a pseudo-christian, or (to use the language of the 17th century) a 'false

professor'. This view was given its classical and richest exposition by John Owen.[8] According to this line of thought the 'enlightenment' of 6:4–6 falls short of true Christian conversion. All who are regenerate are enlightened, but not all who are enlightened are regenerate. Enlightenment is something which happens once and for all in such a way that it is of necessity incapable of repetition, yet it does not amount to conversion. Within the visible church, the argument runs, it is impossible in the early stages to distinguish between wheat and tares. (Actually the field in Matthew 13 'is the world' – v.38.) Such enlightenment brings salvation and life within one's grasp , making it possible to share within the visible church in all the blessings of the gospel. Yet such a person is still not regenerate, still not a true Christian. For A.C.Custance the experience of the pseudo-christian of Heb.6 is 'more like wishful thinking than firm conviction.'[9] The high Calvinist John Brine speaks in language characteristic of this style of thinking when he writes 'On the great difference between real conversion and the mere semblance of it'. In Brine's thinking a person may be convicted by the law, accept the doctrines of the gospel, see the guilt of his sin, take pleasure in the gospel, be conscientious and sincere, be sorry for sin, and yet not be a Christian.[10]

6. A variant of the previous approach is to suggest that the condition of the apostates is expressed in terms of what they claimed. The writer supposedly takes this at face value as a 'judgement of charity'. R.Nicole thinks William Gouge adopted this approach.[11] (In my opinion Gouge ought to be classed rather with the previous option and resembles Owen in his exposition.[12] Yet such an approach is a possible one.)

7. A proposal rather similar to the previous two but without its introspective note is found in writers who stress the Jewishness of the readers and the fact that Hebrews relates to a period of transition from Old Covenant to New Covenant. F.C.Synge maintains that 'the people addressed are not Christians . . . they have not made the leap of faith and the abandonment of Jewry which are necessary in order to join their ranks . . . . They are Jews, attracted by the Gospel, but unable to make up their minds. They have, as adherents of the congregation, experienced the gifts and powers of the age to come.'[13] Similarly J.F.Strombeck takes the admonitory passages of Hebrews to be directed against 'the unsaved within the churches'. These are 'early groups of Jewish Christians trusting in the sufficiency of ceremonial worship and the kingdom teachings, but without a personal faith in the Saviour indispensable to salvation'.[14] This view is held with minor variations by K.S.Wuest[15] and N.Weeks.[16]

8. Another approach suggests that the sin described in Hebrews 6 is committed only where there is active hostility to Christ, persisted in for a long time. On this view the key factor is deliberateness. Thus W.L.Lane identifies 'a deliberate, planned, intelligent decision to renounce publicly association with Jesus Christ.'[17] For R.Jewett, the sin is a matter of 'rejecting relationship' with Jesus.[18] B.F.Westcott

speaks of 'active, continuous hostility to Christ'.[19] This approach apparently seeks to avoid the introspective element in the classical Calvinist view. W.H.Thomas writes along these lines: 'It is no ordinary or general fall, but a deliberate apostasy.' 'Active hostility to Christ ever persisted in cannot be a matter of restoration.'[20] Those who are not 'actively hostile' to Christ need have no fear.

9. Others believe the case is hypothetical. Although it refers to apostasy the writer does not envisage that such apostasy will actually take place. The warning itself is a means of securing that the sin will not be committed. W.Manson thus thought 'the catastrophe predicted . . . was hypothetical rather than real.'[21] T.Hewitt favours this view,[22] and A.Mugridge, who writes: 'There seems to be no reason to deny that these five phrases describe Christians', continues, ' . . . we must assume that they fit the description up until the last item and that he is describing what would be the result for them if they were also to fit the last item.'[23]

10. A number of interpreters relieve the severity of the warning by emphasizing particular words or aspects of the passage. Some have adopted a weaker interpretation of *adunatos*, taking it to mean 'very difficult' or 'impossible for men and women but not impossible for God'.[24]

11. Others emphasize that it is not salvation but initial repentance that cannot be the subject of renewal. Solani understands that 'the experience of *metanoia* is so unique that it can scarcely be re-created within the individual'; 'an apostate cannot experience a new *metanoia* because he rejects the very source of repentance.'[25] Sometimes this view is held by those who do not believe in the possibility of loss of salvation. L.Morris thinks that 'nothing in this passage says that genuine Christians may fall away' (i.e. fall from salvation) and that 'it is the impossibility of repentance of which he writes, not that of forgiveness'.[26] This point is stressed by J.Héring: 'It is . . . the impossibility of repenting which is being affirmed, and it is not a question of knowing whether fresh forgiveness can be obtained if one does repent . . . the many discussions about the possibility of renewed forgiveness are quite irrelevant to the question which is raised and resolved in this passage.'[27]

12. Since evangelical Arminians dislike the idea that restoration should be impossible, just as Calvinists dislike the idea that apostasy is possible, a common Arminian interpretation is to follow the English RV and RSV in reading the participle *anastaurountos* as a time-clause, 'while they crucify' (Heb.6:6).[28] This overlooks the importance in Hebrews of the idea of an 'oath', after which God will not 'change his mind'.

13. V.D.Verbrugge suggests a new interpretation in emphasizing the communal aspects of the sin envisaged in Heb.6:4–6. The passage then resembles Rev. 2:5 in implying that a church or community may lose the effectiveness of its testimony.[29] This view is refuted, in my opinion, by the fact that Heb.3:12 refers to the evil heart of unbelief

'in any one of you' (*en tini humon*). The thought of the individual falling cannot be dismissed. Individual language is also used in 12:16 which is clearly parallel to 6:4–6.

14. Some suggest that only temporal judgements are in view. Just as the Israelites in the wilderness died without reaching Canaan, and just as the wilful sin of Ananias and Sapphira resulted in their death, so there is a 'sin unto death' into which the Christian may fall. In such a case death follows but loss of salvation is not involved. G.H.Lang held such a view,[30] as does Z.Hodges[31] and M.De Haan[32].

15. An approach which is difficult to understand and difficult to apply pastorally is found among those who see in Hebrews 6 an antinomy or dialectic. Scholars who adopt such an approach see here a reference to apostasy but maintain that it is 'one side of the coin' or is 'only' pastoral in intention and should not be taken as serious teaching. Thus J.K.Solani can write: 'The author here was writing as a pastor of souls . . . He did not intend to raise the dogmatic question.' Evaluation of Hebrews 6 and 10 'must be made in keeping with the paraenetic genre in which it is expressed'. Following this line he concludes that 'it is not necessary or even possible, for theologians to "harmonize" the doctrine of Hebrews with the penitential discipline of the Church of a century after its composition.'[33] Similarly D.A.Hagner writes: 'Can Christians, then, fall away and lose their salvation? The answer again consists of a yes and a no . . . .Christians can apostasize . . . .Yet, paradoxically, if they become true apostates, they show that they were not authentic Christians.'[34] He thus comes in the category of those who see antinomy here. Yet his view could also be categorized in the fifth of the groups listed above. R.Brown seems to follow such a line when he expounds this section as a 'partial truth'.[35] For A. Murray, whose position is similar, 'every truth has two sides'.[36]

Mention might be made at this point of those writers whose position is difficult to detect since they do not precisely state any at all. Perhaps they too see antinomy here.[37] Since this approach is widespread and is sometimes thought to be rather wise and discerning it may be worthy of further comment. Often in one's understanding of Scripture one has to hold together ideas that are equally taught but seem impossible to reconcile. The reality of God's sovereignty and human responsibility is a well-known example. The 'mystery' of holding two incompatibles together is often stressed. Yet it must be said that some antinomies can be lived with and others cannot. It is quite possible to worship Jesus as God and yet know his great sympathy as a fellow human being, without having to resolve the enigma of Jesus' being God as though he were not man, and man as though he were not God. This is a mystery that can be lived with. I doubt however whether it is possible to practically hold the view that it both is and is not possible for the Christian to lose salvation. In practice the fear that it is possible will override the conviction that it is not. For those who have a low view of Scripture the 'antinomy' approach to Hebrews 6 and eternal security may be adequate. To those who wish to practise their faith, it is an impossible antinomy. If it is possible to lose one's salvation, then that is the end of the matter. To believe at the same time that it is and that it is not possible to lose justification-regeneration is itself impossible! Any one who tries it believes only one side of the antinomy and feels himself able to lose salvation.

16. I personally was taught and held for many years the fifth of the views mentioned above. But further thought on its practical consequences and the overall message of Hebrews have led me in a different direction. A sixtenth view – which I believe is basically correct – is held by a few who understand the 'falling away' of Hebrews 6 as referring not to apostasy but to a persistent rebelliousness comparable to the Israelites' failure of faith in the wilderness. On such a view the 'impossibility of restoration' and the 'fiery expectation of judgement' refer to a serious chastening in which God does not permit perfection, usefulness is forfeited, and fearful chastening is experienced – but without loss of salvation. This approach is comparatively more infrequent. With minor variations it is found in works by M.R.De Haan,[38] R.G.Gromacki, [39] Z.Hodges,[40] R.T.Kendall,[41] G.H.Lang,[42] J.Vernon McGee[43] and H.A.G.Tait[44]. Some of these writers think that the judgement in view is only temporal, and thus also come in the thirteenth category above.

A HOLISTIC APPROACH

While it is impossible to supply a thorough study of Hebrews in a few pages I propose to introduce my own view by presenting the theme of Hebrews holistically. Interpretations of the warning passages of Hebrews (2:1–4; 3:7–4:13; 6:1–8; 10:26–31; 12:15–17,25) tend to coalesce. Most scholars (all that I know of) identify one main strand of warning as appearing intermittently throughout the letter so that interpretations of chapter 6 cohere with similar interpretations of the other passages. I do not know of any writer who takes chapter 6 in an Arminian fashion but interprets chapter 10 in a Calvinist fashion, or vice-versa.[45]

My only concern here is with the bearing of this passage on a non-legalistic theology in which the Christian is viewed as having an absolute assurance of salvation. The only 'introductory' question needing attention concerns the state of the readers.[46] I take it that they are Christians, but Christians in a sluggish and weary state, inclined to give way to the pressures they are experiencing. They are inclined to abandon not their intial faith in Jesus but their bold profession of faith and their willingness to hold on their confidence in the face of adversity. I take it that they are Jews, that they are suffering from the hostility of their compatriots, that they are tempted to dilute their Christianity in the interest of something more visibly Judaistic.

INHERITANCE IN HEBREWS

We may approach the matter first of all by considering the theme of inheritance in Hebrews – a topic that was omitted from the survey of inheritance in the pages above.

According to Hebrews, Jesus, the God-man, became an heir because of his diligent obedience. When the author says (1:2) that Jesus was 'appointed the *heir*' he has the obedience of Jesus and the resurrection-ascension in mind. It was because of his obedient suffering ('therefore' – cf.Phil.2:9) that Jesus was highly exalted. The same point is made in 1:3b–4. Having suffered, Jesus became greater than the angels. Before that time he was for a little while lower than the angels but because of the suffering of death was 'crowned' (2:9). Thus early in the epistle we learn that inheritance is reward.

In 1:14 we are introduced to the thought that we are to 'inherit' salvation. I take it that eschatological salvation is in view and that this includes reward.[47] Jesus was helped by the angels to achieve his inheritance (if Lk. 22:43 throws any light on Heb.1:14); the Christian is likewise helped by the angels to achieve the reward that accompanies final salvation. It must be remembered however that in the thought of Hebrews the Christian is 'sanctified for ever'. No further help is needed to achieve that.

Chapter 2 develops the theme. Humankind was designed for glory (2:5–8a) but was to achieve this through the work entrusted to it (2:7c–8a). As one looks at the human race it is apparent that it has not yet arrived at this glory (2:8b). Instead Jesus has followed the pathway that humankind should have followed; he has got to glory and honour. The only way humankind can fulfil its original destiny (mentioned in 2:5–8a) is through Jesus. He died for the human race so this way of getting to glory is 'on offer' for all. Heb.2:10 mentions 'sons' for the first time in this connection. Before one can attain eschatological honour one must become a 'son'. In context, 'getting many sons to glory' must refer to reward. The glory that humankind was destined for but lost was a glory that would come through having served God. He was to put all things beneath his feet and by so doing attain to glory. Jesus was 'crowned' with glory because of his obedience. He is a sympathetic saviour who is able to bring his people along after him along the route that he has already followed, and so bring them to get their 'crown' of glory.[48]

Hebrews 6:12 picks up the same point. God promises that those who keep an open ear to his voice (3:7), endure amidst trials (3:8) and get to know his ways (3:10) will attain an inheritance. The language of 6:12 implies that something is promised to the Christian beyond conversion-initiation, something analogous to Israel's promised land, requiring diligent faith for its attainment. Hebrews 6:13–20 links the mention of inheritance in 6:12 with that of oath. There are two reasons for the inclusion of 6:13–20. (i) Jesus is the 'seed' that was promised to Abraham. Because he was the subject of the oath of Genesis 22 this

part of the Christian's encouragement is immutable. As the fulfilment
of the oath to Abraham, Jesus is an 'anchor' that will not fail. He 'ever'
lives (unlike the Aaronic priests who died), never sins (unlike the
Levitical high priest who sinned) and cannot be the subject of any
'change of mind' upon the part of God (in distinction from the
Levitical priesthood who were the subject of a 'change in the
priesthood', 7:12). (ii) A second reason for 6:13–20 is that it sets forth
not only the immutability of Jesus' priesthood but also the possibility
of the same oath occuring in the life of the believer. Believers, who
live on the oath to Abraham concerning his 'seed' (Jesus) are
encouraged to seek an oath for themselves. The 'heirs' of 6:17 are
Christians. The fact that 'promise', 'heir' and 'oath' occur in the same
verse indicates that heirship, inheriting, promise-language and oath-
language form part of one circle of ideas.

Hebrews 9:15 makes the point that because of ('Therefore') a
radically effective atonement it is possible for the Mosaic set-up to be
abolished and a radically new kind of covenant inaugurated. In the old
arrangement obedience to a law-covenant could lead to Israel's 'living
long in the land'. In the New Covenant also there are promises of
inheritance. Jesus administers it. He puts his will before us (we 'hear
his voice' – 3:7), looks to us to endure trials (3:8). As the believer
responds Jesus ministers the promises of 8:10–12. The radically
effective nature of his offering allows the Christian to pursue the
inheritance without any distraction arising from guilt. This kind of
covenant is virtually identical to the first century 'testament' (but two
other kinds of covenant have no resemblance to a testament), so the
writer can briefly switch to a contemporary (i.e.1st century AD) use of
the term *diatheke* to illustrate his point (Heb.9:16–17).[49]

In Hebrews 11:7 the words *kata pistin dikaiosunes . . . kleronomos*
are parallel to Titus 3:7. To translate 'heir of righteousness'[50] is
misleading. The genitive is 'immensely versatile'[51] and the phrase
surely means 'an heir originating from righteousness by faith'. It is a
genitive of origin or definition.

Hebrews 12:17 provides an illustration of a Christian lacking interest
in their 'inheritance'. We shall return to it a few lines below. In the
light of the theme of inheritance that flows throughout Hebrews how
must the warnings of Hebrews be taken? What is the sin? What is the
loss threatened? In the light of the inheritance-theme surely it is
unlikely that the introspective apprach is correct. The writer is not
addressing 'imitation Christians' or merely 'enlightened' seekers. He is
addressing those who are Christians, urging them not to throw away
their confidence but to hold on in faith until they reach their reward.
This is explicit in 10:35.

THE WARNINGS AND INHERITANCE

We shall consider the warnings in the light of the inheritance-theme
which flows throughout the letter. In 2:3 the author urges that 'we' –
the Christians including himself – should not 'neglect' salvation. The

verb is *ameleo*, which means not so much 'reject' as 'neglect', 'show little concern', 'disregard', 'pay no attention'[52]. It suggests that the readers are Christians but are in danger of not making use of their salvation. They are in great danger if they do neglect salvation. He asks, 'How shall we escape?' – although he does not at this point say what the penalty would be for such neglect.

The longest warning pasage extends from 3:7 to 4:13. It is important to remember that when one reaches the warning of 6:3–6 a great deal has already been said in chapters 3 and 4. The sin referred to is that of the Israelites who were 'redeemed by the blood of the lamb' but did not press on to achieve what they were redeemed for. They did not heed God's voice (3:7); they hardened their hearts (3:8), rebelled against God (3:8), did not learn anything from the ways of God which they observed (3:9). A crucial verse is 3:10, which refers back to the oath of Num. 14:22. This is a vital point. I have already have argued that the divine 'oath' is the point at which God 'makes up his mind' and marks decision that certain promises have been gained or lost.[53] In Num.14 an oath is taken, following which the first generation of Israelites cannot enter Canaan, even though they try (14:39–45). They could not return to where they were before the event of 14:22. Nothing Moses said or did could renew their position so that they now could inherit Canaan. The precise nature of the loss is important; it did not involve a return to Egypt. This would have negated the event achieved by the blood of the passover lamb. The loss consisted in God's deciding that they should not inherit what they should have inherited, what they were redeemed for.

In a lengthy digression, Heb.5:12–6:12 contains the crucial warning of 6:3–6. The whole warning is really contained in 6:3. Verses 4–6 (beginning 'For . . . ') explains v.3. Verse 3 is really quite clear. It implies that God may take a decision that means it is not possible for the Hebrew Christians to press on to perfection. The resemblance between 3:10 and Num.14 will be noticed. What then is the sin envisaged? Too much must not be read into the word *parapipto*. It is not at all necessary to translate it 'commit apostasy' as though some turning away from saving faith were envisaged. There are clearly attested instances where the verb is used but where recovery is envisaged (although I do not suggest that recovery is envisaged in Hebrews 6)[54].

In the context of the argument of Hebrews, to 'fall by the wayside' (*parapipto*) means to so persistently rebel (like the Israelites in the wilderness) that God takes an oath of wrath (cf. Heb.3:10) and no further progress in the Christian life is made (cf.Num.14:39–45). It is likely that the implied subject of the verb 'renew' is the writer himself: 'we have much to say . . . Let us leave . . . This we shall do if God permit . . . For it is impossible [for me the writer] to renew again . . . those who . . . fall by the wayside'.

The writer is thinking of the Hebrew Christians' achieving what they were redeemed for. He is thinking of works of diligent faith. Refusal to progress is likely to incur the displeasure of God and thus the experience of his oath. In such a case no further spiritual progress will be made. None of this asserts 'falling away' in the Arminian sense of the term, and the analogy of Numbers 14 to which the writer has referred is against the idea.

The illustration in vv.7f. shows that the writer is thinking about the fruitfulness that should come when rain (the continued ministry of Jesus) falls on ground (the Hebrews). It should produce fruit. What happens after the rain leads either to further blessing (the oath of God's mercy – 6:15–18) or to a curse (the oath of God's wrath – 3:10). Verses 9–12 are also important. The writers refers to God's justice in blessing the reader's works. The Puritan view of this passage surely receives refutation here. Is the writer saying: go on in good works and then God will give you salvation? No Puritan held such doctrine! Surely his line of thought is: go on in works of faith and you will – in the justice of God – receive your reward. It is also significant that the writer says not, 'We are persuaded of your salvation' but, 'We are persuaded of better things that accompany salvation.' Here he distinguishes between salvation and the fruitfulness that ought to accompany salvation. The themes here are works, diligent faith, and reward. They contrast with lack of diligent faith, refusal to move on with God, the experience of the oath of God's wrath – and no further progress in the Christian life. Significantly, v.12 continues the theme when it speaks of persistent faith: they already have faith but will they persist in trying cirucmstances? And over against the loss of progress mentioned in vv.3–6 he speaks of 'inheriting' promises.

Hebrews 10:29–39 follow similar lines. The readers are Christians and their present salvation is not disputed. They have received the truth (10:29); they have been sanctified (10:29); they know God (10:30); they are his people (10:30). The danger threatening them is that they may not use the covenant-ministry of Jesus (10:29), not use the ministry of the Spirit working in their lives (10:29). Behaving thus, they are setting themselves up for a fiery judgement. This judgement has often been understood as hell, in the traditional sense. But we notice that the contrasting term the writer uses in v.35 is reward. If they hold on they will be (not 'saved but) 'richly rewarded'. The clear implication is that the author's theme is not salvation but reward.

By interpreting Heb.10 along these lines we disclose a striking similarity with 1 Cor.3. Both mention building on what one already has; both mention reward and loss of reward; both mention fiery judgement. That this does not involve loss of salvation is explicit in 1 Cor. 3 (v.15) but not so explicit in Heb. 10. Yet in the light of statements that the sanctification that the believers possess is eternal (Heb.9:12), Heb.10 must be understood as exactly parallel to 1 Cor. 3, especially v.15.

Hebrews 12:17 provides an illustration of a Christian who lacks interest in the 'inheritance'. By the Mosaic law (Dt.21:17) a firstborn son was lined up for a distinct inheritance. Yet it could be forfeited (cf.1 Chr.5:1,2; a pre-Mosaic case is Gn.49:3,4). Esau was an heir, due for inheritance, but explicitly said he was not interested in it ('What profit shall the birthright do to me?'). This lack of interest was confirmed by a divine oath (Gn.25:31,33) which made the matter fixed. He found no place for a change of mind in his father (cf. ASV). G.H.Lang comments: 'Of Esau himself the history gives, as a final picture, a man who has risen above his earlier hatred of his brother, welcomes him back with love, is ready to protect him and his substance (Gen.32–33), and who at last joins him at the graveside of his father (Gen.35:29). Thus he is the type of one of the family of God who lapses into carnality and bitterness, but years after is restored in soul, yet who nevertheless cannot regain the full position . . . He is the first that shall be last though still in the family.'[55]

The last word of warning in the letter is Heb.13:25–29. It does not add to what we have already seen but again makes the point (as in 2:1–4) that judgement under the new covenant is more severe than judgement under the old covenant.

In all of this three points are worthy of note: (i) At no point does the writer query the conversion of his readers or of those who have left the fellowship. (ii) The sin in question is committed by a Christian who has hitherto had much personal experience of God. (iii) The writer does not suggest that the 'eternal redemption' received by these Christians or the 'eternal sanctification' conferred upon them has been in any way withdrawn. Since Jesus intercedes for his people and his priesthood has been the subject of an oath, it is of the very essence of the writer's position that such saving mediation cannot be withdrawn.

What can be lost is what is built – or fails to be built – on the mediation of Jesus. It is possible to be 'redeemed by the blood of the lamb' and yet not 'inherit Canaan'. Yet the one who has forfeited Canaan does not therefore return to Egypt. Redemption by the blood of the lamb is secure.

16

Prospects for a Non-Legalistic Theology

We are now in a position to review the position we have reached and to draw some conclusions.

A LAW-CENTRED SOTERIOLOGY

I have drawn attention to a theological problem, the place of law in soteriology, especially in relation to assurance of salvation. The church has repeatedly fallen into a law-centred doctrine of salvation. Since the days of Aquinas this tendency has intensified, with the result that the Christian church has been under the influence of a detailed law-code consisting of moral principles extrapolated and extended from the decalogue.

While the Reformation saw a renewed emphasis on grace, the place of the decalogue was not drastically reconsidered. Although Luther rejected the law as a means of salvation he still maintained it was needful in convicting of sin. Calvin went further and held the law was 'chiefly for the righteous man' as a guide to his life. In post-Reformation Protestantism this trend developed further still and a heavy emphasis on 'the law' came into being. Although this 'law' sometimes included ingredients from the whole Torah, yet in popular evangelism and Christian counselling it took the form of a heightened and spiritualized version of the Decalogue. As a result the heirs of the Reformation frequently became extremely introspective. Other elements, such as an ultra-logical doctrine of limited atonement, and an interpretation of Hebrews 6, enhanced the introspective theology of the heirs of the Reformation.

The eighteenth century saw the rise of Wesleyan Arminianism, building on the Arminianism of the late 16th and early 17th centuries. The Arminians broke away from Calvinistic introspection but only at the cost of a heavy emphasis on 'free-will' and while retaining the same view of the law as had been held by the Puritans. Consequently twentieth century evangelicals have inherited a theology which remains heavily indebted to the excessively legalistic emphasis of the two major soteriologies of their forefathers.

A BIBLICAL DOCTRINE OF SALVATION

I have made a selective and preliminary attempt to set forth what would be the main planks of a revised soteriology to replace the introspective ones. Removing the law from its intimidating position creates an opening for some theological themes which are much more inspiriting than the traditional approaches. We have identified some richly encouraging aspects of biblical soteriology: the faith of Christ, fearless vulnerability to the charge of antinomianism, a doctrine of justification that is more reassuring than its predecessors. Yet it would be natural to ask whether along with the threats of the law we may have removed every kind of sanction from the Christian life. Is there, in fact any equivalent motivating factor in the revised theology outlined here? Could any similar emphases operate once the Torah has been removed from its rather central position in evangelicalism, including the demand for conviction by the law before conversion?

We have seen that in fact motivation is not absent from such a revised theology; the theme of inheritance to be sought and achieved is a strongly motivating factor in the Christian life, although it does not at all threaten the Christian's salvation or security. In this connection we have seen how the warnings of Scripture have a place in the Christian's thinking about his or her position before God. Although these warnings are severe and sobering, yet we have seen that they need not give rise to introspective questionings, for none of them takes the form that has been generally assumed in evangelical theology. They do not demand that Christians should constantly scrutinize their conversion or doubt their past experience with God. Nor do they give rise to the terrifying possibility of a totally lost salvation.

In fact, there is a biblically rooted theology which is free both from the legalism of 'Arminianism' (the phenomenon is wider than the use of the name) and the introspection of the Calvinism that has prevailed between the 17th and 20th centuries.

The whole of Scripture needs to be reconsidered in the light of this approach. This study has concentrated only on certain limited areas and the picture has been painted with a large brush. The ultimate question is: what must I believe and what must I preach? There are many aspects of the matter that cry for attention and this study is merely an interim report. In it I have sought to present wide-ranging sketches of a theology that does not tie together grace and law so tightly as to either terrify the sensitive or induce complacency. If it appears somewhat 'dangerous' – is not grace itself 'dangerous'? On the other hand, it holds out possibilities of motivation without discouragement. If law and grace are tied together, then 'assured' Christians – the Pharisees – may be sure of salvation but their obedience is *too* guaranteed. Alternatively they are unsure of salvation and work for God in order to feel that they possess it. Loosening this bond offers possibilities of a theology which is reassuring, and yet which presents a further challenge for the Christian: the challenge of obedience to the Spirit and entering into inheritance here and hereafter.

SOME IMPORTANT QUESTIONS

Among the many residual questions arising from this study three deserve special attention in the future.

1. What is the relationship between resurrection and reward? Are there variations in final glory which correlate with variations in the honour attending resurrection?

2. What is the nature of the 'fire' referred to in 1 Corinthians 3:15? What are the implications of the Christian's experiencing a 'fire' which is not destructive of salvation? What is the significance of the passages where Gehenna is held out as a possibility for the Christian? Is there a temporary Gehenna? What does it mean to be 'hurt' by the second death? What does Ephesians 5 imply when it speaks of Christians sharing in a revelation of wrath which was not designed for them?

3. What is the nature of the Christian's inheritance? Is it honour? Further service of God? What else may be involved?

THE CHRISTIAN LIFE

The interpretation outlined here presents the Christian life as starting in a radical and gracious acceptance by God which has not the slightest connection with 'works'. Jesus has lived for me; Jesus has died for me; all I need is Jesus. This leaves room for sudden conversion. Can anyone with any kind of faith in the New Testament believe anything else? One is staggered by the degree of acceptance and assurance that may come with no preparation for grace at all. No wonder Calvin wrote, 'Away with all this talk about preparation' (*Inst.*2:2:27). I believe the Christian is released totally and radically from condemnation and is placed in a kingdom of grace with day-by-day access to God through Jesus. I believe in a baptism with the Holy Spirit in which the love of God is shed abroad in the heart, 'sealing' all that the Christian objectively possesses in Christ. Such Christians have no doubts about resurrection to glory because they feel as if they are in glory already.

> 'A debtor to mercy alone,
>   Of covenant mercy I sing;
> Nor fear with Thy righteousness on,
>   My person and offering to bring.
> The terrors of law and of God
>   With me can have nothing to do;
> My Saviour's obedience and blood
>   Hide all my transgressions from view.'

Is this licentiousness? I would not be surprised if anyone thought so, because any gospel that *is* a gospel must be vulnerable to the charge of licentiousness. But no, it is not moral licentiousness; it is grace.

Yet warnings abound in the New Testament. In respect of inheritance, the Christian's secure status means only qualification to receive it. Heaven is secure but there is such a thing as being saved by fire. Is Arminianism the way of the New Testament or does it not cast a legalistic shadow over the gospel? Is scholastic Calvinism the answer or does that not also cast one into the depths of introspection? Surely the New Testament balance is one of absolute freedom, an assurance that one will 'never thirst again', a knowledge that 'nothing in all creation is able to separate us from the love of God in Christ'. Yet from this basis of radical assurance spring profound challenges, the challenge to accept responsibility, the challenge to work out one's salvation, the challenge to lay up treasure in heaven, the knowledge that there is something to be 'laid hold of', rewards to be won. Yet all along the way there is no need to fear that I am working for my eternal salvation.

What paradoxes! Amazing grace and profound challenge; incredible assurance yet awe-inspiring responsibility; freedom to be myself yet the knowledge that Jesus achieves all in me. Here is a theology that motivates but does not discourage – a theology of encouragement. But is not this the gospel? I believe it is.

Notes to Chapters

NOTES TO CHAPTER ONE

1 B.Tyler & A.A.Bennett, *The Life and Labours of Asahel Nettleton*, (repr. Banner of Truth, 1975), p.30.

2 D.R.Smith, 'John Fletcher: an Arminian Upholder of Holiness', in *The Manifold Grace of God, Papers read at the Puritan and Reformed Studies Conference, 1968*, (London: PRSC, 1969), p.73; J.Fletcher, Works (Salem: Schmul, 1974, vol.1, pp.170f., p.95.

3 Fletcher, *Works*, vol.1, pp.117f.

4 F.K.Smith & T.W.Mellish, *Teach Yourself Greek* (EUP, 1947, pp.153f.).

5 E.Schaeffer, *Lifelines: The Ten Commandments for Today* (Hodder, 1978), pp.97,99.

6 T.F.Torrance, *The Doctrine of Grace in the Apostolic Fathers* (Oliver & Boyd, 1948), p.133.

7 Torrance, *Grace*, p.136.

8 Torrance, *Grace*, p.137. Italics are original.

9 G.Bourgeault, *Decalogue et Morale Chrétienne* (Paris: Desclées, 1970), p.417. The conclusions regarding patristic evidence are summarised on pp.405–418.

10 H.Röthlisberger, *Das Weg Der Kirche Am Sinai* (Zwingli, 1965), p.50.

11 C.F.Allison, *The Rise of Moralism* (Morehouse Barlow, 1966), passim.

12 R.T.Kendall, *Calvin and English Calvinism to 1649* (OUP, 1979) passim.

13 The phrase is traditional in English-speaking Reformed theology and is found, e.g. in ch.19, section 6 of the Westminster Confession of Faith. See WCF (e.g. The Confession of Faith; The Larger and Shorter Catechism (Inverness: Free Presbyterian Church of Scotland, 1976) p.82.

14 See WCF, ch.9, cited above. A neo-Puritan exposition of the same viewpoint is found in W.Chantry, *Today's Gospel* (Banner of Truth, 1970) esp.ch.2. Chantry thinks that sustained preaching of the Decalogue is a primary tool of evangelism (pp.35–46). P.Helm also speaks of 'the clear teaching of Scripture regarding the priority of the preaching of the law over against the preaching of the gospel' (*The Beginnings: Word and Spirit in Conversion*, Banner of Truth, 1986, p.103).

15 G.Kawerau, *Johannes Agricola von Eisleben* (Berlin: Wilhelm Hertz 1881) J.Rogge, *Johannes Agricolas Lutherverständnis*, 1960.

16 D.Hall, *The Antinomian Controversy, 1636–1638* (Wesleyan University, 1968), esp. pp.3–20; E.Emerson, *Puritanism in America 1620–1750* (Boston: Twayne, 1977), pp.72–79; L.Ziff, *The Career of John Cotton* (Princeton, 1962), pp.106–148; R.T.Kendall, 'John Cotton – First English Calvinist?' in The *Puritan Experiment in the New World; Papers read at the 1976 Conference* (Huntingdon: Westminster Conference 1977), pp.38–50.

17 See Kevan, *Grace*; Campbell, *Antinomian Controversies*, pp.61–81.

18   R.Dabney, 'Theology of the Plymouth Brethren', in *Discussions: Evangelical and Theological*, vol.1 (Banner of Truth, 1967), pp.169–228.

19   Malan was accused of being 'an unprincipled antinomian' because of his teaching concerning faith and justification. His godly character and evangelistic zeal were conceded and admired. See C.Malan, *Theogenes, or A Plain and Scriptural Answer to the Solemn Question, Am I, or Am I Not, a Child of God* (Nisbet, 1828); Malan (one of César Malan's sons; name unidentified), *The Life, Labours and Writings of Caesar Malan* (Nisbet, 1869); C.Malan, *The True Cross* (Nisbet, 1848).

20   See the account of the two men, Luther and Agricola, in J.Mackinnon, *Luther and the Reformation* (4 vols London, 1925–30), vol.4, pp.161–179.

21   From the 17th century descriptions of 'antinomians' by Samuel Rutherford one would think them wholly evil (see Rutherford, *Survey*, passim). However this was part of the mechanics of controversy more than a realistic appraisal of their lifestyle. On the other hand Charles Spurgeon said of Tobias Crisp and the 17th century controversy concerning him, 'He was called an Antinomian, but the term was misapplied . . . There need not have been such an outcry' ('The Downgrade', *Sword and Trowel*, March 1887) p.124). F.Heal points out that even the 'familists', the 17th century sect that sprang from the 'revelations' of Henry Niclaes, 'rarely seem to have deserved the epithet 'libertine' which was often applied to them, and Niclaes stressed that his revelations fulfilled the law rather than overthrowing it' ('The Family of Love and the diocese of Ely' in *Schism, Heresy and Religious Protest*, (CUP, 1972), p.214.

Similarly the pioneer of 17th century English 'antinomianism', John Eaton, wrote *The Discovery of the Most Dangerous Dead Faith* (1642) in which he spoke of 'the horrible filthinesse of sin before God'. He was not in any way licentious and could be quite legalistic. He believed in preaching the law, the main points of which, he said, should 'be clearly and diligently pressed upon sleeping consciences . . . until the most upright, honest, yea, and most sanctified man in works may feel himselfe slaine by the law, especially the tenth commandment'. Eaton tended however to hold the doctrine of justification in such a way as to maintain that God sees no sin in his people. See Eaton, *Discovery*, pp.89,108,39 respectively).

In *The Honey-combe of Free Justification by Christ Alone* (1642) it is clear that Eaton's main concern was assurance of salvation (see esp. p.15). No one reading the *Honey-Combe* could conceive of Eaton's having any sympathy with any kind of licentiousness. In the 17th century copy belonging to the British Museum, there is a scribbled note evidently going back to a contemporary. It spoke of his zeal, patience and piety, saying that he was 'exceedingly admired in the neighbourhood where he lived, and strangely valued for many years after his death'.

22   See I.H.Marshall, *Acts* (IVP, 1980), p.203.

NOTES TO CHAPTER TWO

1   I.Murray, 'Will the Unholy Be Saved?' (review article in *The Banner of Truth*, no.246, March 1984), pp.1–15, esp.p.2; R.F.White, Review of *The Gospel Under Siege: A Study of Faith and Works* [Dallas: Redencion Via, 1981], by Z.Hodges, WTJ, 46, no.2, Feb 1984, pp.426–430.

2   See M.A.Eaton, *Baptism With the Spirit* (IVP, 1989), pp.51–53. See also A.McGrath's study of the matter in P.Avis (ed), *The History of Christian Theology*, vol.1, 'The Sources of Theology' (Marshall Pickering, 1986), pp.154–164; and R.T.Kendall, 'The Puritan Modification of Calvin's Theology', in *John Calvin: His Influence in the Western World* (Zondervan, 1982), pp.199–216.

3   See the catena of citations from Augustine in J.Owen, *Death of Death* (repr. Banner of Truth, 1959), p.311f.

4   See J.Usher (17th century Archbishop of Armagh), *Gotteschalki et praedestione controversiae ab eo notae historia*, Dublin 1631, reprinted in *The Whole Works of . . . J.Usher*, Dublin, 1848–64, pp.1–233.

5   Lombard's words are: 'obtulit pro omnibus, quantam ad pretii sufficientam; sed pro electis tantum quantum ad efficaciem' (Sententiarum Libri Quattuor 3:20:3, MPL, 192, col.799).

6   J.Calvin, *The Gospel According to St.John . . . and the First Epistle of St.John* (Eerdmans, 1961), p.244.

7   Luther interprets 'the many' as 'believers' and in the glosses on Romans 5:20 comments 'He says "Many" and not "All." ' See Luther: *Lectures on Romans*, 1961 ed., p.174; DMLW, pp.53f.,318.

8   'He says many meaning all, as in Rom.5:15' (Calvin, *Hebrews* (Oliver & Boyd, 1963), p.131.

9   H.Roberts, 'Particular Redemption in Perspective', *Reformation Today* no.42, Mar.-Apr.1978, pp.12–18.

10   Dodsworth, *General Redemption*, pp.ix,x.

11   The sermon ('Particular Redemption') was preached by James Spurgeon, Charles's brother. See J.Spurgeon, 'Particular Redemption', *New Park Street Pulpit* vol.7, 1884, pp.313–318.

12   R.B.Kuiper, *God-Centred Evangelism* (Banner of Truth, 1966), p.23.

13   J.Cheeseman et al., *Grace of God in the Gospel* (Banner of Truth, 1972), p.79.

14   J.Murray, Redemption Accomplished and Applied (Banner of Truth, 1961), p.65.

15   Owen, *Works*, 10, p.450.

16   Cheeseman, *Grace*, p.89.

17   Calvin, John, vol.1, p.74.

18   Cheeseman, *Grace*, p.92; Perkins, *Galatians*, p.219.

19   Cheeseman, *Grace*, p.92.

20   Calvin, John, p.74.

21   J.Murray, *Collected Writings of John Murray*, vol.2 (Banner of Truth, 1976), pp.264–265.

22   Murray, *Redemption*, p.154.

23   Murray, *Redemption*, pp.154–156.

24   Murray, *Redemption*, pp.152–153.

25   Murray, *Writings*, vol.2, p.267,271.

26   Murray, *Writings*, vol.2, p.271.

27   See the expositions of C.Hodge (*Romans* rp. Banner of Truth 1972, pp.191–220); R.Haldane, (*Romans*, pp.237–284), J.R.W.Stott, *Men Made New: An Exposition of Romans 5–8* (IVP, 1966), p.42. Stott explicitly reveals a fear of antinomianism (p.33) and repudiates the 'Keswick' interpretation of 'dying to sin' that relates it to sanctification (pp.37–41). See also D.N.Steele & C.C.Thomas, *Romans: An Interpretive Outline* (Presbyterian & Reformed, 1963), pp.54–55; G.B.Wilson, *Romans: A Digest of Reformed Comment* (Banner of Truth, 1969), p.114.

28   See throughout the section on 'the assurance of faith' in Murray, *Writings*, vol.2, 264–274.

29   Murray, *Writings*, vol.2, p.265.

30   See Kendall, *Puritan Modification*, pp.205–206.

31   See Calvin, *Hebrews . . . Peter*, p.334.

32   See Murray, *Redemption*, 1955, p.191.

33   G.Petter, *Mark*, 1661, p.48.

34   G.Petter, *Mark*, 1661, p.48–50,52

35   Wilson, *2 Corinthians*, p.171.

36   Wilson, *Colossians and Philemon*, p.38.

37   Wilson, *Revelation*.

38 As the Baptist radical Puritan John Bunyan wrote (*The Pilgrim's Progress*, Penguin Classics 1965 ed, p.205).

39 See B.Tyler & A.A.Bonar, *Nettleton and His Labours* (Banner of Truth, 1975), p.30.

40 See O.R.Johnstone, 'Thomas Shepard's "Parable of the Ten Virgins" ', in *Servants of the Word*, 1957 Puritan Conference Papers informally distributed, pp.25–35). Shephard wrote much on the 'gospel hypocrite' and the 'knowledge of Christ which does not save' (Johnstone, 'Shepard's Parable', pp.31–34).

41 'John Bunyan and His Experience', *Servants of the Word*, 1957, pp.36–45). It must be noted that Bunyan comes to faith in Christ at the beginning of his story. His subsequent distress is typical Puritan experience.

42 'Daily Life Among the Puritans', *Servants*, 1957, pp.59–71, esp.p.65.

43 'The Puritans and the Doctrine of Election', *The Wisdom of Our Fathers*, (1956 Puritan Conference Papers informally distributed) pp.1–13, esp.pp.10f.

44 See G.Hemming, 'The Puritans' Dealing With Troubled Souls', in *The Wisdom of Our Fathers*, pp.26–37. Hemming comments on the place of the law in the dealing with 'troubled souls' (p.27)).

45 O.R.Johnstone, 'Richard Greenham and the Trials of a Christian', in *The Wisdom* pp.59–69, esp.p.59).

46 P.Cook, 'Becoming a Christian – In the Teaching of Richard Rogers and Richard Greenham', in *Becoming a Christian*, 1973, pp.58–67).

47 R.Horn, 'Thomas Hooker – The Soul Preparation for Christ', in *The Puritan Experiment in the New World*, 1976, pp.19–37, esp.p.35.

48 See W.Guthrie, *The Christian's Great Interest*, reprinted 1982; D.Mingard, 'William Guthrie on the Trial of a Saving Interest in Christ', in *A Goodly Heritage*, 1959, pp.27–33).

49 'Heaven on Earth, A . . . Discourse Touching . . . Assurance', in *The Works of Thomas Brooks*, 1866, vol.2, pp.301–534.

50 W.H.Davies, 'Oliver Heywood the Northern Puritan', in *One Steadfast High Intent*, 1967, pp.45–55).

NOTES TO CHAPTER THREE

1 *A Collection of Hymns for the Use of the People Called Methodists*, 1876, no.34, v.7. Wesley used expressions that could only have been offensive to his Calvinist opponents: 'Will you let him die in vain?' (Hymn 6, v.2); 'After all his waste of love . . . why will you resolve to die?' (Hymn 8, v.1).

2 Wesley, *Hymns*, no.39, vv.4,5.

3 J.Arminius, *Works of James Arminius*, vol.2 (Longman et al. 1828), p.726.

4 *The Meaning of Salvation* (Hodder, 1965), p.231,235.

5 See the fivefold work, 'First . . . Second . . . Fifth Check to Antinomianism', in *The Works of John Fletcher*, vol.1, 1829 (reprinted Schmul, 1974), pp.115–445.

6 See D.R.Smith, 'John Fletcher: An Arminian Upholder of Holiness', in *The Manifold Grace of God* (PRSC, 1969), pp.62f.,67f.

7 Smith, 'Fletcher', p.71.

8 Smith, 'Fletcher', p.72.

9 Smith, 'Fletcher', p.73; Fletcher, *Works*, vol.1, pp.170–171.

10 Fletcher, *Works*, vol.1, p.174.

11 Fletcher, *Works*, vol.1, p.201.

12 Fletcher, *Works*, vol.1, p.195.

13 Fletcher, *Works*, vol.1, p.198.

14 Fletcher, *Works*, vol.1, p.95.

15 Fletcher, *Works*, vol.1, p.196.

16 See J.Arminius, *Works*, vol.2, pp.454, also pp.456–469.
17 Fletcher, *Works*, vol.1, pp.117f..
18 Fletcher, *Works*, vol.1, p.179.115b,442,444.
19 R.C.H.Lenski, *The Interpretation of I and II Corinthians*, 1957, p.388.
20 R.C.H.Lenski, *The Interpretation of St.John's Gospel*, 1943, p.1139. See also Lenski's comments on Jn.15:6 (pp.1037–1040).
21 R.Shanks, *Life in the Son*, 1961, pp.333–337. The texts are Mt.18:21–35; 24:4,5,11–13,23–26; 25:1–13; Lk.8:11–15; 11:24–28; 12:42–46; Jn.6:66–71; 8:31,32; 8:51; 13:8; 15:1–6; Ac.11:21–23; 14:21–22; Rom.6:11–23; 8:12–4,17; 11:20–22; 14:15–23; 1 Cor.9:23–27; 10:1–21; 11:29–32; 15:1,2; 2 Cor.1;24; 11:2–4; 12:21–13:5; Gal.5:1–4; 6:7–9; Eph.3:17; Phil.2:12–16; 3:4–4:1; Col.1:21–23; 2:4–8; 2:18–19;1 Thess.3:1–8; 1 Tim.1:3–7,18–20; 2:11–15; 4:1–16; 5:8; 5:11–15,5,6 [sic]; 6:9–12; 6:17–19; 6:20,21; 2 Tim.2:11–18; 2:22–26; 3:13–15; Heb.2:1–3; 3:6–19; 4:1–16; 5:8,9; 6:4–9; 6:10–20; 10:19–31; 10:32–39; 11:13–16; 12:1–17; 12:25–29; 13:9–14; 13:17,7 [sic]; Jam.1:12–16; 1:21–22; 2:14–26; 4:4–10; 5:19,20; 1 Pet.1:5– 9,13; 2 Pet.1:5–11; 2:1–22; 3:16,17; 1 Jn.1:5–2:11; 2:15–28; 2:29–3:10; 5:4,5; 5:16; 2 Jn.6–9; Jude 5–12; 20,21; Rev.2; 7; 2:10,11.
22 See G.Duty, *If Ye Continue* (Bethany, 1966), passim.
23 See Marshall, *Kept*, 1969, passim.
24 W.Barclay, *The Letters to the Philippians, Colossians and Thessalonians* (rev.ed., St Andrews, 1975), p.40.

NOTES TO CHAPTER FOUR

1 J.I.Packer, 'Infallible Scripture and the Role of Hermeneutics', in *Scripture and Truth*, ed. D.A.Carson & J.D.Woodbridge (IVP, 1983), p.325.
2 See the 'Preface to the Complete . . . Latin Writings', 1545, in Luther's *Works*, American ed, vol.34, pp.323–338; the excerpt appears on pp.336f.
3 J.I.Packer, 'Upholding the Unity of Scripture Today', JETS, 25, 1982, pp.409f.
4 See J.I.Packer, 'Sola Scriptura in History and Today', in *God's Inerrant Word* (Ed. J.W.Montgomery, Bethany, 1973), pp.59f.
5 Luther queried the canonicity of James, because of the disagreement he perceived between Paul and James. See N.B.Stonehouse, 'Luther and the New Testament' in *Paul Before the Areopagus* (Tyndale, 1957), pp.186–197. If Luther's 'Table Talk' is trustworthy, then as late as 1542 he argued that 'We should throw the epistle of James out of this school for it doesn't amount to much . . . the ancients . . . didn't acknowledge this letter' (*Works*, vol.54, 1967, pp.424ff). Luther was quite clear that James 'is flatly against St.Paul and all the rest of Scripture' (*Works*, vol.35, 1960, p.396).
6 See e.g. H.Räisänen, *Paul and the Law* (Mohr, 1983); E.P.Sanders, *Paul, the Law, and the Jewish People* (Fortress, 1983); H.Hübner, *Law in Paul's Thought* (Clark, 1984).

NOTES TO CHAPTER FIVE

1 D.M. Lloyd-Jones, *New Man*, 1972, pp.9f.
2 G.D.Fee, *1 Corinthians* (NICNT, Eerdmans, 1987), pp.142–145. The full weight of this verse needs to be explored.

NOTES TO CHAPTER SIX

1 The classic exposition is John Owen's magisterial work *The Death of Death in the Death of Christ*, 1647 (Owen's *Works*, vol.10, pp.139–428). Modern statements are

found in J.Murray, *The Atonement and the Free Offer of the Gospel*, in *Writings*, 1, 1976, pp.59–85, esp.74–80; R.B.Kuiper, *For Whom Did Christ Die?* (Baker, 1959). The early history of the doctrine is surveyed in W.R.Godfrey, 'Reformed Thought On the Extent of the Atonement', *WThJ*, 37, 1974–1975, pp.133–171.

2   See E.H.Palmer, *The Five Points of Calvinism*, (Guardian, 1972, pp.43–50) with subsidiary appeal to others that are 'less useful as "proof texts" ' (e.g. Mt.1:21; Ro.8:32).Only Jn.10:10–29 and Ephesians 5:27–27 are positively expounded by Murray (*Writings*, 1, pp.74–78). Other texts that might be cited are Isa.5:11; Mt.1:21; 15:24; 20:28; Mk.10:45; Jn.17:9; Acts 20:28; Ro.8:31–39; Gal.3:13; Hb.9:28.

None of these really amounts to much. (i) Texts which speak of 'us' or God's people being saved do not deny that an objective provision was made for everyone. Christ died for all to win some. (ii) The term 'many' cannot be used to introduce a restriction for the atonement. That it may be a Hebraism for 'everyone' is indisputable. (iii) Deductions from the doctrine of election are precisely that: deductions and no more. (iv) Both Eph.5:25 and Jn.10:15 contain strong metaphors (sheep/shepherds; marriage) which necessarily focus on the sheep or upon the bride. To use them to cancel out passages with a more universal emphasis is surely to over-press them in the interests of a logic which is more Aristotelian than biblical. See J.B.Torrance, 'The Incarnation and "Limited Atonement" ', *SBET*, no.2, 1984, pp.32–40.

3   W.Hendriksen, *Matthew*, pp.750, 911; *Mark*, pp.415f., 575.

4   So Jerome ('*id est pro his qui credere voluerint*', cited by McNeile, *Matthew*, p.290).

5   McNeile, *Matthew*, pp.290f..

6   Calvin *Harmony*, 2, p.277.

7   Matt.20:28; 26:28; Mk.10:45; 14:24 echo Isaiah 53; *polloi* is the equivalent of *rabbim* in Is.53:11–12 (see Cranfield, *Mark*, 1966, p.444); R.T.France, *Jesus and the Old Testament* (IVP, 1971), pp.116–121. See also J.Jeremias, *polloi*, in *TDNT*, 6, pp.536–545, esp.p.536, nn.3,4. Further data is provided by Jeremias from gospel parallels and Old Testament usage.

8   B.B.Warfield, *Biblical and Theological Studies* (Presbyterian & Reformed, 1952), pp.505–522.

9   Calvin, *John*, pp.73f.

10   See C.Spicq, *Epîtres Pastorales*, vol.2, 1969, p.637.

11   The present tense of the Vulgate and other translations goes back to a weakly attested variant.

12   Hb.4:15; 6:20; 7:25.

13   Hb.1:3; 2:9,14; 7:27.

14   *Works*, vol 10, pp.362–368.

15   A.D.Chang, 'Second Peter 2:1 and the Extent of the Atonement', *Bib. Sac.*142, 1985, pp.52–63.

16   *Inst.*3:24:4.

17   'Christ . . . is the mirror wherein we must, and without self-deception may, contemplate our own election' (*Inst.*3:24:5).

18   *Concerning the Eternal Predestination of God*, ET, 1961, p.130).

19   T.Beza, *A Briefe and Pithie Summe of the Christian Faith*, 1565, p.36a,37, quoted by R.T.Kendall, *John Cotton*, p.40.

20   *Predestination*, p.130.

21   *John*, p.73. My italics.

22   *John*, pp.73f.

NOTES TO CHAPTER SEVEN

1   M.A.Eaton, *Living Under Grace: Romans 6:1–7:25* (Nelson Word, 1994,1989), pp.290–349.

2 D.J.Wiseman points out that 'there has been a growing awareness that the collections of ancient laws from Mesopotamia are not 'codes' of laws, but case-laws or decisions based on the facts of isolated and particular cases'. 'It is certain that among the whole corpus of legal literature from the ancient near East we have no 'code' of laws in our modern sense' ('Law and Order in the Old Testament', *VE*, 8, 1973, pp.9f.).

3 Omissions may be noted when the Torah is compared with the Law of Eshnunna, in R.Yaron, *The Law of Eshnunna* (Magnes, 1969), p.136. B.S.Jackson points out that 'Biblical law does not deal with theft of slaves, unlike the Ancient Near Eastern corpora' (*Theft in Early Jewish Law* (OUP, 1972), p.118).

4 Many writers point to what on a *prima facie* reading of the old Testament is pre-Mosaic legislation and use it as evidence for Israel's legislation (e.g. H.McKeating, 'The Development of the Law on Homicide in Ancient Israel', *VT*, 25, 1975, pp.46–49, concerning the rape of Dinah). One must remember however that allusion to local pre-Mosaic law does not mean that such law has any divine sanction.

5 Hyatt says the chapter 'presupposes the law of the Sabbath promulgated at Sinai (*Ex.*, p.178). I prefer to think that it anticipates and prepares for the Sinaitic fourth commandment. The anarthrous construction in Ex.16:23,25 may signify the innovative nature of the Sabbath command at this point (see H.P.H.Dressler, 'The Sabbath in the Old Testament', in *From Sabbath to Lord's Day* (ed. D.A.Carson, Zondervan, 1982), pp.24–26,37.)

6 If 'justification' is the foundational element in the Christian life, as I think it is, and if Abraham is the classic model of justification, as Paul maintained, then I think it is correct to use the term 'salvation', as long as one bears in mind that the New Testament treats pre-Christian believers as seeing the promises 'from afar' (Hb.11:13). See J.S.Feinberg, 'Salvation in the Old Testament', in *Tradition and Testament*, 1981, pp.39–77; G.W.Grogan, 'The Experience of Salvation in the Old and New Testaments', *VE*, 1967, pp.4–26.7.

7 D.J.Wiseman, 'Ur of the Chaldees', *NBD*, p.1305.

8 See also Gen.24:7 ('Yahweh . . . who took me from the house of my father'). 'Take' (*laqach*) is also used as a verb of election in Dt.4:20.

If Gen.15:7 and Nehemiah 9:7 (also Philo, *De Abrahamo*, 71; Josephus, *Antiquities*, 1:7) bear witness to a call of Abraham from Ur, then Abraham's disentanglement from reliance on his family went through several stages, according to the biblical witness. E.Haenchen points out (*Acts*, 1971, Blackwell, p.278) that the words 'from your father's house' are omitted from Acts 7:2, which seems to refer to an earlier call than the one mentioned in Gen.12:1. Perhaps we are meant to think of Abraham's discovering progressively that a break from his 'father's house' would mean more than he initially realised.

9 In Puritan thinking 'the moral Law is so closely bound up with the rational nature of which man is possessed, it is sometimes spoken of as the Law of nature' (E.F.Kevan, *Grace*, p.54). John Lightfoot in 1629 wrote that 'Adam heard as much in the garden, as Israel did at Sinai, but onely in fewer words and without thunder' (*Erubhin: or Miscellenies Christian and Judicial*, London, 1629, p.182, cited in Kevan, *Grace*, p.60). See also WCF, sections VII and XIX ('God gave to Adam a law, as a covenant of works'). For this viewpoint in the significant Puritan thinker William Ames, see L.W.Gibbs, 'The Puritan Natural Law Theory of William Ames', *HThR*, 64, 1971, pp.37–57.

10 A.Jepsen, *'aman*, in *TDOT*, 1, pp.292–293.

11 It is possible to take Abraham as the subject as was done by the 13th century Spanish rabbi Nachmanides (see Rambam (Nachmanides), *Commentary on the Torah: Gen.* (Shiloh, 1971), p.197. Van Selms holds a similar view (*Genesis.*, vol.1, Callenbach, 1984, p.215). But on that view there is no antecedent of the suffix.

12 J.A.Motyer, 'Covenant and Promise', *Evangel*, vol.1, pt.1, 1983, p.4.

13 Recently the consensus of opinion has viewed the passage in the light of Jer.34:18–19 and treated the dismemberment of the animals as a self-imprecation in the event of the covenant's being broken. Although there are differences between Gen.15:7–21 and Jer.34:18–19 and no precise extra-biblical parallel is known, it is clear that the rite inaugurates a treaty and involves self-malediction upon the potential treaty-breaker (see fully Hasel, 'The Meaning of the Animal Rite in Gen.15', *JSOT*, 19, 1981, pp.61–78).

14 Motyer, 'Covenant', p.4.

15 The promise to Abraham concerned 'a land that I will show (*'ar'eh*) you' but 'unto your seed I will give (*'etten*) this land'. The difference in wording in Gen.12:1,7 ('show' versus 'give') is significant. I owe this observation to the rather eccentric writer A.W.Pink. Even eccentricity does not prevent the observation of some basic data! See A.W.Pink, *The Divine Covenants* (Baker, 1973), p.103. As I understand the relation of Gen.22 to the rest of salvation-history, the modern Christian depends on the oath given to Abraham. An oath is irrevocable. It is the fact that blessings to believers flow from Abraham's obedience that warrants the term 'mediator'.

16 The philological 'meaning' of the vocables *'l shdy* remains obscure, as is emphasized by many, e.g. W.F.Albright, 'The Names Shaddai and Abram', JBL, 54, 1935, pp.180–193). Examining usage is preferable to exploring etymologies.

17 Motyer, *Revelation of the Divine Name* (Tyndale, 1959), p.29.

18 O.P.Robertson believes that the lateness of the statement in Gen.15:6 (in ch.15 rather than ch.12) is intended to underline the fact that after the faith of ch.12 'nothing has been added to faith as the way to righteousness' (*New Covenant*, p.267). In this he follows Calvin (*Genesis* (Banner of Truth, 1975), p.409).

19 See F.J.Helfmeyer, [*halak*], *TDOT*, 3, p.388.

20 Weinfeld points to the similarity of the Abrahamic and the 'grant' type of covenant (see below, pp.76f.). The 'grant' of land would be given to one who 'walked in perfection' and 'kept the charge of my kingship' (see M.Weinfeld, *Deuteronomy and the Deuteronomic School*, OUP, 1972, pp.75f.).

21 See P.K.McCarter, *1 Samuel* (Doubleday, AB, 1980), pp.247f..

22 F.D.Kidner, *Psalms* (IVP, 1973), pp.58f..

23 See GK 110(f); cf. Gen.42:18 ('this do and live'), Am.5:4,6.

24 Motyer, *Revelation*, p.29.

25 J.A.Motyer, 'Covenant', p.4.

26 Much depends on how the term 'regeneration' is used. If one thinks of it as identical to the New Testament gift of the Spirit, the statement in the text is not warranted. However I distinguish between a work of the Spirit which initiates new life and a work of the Spirit sealing new life. Abraham is portrayed as already a man of faith. On my definition he is already 'regenerate'. Circumcision 'seals' what has already happened to him. See G.W.Grogan, 'Experience', *VE*, 5, 1967, pp.4–26; J.Rea, 'The Personal Relationship of Old Testament Believers to the Holy Spirit', in *Essays on Apostolic Themes*, 1985, pp.92–103; L.J.Wood, *The Holy Spirit in the Old Testament* (Zondervan, 1976), pp.105f..

27 This point is, in my opinion, insufficiently recognised. It is found in some evangelical circles (see A.W.Pink, *Divine Covenants* (Baker, 1973), p.103; F.P.Moller, 'Objections to Infant Baptism', in *Infant Baptism* (UNISA, 1984), p.80). To deal with the matter fully would require a study of the term 'seal'. In my understanding the term always has the notion of an irrevocable and infallible guarantee. For this reason I am unhappy with the Reformed custom of calling the sacraments 'seals'. G.C.Berkouwer maintains that to call the sacraments seals 'does not mean that these signs and seals can in themselves perform the miracle of strengthening our faith (*The Sacraments*, Eerdmans, 1969, p.135). But this is to weaken the meaning of 'seal'. A 'seal' does in itself perform the miracle of strengthening faith. I agree in this matter with A.Carson: 'That baptism and the Lord's

Supper are seals of the new covenant, is a doctrine so common, and a phraseology so established, that it is received without question as a first principle . . . I strongly protest against it as unscriptural' (*Baptism, Its Mode and Its Subjects*, National Foundation for Christian Education (USA), 1969 (original 19th century), p.234). I agree with G.R.Beasley-Murray (*Baptism in the New Testament*, Paternoster, 1962, pp.171–177) and J.D.G.Dunn (*Baptism in the Holy Spirit*, SCM, 1970, pp.131–134, 156) in relating circumcision to the baptism with the Spirit, understood experientially not sacramentally.

If it be said 'But this makes circumcision have a different meaning for Abraham compared to the meaning it has for his descendants', I reply, 'On the contrary, circumcision retains the same meaning for Abraham and for his descendants. It told Abraham that his way of salvation was the way of salvation; it told his descendants that Abraham's way (not their own way) of salvation was the way of salvation. The meaning stays the same. It points to Abraham's being justified by faith. But this means that the term 'seal' (infallible guarantee) is appropriate to Abraham only. It seals Abraham's faith and calls all others to follow in his steps.

The only entity that infallibly 'seals' believers in the New Testament is the Holy Spirit. It is no accident that the New Testament applies the term *sphragis* to the circumcision of Abraham and to the work of the Spirit. They are in my opinion exactly analogous.

28 I quote from p.8 of the informal notes issued by the Theological Students' Fellowship, London, of J.A.Motyer's lectures on 'Old Testament Covenant Theology' (1972–73). The published version (see 'Covenant and Promise', p.4) is slightly less emphatic but makes the same point.

29 I translate the text in this way because the English word 'now' is often merely an otiose introductory particle. But *'attah* must be given its full weight, 'at this time', as in Ex.18:11; Jdg.17:3; 1 Ki.17:24; Ps.20:7(Heb). The weak use of 'now' does not seem to exist in Hebrew.

30 On the linguistics of oath-language, see H.S.Gehman, 'The Oath in the Old Testament: Its Vocabulary, Idiom and Syntax in the Massoretic Text and the Septuagint', in *Grace Upon Grace* (Eerdmans, 1975), pp.51–63. Gehman does not reflect on the connection between oath-taking and the end of any possible change of mind, but comes close to doing so when alluding to Ps.110;4: 'the oath was final, and he would not change his mind' (pp.51f.). M.R.Lehman surveys biblical oath-formulae in the light of ancient near eastern practise, in 'Biblical Oaths', *ZATW*, 81, 1969, pp.74–92.

31 See A. König's comment on Jer.4:28 in *Here*, p.66 ('This assurance presupposes that there might well be decisions which he can go back on and over which he might repent'). R.T.Kendall's sermonic treatment of the same theme is stimulating ('Does God Change His Mind?' in *Jonah* (Hodder, 1978), pp.201–210). H.Berkhof points to the opposite tendency in much modern theology and comments 'In its doctrine of God, theology will always drift about between Aristotle and Hegel' (i.e. between the static and the changeable). See 'The (Un)Changeability of God', in *Grace Upon Grace*, 1975, p.25.

32 W.Bruggemann discusses the theological significance of God's testing. 'In our sophistication', he writes, 'we may find the notion of "testing" primitive' (*Genesis*, p.190; see more generally pp.18–194). My own view is that 'testing' is part of the sequence: provisional promise – delay – supreme test – oath. The promises of God could have been aborted by disobedience. A time gap is present that requires 'faith and patience' (cf. Heb.6:12) for the promise to be inherited. The delay is itself a test of faith. At the end of the painful delay comes an even greater test of faith. When the test is passed it leads to God's oath.

Something similar is found with the threats of God, and with the disobedience of God's people. In Ex.-Numbers the Israelites exhibit repeated disobedience. Delay in getting to Canaan is a painful test. When the people test God, God is testing them, at

Massah (Heb. *nissah* = to test). The oath in Nu.14:22,28 is a turning point. After that they cannot enter Canaan. 'Testing' is of the essence of the life of faith. It is a central ingredient in the pilgrimage towards inheriting or not inheriting what is promised.

33 G.E.Mendenhall, 'Covenant', in *IDB*, 1, p.714.

34 Mendhenhall, *Covenant*, p.720. See further G.M.Tucker, 'Covenant Forms and Contract Forms', *VT*, 15, 1965, pp.488–490. Tucker concludes that: 'the extra-biblical and the biblical evidence for the name of the contract form speak with one voice: Covenants . . . are also called oaths' (p.490).

NOTES TO CHAPTER EIGHT

1 J.A.Motyer, *Law and Life: A Study of the Meaning of Law in the Old Testament* (Lawyers Christian Fellowship, 1978), pp.5f.

2 Leupold, *Genesis*, p.720.

3 Some argue that 'obligation' (*Verpflichtung*) is a better translation (see E.Kutsch, 'Gesetz und Gnade', *ZATW*, 79, 1967, pp.18–35; E.Kutsch, 'Der Begriff [*berith*] in vordeuteronomischer Zeit', in *Das Ferne und Nahe Wort: Festchrift Leonard Rost*, BZAW, 105, 1967, pp.133–143; W.Eichrodt dismisses views that regard covenant as contract as 'long-obsolete argumentation of Kratzschmar, from the year 1896 . . . revived with no new support' (Covenant and Law: Thoughts on Recent Discussion', *Inter*, 20, 1966, pp.302–321, esp.p.304). A survey of the linguistic data concerning *berith* is found in P.Buis, *La Notion d'Alliance dans L'Ancien Testament* (Cerf, 1976). Older discussions are summarized by F.R.VanDevelder, *Form and History*, pp.12–35.

4 Covenant terminology is not to be found in Genesis chapter 3. For interpretations of Hos.6:7, see H.W.Wolff, *Hosea*, (Fortress, 1974), pp.105, 121f.; J.L.Mays, *Hosea*, (SCM, 1969), pp.99f.; W.Rudolph, *Hosea*, KAT, 1966, pp.141f. (who emend to *b'dm* instead of *k'dm*, and F.I.Andersen, *Hosea*, AB, 1980, pp.438f., who does not emend the text but still thinks Adam is a place name.

5 *The Biblical Archaeologist Reader*, vol.3, 1970, pp.25–53, reprints Mendenhall's articles, 'Covenant Forms in Israelite Tradition' (*BA*, 17, 1954, pp.50–76), 'Ancient Orient and Biblical Law' (*BA*, 17, 1954, pp.26–46).

6 Mendenhall, *Archaeologist Reader*, 3, p.31. Independently of Mendenhall, K.Baltzer came to similar conclusions in *Das Bundesformular*, 1964.

7 Among dozens of examples see D.J.McCarthy, *Old Testament Covenant* (Blackwell, 1972), p.12; Kitchen, *Ancient*, pp.92–93; D.R.Hillers, *Covenant: the History of a Biblical Idea* (John Hopkins, 1969), pp.29–37.

8 See Kitchen, *Bible*, p.81.

9 See Kitchen, *Ancient*.

10 M.Weinfeld, 'The Covenant of Grant in the Old Testament and in the Ancient Near East', *JAOS*, 90, 1970, pp.184–203; also his *Deuteronomy*, pp.75f.

11 Weinfeld, *Covenant of Grant*, p.202.

12 By 'secular' I mean that God is not one of the parties involved in giving or receiving the oath. All covenants were closely linked with religious faith.

13 These are the covenants between Abram and his allies (Gn.14:13; on 'alliance of defence', see Wiseman, 'Abraham the Prince', pp.229f., and the Assyrian secular parallel in Wiseman, *Vassal-Treaties*, p.41 (lines 162–168), the covenants between Abram and Abimelech (Gen.21:27,32), between Isaac and Abimelech (Gen.26:28), between Jacob and Laban (Gen.31:44). Such agreements may take place between kings. There were mutual treaties of peace between Asa and Ben-Hadad I of Aram (1 Ki..15:19; 2 Chr.16:2), as there had been between Asa's father, Abijah, and the father of Ben-Hadad (1 Ki..15:19; 2 Chr.16:2). There was such a pact also between Ben-Hadad I and Baasha of Israel (1 Ki..15;19; 2 Chr.16:3). We have mention of a

covenant-brotherhood between David and Jonathan (1 Sa.18:3; 20:8; 23:18;). We have the covenant between David and Abner of the house of Saul (2 Sa.3:12f.), between Solomon and Hiram (1 Ki..5:12), and between Ahab and Ben-Hadad II (1 Ki..15;19; 2 Chr.16:3). We have mention of a covenant-brotherhood between David and Jonathan (1 Sa.18:3; 20:8; 23:18; McCarter suggests that more than friendship is involved and that 1 Sa.18:3 records Jonathan's transfer of his position as heir apparent; see *1 Samuel*, pp.305,340f.). We have the covenant between David and Abner of the house of Saul (2 Sa.3:12,13), between Solomon and Hiram (1 Ki..5:12), and between Ahab and Ben-Hadad II (1 Ki.20:34).

14 Young, *The Prophecy of Daniel*, (Eerdmans ,1949), p.242.

15 Mendenhall in 1962 spoke of four types of secular covenant: parity, suzerainty, patron and promissory ('Covenant', *IDB*, vol.1, pp.716–717). I put 'patron' and 'promissory' covenants together as basically of one kind.

I do not believe that the covenants of 2 Ki.23:3; Neh.10:28f.; Ezr.10:3 belong to the same type of covenant as Jer.34:8–22 (pace Mendenhall, 'Covenant', p.717). These seem to be law-covenants voluntarily entered into. The people 'took a curse and oath to follow the law of God' (Ne.10:30, EVV 10:29). They are renewals of a suzerainty type of covenant (see Fensham, *Ezra, Nehemiah*, NICOT, 1982, p.134; Baltzer, Covenant, pp.47f.; J.B.Myers, *Ezra, Nehemiah*, AB, 1965, p.83). As Mendenhall suggests Ne.5:11–13 is possibly to be seen as a promissory covenant, despite the absence of the term (Mendenhall, Covenant, p.717). Fensham rightly says 'Curse (*'ala*) is sometimes so closely related to covenant that it functions as a synonym for covenant' (*Ezra, Nehemiah*, p.238; see also Craigie, *Deuteronomy*, p.359).

16 See McCarter, *1 Samuel*, pp.202f.

17 The major commentators however agree in referring v.19 to the oath of loyalty to Babylon, taken by the Israelite king (see W.Zimmerli, *Ezekiel* (Fortress, 1969), pp.365f.; G.C.Aalders, *Ezekiel*, COT, vol.1, 1955, p.288; M.Greenberg, *Ezekiel 1–20*, AB, p.315; J.W.Wevers, *Ezekiel*, NCB, p.107). The oath is God's oath because it is made before God and required by God (see W.Eichrodt, *Ezekiel*, SCM, 1970, p.227).

18 Fensham, *Ezra, Nehemiah*, p.268.

19 See C.F.Keil, *Ezra, Nehemiah, Esther* (Eerdmans, n.d.), p.245.

20 M.Weinfeld comments 'The covenant with Abraham, like the covenant with David, belongs to the 'grant' type which differs from the 'vassal' type of covenant (*Deuteronomy*, p.74). On renewals of the Sinai-covenant, see D.J.McCarthy, 'Compact and Kingship: Stimuli for Hebrew Covenant Thinking', *Studies in the Period of David and Solomon* . . . (Eisenbrauns, 1982), pp.75–92; D.J.McCarthy, 'Covenant and Law in Chronicles-Nehemiah', *CBQ*, 44, 1982, pp.41–43.

21 In interpreting 'kingdom of priests' two guidelines seem important: (i) the parallel expressions *khnym mmlkt* and *gwy qds* suggest that *mmlkt* is the main noun and that *khnym* has qualifying and adjectival force (so W.L.Moran, 'A Kingdom of Priests', in *The Bible in Current Catholic Thought* (Herder, 1962), p.7; R.B.Y.Scott, 'A Kingdom of Priests, Ex.xix.6', *OTS*, 8, 1950, p.216). (ii) The parallelism of the two expressions suggest that the whole nation is envisaged as having a priestly ministry to the world. (If Moran is correct in his argument that *mmlkt* means 'kings' rather than 'kingdom', it would still be the whole nation that is in view). Although some Israelites would function as a particular priesthood, the central point is emphasizing what the whole nation would be (See Hyatt, *Exodus*, p.200).

22 Childs, *Exodus*, p.367. The corporateness of this covenant is emphasized also by J.B.Bauer, 'Könige und Priester, ein heiliges Volk (Ex.19,6)', BZ, 2, 1958, pp.283–286.

23 This is frequently observed. D.J.McCarthy can even say of late usage of *diatheke* in the LXX that often 'rules' would come closer to the feel of the word' ('Covenant in Narratives from Late OT Times', in *The Quest for the Kingdom of God* (Eisenbrauns, 1982), p.81).

24   Nu.10:33; 14:44; Dt.10:8; 31:9,25,26; Jos.3:3, 6(x2), 8, 11, 14, 17; 4:7, 9, 18; 6:6,8; 8:33; Jdg.20:27; 1 Sa.4:3,4(x2),5; 2 Sa.15:24; 1 Ki..3:15; 6:19; 8:1,6; 1 Chr.15:25,26,28,29; 16:6,37; 17:1; 22:11; 28:2,18; 2 Chr.5:2,7; Jer.3:16.

25   See J.E.Latham, *The Religious Symbolism of Salt* (Duchesne, 1982), esp.p.62, for salt as symbolism of covenant.

26   Other explicit mentions of the Sinai-covenant are Ps.50:15, recalling Ex.24:3–8 (see Kidner, Psalms, p.86), Jer.34:13,18(x2) (see Thompson, Jeremiah, p.343); Ezk.16:59 referring back to Dt.29:11,12; Ezk.16:60,61 referring to Lv.26:42,45 (see C.F.Keil, *Ezekiel*, vol.1, rp. Eerdmans, 1966, p.230).

27   See the helpful survey in M.Weinfeld, 'Covenant, Davidic', *IDB* Suppl.Vol. p.188. Weinfeld points to the 'analogous typology' between the Abrahamic and Davidic covenants (p.189), to its being modelled on the royal grant (p.189), and to its unconditionality (pp.189,191). He comments 'The Abrahamic and Davidic covenants are then a promissory type, while the Mosaic covenant is an obligatory type' (p.189).

28   Leupold, *Isaiah*, 2, p.325.

29   In the survey above I have not mentioned figurative uses of *berith* in Job.5:23; 31:1; 41:4; Is.28:15,18; Jer.33:20(x2),25. In the interests of space I have largely kept myself to passages of the Old Testament where mention of *berith* is explicit. The material would have been much enlarged if other terms (*eduth*, *'alah*, etc) had been taken into consideration. See Fensham, 'Common Trends in Curses of the Near Eastern Treaties . . . ', *ZATW*, 75, 1963, pp.155–175, for links between covenant and malediction. Even considering these terms would not exhaust the matter, so pervasive is covenant language and metaphor in the Old Testament. See M.Fox, '*Tob* as Covenant Terminology', *BASOR*, 209, 1973, pp.41f.; H.B.Huffmon, 'The Treaty Background of Hebrew *Yada*'', *BASOR*, 181, 1966, pp.31–37, W.L.Moran, The Ancient Near Eastern Background of the Love of God in Deuteronomy, *CBQ*, 25, 1963, pp.78–87. See also J.Hempel, Bund, in RGG, col.1514, for other covenant terms.

30   Law 'Covenant', *WTJ*, 27, 1964–65, p.3; see also *By Oath Consigned*, p.16. Mendenhall remarks 'the covenant with Abraham (and Noah) is of completely different form . . .it is Yahweh himself who swears to certain promises to be carried out in the future. It is not often enough seen that no obligations are imposed upon Abraham . . .The covenant of Moses, on the other hand, is about the exact opposite' (Law and Covenant, pp.35f.). Others who see antithesis between Abraham-type and Sinai-type of covenants include W.Zimmerli, 'Sinai-bund und Abrahambund: Ein Beitrag zum Verständnis der Priesterschrift', *TZ*, 16, 1960, pp.268–280.

31   The question of the origins of the people of Israel is much disputed. See F.D.Kidner, 'The Origins of Israel', *TSF Bulletin* (British), no.57, Summer 1970, pp.3–12.

The date, origin and unity of the decalogue are also a matter of dispute. Nowadays there is a trend which recognises its antiquity. See surveys in J.J.Stamm, 'Dreissig Jahre Dekalogsforschung', *TR*, 17, 1961, pp.189–239; H.G.Reventlow, *Gebot und Predigt in Dekalog*, 1962; J.Schreiner, *Die Zehn Gebote im Leben des Gottesvolkes*, 1966; J.J.Stamm & M.E.Andrew, *The Ten Commandments in Recent Research*, 1967; E.Nielsen, *The Ten Commandments in New Perspective*, 1968.

32   The Israel-centred aspect of the giving of the law must be asserted despite widespread assumptions to the contrary. R.Stewart asks the question 'For whom was the Decalogue intended?' and answers 'For all mankind, in potential' ('Ancient Israel: A Model for Today?' *SBET*, 3, 1985, p.33). This seems to be an inaccurate reading of the text of the Torah itself, and neglects Paul's distinction between those who do and those who do not have the law (Ro.2). It runs into special difficulties in the case of the Sabbath. Stewart says the fourth commandment 'binds the Christian also' but clearly would not want the Sabbath law to be literally applied to the Christian as he himself hints (p.29).

33 See J.A.Motyer, *Day of the Lion*, (IVP, 1974), pp.35–37, who points to the similarity to Romans 2.

34 See Phillips, *Criminal Law* (Blackwell, 1970). R.L.Wilson says that 'the Decalogue cannot itself be considered law in a strict sense because it lacks prescriptions for communal action against offenders ('Enforcing the Covenant: The Mechanisms of Judicial Authority in Early Israel', in *The Quest for the Kingdom of God*, 1983, p.59). This is the case only if one isolates the decalogue from its context in Exodus 19–24, and from the Torah as a whole.

35 C.H.H.Wright, 'The Israelite Household and the Decalogue: The Social Background and Significance of Some of the Commandments,' *TB*, 30, 1979, pp.101–124. esp p.102.

36 See A Goetze, *The Laws of Eshnunna*, *AASOR*, 31, 1951–52 (published 1956), pp.24ff.

37 See G.R.Driver & J.C.Miles, *The Assyrian Laws*, 1935

38 M.Resnick, *Punishment in Civil Delicts According to the Old Testament Akkadian Codes and the Qur'an*, unpublished M.A., 1979, p.259.

39 Z.W.Falk, *Hebrew Law*, chs.5–10. S.Amsler's survey of motivation in Deuteronomy reveals the nationalistic emphasis of the motivation-clauses (see 'La Motivation de l'Ethique dans la Parenèse du Deuteronome', in *Beitrage zur Alttestamentlichen Theologie*, 1977, pp.11–22, esp. p.19. Much the same point is revealed in C.M.Carmichael's *The Laws of Deuteronomy*, 1974; see also S.M.Paul, *Studies in the Book of the Covenant in the Light of Cuneiform and Biblical Law*, VTS 18, 1970

40 The Old Testament prescribed the death penalty for murder (Nu.35: 16ff), various sexual offences (Dt.22; Lv.28), kidnapping (Dt.24:7), defiance of parents (Dt.21:18–21), blasphemy or incitement to apostasy (Lv.24:16; Dt.13). See F.D.Kidner, *The Death Penalty*, 1963, pp.10–11. Rushdoony gives a fuller list (*Institutes*, p.77.)

41 Williams, 'Penology', *Bib.Sac.* 133, 1976, p.43, 45–49.

42 F.D.Kidner, *Hard Sayings*, 1972, p.22

43 See G.Wenham, in Kaye, *Law, Morality and the Bible*, 1978, p.39. Theft of booty in holy war was an exception. A survey of penalties for theft is provided by B.S.Jackson, *Theft*, pp.130–199.

44 G Wenham, *The Book of Leviticus*, *NICOT*, 1979, p.241.

45 See J.Milgrom, 'Prolegomenon to Leviticus 17:11' *JBL*, 90, 1971, pp.154–156.

46 This receives support from LH 154, compared with Lv.20:17.

47 Kaye & Wenham, *Law*, p.44; Jackson, *Theft*, p.154ff. Fines other than compensation, and imprisonment, were not modes of punishment in the Torah.

48 Wenham, in Kaye and Wenham, *Law*, p.12.

49 T.H.Gaster, 'Sacrifice', *IDB*, vol.4 pp.147–159,esp. pp.151–152.

50 H.H.Rowley, 'The Meaning of Sacrifice in the Old Testament,' in *From Moses to Qumran*, 1963, pp.92–93.

51 Rowley, 'Meaning of Sacrifice,' p.94.

52 Lehman, 'Oaths,' *ZATW*, vol.81, 1969, p.74.

53 See G.J.Wenham, 'The Deuteronomic Theology of the Book of Joshua,' *JBL*, 90, 1971, pp.146–148, concerning the law in Joshua.

54 Young, *Introduction*, p.43.

55 It appears from the statement in Heb.1:7 that in the first century theophany could be interpreted as angelic manifestation.

56 See Heb.8:8 ('finding fault with *them*' – assuming that the text should read *autous* rather than *autois* attached to *legei*.) See also W.C. Kaiser, 'The Old Promise and the New Covenant in Jer.31,31–34,' *JETS* 15, 1972, pp.11–23, esp. p.17.

57 See M.A.Eaton, *Living Under Grace*, pp.175–177.

58 J.Herrman, 'Das Zehnte Gebot,' in *Beitrage zur Religionsgeschichte und Archaeologie Palestinas*, 1927, pp.69–82.

59   See A.Alt, *Kleine Schriften*, vol.1, p.334, n.1. The line in Phoenician is *'m 'p ychmd '[y]t h grt z* (see H.Donner & W.Rollig, *Kanaanische und Aramaische Inschriften*, Band 1, 1971, p.6, Text no.26, C IV 16–17.

60   L.Koehler, *Hebrew Man*, 1956; Stamm and Andrew, *Ten Commandments*, 1971. I have not had access to the works of Proksch and Volz.

61   See Moran, 'The Conclusion of the Decalogue (Ex.20,17 = Dt.5,21), *CBQ*, 29, 1967, pp.543–554.

62   Gordon, *Ugaritic Textbook*, p.397.

63   Eaton, *Ecclesiastes*, p.61.

NOTES TO CHAPTER NINE

1   J.W.Drane (*Paul Libertine or Legalist?* SPCK, 1975) sees development in Paul's thinking. Others see incoherence (see E.P.Sanders, *Paul, The Law and the Jewish People* Fortress, 1983; H.Räisänen, *Paul and the Law Mohr*, 1983; H.Hübner, *Law in Paul's Thought* Clark, 1984).

2   See also Eaton, *Living under Grace* (Nelson Word 1994).

3   It has been debated whether Paul addresses himself to two enemies, legalists and libertines; so W.Lutgert, *Gesetz und Geist*, (Gütersloh, 1919); H.J.Ropes, *The Singular Problem of the Epistle to the Galatians*, (Cambridge, USA, 1929) or to only one, the Judaizers (so most commentators; see J.B.Lightfoot, *Galatians*, 1896[10], 27–35 and throughout; H.D.Betz, 'Geist, Freiheit und Gesetz: Die Botschaft des Paulus an die Gemeinden in Galatien, *ZTK* , 71, 1974, pp.78–93). The precise identity of 'Galatia' has been contested especially since the days of Ramsay (see W.M.Ramsay, *Historical Commentary on . . . Galatians*, 1899, rp 1978).In modern times F.F.Bruce has been the most notable supporter of Ramsay's views (see his *Galatians*, NIGTC, Paternoster, 1982; *Acts: Greek Text*: Tyndale Press 1951, pp.240f.; *Paul Apostle of the Free Spirit*, Paternoster, 1980, pp.148–159, and other works by Bruce. See also R.P.Martin, 'The Setting of 2 Corinthians', *TB*, 37, 1986, pp.4–6; C.J.Hemer, 'Acts and Galatians Reconsidered', *Them.2*, 1976–77, pp.81–88). The place of Galatians in the sequence of Paul's letter and the relationship between Gal.2:1–10 and the different incidents in Acts have been matters of varied opinion (see references a few footnotes below). The precise nature of the literature we call Galatians has been discussed (see H.D.Betz, 'The Literary Composition and Function of Paul's Letter to the Galatians', *NTS*, 21, 1974–75, pp.353–374) with special interest taken in its rhetoric (on which see also J.D.Hester, 'The Rhetorical Structure of Galatians 1:11–2:14', *JBL*, 103, 1984, pp.223–233). It has been questioned not only whether 'justification by faith' is the centre of the New Testament (see C.K.Barrett, 'The Centre of the New Testament and the Canon', in *Die Mitte des Neuen Testaments*, Vandenhoeck, 1983, pp.5–21, esp.pp.15–16), and whether it is the centre of Paul (see the survey by R.Y.K.Fung, 'The Status of Justification by Faith in Paul's Thought', *Them.*, 6:3, April 1981, pp.4–11; J.D.G.Dunn, 'The New Perspective on Paul', *BJRL*, 65, 1983, pp.95–122), but also whether it is the centre of Galatians (see C.H.Buck, 'The Date of Galatians', *JBL*, 70, 1951, pp.121f.). Given that Paul's main opponents are Judaistic, the precise nature of the judaising Christianity has been a matter of debate. Is it orthodox Pharisaism (so H.J.Schoeps, *Paul:* 1961, pp.74–76)? Is it Jewish gnosticism (W.Schmithals, 'Die Häretiker in Galatien', *ZNTW*, 47, 1956, pp.26–67)? Or are we dealing with Judaizing gentile Christians? (J.Munck *Paul and the Salvation of Mankind*, SCM, 1959, pp.87–89). Yet it is likely that Gal.6:13 refers to gentile Christians who have succumbed to Jewish pressure. The ultimate foe could still be Jewish). Other possibilities have been canvassed (J.B.Tyson 'Paul's Opponents in Galatia', *NovT*, 10, 1968, pp.241–254. R.Crownfield 'The Singular Problem of the Dual Galatians', *JBL*, 63, 1945, pp.491–500; R.Jewett 'The Agitators and the

Galatian Congregation', *NTS*, 17, 1970–71, pp.198–212). For the view that there was a substantial law-observant mission to gentiles in Galatia, see J.L.Martyn, 'A Law-Observant Mission to Gentiles . . .', *SJT*, 38, pp.307–324.

4   The chronology of these times as best as one can see might be as follows:

Death of Jesus	AD 33, April
Day of Pentecost	AD 33, May
Events of Acts 2–9	Mid-33 to mid-34
Conversion of Paul	Summer 34
First visit to Jerusalem	Summer 36
Paul in Tarsus	AD 36–46
Evangelistic success among gentiles	AD 45
Barnabas is sent from Jerusalem	AD 45/46
Paul comes from Tarsus to Antioch	AD 46
A year's ministry in Antioch	AD 46–47
Paul's second visit to Jerusalem	AD 47 (14 years after AD 34 reckoned inclusively)
Paul and Barnabas in Galatia	Spring-Autumn AD 47
Events of Galatians 2:11–14	Early AD 48
Bad news from Galatia	AD 48
The epistle to the Galatians written	AD 48
The consultation at Jerusalem	Early AD 49

Of course the chronology of Acts and of Paul's life is a difficult matter. This chronology accepts the basic reliability of Acts and Galatians, and links Gal.2:1–10 with Acts 11:27–29. I am aware of certain difficulties in this reconstruction (Acts 2–9 seem to include many events in a short time) yet I think that, all things considered, this is a likely chronology with which to work as a hypothesis.

A totally different approach to Pauline chronology is found in R.Jewett, *A Chronology of Paul's Life*, 1979; J.Knox, 'Fourteen Years Later, A Note on Pauline Chronology', *JR*, 16, 1936, pp.341–349; J.Knox, 'The Pauline Chronology', *JBL*, 58, 1939, pp.15–40, and G.Lüdemann, *Paul Apostle to the Gentiles*, SCM, 1984. These works assume Acts has deficiences as a dependable source. See A.J.M.Wedderburn, 'Some Recent Pauline Chronologies', *ExT*, 92, 1980/81, pp.103–108.

5   See Kümmel, *Introduction*, pp.301–304. Some regard Acts 11 and Acts 15 as duplicate accounts (see Haenchen, *Acts*, pp.455–472; D.R.Catchpole, 'Paul, James and the Apostolic Decree', *NTS*, 1977, pp.435f.). A radical and speculative reconstruction is offered by J.Knox, *Chapters in a Life of Paul*, (Black, 1954), pp.74–88. Many British scholars, notably F.F.Bruce and his pupils, follow Ramsay in linking Ac.11 and Gal.2. See Bruce, *Acts: Greek Text*, pp.31f.; E.E.Ellis, *Paul and His Interpreters*, Eerdmans, 1961, pp.16f.; R.N.Longenecker, *Acts* in *Expositor's Bible Commentary*, vol.9, Zondervan, 1981, pp.404f.; R.N.Longenecker, *Galatians* (Word, 1993), pp.lxi-lxx, lxxvii-lxxxiii; C.S.C.Williams, *Acts*, (Black, 1957), pp.22ff. This has the advantage of explaining why Paul should make no mention of the famine visit of Acts 11 if the majority view is correct, accounting for the non-mention of the public Jerusalem consultation and non-mention of the Jerusalem decisions. It makes it easier to understand Peter's defection mentioned in Gal.2:11–14. (P.J.Achtemeier from a less conservative standpoint also thinks Gal.2:1–10 has 'its clearest echo' in Acts 11; see 'An Elusive Unity: Paul, Acts, and the Early Church', *CBQ*, 48, 1986, pp.1–6, esp.p.17).

True, it is somewhat difficult chronologically, especially if Jesus' death is dated in AD 33. But see W.B.Decker, 'The Early Date of Galatians', *Restoration Quarterly*, 2, pp.132–138, C.J.Hemer, 'Observations on Pauline Chronology', in *Pauline Studies*, (Paternoster, 1980), pp.3–18. On any view Acts 15 and Gal.2 refer to two meetings.

Acts 15 was public; Gal.2 was private. The whole matter is discussed fully by Guthrie, *New Testament Introduction* (Tyndale, 1970), pp.85f.

6 See G.Lyons, *Pauline Autobiography* (Scholars, ch.3), esp.pp.170–176. J.M.G.Barclay, 'Mirror-Reading a Polemical Letter: Galatians As a Test case', *JSNT*, 31, 1987, pp.73–93, surveys the issues involved.

7 One view of this matter is that the incident concerning Titus took place at the Jerusalem meeting. There are difficulties with this view (see R.Y.K.Fung, *Galatians*, Eerdmans, 1988, p.91).

A second approach (see G.S.Duncan, *Galatians*, Hodder, 1934, p.42) follows the Western text (omitting *ois oude*) in which case it would mean Paul was not compelled to circumcise Titus but yielded to the need of the occasion. Perhaps Paul felt he should not offend anyone in a matter of indifference (cf. 1 Cor.7:19; 10:32).

A third view suggests the question was raised later by sham Christians. Vv.3–5 are parenthetical, and verses 4f. are a digression within the parenthesis. B.Orchard especially has argued this (see 'A New Solution of the Galatians Problem'. *BJRL*, 28, 1944, pp.154–174; 'A Note on the Meaning of Galatians ii.3–5', *JTS*, 43, 1942, pp.173–177; 'The Ellipsis between Gal.2,3 and 2,4, *Bib.*, 54, 1973, pp.469–481; 'Once Again the Ellipsis between Gal.2,3 and 2,4', *Bib.*, 57, 1976, 254–255. He suggests the words '. . . the liberty of the gentiles is now in danger' or 'this question has now arisen' should be assumed.

I am suggesting that the false brethren slipped in *shortly* after the discussion, not at an altogether different occasion. This has three advantages. It fits the impression we have that Paul is dealing with one occasion not with two entirely different incidents. It explains the fact that Paul first says Titus was not circumcised, but then feels he has to explain something. The two things are that Titus was not circumcised but then that false disciples, *not as a participant in the meeting but shortly afterwards* came in to see and to subvert the freedom given. The assumed ellipsis, 'this matter arose', is a very simple one, more natural than that suggested by Orchard. Compare now Longenecker's, 'Now this happened . . . ' (*Galatians*, p.50).

8 Dunn's view is that Gal.2:16 asserts that Jewish believers are justified by covenantal nomism on the proviso that they have faith in Jesus the Messiah ('Perspective', pp.103–118, esp.p.112; J.D.G.Dunn, *Galatians*, Black, 1993, p.137). This neglects the fact that *ei me* or *ean me* 'is sometimes used to introduce an exception to something more general than that which has actually been mentioned' (J.H.Skilton, *Machen's Notes on Galatians*, Presbyterian and Reformed, 1973, p.77). For example, Matt.12:4 is not to be translated 'what it was not lawful for David to eat, nor for those who were with him except for the priests'. Rather we do well to translate as a fresh thought: 'It is *only* for the priests' (see also adversative uses of *ei me* in Gal.1:7; Lk.4:26–27). Similarly *ean me* in Gal.2:16 wholly excludes the previously mentioned justification by works of law: 'he is only justified by the faith(fulness) of Christ'. See also Bruce, Galatians, p.138. See also the Greek of Lk.4:26,27; Rv.21:27.

(ii) Dunn's view makes Paul begin by saying 'We are not justified by the works of the law except through faith . . . ', only to end by saying 'We are justified by faith and not by works of the law'. Paul's thought may have developed but he surely did not leave a contradiction within one sentence.

(iii) Dunn's view means that Eph.2:8–10 is a radical departure from Paul's words in Galatians. Even if Ephesians is not by Paul it at least shows how a close disciple understood him.

9 L.Morris, *Apostolic Preaching of the Cross* (Tyndale, 1965), pp.251–298; Murray, *Romans*, vol.1, (Eerdmans, 1968), pp.336–362; Cranfield, *Romans*, vol.1, (Clark, 1975), pp.92–95. His statement, 'This conclusion is surely forced upon us by the linguistic evidence' (p.95) seems correct.

10 E.D.Burton, *Galatians* (Clark, 1920).

11 Dunn, 'Perspective' *BJRL*, 65, 1983, pp.93–122, esp.p.107, 111.

12   D.Fuller, 'Paul and the 'Works of the Law', *WTJ*, 38, 1975–76, pp.31–33; D.Fuller, *Gospel and Law* (Eerdmans, 1980), pp.90–99,199–204; C.H.Cosgrove, 'The Mosaic Law Preaches Faith . . . ', *WTJ*, 39, 1976–77, pp.153–158; C.E.B.Cranfield, 'St.Paul and the Law', *SJT*, 17, 1964, pp.43–68, Cranfield, *Romans*, vol.2, 1979, pp.845–862; C.F.D.Moule, *Obligation in the Ethic of Paul* . . ., (CUP, 1967), pp.392–398.

13   See D.J.Moo, 'Law', p.91; G.Bertram, art.[*ergon ktl.*], *TDNT*, 6, pp.645–647.

14   Moo, 'Law', p.94.

15   The other possibility is that Paul is dealing with a logical conclusion from correct premises (see Lightfoot, *Galatians*, p.116f.; Burton, *Galatians*, pp.127–130; Fung, *Galatians*, p.119). Yet, as Fung points out (*Galatians*, p.120), *me genoito* is used by Paul only to negate a false conclusion from premises taken for granted.

16   Some interpretations of *hamartia* and *hamartolos* in vss.15,17 (twice) involve referring only to breaches of ceremonial law (see J.Lambrecht, 'The Line of Thought in Gal.2.14b-21', *NTS*, 24, 1978, p.485).

17   The verse has also been taken (i) as a warning against sin after experience of grace (mentioned by H.Olshausen but without agreement, *Galatians, Ephesians, Colossians and Thessalonians*, Clark, 1864, p.50); (ii) as a refutation of a false premise, the Judaizer's approach to justification (D.Guthrie, *Galatians*, Oliphants,1974, p.88; Hendriksen, *Galatians*, Banner of Truth, 1969, p.100); (iii) as a protest in the mouth of opponents (so C.F.D.Moule, 'A Note on Galatians ii.17,18', *ExT*, 56, 1944–45, p.223) giving a different accentuation to *ara*). Other views are mentioned by Hendriksen, *Galatians*, p.100; Burton, *Galatians*, pp.128f.; and a further view is maintained by W.Macdonald, *Galatians*, Illinois: Emmaus, n.d., p.23 (Christ is a minister of sin in failing to fulfil his promises, on Judaisers' presuppositions).

J.Lambrecht ('The Line of Thought in Gal.2.14b-21', *NTS*, 24, 1978, pp.484–495) deals with different ways of tracing the thought. (i) v.18 may be regarded as a parenthesis. So G.Klein, 'Individualgeschichte und Weltgeschichte bei Paulus', *EvTh*, 24, 1964, pp.132f. In which case v.19 either explains v.18 (so F.Mussner, *Der Galaterbrief*, Herder, 1974, p.179) or the end of v.17 (so Klein, loc.cit.). (ii) A smoother line of thought is followed if v.18 explains *me genoito* – the approach I have followed. (iii) Moule's view, cited above, takes v.18 as the voice of an objector. (iv) Lambrecht himself sees the gar as not explanatory but continuative ('But . . . ') and introducing a slightly new line of thought. I prefer to see the *gar* as authentically explanatory of v.17, and the *gar* of v.19 as authentically explanatory of v.18.

18   Barrett, *Freedom*, p.20

19   Osiek, *Galatians* (Dublin: Veritas, 1980), p.30.

20   Ramsay, *Galatians*, p.327.

21   This is stated in v.5 regardless of the meaning of *pascho* which could refer to general Christian experience (see RSV, NEB) or to suffering (so Guthrie, *Galatians*, p.93; Koehler, *Galatians*, p.73).

22   So Betz, *Galatians*, p.128, n.3.

23   This is favoured by R B Hays, *The Faith of Jesus Christ* (Scholars, 1983), p.147.

24   So J.Bligh, *Galatians* (St Paul, 1969), p.225.

25   So Lightfoot, *Galatians*, p.134; Burton, *Galatians*, p.147; Lagrange, *Galates*, p.59; Ridderbos, *Galatia*; p.113, Guthrie, *Galatians*, pp.92f..

26   Hays, *Faith*, p.143–149.

27   Schmithals, *Paul*, p.47. The assumption is widespread.

28   See Betz, *Galatians*, pp.139f. and sources cited there.

29   Betz, *Galatians*, p.139.

30   See Fung, *Galatians*, pp.141–143; F.F.Bruce, 'The Curse of the Law', in *Paul and Paulinism*, (ed. M.D.Hooker & S.G.Wilson, SPCK, 1982), pp.28–29; M.Noth, 'For all who rely on works of the law are under a curse', *The Laws in the Pentateuch*,

(Oliver & Boyd, 1966), p.131. In addition, one notes the 'all' of Dt.28:1 and the words *hktbym bspr hzh* in Dt.28:25, both of which Paul draws upon.

31   Interpretations are (i) 'The righteous shall live by his (own) faith.' See C.C.Cavallin 'The Righteous Shall Live By Faith . . . *ST*, 32, 1978, pp.33–43; (ii) 'The righteous shall live by His (Jesus') faith'; cf. LXX *mou* referring to God. (iii) 'The righteous-by-faith shall live' (Fung, *Galatians*, p.143; (iv) The Righteous One (Jesus) shall live by faith (A.T.Hanson, *Studies in Paul's Technique*, 1974, p.47; Hays, *Faith*, 1983, 151–154; Cranfield, *Romans*, p.521). The MT is also ambiguous.

32   Calvin, *Romans*, p.223; Calvin, *Galatians*, pp.55, 198.

33   The Scofield Reference Bible of 1917 spoke of 'legal obedience as the condition of salvation' (sub Jn.1:17).

34   Bruce *Galatians*, p.163.

35   Reprinted in K.Stendahl, *Paul Among Jews and Gentiles*, (SCM, 1977), pp.78–96. A more recent consideration is found in J.M.Espy, 'Paul's 'Robust Conscience' Re-Examined', *NTS*, 31, 1985, pp.161–188.

36   J.D.G.Dunn, 'The Incident at Antioch (Gal.2:11–18)', *JSNT*, 18, 1983, pp.3–57; Dunn, 'Perspective', *BJRL*, 65, 1983, pp.93–122; J.D.G.Dunn, 'Works of the Law and the Curse of the Law (Galatians 3.10–14)', *NTS*, 31, 1985, pp.523–542.

37   Fuller, *Gospel*, pp.88–105; D.P.Fuller, 'Paul . . . ', *WTJ*, 38, 1975–76, pp.28–42, esp.37–40.

38   See C.E.B.Cranfield, 'St.Paul and the Law', *SJT*, 17, 1964, p.55; C.F.D.Moule, 'Obligation', 1967, pp.392f.; F.Flückiger, 'Christus und des Gesetzes telos', *ThZ*, 11, 1955, pp.153–157, esp.154.

39   See D.Bourke (ed), *Summa Theologiae*, vol.29, (Eyre & Spottiswoode, 1969) *passim*.

40   See E.P.Sanders, *Paul, the Law and the Jewish People*, (Fortress, 1983), p.72,81; Bruce, *Galatians*, p.166f.; Bonnard, *Galates*, pp.68f. and others.

41   Fung, *Galatians*, 167.

42   T.L.Donaldson, 'The 'Curse of the Law' and the Inclusion of the Gentiles: Galatians 3:13–14', *NTS*, 32, 1986, pp.94–112.

43   Donaldson, 'Curse', p.106.

44   J.J.Hughes points to the strong likelihood that 'covenant' not 'testament' is in mind here. See J.J.Hughes, 'Hebrews IX 15ff and Galatians III 15ff', *NovT*, 21, 1979, pp.66–92. A central point in his argument is the fact that all 'wills' – whether Hellenistic, Egyptian or Roman – could be changed, added to or modified. But once an oath has been taken a covenant cannot be changed; it can only be broken. Ramsay was mistaken in wanting to see the heavy influence of Greek law here. (See Bruce, *Galatians*, p.171; Ramsay, *Galatians*, pp.349–374). Hughes thinks the 'ratification' refers to Gen.15 but it more likely refers to Gen.22.

45   Two quite distinct types of exegesis of 'the seed' occur in early jewish literature. (M.Wilcox, 'The Promise of 'The Seed' in the New Testament and the Targumim', *JSNT*, 5, 1972, pp.2–20.

46   The incorporative aspect of the idea is emphasized by A.König, *Die Doop As Kinderdoop en Grootdoop*, (Pretoria: NGKB, 1986), p.119

47   See D.J.Lull, 'The Law was Our Pedagogue: A Study in Galatians 3:19–25', *JBL*, 105, 1986, p.482.

48   See AG, *charin*. AG themselves list Gal.3:19 under 'goal' rather than 'reason'.

49   The interpretations of Romans also vary; see Lull, 'Law', pp.483–485.

50   The natural phenomena of Ex.19–24 are interpreted as produced by angels as in Jubilees 2:2; 1 Enoch 60:11–24; LXX Dt.33:2; LXX Ps.67:18 and elsewhere. See T.Callan, 'Pauline Midrash: The Exegetical Background of Gal 3:19b', *JBL*, 99, 1980, pp.551–554).

51   Bruce, *Galatians*, p.179.

52   Bruce, *Galatians*, p.179; A.Vanhoye, 'Un méditeur des anges en Ga 3, 19–29', *Bib.*, 59, 1978, pp.4–3–411. See also Longenecker, *Galatians*, p.140.

53　Belleville discusses the positive, negative and neutral senses of *sugkleio* ('Under Law', p.56). The neuter plural *panta* refers to an all-pervasive state of affairs (see Belleville, 'Under Law', p.56; BDF, section 138:1).

54　Belleville, 'Under Law', pp.59–62; G.B.Caird, *Principalities and Powers* (OUP, 1956), p.41. The *stoicheia* have been interpreted as elemental forces of flesh and law (A.J.Bandstra, *The Law and the Elements of the World*, Kok, 1964) or as planetary bodies or the phrase is thought to refer to angelic powers. Most likely it refers to elementary principles of law instinctively followed by all.

55　*Galatians*, p.84

56　As P.Bonnard observes, '*akouo* signifie ici comprendre' (Galates, p.95). Betz thinks that *nomos* is deliberately used ambiguously here (*Galatians*, p.241).

57　A.T.Hanson, (*Studies in Paul's Technique and Theology*, 1974, pp.91–94) shows that the verb in *hatina estin allegoroumena* (3:24) means 'to be expressed symbolically' not 'to be understood symbolically'. We translate: 'these things express a deeper meaning'. The Antiochene exegetes observed that Paul's use of *allegoroumena* does not have to refer to 'allegory' in the way in which the later church used the term (see Bligh, *Galatians*, p.393; R.J.Kepple, 'An Analysis of Antiochene Exegesis of Galatians 4:24–26', *WTJ*, 39, 1976–77, pp.239–249.

58　See *Inst.*II:10:2; A.J.Bandstra,' Law and Gospel in Calvin and Paul', *Exploring the Heritage of John Calvin* (Baker, 1976), pp.21–31.

59　See B.M.Metzger, *A Textual Commentary on the Greek New Testament* (UBS, 1971), p.596. Although *gar* may not be original, C.H.Cosgrove points to Wis.11:25 as proof that *de* may still indicate logical subordination ('The Law Has Given Sarah No Children (Gal.4:21–30)', *NovT*, 1987, p.227, n.33.

60　So Betz, *Galatians*, p.248. Others identify the heavenly Jerusalem with the church (Schlier, *Galater*, p.223; L.Goppelt, *Typos*, p.139). Isa.54:1 was used similarly at Qumran (see Bruce, *Galatians*, p.222) and in 4 Baruch 5:35 (see Cosgrove, 'The Law', p.230–231).

61　See Cosgrove 'The Law', p.234.

62　In Jewish haggadah, Gn.21:9 was interpreted as malicious attack. See Betz, *Galatians*, p.249.

63　Mk.10:30: 'now in this age . . . and in the age to come' (following the use of 'inherit' in Mk.10:17).

64　B.Wintle thinks Paul used the term 'law' in order to avoid the charge of antinomianism ('Paul's Conception of the Law of Christ and Its Relation to the Law of Moses', *RTR*, 38, 2979, pp.42–50, esp.p.49.

65　The term is that of D.Moo, 'Paul and the Law in the Last Ten Years', *SJT*, 40, pp.287–307, esp.p.287.

66　See Räisänen, *Paul*, 1983; 'Paul's Conversion and the Development of His View of the Law', *NTS*, 33, 1987, pp.404–419; Sanders, *Paul*, 1983. Even severer views of Paul's incoherence are maintained by Hübner, *Law*, 1984. See discussions of these works in A.J.M.Wedderburn, 'Paul and the Law', *SJT*, 38, pp.613–622 (reviewing Sanders's work); T.R.Schreiner, 'Paul and Perfect Obedience to the Law: An Evaluation of the View of E.P.Sanders', *WTJ*, 47, 1985, pp.245–278; T.Duidun, 'E.P.Sanders: An Assessment of Two Recent Works', *HJ*, 17, 1986, pp.43–52; W.D.Davies, 'Paul and the Law: Reflections on Pitfalls in Interpretation', in *Paul and Paulinism*, (ed. M.D.Hooker & S.G.Wilson, SPCK, 1982), pp.4–16; J.M.G.Barclay, 'Paul and the Law: Observations on Some Recent Debates', *Them.*, 12, pt.1, Sept 1986, pp.5–15; D. Moo 'Paul and the Law'. T.R. Schreiner's *The Law and its Fulfillment* (Baker, 1993) responds to the trend of the 1990s.

67　See R.H.Gundry, 'Grace, Works, and Staying Saved in Paul', *Bib.*, 66, 1968, p.8.

68　J.B.Webster, 'The Imitation of Christ', *TB*, 37, 1986, p.105.

69　L.B.Smedes, *Mere Morality* (Eerdmans, 1983), p.234. There are curiously contradictory opinions on this matter. L.H.Marshall (*The Challenge of New Testament*

Ethics, Macmillan, 1966, pp.224–232) writes: 'with unwearying and almost tiresome insistence he is constantly inveighing against the idea that any law or code (i.e. any external control), even though it be what he devoutly regarded as the divinely given Law of the Old Testament, is inadequate to the ethical needs of man' (p.224). On the other hand H.N.Ridderbos discusses whether Paul holds to a *'tertius usus legis'* (*Paul*, Eerdmans, 1975, pp.278–288) and holds that 'he time and again harks back to the law . . . when he wishes to define the content of the new obedience' (p.279). Ridderbos is treating any kind of call to obedience as a reference to law. This is a *non sequitur*. A closer look at the texts he cites reveals that they are general references to God's right to command (1 Cor.7:19) or to the statement that love fulfils the law (Rom.13:8–10; Gal.5:14) or to the fact that Paul is *ennomos to(i) Christo(i)* (1 Cor.9:21; Gal.6:2). None of this really amounts to using specific citations of the law as a guide to godliness. The only text which actually includes reference to the specific content of the law seems to be Eph.6:1–4. Here Paul shows that life in the Spirit (Eph.5:18–20) is fulfilled in various relationships and coheres with the commandment concerning honouring parents. I have no objection to citation of the decalogue (although the Sabbath requires radical alteration to be workable!) but the method of approach to them is, in my opinion, an indirect one. Nine of the ten commandments are fulfilled virtually to the letter by walking in the Spirit; over two thousand verses of legislation are also fulfilled – but not to the letter – by walking in the Spirit. The fact that Paul can refer to some of the commands of the decalogue does not negate the fact that he makes minimal use of the Torah in his exhortations to Christian godliness.See also J.Barclay, *Obeying the Truth*, Clark, 1988, p.234.

70 C.F.H.Henry, *Christian Personal Ethics* (Baker, 1957), pp.330–334.

71 Henry, *Ethics*, pp.330–334.

72 In the order in which they are quoted they are: 1 Cor.8:4ff, Rom.1:23; Ac.17:29; Jn.1:18; 4:24; Rom.2:24; 1 Ti.6:1; Jm.2:7; Tit.2:13; 2 Cor.4:4; Col.1:15; Mk.2:28; Mk.2:23; Jn.9:14; 5:9; 9:7; 7:22f; Col.2:16; Ac.20:7; 1 Cor.16:2; Eph.6:1ff; Col.3:20; 1 Tim.5:4; 2 Cor.12:14; Col.3:21; Rom.1:30; Rom.13:8ff; 1 Pet.4:5; 1 Jn.3:15; Jam.4:1f; Rom.2:21f; Eph.4:25ff; 1 Cor.15:15; 1 Jn.2:22f,27; 1 Cor.12:31; Rom.7:7; Eph.5:3ff; Heb.13:5; 1 Cor.5:10f; 6:10; Rom.1:29; 2 Cor.9:5; Eph.5:3; Col.3:5; 1 Thess.2:5; 1 Tim.6:10.

NOTES TO CHAPTER TEN

1 R.H.Smith, *Easter Gospels: The Resurrection of Jesus According to the Four Evangelists* (Augsburg, 1983), p.55. See G.Barth, 'Matthew's Understanding of the Law', in *Tradition and Interpretation in Matthew* (SCM, 1982), pp.159– 164; G.R.Hümmel, 'Die Auseinandersetzung zwischen Kirche und Judentum im Matthäusevangelium', *BEvT*, 33, 1966; C.E.Carlston, 'The Things That Defile (Mk.VII.14) and the Law in Matthew and Mark', *NTS*, 15, 1968, pp.75–96; E.Cothenet, 'Les Prophètes Chrétiens dans l'Evangile selon saint Matthieu', in *L'Evangile selon Matthieu* (ed. Didier, Duculot, 1972), pp.281–308; H.D.Betz, 'Ein Episode im Jungsten Gericht (Mt 7,21–23)', *ZTK*, 78, 1981, pp.1–30.

2 See B.W.Bacon, *Studies in Matthew* (Holt, 1930), p.348. W.D. Davies, *The Setting of the Sermon on the Mount* (CUP, 1964); W.Trilling, *Das Wahre Israel: Studien zur Theologie des Matthäus-evangeliums*, (Kosel, 19643) ; J.Rohde, *Rediscovering the Teaching of the Evangelists* (Westminster, 1968); A.Sand, 'Die Polemik gegen "Gesetzloskeit" im Evangelium nach Matthäus und bei Paulus', *BZ*, 14, 1970, pp.112–125; G.Strecker, *Der Weg der Gerechtigkeit: Untersuchung zur Theologie Matthäus* (Vandenhoeck, 1962); D.Hill, 'False Prophets and Charismatics: Structure and Interpretation in Matthew 7,15–23', *Bib*, 57, 1976, pp.327–348.

3 J.P.Meier, *The Vision of Matthew*, (Paulist, 1979), p.161.

4   Meier, *Vision*, 1979, p.3. D.E. Garland (*The Intention of Matthew 23*, Brill, 1979) regards Matthew's task in chap.23 as two-pronged. He thinks that Matthew is wrestling with the problem of the rejection of Jesus by Israel but that Matthew's severe statements are also a warning to the church not to go the same route: 'The Christian is to see himself potentially mirrored in the scribe'. 'Matthew would probably wish to say to Christian leaders . . ."Do you not see all these things?" '(p.215). This is a more convincing way of handling the extreme severity of Mt.23 and does not demand rejecting the historical nature of Matthew's material. Despite Meier's warning he still feels free to exegete Mt.5:17–20 atomistically, commencing with v.18 (see *Law and History in Matthew's Gospel*, 1976, p.45).

Two works that are very holistic in their approach are J.D.Kingsbury, *Matthew As Story*, 1986, and D.Patte, *The Gospel According to Matthew: A Structural Commentary* (Fortress, 1987).

5   G.Bornkamm, 'End-Expectation and Church in Matthew', in *Tradition and Interpretation in Matthew*, (SCM, 19822).

6   For a survey of opinions concerning structure, see W.D.Davies & D.C.Allison, The *Gospel According to Saint Matthew*, (Clark, 1988), pp.58–72.

7   H.Hübner considers Mt.5:18; 5:19; Lk.16:16–17; Mt.5:17; 5:20 in that order as five distinct sayings. This inevitably leads to neglect of any thread of argument throughout 5:17–20. One does less than justice to Matthew if one does not look at Matthew 5:17–20 as a whole. The redactor clearly put in connecting links ('therefore', 'for'). See H.Hübner, *Das Gesetz in der Synoptischen Tradition* (Luther, 1973), p.32. S.H.Brooks's similar method in Matthew's Community (JSNTS, 1987), frequently results in his treating nearby verses as in tension (see pp.25–30) and even as the result of conflict between Palestinian and Hellenistic communities (p.29).

For a recent presentation of the coherence of the Sermon on the Mount as an integral part of Matthew's Gospel, see G.N.Stanton, 'The Origin and Purpose of Matthew's Sermon on the Mount', in *Tradition and Interpretation in the New Testament*, 1987, pp.181–192.

8   A.M.Honeyman, 'Matthew 5:18 and the Validity of the Law', *NTS*, 1, 1954–55, pp.141f. See also W.J.Dumbrell, 'The Logic of the Role of the Law in Matthew V 1–20', *Novt*, 23, 1981, p.19.

9   Bahnsen, *Theonomy*, pp. v, 39–86. On this view *pleroo* means 'confirm', as he argues (*Theonomy*, pp.69–70). When facing the question 'Are Christians required to observe the Older Testament ritual?' Bahnsen's answer is 'yes and no' (p.207). At this point Bahnsen seems to contradict himself and take another view of Matthew 5:17. 'The meaning of the cermonial laws receive permanent validity and embodiment in Christ' (p.207). Exactly so! Yet this is (in my opinion) true of the whole law including every jot and tittle. Bahnsen does not really maintain the present normativity of every jot and tittle as mandatory for the Christian.

10   R.Alderson, *No Holiness, No Heaven* (Banner of Truth, 1986), pp.19–21; J.I. Packer (*Our Lord's Understanding of the Law of God*, Westminster Chapel, 1962, p.12); D.Wenham, Jesus and the Law, pp.92–96.

11   A.H.McNeile, *Matthew*, (Macmillan, 1965, orig. 1915), p.58; Bahnsen lists 13 works that take this approach (*Theonomy*, p.52, n.47) to which may be added O.Hanssen, *Zum Verständnis der Bergpredigt, in Der Ruf Jesu und Die Antwort der Gemeinde* (Vandenhoeck, 1970), pp.94–111; A.Feuillet, 'Morale Ancienne et Morale Chrétienne d'apres Mt.5.17–20 . . . , *NTS*, 17, pp.123–137, esp.p.124.

12   D. Martyn Lloyd-Jones, *Studies in the Sermon on the Mount*, (IVP, 1959,1960) vol.1, pp.185f.; H.Ljungmann, *Das Gesetz Erfüllen: Matth.5,17ff. und 3,15 untersucht* (Gleerup, 1954); R.C.H.Lenski, *Interpretation of the New Testament: Matthew* (Augsburg, 1943), p.207.

13   Kevan, *Law*, p.70.

14   J.A.Alexander, *Matthew*, (1873, rp Banner of Truth), p.127 (cited by Bahnsen, *Theonomy*, p.53); B.B.Warfield, 'Jesus' Mission According to His Own Testimony',

Princeton Theological Review, 13, 1915, pp.557–559, cited by Bahnsen, *Theonomy*, pp.45,53.

15   H.Ljungman, *Das Gesetz*. See also D.Moo, 'Jesus and the Mosaic Law', *JSNT*, 20, 1984, p.24.

16   Deuteronomy clearly draws distinctions between 'the great commandment' and ancillary commandments (see Kline, *Treaty of the Great King*, 1963, pp.62,79) and there is gradation within the law in the teaching of Jesus.

17   C.F.D.Moule notes that promise-fulfilment language in the New Testament can refer to at least three polarities: i. prediction-verification, ii. initiation-termination and ii. promise-consummation. He surveys the usage of *pleroo* and *male'* in the Old Testament, Qumran, other Jewish writings, secular literature, the New Testament and early Christian literature.Under the rubric (i) *prediction-verification*, he lists Lk.1:45; 18:31; 22:37; Jn.19:38; Ac.4:28; 13:29; 2 Pe.3:2. Under (ii) *initiation-termination* he lists Mt.10:23; 11:13,53; 19:1; 26:1; Mk.13:4; Lk.2:39,43; 4:2,13; 12:50; 14:10; Jn.4:34; Ac.20:24; Ro.2:27; 13:6; 15:8; Phil.1:6; 2 Ti.4:7; Hb.7:11; 8:8; Jm.2:8; Rv.10:7; 11:7; 15:1,8; 17:17; 20:3,5,7. Under (iii) *promise-consummation* he lists Mt.1:21; 2:15; 4:14; 12:17; 21:4; 2:23; 7:17; 13:35; 2:17; 27:9; 3:15; 5:17; 13:14; 26:54,56; 23:32; 14:26; 19:21; Ro.8:14; 13:8,10; Gal.5:14; 6:2; Col.4:17; 1 Th.2:16; 2 Th.1:1; Jm.2:23. I have left out verses Moule rightly labels 'less relevant' and have omitted Mk.15:28 where the reading is not original. See C.F.D.Moule, 'Fulfilment-Words in the New Testament', *NTS*, 14, 1967–68, pp.293–320.

It could be argued that *pleroo* in Mt.5:17 is quite distinct from *pleroo* elsewhere in Matthew, that Moule's category (iii) must not be assimilated to his category (i). The fact that he explicitly includes 'the prophets' surely makes it likely that *pleroo* in 5:17 must be related to *pleroo* in the fulfilment formulae.

18   See J.Schneider, [*Erchomai, ktl*], *TDNT*, 2, p.682.

19   See France, *Matthew* (IVP, 1985), pp.333–349, and his *Jesus and the Old Testament* (Tyndale Press 1971), pp.227–239.

20   See AG, p.48a.

21   McNeile, *Matthew*, p.60.

22   Lloyd-Jones, *Sermon*, 1, pp.199–209.

23   Whether the added phrase deals with oral law or not is debateable. See R.Banks, *Jesus and the Law in the Synoptic Tradition* (CUP, 1975), pp.186f., where the conclusion is reached that 'the whole of v.21 must be considered an expression of the Old Testament position (p.187; so also Gundry, *Matthew, a Coimmentary on his Literary and Theological Art* (Eerdmans, 1982), p.84.

24   My thesis, *A Theology of Encouragement. A Step Towards a Non-Legalistic Soteriology* (unpublished, UNISA, Nov.1989), contains documentation, too extensive to be included here. See especially W.A.Heth & G.J.Wenham, *Jesus and Divorce* (Hodder, 1984).

25   Probably *me anistemai to(i) ponero(i)* refers to foregoing legal rights.

26   Banks, *Jesus*, p.200.

27   See *Dem.2.3*; *j.Shabb.3c*.

28   See D.A.Carson, 'Jesus and the Sabbath in the Four Gospels', in *From Sabbath To Lord's Day*, ed. D.A.Carson (Zondervan, 1982), p.61. See pp.60f.1, 87, for other interpretations of the 'crime'.

29   See further Hümmel, 'Auseinandersetzung', pp.42f.; L.Goppelt, [*Peinao*], *TDNT*, 6, p.19.

30   The eight are: (i) the Sermon on the Mount (Mt.5:17–48; 7:12); (ii) the issue of table-fellowship (9:9–13; 11:19); (iii) sabbath-controversies (12:1–8); (iv) ritual uncleanness (15:1–20); (v) divorce (19:3–12); (vi) the young ruler (9:16–22); (vii) the greatest commandment (22:34–40); (viii) the denunciation of scribes and Pharisees (23:1–36).

31   The verb is plural in Mt.16:15.

32   See Banks, *Jesus*, pp.92–93; J.Liver, 'The Half-Shekel Offering in Biblical and Post-Biblical Literature', *HThR*, 56, 1963, pp.178–191.

33   See France, *Matthew*, p.82.

34   Mishnah *Gittin* 9:10; Josephus, *Antiquities* iv:253; Josephus, *Life*, 426.

35   NIV. See D.A.Carson, 'Matthew', in *Expositor's Bible Commentary*, vol.8, (Zondervan, 1984), p.411.

36   Carson, Matthew, sub. loc.

37   J.Dupont, 'Mariage et Divorce dans l'Evangile: Matthieu 19, 3–12 et Parallèles' (1959), cited by Heth and Wenham and given detailed consideration in Heth & Wenham, *Divorce*, pp.56–68.

38   Early expositions are J.Calvin, *Harmony of the Gospels* (1555 rp. St.Andrews, 1972), vol.2, pp.252–258; D.Dickson, Matthew, 1981 ed. (rp Banner of Truth 1981), pp.258–260. See also 'Sermons on Mark x.17–27' in *The Complete Works of Thomas Manton*, (rp. Maranatha, 1974(?)), vols.16, pp.409–494, and 17, pp.3–93 and W.J.Chantry, *Today's Gospel* (Banner, 1970).

39   B.B.Warfield, 'Jesus' Alleged Confession of Sin', *PTR*, 12, 1914, pp.177–228; I quote from the reprinted version in Warfield, *Person and Work of Christ* (Presbyterian and Reformed, 1950), p.149.

40   Warfield, 'Jesus' ', p.151.

41   Hendriksen, *Matthew* (Banner, 1973), pp.725f.

42   In Heb.1:14 the writer speaks of 'inheriting salvation'. Yet 'inheriting' is a term generally associated with reward, and elsewhere 'salvation' and reward are distinguished. The readers of Heb.1:14 are Christians yet their reward has not yet come as Hebrews 10:35 makes clear.

43   In Matthew 24 the disciples wrongly tie together the fall of Jerusalem and the end of the age, but Jesus without initially drawing attention to the error implicitly corrects them ('When you see these things . . . it is near . . . But no one knows of that day . . .').

44   W.C.Kaiser, 'The Weightier and Lighter Matters of the Law: Moses, Jesus and Paul, in *Current Issues in Biblical and Patristic Interpretation* (ed.G.F.Hawthorne, Eerdmans, 1975), p.183.

45   See G.Bertram, [*kremannumi, ktl*] *TDNT*, 3, pp.915–921, esp.p.919f.

46   K.Berger, *Die Gesetzauslegung Jesu*, (Neukirchener Verlag, 1972), pp.227–232, cited by Carson, *Matthew*, p.465.

47   *Berkôt* 63a (*ca.*220 AD);

48   See Kaiser, 'Weightier', pp.182f..

49   D.Moo's article, 'Jesus and the Mosaic Law', *JSNT*, 20, 1984, pp.3–49, debates the question whether Jesus refers to the 'priority of love over law' or 'the priority of love within the law' (esp.p.11). Possibly it is a needless contrast. There is a priority of love within the law, but in practical day-to-day considerations this becomes a rule of thumb (see Mt.7:12) which is above the law itself, although 'fulfillng' it.

50   E. Schweizer, *The Good News According to Matthew*, SPCK, 1975, p.425; see also G.Bornkamm, *Das Doppelgebot der Liebe, Geschichte und Glaube*, I (Kaiser, 1968), pp.37–45.

51   The love-command is not a 'summary' or the 'essence' of the law. See R.A. Guelich, 'Not To Annul the Law Rather to Fullfill the Law and the Prophets, (Dissertation, Hamburg, 1967), p.102.. It is simply that despite its obscure position (in Lv.19:18), it was destined to have more significance than any other regulation in the Torah.

52   Bornkamm, *End-Expectation*, p.24. See also E.Haenchen, 'Matthäus 23', *ZTK*, 48, 1951, pp.38–40; G.Barth, 'Matthew's Understanding', pp.71,86.

53   Bahnsen, *Theonomy*, pp.119f.; R.J.Rushdoony, *Institutes of Biblical Law* (Craig, 1973), p.7.

54   N.B. Stonehouse, *Witness of Matthew and Mark to Christ* (Tyndale Press, 1944) p.196.

55 Meier, *Law*, 1976, pp.106,119,156.
56 Garland, *Matthew 23*, p.20.
57 See W.Grundmann, *Das Evangelium nach Matthäus* (Evangelische, 1968) p.484; Schweizer, *Matthew*, p.437.
58 France, *Matthew*, p.324; Carson, *Matthew*, p.473.
59 Garland, *Matthew 23*, p.140.
60 Carson, *Matthew*, p.481; my italics.
61 Other opinions are (i) The verse exhibits legalism. (ii) The tithe is still mandatory in its Mosaic form. (iii) This concession is a foil to the remainder of the verse ('Keep your observances if you like, but your sin is seen not in declining to tithe but in declining to . . .').
62 This approach is developed by J.Murray, 'The Interadventual Period and the Advent: Matthew 24–25, in *Writings*, 2 (Banner, 977), pp.387–400.
63 France, *Matthew*, pp.333–349; also R.T.France, *Jesus*, pp.227–239. France's view was also presented earlier by M.Kik, *Matthew Twenty-Four*, 1948 (available as pp.51–173 of M.Kik, *An Eschatology of Victory*, Presbyterian and Reformed, 1971).
64 That these words are indeed a commissioning is argued by B.J.Hubbard, *The Matthean Redaction of a Primitive Apostolic Commissioning* (Scholars, 1974). P. O'Brien agrees ('The Great Commission of Matthew 28:18–20. A Missionary Mandate or Not?' *RTR*, 25, 1976, pp.66–78).
65 R.H.Smith, *Easter Gospels*, p.77.
66 Hubbard, Apostolic Commissioning, passim.

NOTES TO CHAPTER ELEVEN

1 In the 17th century John Eaton the 'antinomian' and Anne Hutchinson (of the 'antinomian controversy' in New England) refer to the 'faith of Christ'.
2 J.Haussleiter, 'Der Glaube Jesu Christi und der christliche Glaube' *NKZ*, 2, 1891, pp.109–145,205–230.
3 A.G.Hebert, ' "Faithfulness" and "Faith" ', *Theol*, 58, 1955, pp.373–379.
4 T.F.Torrance, 'One Aspect of the Biblical Conception of Faith', *ExT*, 68, 1956–57, pp.111f.; K.Barth, *Romans*, 6th ed. (ET 1933 rp OUP 1977), pp.91, 104, also pp.41,96; G.Kittel, '[*pistis Iesou Christou*] bei Paulus', *TSK*, 79, 1906, pp.419–436; Edwin R. Goodenough & A.T.Krabel, 'Paul and the Hellenization of Christianity', in *Religions in Antiquity* (*Brill*, 1967), Studies in the History of Religions, Supplements to *Numen*, vol.15,pp.35–80; M.Barth, 'The Faith of the Messiah', *HJ*, 10, 1963, pp.363–370.
5 C.F.D.Moule, 'The Biblical Conception of Faith', *ExT*, 68, 1956–57, p.157, with Torrance's reply (p.221) and further comment (p.222); Murray, *Romans*, pp.362–374; J.Barr, *The Semantics of Biblical Language* (OUP, 1961), ch.7. A.J.Hultgren has a number of objections: Paul does not use the phrase *he pistis tou Christou*; when Paul uses a subjective genitive with *pistis* the article is invariably present; syntactical observations do not suggest a subjective genitive ('The *Pistis Christou* Formulation in Paul', *NovT*, 22, 1980, pp.248–263). L.T.Johnson replied to the theological arguments of Hultgren ('Romans 3:21–26 and the Faith of Jesus', *CBQ*, 44, 1982, pp.77–90) and S.K.Williams replied to the syntactical arguments ('Again *Pistis Christou*', *CBQ*, 49, 1987, pp.431–447).
6 See H.Ljungman, *Pistis* (Gleerup, 1964), pp.38–40,44,47; G.M.Taylor, 'The Function of [*PISTIS CHRISTOU*] in Galatians', *JBL*, 85, 1966, pp.58–76; G.Howard, 'On the 'Faith of Christ'', *HThR*, 60, 1967, pp.459–465; J.Bligh, 'Did Jesus Live By Faith?' *HJ*, 9, 1968, pp.418f.; Bligh, *Galatians* (St.Paul, 1969), pp.203–205; G.Howard, 'Romans 3:21–31 and the Inclusion of the Gentiles', *HThR*, 63, 1970, pp.228–231; D.W.B.Robinson, "Faith of Jesus Christ" – a New Testament Debate', *RThR*, 29,

1970, pp.71–81; G.Howard 'The "Faith of Christ" ' *ExT*, 85, 1973–74, pp.212–214; R.N.Longenecker, 'The Obedience of Christ in the Theology of the Early Church' in *Reconciliation and Hope* (ed. R.J.Banks, Paternoster, 1974), pp.142–152, esp. pp.145–148; R.B.Hays, 'Psalm 143 and the Logic of Romans 3', *JBL*, 99, 1980, pp.107–115. S.K.Williams, 'The Righteousness of God in Romans', *JBL*, 99, 1980, pp.241–90, esp. pp.272–277. A.J.Hultgren reviewed scholarly writings on the subject in 1980 ('The *Pistis Christou* Formulation in Paul', *NovT*, 22, 1980, pp.248–263).

7 LS, p.1408; MM, 515.

8 See R.B.Hays, 'Jesus' Faith and Ours: A Re-Reading of Galatians 3', *TSF Bulletin* (American), vol.7, no.1, Sep–Oct 1983, pp.2–6, esp. p.3.

9 Mt.9:2,22,29; 15:28; Mk.2:5; 5:34; 10:52; Lk.5:20; 7:50; 8:25,48; 17:19; 18:42; 22:32; Ro.1:8,12; 3:3; 4:5,12,16; 1 Cor.2:5; 15:14,17; 2 Cor.1:24; 10:15; Phil.2:17; Col.1:4; 2:5; 1 Th.1:8; 3:2,5,7,10; 2 Th.1:3; 2 Ti.2:18; Ti.1:2; Jm.2:18(x2); 1 Pe.1:7,21; 2 Pe.1:5; 1 Jn.5:4; Ju.20; Rv.13:10.

10 Mk.11:22; Ac.3:16; Ro.3:22,26; Gal.2:16,16,20; 3:22; Eph.3:12; Phil.1:27; 3:9; Col.2:7; 2 Th.2:13; Jm.2:1; Rv.2:13; 14:12.

11 See G.Howard, 'On the "Faith of Christ" ', *HTR*, 60, 1967, pp.459–465.

12 Robinson, 'Faith', p.74.

13 Richard Watson (1781–1833) thought of it as part of a 'gross corruption of christian faith' (see Ed.R.S.Taylor, *Leading Wesleyan Thinkers*, vol.3 (Beacon Hill, 1985), pp.23–49, esp. p.42. This hostility goes back to John Fletcher who spoke of the 'bare-faced Antinomian, who expects to be justified in the great day by Christ's imputed righteousness without works' (*Works*, 1, p.303). Less forcefully Wesley also rejected the idea (see P.Toon, *Justification*, pp.105–106).

14 See J.Murray, *Writings*, 2, pp.212–214; Hughes, *Second Corinthians*, p.212; Morris, *Apostolic Preaching*, pp.281–282; Stott, *Cross*, p.200. The idea has roots in Calvin who said, 'We hold that Christ is their only righteousness . . . By His obedience he has wiped off our transgressions' (see Calvin's 'Reply to Sadoleto', in *A Reformation Debate* (ed.J.C.Olin, Baker, 1976, p.67).

15 Luther: *Letters of Spiritual Counsel*, p.110. (My attention was drawn to this letter by Stott, *Cross*, p.200).

NOTES TO CHAPTER TWELVE

1 See G.S.Faber, *The Primitive Doctrine of Justification*, 1837; J.Buchanan, *The Doctrine of Justification*, (1867, rp. Banner, 1961), p.94.

2 McGrath, 'Justification – "Making Just" ', p.45). Augustine's teaching is summarized by Toon (*Justification*, pp.48–50).

3 See A.E.McGrath, 'The Article by which the Church Stands or fall', *EQ*, 58, 1986, p.207; A.E.McGrath, 'Der articulus justificationis als axiomatischer Grundsatz der christliche Glaubens', *ZTK*, 81, 1984, p.383. For a survey of Luther's teaching concerning justification, see J.Heinz, *Justification and Merit, Luther vs. Catholicism* (Andrews University, 1981), pp.13–248; P.Althaus, *Theology of Martin Luther* (Fortress, 1966); A.Peters, *Glaube und Werk Luthers Rehctfertigungslehre im Lichte der Heiligen Schrift*, Berlin, 1967; O.H.Pesch, *Die Theologie Der Rechtfertigung Bei Martin Luther und Thomas Von Aquin*, Matthias-Grunewold, 1967).

4 See A.E.McGrath, 'Forerunners of the Reformation? . . . '*HTR*, 75, 1982, p.225).

5 A.E.McGrath points to ocasions when Luther could regard justification as process as well as event ('Justification – "Making Just" or "Declaring Just"?' *Churchman*, 96, 1982, p.46). The stronger antithesis between forensic justification and regeneration originated with Melanchthon (McGrath, 'Justification – "Making Just" ', p.47).

6 See especially J.Fletcher, 'Fourth Check to Antinomianism', in *Works*, vol.1 (rp. Schmul, 1974), pp.209–331.

7 J.Gill, *A Body of Divinity*, 1971 rp. Sovreign Grace, p.503.

8 J.W.Baker, 'Sola Fide, Sola Gratia: The Battle for Luther in Seventeenth Century England', *The Sixteenth Century Journal*, 16, 1985, pp.115–133.

9 See A.E.McGrath, 'John Henry Newman's "Lectures On Justification": . .', *Churchman*, 97, 1983, pp.112–122.

10 H.Küng, *Justification*, 1964. E.Käsemann, ' "The Righteousness of God" in Paul', in *New Testament Questions of Today* (SCM, 1969), pp.168–183; see D.Demson, ' "Justification By Faith": . . .', *Toronto Journal of Theology*, 2, 1986, pp.63–78; J.Plevnil, 'Recent Developments in the Discussion Concerning Justification By Faith', *TJT*, 2, 1986, pp.47–62; A.E.McGrath, 'Justification: Barth, Trent and Kung', *SJT*, 34, 1981, pp.517–529.

11 See L.Morris, *The Apostolic Preaching*, chs.8,9, and A.E.McGrath, *Iustitia*, vol.1, pp.1–16, for a recent survey of the linguistic data.

Some Catholic theologians (K.Kertelge, R.Kosters, H.Küng, M.Schmaus) acknowledge that *dikaioo* is a forensic term. See Heinz, *Justification*, 1981, pp.37–45. Kosters admits that 'der forensische Grundcharakter der Rechtfertingung wird auch katholischer Seite mehr und mehr anerkannt' ('Die Lehre von der rechtfertigung . . . , *ZKT*, 90, 1968, p.313. The evidence for the forensic interpretation of the verb is summarized by Kung, *Justification*, pp.201f.

This does not mean that the Protestant doctrine has been conceded. But it does perhaps give some justification for my proceeding to explore further the Protestant doctrine in a non-legalistic context.

12 H.Küng says 'the reality of justification . . . is much richer than what is directly signified by the word justification' (p.208). This is apparently the approach of M.Schmaus (*Justification and the Last Things*, Sheed and Ward 1977).

13 'Definitive Sanctification', *Collected Writings*, 2, p.278.

14 See D.M.Lloyd-Jones, *The Gospel of God* (Banner, 1985), p.134.

15 Stott, *Cross*, p.187–8.

16 See M.A.Eaton, *Living Under Grace* (Nelson Word, 1994), p.97; see also M.A.Eaton, *How To Live A Godly Life* (Sovereign World, 1993), chs.8,9.

17 See C.F.Allison, *The Rise of Moralism* (Morehouse Barlow, 1966), passim; also A.E.McGrath, 'The Emergence of the Anglican Tradition on Justification, 1600–1700', *Churchman*, 98, 1983, pp.28–43, esp. pp.33,39.

18 Heinz, *Justification*, p.217f..

19 See Heinz, *Justification*, p.73.

20 Toon, *Justification*, pp.141f. McGrath thinks Toon is more generous to Newman than he ought to be (see P.Toon, 'A Critical Review of John Henry Newman's Doctrine of Justification', *Churchman*, 94, 1980, pp.335–344; A.E. McGrath, 'John Henry Newman's "Lectures on Justification": . . .', *Churchman*, 97, 1983, p.121).

21 Rahner, 'Controversial Theology, or Justification' in *Theological Investigations*, vol.4 (Darton, 1974), pp.189–218, esp. p.199.

22 Some confusion is introduced when the difference between biblical language and systematic theological language is overlooked. It is not difficult to show that the New Testament envisages that the Christian is objectively consecrated and sanctified 'in Christ' from conversion onwards. J. Murray rightly says that 'a considerable part of New Testament teaching places sanctification in this category' (*Collected Writings*, 2, pp.277–293). At this point there is no need to look for a complex *ordo salutis*. The idea of 'complementary models' is in this aspect entirely appropriate. But in the language of the church over the centuries 'sanctification' has generally referred to progressive growth in godly living, progressive conformity to Jesus, the deepening and growing work of the Spirit in conforming us to the image of Christ. In this sense there is priority of justification (which is objective, positional, definitive, confers an 'alien' righteous-

ness and is the ground of a total security in Christ) over against ongoing sanctification (which is subjective, practical, admits of variation and inconsistency, and is entirely inadequate to be the basis of assurance of salvation).

NOTES TO CHAPTER THIRTEEN

1   J.Fletcher, *Works*, 1, p.489.

2   A.A.Hoekema, *The Bible and the Future* (Paternoster, 1978) p.259.

3   They are the verbs *chalal, nachal, yarash*, and the nouns *cheleq, morashah, nachalah* and *yerushah*.

4   *BDB*, p.439.

5   F.F.Bruce comments 'The inheritance is associated with sanctification rather than with forgiveness' and compares Dt.33:3–4 where *hegiasmeno* and *kleronomia* are linked (*Acts: Grk Text*, p.445).

6   Mark 10:17 is best interpreted as a question about reward. Jesus' way of pointing to a level of spirituality that outstrips the law of Moses is to give the traditional answer (10:19) and then pointedly indicate that there is a level of spirituality that goes beyond it (10:21): uncovetousness and a direct relationship to Jesus. The result is not 'heaven' but 'treasure in heaven'. There are probably a few occasions where even the word 'salvation' refers not to initial conversion but to final salvation with its attendant reward. Mk 10:26 uses this language. Jesus accepts such language (on the lips of disciples) but vv.29–31 make it clear that he is still speaking of reward.

In Lk.10:25 Jesus again deals with a compassion which outstripped the law, was not demanded by the law and even contravened the law (a contaminating contact with Samaritans). The parable deals with what one 'does' (10:37). Lk.18:18 accepts the law but then deliberately goes beyond it. It leads into questions concerning reward (18:28–30).

7   See RSV and AG, p.73.

8   If one assumes that inheritance is tightly correlated to justification and conversion-initiation then it is natural to read 'born again . . . to an inheritance' as teaching an inexorable and inevitable inheritance for every Christian. But if one comes to 1 Peter with the Old Testament background in mind, no one could think of a person's being born to the automatic and inexorable acquirement of inheritance. (The resurrection of Jesus is a foretaste of and a guarantee of final resurrection to reward). The NASV reads: 'to obtain an inheritance'. This is surely legitimate. The Greek *eis* frequently refers to purpose. So 1 Pet.1:3–4 may read: 'God . . . who . . . has caused us to be born again to a living hope . . . in order that we may obtain an inheritance . . .'. It is reserved in heaven on the assumption that we obtain it. One might compare the use of *eis* in Lk.5:4 where *eis agran* means ' . . . in order that you may obtain a catch'. The structure and grammar are identical to 1 Pet.1:4.

The tangled complexities of 1 Pet.1:3–4 are surveyed in D.C.Arichea & E.A.Nida, *A Translator's Handbook on the First Letter From Peter* (UBS, 1980) pp.13–18. That a purpose clause is to be seen here ('in order that you may obtain an inheritance') is confirmed by 1 Peter 3:7 where husband and wife are fellow-heirs of the grace of life (i.e. are both due for inheritance) but where the husband's harshness could hinder the prayer-life that leads to inheritance. The 'heirship' is not irresistibly carried forward.

9   Eph.1:3–14 moves from the planning of salvation ('He chose us . . . he predestined us') to the present enjoyment of salvation ('redemption . . . forgiveness') and then to the future possibilities of salvation ('inheritance . . . redemption of the possession'). (The reference to inheritance (*eklerothemen*) in Eph.1:11 has been taken to refer to (i) predestination (see RSV), (ii) God's inheritance in his people ('claimed by God as his portion', Bruce, *Colossians . . . Ephesians*, p.262), (iii) 'heaven' or final salvation (so M.Barth, *Ephesians 1–3*, Doubleday, 1981, pp.115–119). The three possibilities are considered by M.Barth (*Ephesians 1–3*, pp.92–94). He thinks that

'purely philological considerations do not permit a final decision' (p.94), but opts finally for a reference to the eschatological aspect of salvation (pp.115–119).) The emphasis of the chapter is surely on the amazing possibilities of salvation. There is a predestined inheritance (1:11). Yet it is important to note that inheritance in Ephesians is not irresistibly predestined. Where human works are involved God may put a plan before his people and ask them to see that it is implemented. The latter is surely the case with inheritance. As in ancient Israel the nation were repeatedly asked to take what God planned to give, so in the life of the Christian there are good works that God has foreordained (Eph.2:10) but he has foreordained 'that we should walk in them' (Eph.2:10). Eph.1:11 mentions this plan but it must not be thought of as irresistible in the same way that Eph.1:5 is irresistible. 'Adoption as sons' comes without works. The question of resistance does not enter into the situation in my opinion. 'Inheritance' is a matter of reward; the question of resistance does come in.

I am not presenting here any detailed consideration of election, although much in this work leads on to it. I suspect there is a difference between irresistile predestination to salvation, and resistible predestination to inheritance. My approach then to Rom.8:28–30 and 9:6–29 is thoroughly – but unspeculatively – 'Calvinistic'. Yet this does not predetermine the interpretation of predestination to inheritance or the interpretation of Eph.2:10. When it speaks of *ergois agathois ois proetoimasen ho theos hina ev autois peripatesomen* the human factor ('that we should walk in them') implies we are not dealing with sheer gracious gift but with human co-operation. At this point an 'Arminian' exposition is more convincing (along the lines at this point of the stridently Arminian theology of C.H.Pinnock, (ed.) *Grace Unlimited* (Bethany, 1975). There may be 'irresistible grace' in Eph.2:8–9, but not in Eph.2:10 – a possibility that has not so far as I know been adequately considered.

Ephesians 1:18 proceeds to pray that the believers' eyes will be open to the vast possibilities before them. However the fact that the hope, the inheritance and the needful power are available does not mean that the Christian experiences them willy-nilly. What would be the point of praying in 1:18–19a and 3:14–21 for something that is inexorable and inevitable? One does not need to pray for what is already and irresistably secured. Paul does not pray for their 'adoption of sons'; he does pray they will reach to the heights of their inheritance. The two are distinct.

At a later stage Eph.3:6 makes the point that the inheritance is lined up for gentile Christians who are in a position of total equality with their Jewish Christian friends.

10 I summarize here what will be more fully expounded in my *Return to Glory* (Nelson Word, 1995?).

11 D.M.Lloyd-Jones, *Romans: Assurance* (Banner, 1971), p.54.

12 D.M.Lloyd-Jones, *Romans: The Final Perseverance of the Saints* (Banner, 1975), pp.257–260.

13 Certain verses have been passed over in this survey. Ac.7:5 deals with the case of Abraham but points to the anomaly that the one who was promised land never received it. Jas.2:5 apparently means that God has predestined (in a manner comparable to Eph.2:10) the poor to be evangelized and that most of his elect are poor. It is notable that inheritance is not linked with 'mere' faith but with being 'rich in faith'. 1 Pe.5:3 uses the term *kleron* in an Old Testament usage in which God's people are in inheritance. Rev.21:7–8 is the last use of inheritance language in the Bible. Again it explicitly connects with human effort ('He who overcomes') and therefore refers to reward in line with Rev.22:12. The consideration of the theme of inheritance in Hebrews is dealt with below. (p.206ff.)'

NOTES TO CHAPTER FOURTEEN

1 N.M.Watson ('Justified by Faith: Judged By Works – An Antinomy?' *NTS*, 29,1983, pp.209–221) thinks warnings are addressed to 'Christians whose faith has

degenerated to a false security . . . Christians in their unbelief' (p.220). But this is problematic. Watson does not face the question of how one knows one is not a Christian whose faith has degenerated. How can one – without self-righteousness – take the passages of assurance to oneself and feel that the warnings do not apply? Should one ever feel that the warnings do not apply? Does it help to think that two categories of Christian are in view? It seems preferable to argue that two closely related but not identical eschatological realities are in view: salvation and reward. The Christian responds to the comfort of one and the warning of the other. This is surely better than being faced with the problem of deciding which type of Christian one is, one who needs comforting or one whose 'faith has degenerated'.

2   E.g. Heb.1:14 and Matthew 19 / Mark 10. The theme of inheriting (Mk.10:17), which is identical with reward, is explicit (note v.21 'treasure in heaven'; v.30 about receiving in the present age houses and brothers, and so on; and the parallel in Mt.19:27 – 'what will there be for us?'). Yet the word 'saved' is used (Mt.19:25).

3   Commentators on Romans who take approximately the line of approach I am about to present here include Calvin, *Romans and Thessalonians* (Oliver and Boyd, 1961); C.E.B.Cranfield, *Romans* (Clark, 1975, 1979); Haldane, *Romans*; W.Hendriksen, *Romans* (Banner of Truth, 1980,1981); C.Hodge, *Romans* (Banner of Truth, 1972); H.P.Liddon, *Romans* (Longmans and Green, 1893); D.M.Lloyd-Jones, *Romans* (Banner, 1970–75,1985,1989); D.Moo, *Romans 1–8* (Moody, 1991); (Morris, *Romans* (Eerdmans, 1988); Murray, *Romans*; H.Ridderbos, *Aan De Romeinen* (Kok, 1977); D.N.Steele & C.T.Curtis, *Romans: An Interpretive Outline* (Presbyterian and Reformed, 1963); G.B.Backhouse, *Romans*.

4   See Moo, *Romans*, pp.568–569. The 'Arminian' interpreters are lamentably weak here. Writers like I.H.Marshall (see *Kept By the Power of God*, p.102) pay little attention to the details of Paul's argument.

5   For the analysis of this passage as answering four underlying problems, see D.M.Lloyd-Jones, *Romans: Perseverance*, pp.370f.

6   Commentaries on John's Gospel which take approximately the same line of approach in understanding the chapter include Calvin, *John, 1–10* (Eerdmans, 1961); *John, 11–21 and 1 John* (Eerdmans, 1961); D.A.Carson, *John* (IVP, Eerdmans, 1991); W.Hendriksen, *John* (Banner of Truth, 1964); G.Hutcheson, *John* (rp from 1841, Banner of Truth, 1972); L.Morris, *John* (Eerdmans, 1971)A.W. Pink, *Exposition of the Gospel of John*, 3 vols (Zondervan, 1956); J.C.Ryle, *Expository Thoughts on the Gospels: John* (3 vols, Hunt, 1865).

7   G.R.Osborne, 'Soteriology in the Gospel of John', in C.H.Pinnock (ed), *The Grace of God, The Will of Man* (Zondervan, 1989), p.250.

8   See Carson, *John*, pp.510–519. Carson dismisses Calvinist writers who wish to translate *airo* in v.2 by 'lifts up' rather than 'cut off', an interpretation apparently pioneered by A.W.Pink (see pp.518f.).

9   E.A.Blum, 'John', in *The Bible Knowledge Commentary* (ed. J.F.Walwoord & R.B.Zuck, Victor, 1984), pp.325f.

10   Carson, *John*, p.563.

11   Bangs, *Arminius*, pp.216–219, 313, 347f.

12   See Shank, *Life*, pp.109f., 127, 171, 239, 335, 359; Marshall, *Kept*, pp.103f.; G.Duty, *If Ye Continue*, 1966, pp.98f..

13   Rom.11:26 refers to the bulk of the nation of the Israel at a certain point in the history of salvation. See Murray, *Romans*, 2, pp.96–100; Morris, *Romans*, p.341, and others. For another approach, see W.Hendriksen, *Romans 9–16*, pp.379–382. Those Calvinist writers who do not see the communal aspect of Paul's argument have more difficulty with this passage. W.Hendriksen's comments are weak (p.376). Hodge is in a stronger position when he says 'Paul is not speaking of the connection of individual believers . . .but of the relation of communities to the church' (*Romans*, p.370).

14   See T.H.L.Parker, *John Calvin* (Lion, 1975), p.181.

15 A.Dallimore, *George Whitefield*, vol.2 (Banner of Truth, 1980), ch.16.
16 See R.H.Bainton, *Here I Stand*, (originally Abingdon, 1950; 1978 rp), pp.248–251.
17 See J.Calvin, *Letters*, (Banner of Truth, 1980), p.71.
18 J.Gerstner (*A Primer on Justification*, Presbyterian & Reformed, 1983, p.16) maintains that 'antinomians' (American dispensationalist evangelicals) sing: 'Free from the Law, O blessed condition, / I can sin as I please and still have remission.' But Bliss's hymn reads: 'Free from the Law, O blessed condition, / Jesus hath bled and there is remission' and continues: 'Children of God', O glorious calling, / Surely his grace will keep us from falling.'
Gerstner's misrepresentation is typical of the hostility faced by American dispensationalists because of their view of freedom from the Torah. I am not an American dispensationalist but when their critics use this style of argumentation I have to ask: which theology really leads to the fulfilment of the love command, that which holds to release from the Mosaic covenant or the preoccupation with Torah that pervades the Reformed tradition? Is this phenomenon not itself rather antinomian?
One thinks also of Luther's behaviour (see M.U.Edwards's chapter 'Against the Antinomians' in *Luther and the False Brethren*, pp.156–179),and the slanderous hostility of Thomas Edwards (1599–1647, author of *Gangraena: or a Catalogue . . . of . . . Errours, Heresies, Blasphemies . . .*, published in 1646).
It is pleasant to record Charles Spurgeon's loving gentleness towards those with whom he had a disagreement over the Mosaic law. He disapproved of the treatment that the Puritan John Flavel accorded to Crisp's writings. 'Antinomianism was the term applied to the teaching of Dr. Tobias Crisp . . . He was a man of strong faith, ardent zeal, holy life, and great devotion and faithfulness in his ministerial work. He was called an Antinomian but the term was misapplied' (see C.H.Spurgeon, 'The Down Grade', *Sword and Trowel*, March 1887, pp.123f.).
19 Wilson, *1 Corinthians*, p.138 .(The words are a citation from Matthew Henry.)
20 G.Fee, *1 Corinthians* (Eerdmans, 1987), pp.433–441, esp.p.440.
21 For a recent statement, see R.Ombres, *Theology of Purgatory* (Dubln: Mercier, 1978). The differences between the fire of 1 Cor.3:15 and the traditional doctrine of purgatory seem to revolve around the following points: (i) its correlation or non-correlation with justification by faith only, (ii) lack of speculation concerning the time involved, (iii) no statement that it is necessary or that the majority of Christians will be 'saved through fire'. When speculative and legalistic interpretations have been ruled out, 1 Cor.3:15 and Heb.10:29 remain.

NOTES TO CHAPTER FIFTEEN

1 R.Shank wrestles with this in a final chapter ('Is Apostasy Without Remedy'), *Life*, pp.309–329. His view is considered below.
2 E.g. G.W.Buchanan, *To the Hebrews* (Doubleday, 1972), p.108; E.Käsemann, *The Wandering People of God* (Augsburg, 1984), pp.136,189; J.Moffatt, *Hebrews* (Clark, 1924), pp.76–82; H.W.Montefiore, *Hebrews* (Black, 1964), p.109; A.Nairne, *Hebrews* (CUP, 1922), p.108; R.H.Smith, *Hebrews* (Augsburg, 1984), pp.80–82. B.Poschman thinks this view 'very prevalent among Protestant theologians' (*Penance and Anointing for the Sick*, Herder, 1964, p.7) but explicitly mentions only H.Windisch. K.E.Kirk thinks we have here a rigorism which gives no hope of restoration to the offender in case of severe sin (*The Vision of God*, 1932, Longmans & Green, 1932, p.160). See similar views in C.E.Carlston, 'Eschatology and Repentance in the Epistle to the Hebrews', *JBL*, 78, 1959, esp.pp.300f.; A.Snell, *New and Living Way* (Faith, 1959), p.87; W.McCowan, 'Unforgivable Sin', *Kardia: A Journal of Wesleyan Thought*, 1, 1985, p.15; G.A.Turner, *The New and Living Way*

(Bethany, 1975), pp.104–107. Also: F.Delitzsch, *Hebrews*, vol.1 (1871, rp. Klock & Klock, 1978), p.288. A similar view seems to have been held in the circle of the Shepherd of Hermas, although the *Shepherd* of Hermas itself dissents from it. See O.D.Watkins, *A History of Penance* (Longmans & Green, 1920), vol.1, p.16. Some emphasize that it is the writer's eschatological outlook which leads him into such severity. There is no second conversion because the parousia is near. See H.Windisch, *Der Hebräerbrief* (Mohr, 1931), pp.53–54; O.Michel, *Die Brief an die Hebräer* (Vandenhoek, 1966), p.424.

3   Tertullian, *De Pudicitia*, 20 (*PL*, 2, p.1021). M.Goguel interpreted the passage similarly in *L'Eglise Primitive* (vol.3 of *Jésus et Les Origines du Christianisme*, Payot, 1947), p.519 ('il n'y a pas de seconde répentance'). I have not had access to the fuller article by M.Goguel ('La Doctrine de l'impossibilité de la seconde conversion dan l'Épître aux Hébreux et sa place dans l'évolution du Christianisme, *Annuaire de l'École pratique des Hautes Études*, Paris, 1931, pp.4–38, which presumably spells out this view in fuller detail.) Novatianism (although apparently not Novatius himself) came to agree with Tertullian's rigorist approach to capital sins. See Watkins, History, pp.213–214. See Athanasius, *Ad Serap*.iv.3 (*PG*, 26, 654f.), Jerome, *Adv. Jovin.* 2:3 (*PL*, 284f.).

4   See Watkins, *History*, p.48; Kirk, *Vision*, pp.165–171.

5   Watkins, *History*, p.220. It ought to be mentioned that this reading of Hermas has been disputed by Poschmann (*Penance*, pp.26–35).

6   See Chrysostom, *Homilies on Hebrews*, Heb.6:4, *PL*, 63, col.79; Ambrose, *De Poenitentia*, bk.2, ch.2, *PL*, 16, col.497–499.

7   See J.K.Solani, 'The Problem of *Metanoia* in the Epistle to the Hebrews' (DST Dissertation, Catholic University of America, 1970), pp.3f.

8   See J.Owen, 'Nature and Causes of Apostasy', 1676, in *The Works of John Owen*, vol.7 (rp. Banner of Truth 1965), pp.2–259; W.H.Davies, 'The Puritan Doctrine of Apostasy' (*Increasing in the Knowledge of God*, pp.40–46) is concerned with Owen's view but others held a similar approach. See also also W.Gouge, *Commentary on Hebrews* (1655, rp. from 1860 ed., Kregel, 1980), pp.395–410.

9   A.C.Custance *Sovereignty*, p.217.

10   J.Brine, *A Treatise on Various Subjects* (James Paul, 1851), pp.62–80.

11   R.Nicole, 'Some Comments on Hebrews 6:4–6 and the Doctrine of the Perseverance of God with the Saints', in *Current Issues in Biblical and Patristic Interpretation* (ed. G.F.Hawthorne, Eerdmans, 1975), p.361.

12   See Gouge, *Hebrews*, pp.395–410.

13   F.C.Synge, *Hebrews and the Scriptures* (SPCK, 1959), pp.49f.

14   J.F.Strombeck, *Shall Never Perish* (Van Kampen, 1952), p.136; the sense would have been clearer if Strombeck had placed the word 'Christian' in inverted commas).

15   K.S.Wuest, *Hebrews in the Greek New Testament* (Eerdmans, 1947), pp.113–119.

16   N.Weeks, 'Admonition and Error in Hebrews' *WTJ*, 39, 1976–77, pp.72–80).

17   W.S.Lane, *Call To Commitment: Responding to the Message of Hebrews*, 1984, p.94).

18   R.Jewett, *Letter To Pilgrims* (Pilgrim, 1981), p.103.

19   B.F.Westcott *Hebrews* (4th ed., Macmillan, 1928), p.153.

20   W.H.Thomas, *Hebrews* (Eerdmans, 1984), p.73.

21   W.Manson, *Hebrews* (Hodder, 1951), p.64.

22   T.Hewitt, *Hebrews* (Tyndale, 1960), p.111.

23   A.Mugridge, 'Warnings in the Epistle to the Hebrews', *RThR*, 46, 1987, pp.76f.).

24   See C.Spicq, *L'Épître aux Hébreux*, vol.2 (Lecoffre, 1953), p.173; B.Poschmann, *Paenitentia Secunda: Die Kirchliche Busse im altesten Christentum bis Cyprian und Origenes* (Hanstein, 1940), p.41; B.Poschmann, *Penance*, 1964, p.13).

25 Solani, '*Metanoia*', pp.153,155
26 L.Morris, *Hebrews* (Eerdmans, 1983), p.58.
27 J.Héring, *Hebrews* (Epworth, 1970), p.46.
28 RV, RSV Heb.6:6; Shanks, *Life*, ch.19; E.M.B.Green, *The Meaning of Salvation* (Hodder, 1965), p.233.
29 V.D.Verbrugge, 'Towards a New Interpretation of Hebrews 6:4–6', *CTJ*, 15, 1980, pp.61–73.
30 G.H.Lang, *Hebrews* (Paternoster, 1951), p.196.
31 Hodges, *Gospel*, p.33.
32 M.De Haan, *Hebrews* (Zondervan, 1958), pp.99,117.
33 J.K.Solani, '*Metanoia*', pp.7, 153, 160.
34 D.A.Hagner, *Hebrews* (Harper, 1983), p.73.
35 R.Brown, *Christ Above All* (IVP, 1982), p.115.
36 A.Murray, *The Holiest of All* (Nisbet, 1895), p.208.
37 E.g. W.Barclay, *Hebrews* (Westminster, 1976), pp.57–59.
38 Haan, *Hebrews*, passim.
39 R.G.Gromacki, *Stand Bold in Grace*: An Exposition of *Hebrews* (Baker, 1984), pp.107–112.
40 Z.Hodges, 'Hebrews', in *BKC*, NT (Victor, 1983), p.794.
41 R.T.Kendall, *Once Saved Always Saved* (Hodder & Stoughton, 1983), pp.131–134.
42 Lang, *Hebrews*, pp.93–110.
43 J.Vernon McGee, *Hebrews* (Pasadena: Thru the Bible, 1977), vol.1, 1977, pp.1ll-118.
44 H.A.G.Tait, 'The Problem of Apostasy in Hebrews', in *Pulpit and People: Essays in Honour of William Still*, ed.Nigel M.de S.Cameron & Sinclair B.Ferguson, Edinburgh: Rutherford House, 1986, pp.131–139.
45 C.E.Carlston rightly says 'These three central passages [Heb.6; 10; 12] must all be interpreted in the same way' ('Eschatology and Repentance in the Epistle to the Hebrews,' *JBL*, 78, 1959, p.296.
46 See D.G.Peterson, The Situation of the 'Hebrews' (5:11–6:12), *RThR*, 35, 1976, pp.14–21.
47 We have now touched upon this matter many times. I have come to the conclusion that sometimes the language of salvation and reward are kept distinct (1 Cor.3:15) but on occasion the word 'salvation' is used as the omnibus description of all that takes place in the *eschaton*.
48 I think it makes more sense of Hebrews 2 to translate *brachu ti* 'for a little while'. See *AG*, p.147. On the whole section see G.W.Grogan, 'Christ and His People: An Exegetical and theological Study of Hebrews 2:5–18', *VE*, 1969 ed., pp.54–71.
49 See E.W.Smith, 'Will (Testament)', in *ISBE*, 4, p.1064.
50 However all translation and commentaries I have consulted translate Hebrews 11:7 this way.
51 C.F.D.Moule, *Idiom-Book*, p.37.
52 See *AG*, pp.44–45.
53 See pp.61ff.
54 Even *ekpipto* need not refer to apostasy, as Rev.2:5 with its mention of repentance makes clear. *Parapipto* is not found elsewhere in the New Testament. It occurs in Ezk.14:13; 18:24; 20:27 (LXX) where it refers to serious sin which brings heavy chastening (the exile), which may cause physical death and which pollutes one's relationship with God. In the LXX of Est.6:10 it means 'neglect' (cf Heb.2:3). In the apocrypha it is used in Wisdom 6:9; 12:2; 2 Macc. 10:4. The word is found in Josephus *Antiquities* 19:285 and in various Greek papyri from NT times. In some instances it is quite clear that the word does not refer to irremediable apostasy. 'Thou dost correct little those who fall by the wayside (Est.12:12). 'They besought the Lord . . . that if

they fell by the wayside . . . he would chasten them in mercy' (2 Maccabees 10:4). 1
Clement 51:1 uses the term: 'For such things in which we have fallen by the wayside
. . .let us pray that forgiveness may be granted to us'. These examples, which I have
translated myself, make it clear that apostasy without remedy is not in the word itself.
   55   Lang, *Hebrews*, p.253.

Index of Main Biblical References

Index of Names

Subject Index